Wanting like a God

Wanting like a God

Desire and Freedom in Thomas Traherne

DENISE INGE

scm press

© Denise Inge 2009

Published in 2009 by SCM Press
Editorial office
13–17 Long Lane,
London, EC1A 9PN, UK

SCM Press is an imprint of Hymns Ancient and Modern Ltd
(a registered charity)
St Mary's Works, St Mary's Plain,
Norwich, NR3 3BH, UK
www.scm-canterburypress.co.uk

All rights reserved. No part of this publication may be reproduced,
stored in a retrieval system, or transmitted,
in any form or by any means, electronic, mechanical,
photocopying or otherwise, without the prior permission of
the publisher, SCM Press.

The Author has asserted her right under the Copyright,
Designs and Patents Act, 1988,
to be identified as the Author of this Work

British Library Cataloguing in Publication data

A catalogue record for this book is available
from the British Library

978 0 334 04147 4

Typeset by Regent Typesetting, London
Printed and bound by
CPI Antony Rowe, Chippenham SN14 6LH

For
Eleanor and Olivia
long desired

Contents

Acknowledgements ix
Abbreviations x
Foreword by David F. Ford xi

Introducing a New Traherne 1

Biography 6
Traherne's Background and Character 6
Career, Friends and Associates 10
Historical Context 13
Sources and Influences 19
The Poet of Felicity? 22

1 Wanting 25

Desire and Sexuality 28
The Passion Imperative 37
Passion and Prudence 41
The Infinite End 50
The Finite Means 63
Wanting Like a God 72

2 Discerning Treasure 81

What is Treasure? 81
Spiritual Discernment 98
Prizing 106
An Economy of Need and Treasure 110

3 Choice 124

In Defence of Liberty 125

The Golden Link	131
Power and Act	146
Free Agency	153
Liberty and Grace	162
Hope	169

4 Difference — 175

Felicity as Unity	176
The Importance of Difference	181
Circulation and Communication	201

5 Communion — 221

Communion and Union	222
On Communion and the Cross	228
On Communion with One Another	238
Desire and Satisfaction in the Circle of Bliss	244
Gratitude	252

Epilogue	262
Appendix 1: Manuscript Discoveries	267
The Ceremonial Law	269
The Lambeth Manuscript	271
Inducements to Retiredness	272
A Sober View of Dr Twisse	275
Love	280
Seeds of Eternity	280
The Kingdom of God	285
Appendix 2: Folios and corresponding chapters for Inducements to Retiredness, A Sober View of Dr Twisse, *and* The Kingdom of God	302
Bibliography	304
Index	307

Acknowledgements

I am indebted to the late Jeremy Maule, whose friendship and discussion greatly aided my early work on this project; to Donald Allchin for his unflagging enthusiasm and scholarly encouragement; to David Ford, Jacqueline Eales and Mark McIntosh, whose interests in Traherne have encouraged me; to Calum McFarlane, Leigh DeNeef and Nabil Matar, who have at an earlier stage offered discussion, debate, and/or the loan of relevant articles; and to the Lambeth Palace Library, the British Library, the Bodleian Library and the Folger Library for allowing me access over the years to manuscripts and for allowing their manuscripts to be copied onto microfilm.

I owe a happy debt to Tom Howard, who introduced me to Traherne many years ago when I was an undergraduate, and to Sam Wells, who brought Traherne to my attention again one day, when my interest in him had lapsed. These two men in their separate ways gave me Traherne and my life has been much richer for it. Without them this book wouldn't have happened. Brian Horne supervised my doctoral work, out of which this book eventually grew, and I am grateful for his quiet support and thoughtful interventions in the early years of this project.

I would also like to thank Bridget Nichols, friend and reader, and the skilful Tom Willet, who translated parts of Italian that were incomprehensible to me. Thanks too to Mary Matthews for her support and patience, to Natalie Watson who has been such a helpful editor, and to Hester Higton whose able copy-editing enhanced the manuscript. I am grateful to Zuzanna Demcakova, whose years of childcare have enabled me to work.

My deepest thanks to John Inge, beloved companion on the road, who reads everything and knows what to say and whose love never fails.

Abbreviations

C	*The Centuries of Meditations*
CE	*Christian Ethicks*
CB	*The Commonplace Book* [Bod.MS.Eng.Poet.c.42]
COH	*Commentaries of Heaven* [BL.MS.Add.63054]
CYB	*The Church's Year-Book* [Bod.MS.Eng.Th.e.51]
EN	*The Early Notebook* [Bod.MS.Lat.Misc.f.45]
FN	*The Ficino Notebook* [B.M.MS.Burney 126]
ITR	*Inducements to Retiredness* [Lamb.MS.1360]
KOG	*The Kingdom of God* [Lamb.MS.1360]
L	*Love* [Lamb.MS.1360]
MSD	*Meditations on the Six Days of Creation*
RF	*Roman Forgeries*
SE	*Seeds of Eternity* [Lamb.MS.1360]
SM	*The Select Meditations*
SV	*A Sober View of Doctor Twisse* [Lamb.MS.1360]
TCL	*The Ceremonial Law* [Folger.MS]

Foreword

David F. Ford

Traherne poses a massive challenge for anyone writing about him. His sheer superabundance in thought, imagination, expression, and the range and interconnection of his topics means that it is extraordinarily difficult to do him justice. In recent years this has been compounded by the discovery of many more writings, some of which add whole dimensions to our conception of him. It is possible, of course, that more such happy surprises are in store for us, but for someone who died at 37, and led a full life apart from writing, the corpus is already large, and while we may hope for more it is becoming less likely. So this is the first time that it is possible to study him as a whole. There has been enough time to make the new works available and to assimilate them in relation to the rest of his writing, but no substantial integrated study of the old with the new material has yet been done. The thrice repeated 'never before' in the opening paragraph of Dr Inge's Epilogue is therefore justified: this book is ground-breaking.

Dr Inge has over many years steeped herself in Traherne and the rapidly growing literature about him, has written on him, and has recently edited a reader that covers the range of his works and is the best available introduction to them.* The present study shows where all that has been heading. It reveals a fine scholar and theologian stretching her mind and imagination to engage with all the main aspects of Traherne's varied life and work. We see Traherne as a theologian above all, and in the light of her description and assessment it is clear that he deserves to take his place as a major classic of Christian theology. He is not only an inspired interpreter of the Bible but also in fruitful conversation with a range of classic and sometimes surprising sources within and beyond the Christian tradition – these are helpfully noted in the book. He emerges as very much of his time, deeply involved with his church and society and also with the sciences during a period of rapid development. He is a Renaissance man in the vast scope of his interests and in the energetic,

---

* *Happiness and Holiness: Thomas Traherne and His Writings*, Canterbury Press, 2008.

open and exploratory way he pursues them. He has a faith that loves knowledge of all sorts. But this is just one part of a love for God and God's creation that is excessive and ecstatic, revelling in the infinite God and his infinite desire for creation.

That this is a God who wants and desires is highlighted in the title and deserves the attention Dr Inge gives this distinctive feature of Traherne's thought. It is obviously a feature of God in the Bible, but has never, so far as I know, been dwelt upon with such thoroughness. Her consideration of this and other key concepts, such as felicity, treasure, choice, difference, circulation, delight, communion, gratitude and, above all, love, amount to a rare and rich theological feast. I was especially fascinated by Traherne's theology of the cross, seen as the tree of life, on fire like the burning bush – with the fire of love.

Traherne the theologian is inseparable from Traherne the visionary, poet, priest, pastor, scholar, debater, friend – and all of these play their part in Dr Inge's account. Not only that, his love of language and facility in its use is echoed by hers, and we are fortunate that this first full treatment of him shows such imaginative and conceptual felicity in expression.

Dr Inge, perhaps wisely, does not attempt to determine Traherne's place among today's theologies. For that to become clearer there would need to be a wider reception of his work than has so far been possible, but I would conclude with a few preliminary thoughts. There is no obvious parallel to Traherne in either the past or the present. He is obviously theological, but much of his work defies categorization in a single genre – theological exegesis, doctrine, systematic theology, philosophical theology, spirituality, sermon, practical theology, or whatever. In this he is like several other English Christian thinkers, such as Julian of Norwich, Bishop Butler, Samuel Johnson (think of his prayers), Samuel Taylor Coleridge or Dorothy Sayers. In theological range and weight he compares favourably not only with them but with other theological classics. Were he to be paired with Richard Hooker, classic Anglican theology would be enriched with fresh depth, wisdom and joy. Academic theology especially needs to beware of neglecting Traherne because he is not in anyone's specialty, and to recognize that this constructive, imaginative theological thinking, bringing together many strands into a lively hybrid, deserves much more of the sort of appreciative and critical engagement given in this book. Above all, it would be wise for theologians to seek in him a source of the reinvigoration and rejuvenation about which he himself was so perceptive.

Cambridge
Ascension Day 2009

Introducing a New Traherne

> Breath after him my soul, take leav to soar,
> And when thou most art lost, then most Adore
> Aspire, Desire, Admire; he is all Lov...
>
> (*COH*, 'Atheist')

For generations Traherne has been known by many as 'the Poet of Felicity' – a secluded country priest, a naive optimist, a visionary, perhaps even a mystic – whose love of nature and celebration of childhood innocence was unparalleled in his time. Yet these innocence and nature themes have estranged as many readers as they have inspired. Bertram Dobell, Traherne's first twentieth-century editor, spoke of Traherne's 'remote otherworldliness'; and as this description lodged itself firmly in the early interpretations of Traherne's felicity, there grew up, very early, a notion of Traherne 'brimming with happiness',[1] in touch with neither the practical realities of everyday life nor the darker side of human nature. As Peter Beal notes, the introduction Traherne received from his first editors 'has virtually defined his literary persona ever since'.[2] In the 1940s, his first biographer, Gladys Wade, did little to alter this image. As Dobell's 'happy soul' and Wade's 'radiant, happy mortal',[3] he is charming but infantile, a naive and childlike man, head in the clouds and feet in paradise.

To be fair, this reading of Traherne and his felicity seems to be supported by his deliberate choice in *Christian Ethicks*, published in the year after his death, to consider virtue to the exclusion of vice. According to this 'virtue-only' reading, what he does see of the world is nature in a kind of glorified state. Such lines as the famous 'The corn was

---

[1] 'Traherne, so brimming with happiness, so anxious to bestow this priceless gift on others, is impotent to impart his joy. So pure and rare a mind cannot face the facts of life.' (Frances Towers, 'Thomas Traherne: His Outlook on Life', *The Nineteenth Century and After*, 87 (1920), pp. 1024–30).

[2] Peter Beal, *Index of English Literary Manuscripts*, Vol. 2, 1625–1700, Part 2, Lee–Wycherley, London: Mansell, 1993, p. 477.

[3] 'He became one of the most radiantly, most infectiously happy mortals this earth has known.' Gladys Wade, *Thomas Traherne*, Princeton: Princeton University Press, 1944, p. 3.

orient and immortal wheat, which never should be reaped, nor was ever sown', from the third *Century*, are the flagships of such a reading. In this view he is often thought of in Romantic, or Pre-Romantic terms, linked with Blake, Wordsworth and Whitman,[4] and his felicity is a kind of innocence revisited. Traherne's great theme of 'Felicity' becomes alienating and over simplistic. Carol Marks, one of the most influential critics of the later twentieth century, voiced the frustration of many readers when she wrote:

> There is a certain naivete about all this; it is too simple ... In the end, that simplicity diminishes our faith in Traherne's sincere but facile professions of practicality. His conviction of man's goodness can inspire us to admiration, perhaps to envy, but not to assent.[5]

This Traherne is not quite human as we are. He either has a mystical vision, or an unusually clear memory of childhood experiences, or a philosophical system that we do not. As Leigh DeNeef has more recently put it, 'there is little sense [in collected criticism] that Traherne ever suffered from the kinds of alienation that besiege either his own contemporaries or his subsequent readers'. DeNeef notes the problem of an unhistoricized Traherne: 'If Traherne had nothing to say to his own age and time, what can he have to say to ours?'[6]

---

4 Such connections are made in, among others: Bertram Dobell, 'Introduction', *The Poetical Works of Thomas Traherne*, London, 1903; Wade, *Thomas Traherne*, p. 148; Elbert Thompson, 'The Philosophy of Thomas Traherne', *Philological Quarterly*, viii:2 (1929), pp. 97–112; Ben Drake, 'Thomas Traherne's *Songs of Innocence*', *Modern Language Quarterly*, 31 (1970), pp. 492–503; Dorothy Sayers, 'The Beatrician Vision in Dante and other Poets', *Nottingham Medieval Studies*, 2 (1958), pp. 3–23, though Sayers also notes some important distinctions between Traherne and Wordsworth. Because Traherne was not 'discovered' as a poet until the turn of the twentieth century none of these poets would have in fact been knowingly influenced by him.

5 Carol Marks, 'Traherne's *Church's Year-Book*', *Papers of the Bibliographical Society of America*, 58(1964), pp. 31–72, 71-2. See Malcolm Day's response to this criticism in *Thomas Traherne*, Boston: Twayne Publishers, 1982, p. 5.

6 A. Leigh DeNeef, *Traherne in Dialogue: Heidegger, Lacan, and Derrida*, Durham, NC: Duke University Press, 1988, pp. 5–6. DeNeef believes the problem is one of historicizing Traherne and so puts him in dialogue with Heidegger, Lacan and Derrida. 'It could be argued, I think, that to the extent that the old historicism failed to historicize Traherne it also kept him conveniently alien to modern readers. ... Alienated from his contemporaries, radically idiosyncratic in both his thinking and his writing, and willfully committed to reimagining a childhood innocence that is either blatantly unrecoverable or simply absurd, Traherne can hardly compete with figures like Donne and Milton for the attention of a modern reader.' New manuscript discoveries, as we will see, have since contributed significantly to the historicizing of Traherne; nevertheless, DeNeef's study throws many valuable new lights onto Traherne.

INTRODUCING A NEW TRAHERNE

In this study I would like to suggest a theological reading of Traherne rooted in his own day and relevant to ours, which incorporates the most recent biographical information and the findings of huge new manuscript discoveries,[7] in which desire is the *leitmotif* and spring of action, and in which felicity is not so much about early innocence or glibly enjoying the world as it is about finding august desires satisfied and renewed.

Two of the significant features of the new manuscript discoveries are that they are mainly prose and that they are seriously theological, and this study reflects this by treating Traherne less as a poet and more as a theologian. Underlying the theme of desire in this study are such questions as: What kind of God does Traherne believe in? In what way might the human soul relate to such a God? These fundamental theological questions, foundational as they are to all of his work, have never been explicitly dealt with across the canon, partly, perhaps, because Traherne has not been considered a serious theologian or even, in some cases, fully Christian,[8] and partly because the canon has so recently expanded. T. S. Eliot once wrote of Vaughan a description that also seems to fit the inherited reading of Traherne: 'Much of his poetry is religious, but is not of the Church.'[9] However, recent scholarship has shown his connection to the events surrounding the Restoration: his 'un-churchy' poetry is, in fact, with his other works deeply rooted in the religious controversies and political events of the seventeenth-century church and state.[10]

---

7 The Appendix of this volume contains a brief description of the newest discoveries. A description of all his known works can be found in D. Inge, *Happiness and Holiness: Thomas Traherne and his Writings*, Norwich: Canterbury Press, 2008.

8 Intimations of pantheism, a general lack of Christology, an avoidance of sin, no clear doctrine of the Trinity or of Atonement are among the criticisms levelled in such works as: Keith Salter, 'Traherne and a Romantic Heresy', *Notes and Queries*, 200 (1955), pp. 153–6, and *Thomas Traherne: Mystic and Poet*, London: Edward Arnold, 1964; Alison Sherrington, *Mystical Symbolism in the Poetry of Thomas Traherne*, St Lucia: University of Queensland Press, 1970; Franz Wohrer, *Thomas Traherne: Growth of a Mystic's Mind*, Salzburg Studies in English Literature, Salzburg: Poetry Salzburg, 1982; Pat Pinset, 'The Image of Christ in the Writings of Two Seventeenth-Century English Country Parsons: George Herbert and Thomas Traherne', *Images of Christ: Ancient and Modern*, Roehampton Institute London Papers, No. 2, Sheffield: Sheffield Academic Press, 1997, pp. 227–38; Peter Maitland, 'Thomas Traherne's Path to Felicity: The Missing Christ', MA thesis, Carleton University, Canada, 1994.

9 T. S. Eliot, 'Mystic and Politician as Poet: Vaughan, Traherne, Marvell and Milton', *The Listener*, 2 April 1930, pp. 590–1, 590.

10 See Nabil Matar, 'The Political Views of Thomas Traherne', *Huntington Library Quarterly*, 57:3 (Summer 1994), pp. 241–53; and 'Mysticism and Sectarianism in Mid-17th Century England', *Studia Mystica*, XI:1 (Spring 1988), pp. 55–65; Michael Ponsford, 'Thomas Traherne, the New Jerusalem, and Seventeenth Century Millenarianism', *The*

This study is interested in his engagement with those events since they historicize him within the larger framework of seventeenth-century theological parlance, and help to locate Traherne as a coherent theologian with a consistent vision of God. Alongside this, the book's primary concern, is to articulate Traherne's distinct contribution to the discussion of desire in God that cuts across the centuries from Gregory the Great and Augustine through to the late twentieth-century and twenty-first-century writers who have picked up again this forgotten thread. Desire is not just one theme among many in Traherne but the backbone of his writing, and the consistency of his vision of a desiring God is unusual if not unique for his period. Drawing as it does on the innovations of science and political science and the emerging models of what we now perceive to be a modern way of thinking, Traherne's theology of desire provides a hitherto unknown link between early Patristic writings on desire in God and more contemporary works, making him a new and exciting partner for dialogue with contemporary theologians.

In a sense, nothing that this study will say is novel. Looking back over the familiar corpus of writings with the influence of the new discoveries, we may see that whatever is new has been intimated in the previously known works. What really *has* changed is that we can now speak with more confidence and clarity about Traherne's theological positions, about the degree of his engagement with controversy, his intense interest in authority, his passion for God. The aim of this study is to do this under the uniting themes of desire and freedom, in a sense to start excavating the implicit theology in Traherne. This is the first study of its kind since the new discoveries have unearthed more of Traherne's theological writings; it cannot be exhaustive, but it may be a door-opening contribution to our newest understandings of Traherne.[11]

Durham University Journal, 87:2 (July 1995), pp. 243–50; Julia Smith, 'Thomas Traherne and The Restoration', *The Seventeenth Century*, III:2 (Autumn 1988), pp. 203–22; and 'Introduction', *Select Meditations,* Manchester, Carcanet, 1997; Denise Inge, 'Thomas Traherne and the Socinian Heresy in *Commentaries of Heaven*', Notes and Queries, 54:4 (2007), pp. 412–16; Denise Inge, *Happiness and Holiness.*

11 Of course, the discussion of Traherne as a serious theologian in a broader context has already begun. See, for instance, Mark McIntosh, *Discernment and Truth*, New York: Herder and Herder, 2004, Ch. 9; David F. Ford, *Self and Salvation: Being Transformed*, Cambridge: Cambridge University Press, 1999, Ch. 11; Donald Allchin, 'The Sacrifice of Praise and Thanksgiving', *Profitable Wonders: Aspects of Thomas Traherne*, Oxford: The Amate Press, 1989; and 'The Whole Assembly Sings: Thomas Traherne', *The Joy of All Creation*, London: New City, 1993, Ch. 1; David Ford, *Christian Wisdom*, Cambridge, Cambridge University Press, 2007.

INTRODUCING A NEW TRAHERNE

Traherne is a fascinating thinker: wide-ranging, exploratory, daring almost to the point of error. His writing, like his thought, is prolific; but he is not, on the whole, systematic. And yet it is difficult to read Traherne attentively without observing certain themes and patterns of thought emerging; it is certainly impossible to discuss his work effectively without offering some framework for that discussion. Sooner or later some kind of system emerges. The one that this book offers is based on the themes of freedom and desire, in an attempt to communicate rather than to limit Traherne's incorrigibly adventurous spirit. Given the already ambitious nature of the project it is not possible to treat the poetry and prose separately; neither, in a theme-driven study, is it necessarily desirable to do so. Nor is it suitable, in this case, to study each work as a separate historical document (although a brief description of the newest works is given in the appendix). Most of the newest discoveries have as yet been only loosely dated if dated at all; several of them that are dated are placed in the already bulging years just prior to his death, when it seems the largest amount of his writing occurred. It is therefore not yet possible (if indeed it ever will be) to read Traherne as a writer of 'early' works and 'late' works to be read in comparison and contrast; almost all of the major works, apart from *Select Meditations*, would be considered 'late'. Similarly, although questions of intended audience must arise in the study of Traherne's work, it does not seem to me advantageous to consider his works primarily in terms that separate his more erudite work from that intended for a lay audience. Much recent scholarship in the field of early modern studies has suggested that the boundaries between public and private, and between popular and erudite writing, may have been more blurred in the seventeenth century than it seems to us now. Private unpublished manuscripts were sometimes circulated widely, and there were published works in the public arena that were in fact addressed privately; the intelligent reader was not just the academic.[12] This may be most true of theology, which, with the advent of print pamphlets, was opening up to lay people as never before.

It seems most advantageous then, to approach his theology thematically and, since the aim of the book is to discover those themes of desire and freedom where they recur over the full range of his writings, his

---

12 See Adam Fox, *Oral and Literate Culture in England, 1500–1700*, Oxford: Clarendon Press, 2000; Roger Chartier, ed., *The Culture of Print: Power and the Uses of Print in Early Modern Europe*, trans. Lydia G. Cochrane, Princeton: Princeton University Press, 1989; Tessa Watt, *Cheap Print and Popular Piety, 1550–1640*, Cambridge: Cambridge University Press, 1991.

works will be referred to more often in terms of their thematic rather than their chronological or generic relation to each other.

Biography

Although there has been scholarly digging, and a large new entry in the *Oxford Dictionary of National Biography*, there is, as yet, no recent biography of Traherne. We have a few dates from parish and college records that form a kind of skeleton of his life, fleshed out with scraps disclosed in his own asides, comments of churchwardens, colleagues, gossip writers; and we have the additional information that we glean from new manuscript discoveries. From all of these a kind of collage image of the man emerges. His probable year of birth is 1637, six years after Donne's death. We have the dates of his entry into Brasenose College, Oxford, in 1652 at the age of fifteen, his BA in 1656 and MA in 1661. We know that he was appointed to the rural parish of Credenhill in Herefordshire in 1657 and ordained in October 1660. He is believed to have become chaplain to Sir Orlando Bridgeman, Lord Keeper of the Seal, in 1669, although recent scholarship suggests that this may have happened as late as 1673. He published his first work, *Roman Forgeries*, in 1673 and died in the first week of October 1674 at Bridgeman's house in Teddington.

Traherne's Background and Character

Apart from what has been written about Traherne's brother Philip, whose posthumous editing of Traherne's poetry confused the early literary critique of the writer, relatively little has been published about Traherne's family background. Anthony A. Wood describes Traherne simply as 'a shoemaker's son of Hereford'. Traherne is thought to have been born in Hereford and it has been suggested that he may have been related to a well-to-do family of Trahernes who lived in nearby Lugwardine, several miles to the north-east, as well as to an older Philip Traherne, twice mayor of Hereford.[13] Gossip writer John Aubrey records

---

13 See H. M. Margoliouth, 'Introduction', *Poems, Centuries and Thanksgivings*, Oxford: Clarendon, 1958, p. xxxii; Malcolm Day, *Thomas Traherne*, Woodbridge, CT: Twayne Publishers, 1982, p. 11; Wade, *Thomas Traherne*, pp. 32–7. Following M. L. Dawson, 'Thomas Traherne', *TLS*, 26, 1927, p. 667, Franz Wohrer, *Thomas Traherne*, pp. 61–4 notes the several textual references to Philip and Lugwardine in 'On Leaping over the Moon' and 'To the Same Purpose', and that his son, Thomas, on entering King's College, Cambridge gave as his arms a suit that perfectly fits the coat of arms of the Lugwardine

a story of Traherne's indicating that there were two apprentices living in the Traherne household,[14] and it is likely that the writer's cobbler father, who was a freeman of the city, may, in fact, have been master craftsman of a small cottage industry and Traherne a member of the rising middle class.[15] In *The Kingdom of God*, Traherne claims to be writing from his own experience when he states: 'One of those Causes that made my Father Delightfull to me upon Earth was the Convenient House and Estate I did inherit by descending from him.'[16]

What kind of person Traherne was is less mysterious. Aubrey described him as 'a learned a sober person';[17] his churchwarden calls him 'a Godlie man ... a devout liver'.[18] He visited the sick and educated the young, a faithful priest who sometimes found the task of loving his flock wearing. He remained unmarried following his own advice, recently discovered, 'To give one Self wholly and Singly to God ... and love all Mankind in him ... That is, evry person in the whole World, with as near and violent affection. As I would my Wife, or my Dearest Friend'.[19] He was well educated, and by all accounts affable.

A friend describes him as 'a man of cheerful and sprightly Temper, free from any thing of the sourness of formality, by which some great pretenders of Piety rather disparage and misrepresent true Religion, than recommend it. And therefore was very affable and pleasant in his Conversation.' He was also so 'wonderfully transported with the Love of God to Mankind ... that those that would converse with him, were forced to endure some discourse upon these subjects, whether they had any sense of Religion, or not'.[20] Well meaning to all, he must have seemed as irksome to the irreligious as he was engaging to the pious.

Traherne confesses that he talked too much. 'Reservation and Silence: are my Desires', he wrote. 'O that I could attain them: Too much

---

Trahernes, still discernible in the parish church at Lugwardine. He also links the 'painted cloth ... wherein [was wrought] some ancient Story' of the poem 'Poverty' to a luxurious tapestry that hung at 'Middle Court', the home of the Lugwardine Trahernes, which, Dawson claims, the new owners of 'Middle Court' sold for a considerable sum. The authenticity of the coat of arms and of Thomas' entitlement to use it have not been verified.

14 See John Aubrey, *Miscellanies upon Various Subjects*, London, 1696, pp. 129–30.
15 See Julia J. Smith's entry on Traherne, *Oxford Dictionary of National Biography*, Vol. 55, pp. 205–8.
16 *KOG*, 445, ll. 11–14.
17 Aubrey, *Miscellanies*, pp. 129–30.
18 Hereford County Record Office, Registrar's files, 1667, 349.
19 *ITR*, ll. 412–13, 430–2.
20 From the Preface to *A Serious and Pathetical Contemplation of the Mercies of God, in several most Devout and Sublime Thanksgivings for the same*, published by Dr Hickes, 1699.

proneness to Speak is my Diseas.'[21] He was passionate about what he believed. His intellectual argument with a notable, eloquent and well-read Papist on the steps of the Bodleian Library, recorded in the Introduction to *Roman Forgeries*, shows Traherne to be as emotionally engaged in his work as he was intellectually keen and meticulous. In *Commentaries of Heaven*, he records two confrontations with the Baptist minister John Tombes at 'his Amsterdam, His Heretical Church in Leominster' in which his questions left the Baptist scholar standing 'Blank, & mute as a Fish'.[22] Traherne could argue his point tenaciously, often jumping in with both feet and saying more than, on reflection, he may have liked to have said. He prayed for divine assistance to overcome this fault: 'O my God make me faithfull, lively, constant; and Since thou hast Given me a Tongue . . . Teach me to use it moderately Prudently Seasonably to thy Glory. Amen',[23] and he resolved to improve: 'I will be more silent when they talk of vanitie. And since I cannot accompany their Imaginations and the thoughts of God; I will either overrule their Souls, or Depart the company' (*SM*, III, 2). But verbosity seemed always a thorn in his side.

His arguments with the Roman Catholic Church and with the 'Independents' were equally strident. Where the Roman Church was a 'Mother of Lyes' and a black-footed 'Peacock',[24] the Independent preachers of his day were 'Ignorant Zealots!' (*SM*, I, 85) and 'Narrow Souls' (*SM*, III, 25; I, 87) whose thoughts were so absurd that it was 'even a part of felicity to detest and hate them'.[25] Such extreme sentiments were the stuff of seventeenth-century life, the ordinary political and religious parlance in a world in which faith was a matter of life and death; and in speaking so vociferously, Traherne is a man of his time. He loved the re-established church in England, speaking possessively of 'the Beautifull union of my Nationall church!';[26] and he would defend her vigorously against 'the Ingratitude of Pious persons, that would tear out the Bowels of that church which gav them a Beginning'.

---

21 *SM*, III, 65.
22 *COH*, fols 194r–v.
23 *SM*, II, 100.
24 *RF*, Ch. 18 ends 'Surely the feet upon which this Peacock stands, are very Black' (p. 214), and he concludes his final chapter by suggesting that the Roman Church, a 'Mother of Lyes', 'espoused to the Father of Lies', has produced an 'adulterate brood' and so is 'defiled with so great an Off-spring of notorious *Impostures*' (*RF*, p. 297). Of Cardinals and Jesuits he writes: 'Cunning Wits such as Cardinals & Jesuits, may perhaps when they are disposed to do it impose upon old Women & ignorant Tradesmen, having no better defence than their narrow reach & shallow Brain' (*COH*, 'Ascension', fol. 139r).
25 *SM*, III, 25.
26 *SM*, I, 85.

'And for every Trifle and for evry Scruple must ye all abandon her and Lay her wast!' he asks. 'O prodigious and unreasonable men! Must we all be Independent, And cannot we Live, unless we pluck up her roots, and pull down her Hedges? ... Is it unLawfull for Kings and Lords and Senetors to Establish Christian Religion in their dominion.'[27]

As many writers do, he took criticisms to heart, licked the wound and defended himself:

> Here I am censured for Speaking in the Singular number, and Saying I. All these Things are done for me ... There it shall be our Glory and the Joy of all to Acknowledge, I. I am the Lords, and He is mine. Every one shall Speak in the first Person, and it shall be Gods Glory that He is the Joy of all. Can the friend of GOD, and the Heir of all Things in Heaven and Earth forbear to say, I.[28]

Yet, as we now know from new manuscript discoveries, he subjected his work to the eyes of a critical reader who pulled no punches, writing such comments as 'This is not soe pertinent and profitable as it is daingerous, and Inconvenient and seemingly Arrogant if not Impious' (*ITR*, l. 1016) and 'This is not well at all for a Junior to say to such a man as this was' (*SV*, I, l. 39).

He seems to have written as prolifically as he talked, judging not only by the comments of his contemporaries but also by his prodigious output (he was still adding to *Roman Forgeries* as it was going to press). And he wrote for a broad range of audiences – *Roman Forgeries* for the general public, *Commentaries* for 'Publick Persons' who were the 'Watchmen & Bulwarks of Christianity' and also for the 'Satisfaction of Atheists', *Inducements to Retirednesss* for 'the pious soul', *Christian Ethicks* for the ordinary layman, the *Centuries* for a friend. And yet, in the midst of this incessant oral and written conversation, he repeatedly highlights the need for quiet, retiredness, introversion and reflection. It was almost as if he craved solitude as much as he needed an audience.

He lived a relatively simple though by no means penurious life – his living was worth £50 per year. This seems to have been more than enough for him both in terms of wealth and station: 'Exhaltations and Honors, among Riches and Beauties, hav persued me, as much as they hav fled from other men', he wrote in *Inducements to Retiredness*. 'I hav tasted the very Cream of Earthly Delights. And hav had many

---

27 *SM*, III, 24, 25.
28 *SM*, III, 65.

Treasures under my Hand by way of Eminence' (*ITR*, ll. 248–50). He enjoyed what he had and he was generous. He was a Brasenose benefactor in 1664, the time at which they were building chapel, cloister and library. He owned several houses in Hereford. In his nuncupative will he gave his books and his best hat to his brother Philip and his second-best hat to his servant, a ring to each of the ladies of the house, and tokens of thanks to all the servants.[29] After his death, the several houses he had owned in the city became almshouses for the poor: an entirely appropriate disposal of the estate of one who is recorded as being, while he lived, 'Charitable to the Poor almost beyond his ability'.[30]

Career, Friends and Associates

Traherne's career was mostly, though not exclusively, parochial. Alongside his parish ministry he worked with the cathedral clergy in Hereford and carried on with his writing. At some point between 1669 and 1673 he became chaplain to Sir Orlando Bridgeman, Lord Keeper of the Seal, in whose Teddington household he died. In contrast to those ministers who took a living but left the care of the souls to a curate, Traherne seems to have been a 'hands on' clergyman according to the testimony of his churchwarden (1673): 'Our minister is continually resident amongst us.'[31] The parish records suggest Credenhill to have been either small or sparsely populated, with only two baptisms, three marriages and three burials in the most lively year, 1667.[32] Yet Traherne went about his work there diligently; his churchwardens describe him as 'a goo[d] & Godlie man well Learned ... a good Preacher of gods word',[33] who visited the poor and did duly 'Instruct the youth'.[34] Traherne's own testimony reveals a man in the thick of ministry, not lost in a world of theoretical felicity but engaged in the knocks and bumps of parish life with its foibles and personalities: 'It is no small matter to Dwell in community or in a congregation, and to convers there without complaint, and to Persevere Faithfully in it until Death' (*SM*, IV, 52). He writes in *Select Meditations*, 'Innocent no man is in

---

29 For a transcription of the will and other biographical details see Margoliouth, *Introduction*.

30 See 'Preface', *Serious and Pathetical Contemplation*.

31 Hereford County Record Office, registrar's files, 1673, 488.

32 One of those buried in 1667, 'Edward Traherne Late of the City of Herefford', may have been a member of Traherne's family.

33 Hereford County Record Office, registrar's files, 1667, 349.

34 Hereford County Record Office, registrar's files, 1673, 488.

this world. much Less a Congregation.' (*SM*, IV, 52). He tried to steer an even course among his parishioners, to be moved to compassion by their sorrows, while remaining unmoved by either their censures or by his own need of approval. He writes from experience:

> if they were miserable as the most are, to be filled with great comp[a]ssion, to retain the Sence of the Eternal Diety. To Lov them as the Saviour of the world doth, not to follow their Opinion, not to be Provoked by their censure, not to approve ones selfe to them, not to give them occation of evill Speech, not to be swayed by their example, are Difficult Things, and He that passeth Thorrow all thes Bryers well, and is in e[v]ry moment prudent shall be more beautifull then if he had never sinned nor been a mong them. (*SM*, IV, 52)

It seems that, for most of his adult life, he spent time in the parish of Credenhill. Evidence of his relationships with parishioners and with local clergy can be found in local records as well as in his writings. The parish register is signed in his own hand from 1664 to 1668 and in 1672. His churchwarden's comment in 1673 that he was continually resident seems odd in light of the fact that Margoliouth claims that he became Bridgeman's chaplain in 1669. It may be that he was a visitor in Bridgeman's London home and did not move to Bridgeman's household until after the Lord Keeper's removal to Teddington in 1673–74, or that, in fact, he was not appointed chaplain until 1673 or thereabouts.

That is not to say that he was intellectually or socially isolated. Other Oxford-educated fellow clergy were within reach of his parish in Credenhill, as were eminent local families. He was close to his younger brother Philip. Somewhere along the way Traherne was admitted to what he describes in *Christian Ethicks* as 'the society and friendship of Great men, where a Nod or a Word is able to prevail more, than the strength of Oxen and Horses'.[35] Some of these friendships went beyond mere sociability: in Bridgeman's household or before it, Traherne discovered by experience what it was like to become a most trusted friend. For he writes: 'they [great men] will entrust their Wives and Children in [a friend's] hands, as I have often experienced; their Gold, their Bonds, their Souls, their Affairs, their lives, their Secrets, Houses, Liberties, and Lands; and be glad of such a Friend in whom to be safe'.[36] Although Traherne valued these close and trusting friendships,

---

35 *CE*, ed. Carol Marks, p. 173.
36 Ibid., p. 200.

they were never enough to satisfy his need to belong to all mankind and all mankind to belong to him. In *Inducements to Retiredness* he confesses, rather disappointedly, 'I hav reason to believ that I hav had as many Strict and Close Amities, with Persons of the Greatest Principles and Bravest Worth. But all that I hav learned from them was Solomons Vanity.' He had high expectations for friendship, believing it required more intimacy and emotional commitment than marriage.[37] His disappointment with human friendship is directly related to a similarly high ambition to love infinitely as God does, for he adds: 'I must be Beloved of all Mankind. And be the Image of the Dietie, and reign Enthroned in the Bosom of God; or els for ever be Dissatisfed.'[38] But it may also be that he had experienced the breakdown of friendship. 'A Close Illimited Friendship is a Divine Enjoyment: could it be always pure, Sincere and perfect', he writes in *Inducements to Retiredness*, 'But so many thousand Things conspire as Ingredients to compose and make up a Perfect friend, that I shall sooner Expect an Angel to be Conversant here on Earth, then such a Person.'[39] He could be speaking theoretically here, but these comments, while not necessarily bitter, seem to suggest a personal knowledge of human affairs. And 'if the Temper be lively and vigorous in my friend, the Resentments will be: if it be flat and insipid, there is an Abatement of the Pleasure. I confess that a Golden and Complying Humor, will smooth and Polish many Asperities'[40] reads as testimonial. Although Traherne acknowledges the limits of human friendship, he never despairs of it entirely: 'for Man is made a Sociable Creature', he admits a few lines later, 'and is never Happy till His Capacities are filled with all their Objects'.[41] Perhaps once bitten twice shy, certainly experienced in human relationships, he concludes: 'It is better only to hav an infinit Benevolence toward all the World, a Moderate friendship with the Good and Excellent: an Intire Illimited friendship with God alone.'[42] This is where his confession of the limits of human friendship is leading – to friendship with God.

As noted above, he worked closely with the clergy of Hereford Cathedral: in 1671 and 1672 he acted as surrogate Dean for the Dean of Hereford's consistory court. This was no sinecure but an appointment that, at its busiest, required him to be present in Hereford as regularly

---

37 See *ITR*, ll. 392–405.
38 *ITR*, ll. 252–4, 255–7.
39 *ITR*, ll. 376–9.
40 *ITR*, ll. 384–7.
41 *ITR*, ll. 272–3.
42 *ITR*, ll. 389–1.

as every Saturday or every other Saturday for months on end.[43] On his death he was described by Thomas Good, Master of Balliol and Prebendary of Hereford as 'one of the most pious ingenious men' he had known. As well as regular contact with fellow clergy, he found companionship among the county families, in particular with Sir Edward Harley of Brampton Bryan, Herefordshire, who referred to Traherne on his death as 'my worthy friend'. There are also the unknown friends of *Select Meditations* abbreviated as 'O my T. G. O my S. H. O my brother!'[44] In addition to these friends and colleagues, Traherne seems to have participated in the manuscript culture of his day, offering his work to be read by others. There is the female friend of the *Centuries*, sometimes thought to be Susanna Hopton. More recently a new manuscript reader has been discovered – Traherne's critical reader of *Inducements to Retiredness* and *A Sober View*. As we have seen above, this reader could be fierce over Traherne's excesses. However, the critical reader praises him too with phrases such as: 'This is a very Accurate and Pertinent description' and 'This is sound and good'.[45] The reader corrected factual errors when they occurred and reprimanded gently: 'all this is Good and True, but you have said it over and over',[46] as well as fiercely. Similarly, the manuscript of the newly discovered unfinished poem *The Ceremonial Law* bears the comments of an enthusiastic and somewhat frustrated reading friend: 'I like this mightily but I pray prosecute it.' That Traherne submitted his work to such readers indicates something of his seriousness as a writer and affirms earlier suggestions that he wrote in the company of colleagues.[47]

Historical Context

The seven years of Civil War in England (1642–49) were the years of Traherne's childhood – years that witnessed bitter and bloody battles,

---

43 The *Acts of Office* records of the Dean's Court for 1671 [7002/1/5] record Traherne's presiding presence in court in February, March, April, May, August, September and December; in 1672, three times in January, twice in February, May and June, and again three times in July, among other occasions. The *Acts of Instance* 1661–72 [7002/1/13] records show a similarly frequent presence. I am grateful to Rosalind Caird for directing me to the relevant records in the Hereford Cathedral Archives.

44 *SM*, II, 38. Could 'T. G.' refer to Thomas Good, cited above (or to Theophilus Gale) and 'S. H.' to Susanna Hopton?

45 *SV*, XIX, l. 76 and *SV*, XVII, l. 120 (marginal note).

46 *SV*, XVIII, l. 18 (marginal note).

47 See Julia Smith, 'Introduction', *Select Meditations*, xxii; and Traherne entry in *Oxford Dictionary of National Biography*, Oxford: Oxford University Press, 2004, vol. 55, pp. 206–7.

the city of Hereford taken and acts of wanton cruelty committed by both sides in the conflict.[48] In June 1645 Charles I stayed at Hereford for 12 days after his defeat in the battle of Naseby. Within days of his departure the city was besieged by parliament's Scottish allies, a siege which lasted over a month, during which the city suffered terrible deprivation. Traherne's early biographer Gladys Wade suggests that Traherne, who would then have been eight or nine years old, may have been among those boys sent out with torches and faggots to set fire to the Scots' earthworks that surrounded the city walls. As the historian Jacqueline Eales notes, when the terrifying siege was lifted by the King's brief return in September 1645 he may also have been among the people described by one eye witness as 'joyfull of the kings' coming... and many came out to meet him'.[49] The mayor at the time of the Scottish siege was the aged Philip Traherne, an innkeeper and, it has been suggested, a relative of Thomas Traherne. A certain John Traherne, probably Thomas's father, was taken prisoner at the fall of Hereford and fined £4 before being released, a fine imposed because John had been a member of the local militia that had defended Hereford against Parliament. Even if subsequent scholarship discovers these persons not to be of his immediate family, their stories, by their very ordinariness, reveal the place of Traherne's childhood to be a city torn by passions and plagued by fear, a city under siege and subject to powerful political and religious upheaval.

It is no wonder that in adult life Traherne welcomed the stability that the Restoration provided. The *Select Meditations* are replete with considerations and asides showing his enthusiasm for the restoration of the king and of an established order. His love of kingship is partly a love of pageantry and of symbol, but it is also indicative of the real and profound need that Traherne sensed in himself and in his nation for an enduring peace. He writes with real relief,

> O Lord, when our citties and Teritories are united by Laws in the fear of thy Name: and are at one accord in Calling upon Thee; when they Move by Consent like an united Army. How Ravishing is their Beauty, How Sweet their Order! It is O my God as if the nation had but one soul.[50]

---

48 For examples of Puritan and Royalist atrocities see Wade, *Thomas Traherne*, Ch. 2.
49 'Thomas Traherne and Royalism: Influences and Networks', the Traherne Association annual lecture, 11 October 2008, College Hall, Hereford.
50 *SM*, I, 85.

The Restoration Church was Traherne's natural home. It is clear from Traherne's attacks, mentioned earlier, on both the Roman Catholic Church and the 'Independents', that Traherne was at home in neither of these forms of Christianity. But the nature of his commitment to the re-established Church of England (or the English Church, as he called it) and the depth of his involvement in the debates that surrounded the developing theology of the re-established Church are just beginning to be understood. In *A Sober View of Dr Twisse*, one of the newly discovered Lambeth manuscript works, we see Traherne closely following the Calvinist/Arminian debate concerning election and free will: do we choose God or does God choose us? In essence, the Calvinists claimed that God chooses and calls irresistibly those who will be saved, whereas the Arminians believed that we choose God. It seems an apparently simple question until one starts unpacking the permutations: do only those whom God has chosen (the Elect) have the chance to choose God? Can the Elect refuse God? and so on. Added to this is the fact that the Calvinist/Arminian conflict was by no means a purely theoretical one but a debate, as we shall see in chapter three, that had highly charged political implications. Traherne follows the debate in the writings of William Twisse (Calvinist), and Samuel Hoard (Arminian), Robert Sanderson and Henry Hammond. The full title of the work, *A Sober View of Dr Twisse his Considerations. With a Compleat Disquisition of Dr Hammonds Letter to Dr Sanderson. And a Prospect of all their Opinions Concerning GODS Decrees* shows something of the exactness Traherne seeks to apply in his consideration of the matter. Not only is he well read in the relevant texts and scrupulous in his attention to Scripture but he is passionate enough to give the matter 28 chapters and to submit his considerations to a critical reader for refinement. This work, though the most significant of its kind in rooting him firmly in the contemporary debate, is not alone. *The Kingdom of God*, another new Lambeth manuscript work, is sprinkled with references to the important ongoing theological and social writings of his day, from fellow priest/poet George Herbert to, as we will see later, the new sciences. *Roman Forgeries*, though concerned with historical documents, is impassioned because of its very strong relevance to the political and theological issues of Traherne's day. And the *Select Meditations* is laced with Restoration political theology. Far from being a man with his head in the clouds, Traherne was grounded both in the nuts and bolts of parish work and in the burgeoning intellectual life of his day.

Traherne was educated in a Puritan college; he was approved by the

Puritans,[51] and placed in the living of Credenhill by the testimonials of several ministers whose Puritan beliefs were such that they refused to subscribe to the Act of Uniformity when it appeared in August 1662 and were expelled from their livings. The Act of Uniformity required clergymen to affirm the *Book of Common Prayer* and to be episcopally ordained before St Bartholomew's Day, 1662. Puritan ministers currently in livings were permitted to remain in their parishes if they complied with these regulations. Smith, Lowe, Voyle and Primrose, who had signed Traherne's certificates, were among the many ministers whose refusal to comply ended their parish careers. And yet Traherne himself remained, not only being ordained but seeking episcopal ordination in 1660, well in advance of needing to do so.[52]

Traherne is described by a contemporary as one who 'became much in love with the beautiful order and *Primitive* Devotions of this our excellent Church'[53] as if he underwent a real process of change from Puritan to conforming priest. This could be an outsider's gloss on Traherne's theological changes; Traherne could have been merely protecting his career but his writings do not suggest that this is so. In *Select Meditations* he confesses his profound relief and joy at the re-establishment of the English Church and his horror of those who oppose it.[54] *A Sober View* assesses the orthodoxy of fellow theologians against the doctrines of the Church of England. And in *Roman Forgeries* and the *Church's Year-Book* we see an almost obsessive interest in the continuity of the Restoration Church with the early apostolic Church. In all of these works he sees the re-established Church as an inheritor of the earlier Church's ritual and order. And so we may see that his love of the English Church was real; yet in a world in which theology and politics were never far from each other, his love of the Church of England was a love of social order and the establishment of national peace and security as well as a love of historic doctrine and practice.[55] The bloodshed and battles were over. The people could live in peace. It was as if for him, at least at the time of the Restoration, the nation at last had one soul.

---

51 Lambeth Palace Library, MS 998 records the patron of Credenhill in 1662: the Puritan Amabella, Countess Dowager of Kent, and names the Puritan ministers who approved Traherne as William Voyle, William Lowe, Sam Smith, George Primrose, Robert Breton, Benjamin Baxter, Joseph Cholmley.
52 The see of Hereford was vacant in 1660 when Traherne was ordained by Robert Skinner, Bishop of Oxford.
53 Preface, *Serious and Pathetical Contemplation*.
54 *SM*, I, 85.
55 See Smith, 'Introduction', *Select Meditations*.

INTRODUCING A NEW TRAHERNE

Yet it was in this settled peace that, for many, intellectual life became unsettled. Straddling as it did the medieval world-view of preceding years and the modern world of Harvey and Hevelius, the seventeenth century saw an unprecedented emergence of sciences – natural, political and social; a kind of collapse and expansion at the same time, which rattled the very foundations of thought. This was especially true for those churchmen whose mindset remained medieval. But whether the church embraced or rejected the new discoveries, those discoveries remain intellectually significant to this day. As G. R. Cragg notes in *The Church and the Age of Reason*, the questions we still discuss about the place of reason, the nature of authority and the character of the universe are questions rooted in this seventeenth-century period of rapid intellectual change.[56]

Traherne was not of the reactionary churchman mould. For him all scientific discovery was a revelation of divine truth. Intellectual changes were afoot, one could sense a building wave and even sense that it might crash against the bulwarks of one's certainties with imponderable force, but for many in the seventeenth century the spiritual and the scientific were still intricately intertwined. It would have been in no sense strange to look into a microscope and see eternity.[57] Traherne revelled in the new infinities revealed by the microscope (c.1610) and the telescope (1608). This love of discovery, and of the sciences in particular, is hinted at many times in his poetry and appears again in the *Centuries of Meditations*; but never has it been more obvious than it is now, in the recently discovered *Kingdom of God*. In his treatise on the atom in Chapter 18 of *The Kingdom of God*, for instance, Traherne devotes ten folio pages to the atom, its properties, immutability, incorruptibility, volatility, strength, power and excellence. In Chapters 19 and 20 we find Harvey and the circulation of the blood, the nature of light, the rules of incidence and the laws of motion, and the operations of the sun. Chapters 21 and 22 consider the annual and diurnal motions of the moon and its description in Hevelius' *Selenographia*, 'new stars lately discovered by the Assistance of Telescopes', calculations of distances between heavenly bodies and contemporary theories positing the inhabitation of the moon. Chapter 23 takes the reader into considerations of the sun from the early Zabii or Chaldean philosophers through the familiar ancients to more modern divines,

---

56 Gerald Robertson Cragg, *The Church and the Age of Reason, 1648–1789*, London: Hodder & Stoughton, 1962, p. 80.

57 Look at the writings of Robert Boyle, such as *Seraphick Love* (1659) and *The High Veneration Man's Intellect Owes to God* (1684–85), which are laced with theology.

philosophers and scientists: Copernicus, Grotius, Descartes (whose *Discourse on Method* was published in the year of Traherne's birth), Gassendi, Hevelius, Dr Charleton, Dr Willis, the learned Gale (who was a contemporary of Traherne's at Oxford), Richardson, Bacon and 'the Incomparable Mr Robert Boyl', to name just a few. His investigations through primary and secondary sources go on in greater or lesser detail for many chapters more. Add to these his own experiments with candles and mirrors inspired by his study of light, and the numerous references to watches, springs, clocks and machines found in *The Kingdom of God*, and one sees a new picture of Traherne emerging. It is a picture of a man deeply engaged in the discoveries and discussions, experiments and theories of his day. The sustained scientific interest shown in *The Kingdom of God*, coupled with the detailed theological writing of *A Sober View*, the academic speculations of *Seeds of Eternity* and the testimonial nature of *Inducements to Retiredness*, together give us a much more mature and well-rounded picture of the man than we have ever had before, affirming and clarifying what had merely been suggested by previously known works. Traherne the naive optimist fades into the background as Traherne the scholar and theologian emerges. There is no whiff of the whimsical here; he may be an amateur scientist, and a dabbler in many other fields, but he is an experienced priest, an able theologian and a serious thinker. His poetry, which takes a back seat in the new manuscript works, does not disappear, but it states with strong conviction:

> Our Dreaming understandings must awake
> And in RIGHT REASON satisfy'd must take
> Their Sovereign Delights . . .
> This brings Men home, and feeds them not with lies:
> Teacheth our duties, and his Laws, to prize:
> And makes Men know in their Inferior State,
> The Joyfull Life of Heaven to Imitate.
> It leads us to a Real Blessedness,
> That we may dayly neer at hand possess:[58]

The belief, suggested above, that a truth revealed in Scripture and in the Tradition must also accord with Reason (C, III, 44, 45, 56) puts him firmly in the Anglican tradition. These three – Scripture, Reason and Tradition – were and remain the triangular cornerstones of the re-established Restoration Church of England.

---

58 'Invisibles are not diminished by', *KOG*, Ch. 23, ll. 272-4, 284-9.

Traherne was a man formed by and informing his world, deeply embedded in his own time, rooted in its cultural past and open to the future it anticipated.

Sources and Influences

The Principal of Brasenose during Traherne's time was the Puritan Dr Greenwood, appointed by the Parliamentary Visitors, and the college was strictly governed. Brasenose grew and flourished during Greenwood's time, the numbers in residence rising from 20 to 120. Both Wade and Keith Salter quote from the *Visitors Register* giving examples of the religious rigour that held sway in Traherne's day: 'every Tutor . . . at some convenient time beween the houres of seven and tenne in the evening' was to 'cause their Pupills to repair to their chambers to pray with them'; and that 'every Lord's Day' all bachelors of arts and undergraduates were to give 'an account . . . of the sermons they have heard, and their attendance on other religious exercises on that day'.[59] Traherne would have received a strong biblical grounding in his Puritan days, and the Bible remains the most prolific and most powerful influence in Traherne's work. We know from his account in the *Centuries* that, at the same period in his life, he read Logic, Ethics, Physics, Metaphysics, Geometry, Astronomy, Poesy, Medicine, Grammar, Music and Rhetoric. He mentions Albert Magnus, Galileo, Hevelius, Galen, Hippocrates, Orpheus, Homer and Lilly.[60] Alongside Scripture there grew up and remained a wide range of other sources and influences, philosophical, literary and scientific.

Throughout his writings, Traherne had the habit of quoting freely from what he had been reading, often without citing his sources. Whole passages are lifted; sometimes altered, sometimes simply planted in the middle of his work and woven in alongside other texts and ideas. Often, in this way, his primary sources go unidentified and whole phrases that are not his own are attributed to him. Conversely, he may cite an author he has met via another author's work so that a name mentioned seems to indicate a primary source that is really a secondary source. Untangling the problems of source for each work is therefore a complicated process. Since the distinctions between primary and secondary sources seemed not to matter much to him, and in order not

---

[59] *Visitors Register*, July 1653 and June 1653. See Wade, *Thomas Traherne*, p. 49 and Keith Salter, *Thomas Traherne: Mystic and Poet*, London: Edward Arnold, p. 80.
[60] C, III, 36.

to make an unwieldy text, I do no more here than note his practice of free borrowing and use. Except where his changes draw attention to the original, I treat his sources more generally as indications of the direction in which his mind was pointed, looking at the movements that moved him and occasionally digging deeper into the vein from which he is drawing.

One much noted group who influenced Traherne were the Cambridge Platonists: Benjamin Whichcote, John Smith, Peter Sterry, Ralph Cudworth, Nathanael Culverwell, John Worthington and Henry More. We know that Traherne read from all the above writers' works from the notes in the *Early Notebook* and in the *Commonplace Book*. Traherne found himself drawn to the same texts to which they were drawn – from the ancient Hermetic writings attributed to Hermes Trismegistus through to Plato and Plotinus and on to the Renaissance writers Ficino and Pico della Mirandola.[61] Plato and Plotinus appear scattered throughout Traherne's work, especially in the *Centuries*, and Traherne's interest in Ficino and Pico della Mirandola has been well documented.[62]

Although ideological and temperamental differences separated him at different points from the men of Cambridge,[63] his thought shows similarities with many of their salient ideas. Throughout his works, Traherne uses the same imagery of light and vision, the eye and the mirror. For him, as for the Neo-Platonists, visual perception links one to the ultimate reality via image or reflection. They all held that there existed in each person a 'natural light', placed there by God, which did

---

[61] Certainly Sterry read Plato, Plotinus and Ficino, these texts being cited among others in his possession in Vivian de Sola Pinto, *Peter Sterry: Platonist and Puritan*, Cambridge: Cambridge University Press, 1934, p. 57. For a fuller account of the literary diet of More and the other Platonists see Carol Marks, 'Thomas Traherne and Cambridge Platonism', *Proceedings of the Modern Language Association*, 81 (1966), pp. 521-3.

[62] See Marks, 'Traherne's Church's Year-Book'; 'Thomas Traherne and Cambridge Platonism', pp. 521-34; 'Thomas Traherne and Hermes Trismegistus' *Renaissance News*, 19 (1966), pp. 118-31; 'Thomas Traherne's Commonplace Book', *Papers of the Bibliographical Society of America*, 60 (1966), pp. 458-65; 'Traherne's Ficino Notebook', *Papers of the Bibliographic Society of America*, 63 (1969), pp. 73-81; and *Christian Ethicks*, Ithaca, NY: Cornell University Press, 1968, introduction.

[63] Psychologically, he has most in common with Peter Sterry, but we know that he read Henry More because he quotes from More's *Divine Dialogues* (London, 1668) in his *Commonplace Book* (s.v. 'Cohaesion', 'Deitie', 'Omnipresence', fols, 26v.2, 33.2–33v.2, and 71v.2–72.1). According to Marks, More's 'spiritual autobiography resembles Traherne's: their responses to the new ideas of space were remarkably alike in feeling, yet Traherne took issue vigorously with More's theories of space and deity, and in general lacked More's intellectual extravagance in the theological matters.' ('Traherne and Cambridge Platonism' p. 521). In support of this, see several entries in *CB* that attack More's theories of space (fol. 33v.1 and fol. 33.2).

not disagree with the light of reason.[64] It is to these 'seeds of natural light', God's 'private Law ... engraven on mens Consciences' that Traherne refers when he speaks of the 'pure and virgin apprehensions' of his infancy and of the 'divine light' in which he was born.[65]

But, significant as they are, the Cambridge Platonists are just one of the very many of Traherne's sources. His patristic and medieval sources are many: Gregory of Nyssa, Gregory the Great, Irenaeus, Athanasius, Augustine, Aquinas, À Kempis, John Chrysostom to name only a few. *Seeds of Eternity* adds to the list of Traherne's sources Cicero[66] and Justin Martyr, as well as the Jesuit scholars of Coimbra University in Portugal, whose Latin translations of Aristotle and others who wrote on the soul were very popular among advanced scholars of the seventeenth century.[67] Traherne was also very much involved in popular Anglican theology. He specifically sets *Christian Ethicks*, his major work on virtue, over against Richard Allestree's *The Whole Duty of Man*, the most popular handbook of holy living in its day. Donald Allchin reminds us that in the *Church's Year-Book*, an unpublished manuscript that both meditates on and expounds the feasts of the church year,[68] Traherne makes use of Lancelot Andrewes, Richard Hooker, Jeremy Taylor, George Herbert, Daniel Fealtry, William Austin and several Commonwealth Prayer Book commentaries. This, coupled with the scholarly digging of *A Sober View*, is indicative of the kind of modern theological scholarship that fed his work. Alongside these philosophical and theological sources come the long list of scientists who also fired Traherne's imagination, some of whom were mentioned

---

64 Culverwell, for instance, refers to 'cleare and undelible Principles, some first and Alphabetical Notions,' which 'are stampt and printed upon the being of man' (Nathanael Culverwell, *An Elegant and Learned Discourse of the Light of Nature*, London, 1652, p. 54). And in Traherne's *Commonplace Book* we find: 'And indeed these common seeds of naturall Light are a private Law, which God has deeply engraven on mens consciences, and is universally extensive unto all, though with a latitude of Degrees; it being in some more, in some Lesse, but in all in great measure obliterated, and defaced since the *fall*. It is also by Divines generally termed the *Light*, or *Law of Nature*, because it flows in, and with, and from Human Nature, eyther immediately, or mediately' (*CB*, s.v. 'Reason', fol. 83, col. 1, quoted from Theophilus Gale, *The Court of the Gentiles*, London and Oxford, 1669–78, vol. I, part II).

65 C, III, 1.

66 Traherne uses the name Tully.

67 See C. Schmitt, *Aristotle and the Rennaisance*, Cambridge, MA: Harvard University Press, 1983.

68 For a fuller account of this work see Donald Allchin, 'The Sacrifice of Praise and Thanksgiving', pp. 22–37. For extracts of the *Year-Book* see Allchin, *Landscapes of Glory*, London: Darton, Longman & Todd, 1989; Inge, *Happiness and Holiness*, pp. 256–7, 297–303.

above, as well as fellow poets such as George Herbert, who appears in the *Church's Year-Book* and in *The Kingdom of God*, and Spenser in *Commentaries of Heaven*.

The Poet of Felicity?

We now see Traherne as much as a prose writer as a poet, and more than ever before as a theologian. We see him involved in the debates of his day and connected to many of the issues that concern us in ours – a reverence for creation, the beauty and priceless worth of the natural world, the capacity of the human soul, the importance of human choice, the spiritual quest, the interplay of science and religion, to name but a few. What kind of reading could we offer that at once honours Traherne's rootedness in his own time and admits his relevance to ours, and that infuses the old understandings of Traherne with new insights? Tempting as it may be, to jettison the 'Felicity' label altogether would be to ignore one of Traherne's major themes and to risk the possibility of developing a critique as lopsided as those that have been outgrown.

Nevertheless, there is a growing awareness in the critical canon from the latter part of the twentieth century onwards, that Traherne's felicity needs to be re-examined not just because an accomplished, easy happiness is alienating for many readers but because it does not resonate with the depth of insights found in other aspects of his work. Already the naive and otherworldly Poet of Felicity as described by Dobell and Wade in the beginning of this introduction is an unrecognizable character.[69] Gone is the 'easy felicity' that was so often viewed as an achieved state and that made Traherne's happiness seem toil-free.

The view that had seen Traherne's felicity as a kind of vague optimism or an abstraction is also changing.[70] Douglas Bush wrote in the 1960s: 'Neither as a Christian nor as philosopher does Traherne seem quite mature'; in his work there is 'a large element of facile, expansive, emotional optimism, the kind of optimism which in the next

---

69 As Joan Webber notes 'No reader of the *Select Meditations* could ever conceive of calling this author a "poet of felicity"' (*The Eloquent I: Style and Self in Seventeenth-century Prose*, Madison, WI: University of Wisconsin Press, 1968. p. 225).

70 See for instance Towers, 'Thomas Traherne'; and Willis Barnestone, 'Two Poets of Felicity: Thomas Traherne and Jorge Guillen', *Books Abroad*, 42 (1968), 14–19. Barnestone's emphasis on abstraction goes so far that he describes Traherne's poetry as 'a form of literary cubism'. It seems to me that Barnestone's felicity seeks to go beyond the world without ever having gone through it. In failing to recognize the sacramental nature of Traherne's vision, he has misunderstood Traherne's relationship to the world.

generations passed easily into deistic sentimentalism and vague aspiration towards infinity'.[71] Justin Miller, however, twenty years later, rejects optimism as another name for felicity. He contends that 'The full meaning of "felicity" cannot be appreciated without viewing it in the context of Traherne's empathy for the pain of the Crucifixion ... The greatness of Traherne's spirit is not in its amiable optimism but in his continued appreciation for the transcended creaturedly and created.'[72] Malcolm Day takes Traherne's optimism seriously; it comes from somewhere and is going somewhere, since it arises out of a 'cosmic' perspective that sees all temporal events in the light of eternity.[73]

As early as 1972, Francis King saw Traherne's felicity as hard won, though revealed not so much in his ecstatic exclamations – which he considered to be floppy thought and language – but in the intense intellectual activity of Traherne's mind:

> the activity of felicity is an intense and learned activity, rather than pure Act ... the conceptual thought working on living memory ... it is this conjunction that radiates felicity, not the flaccid exclamations about Glory, Love, Light, Space, which seem a betrayal of the act of 'Life'.[74]

King is right to locate felicity in action, and right to expect more of it than a kind of enjoyment without labour, a coming home without the journey. But, like others before and after him, he makes felicity largely an activity of the mind. What we see now more than ever before is that Traherne's felicity is a matter of the heart. It is about desire, not intellection. That is why it cannot be easy or abstract or finished. It is weighted by need and winged with longing. Enjoying the world may

---

71 *English Literature in the Earlier Seventeenth Century*, New York: Oxford University Press, 1962, p. 158.

72 Justin Miller, 'Thomas Traherne: Love and Pain in the Poet of Felicity', *Historical Magazine of the Protestant Episcopal Church*, 49 (1980), pp. 209–20, 210 and 220. Miller's thesis is that understanding Traherne's felicity as a kind of unlimited optimism is totally inadequate since it largely ignores Traherne's many references to and identification with the suffering of Christ and the Cross. Miller argues that Traherne's leading of the reader into participation in the life of the Divine must include this suffering, and holds that Traherne's unique gift is that, by appreciation and purgation, he transcends the material world without ever losing his gratitude for it. See also Itrat-Husain, whose understanding of felicity similarly relies on apprehending the significance of the Cross (*The Mystical Element in the Metaphysical Poets of the Seventeenth Century*, Edinburgh: Oliver and Boyd, 1948, p. 294).

73 Day, *Thomas Traherne*, p. 5.

74 Francis King, 'Thomas Traherne: Intellect and Felicity', in Harold Love (ed.), *Restoration Literature: Critical Approaches*, London: Methuen and Co, 1972, pp. 121–43, 129.

be one movement towards it, but felicity itself is more profound.[75] It is about having the continuous want of love and goodness continually supplied.

---

[75] Beachcroft noted this as early as 1930 when he wrote: 'This rarefied rejoicing in natural beauty is apt to be represented as the whole burden of Traherne's Felicity: in truth it is but the first movement towards it' (T.O. Beachcroft, 'Traherne and the Doctrine of Felicity', *The Criterion*, 9 (1930), pp. 291–307). Where Beachcroft deals with the theme of felicity his study is at its most valuable. His broader comments on Traherne's style and structure are, in the light of subsequent discoveries, less accurate.

I

Wanting

> Till all the World be Swallowed up, and Eyd,
> And Taken in, and fed upon, and Known...
> It thirsts, and drinks, and thirsts and drinks again,
> The more it drinks, more Thirsty doth remain
> Its Hunger grows by Eating, and its Thirst
> By Drink's enflamed, till its Paunch doth burst.
>
> (*COH*, 'Avarice I')

Wanting is the dark side to felicity. Traherne knew it, knew about how the shadow made things real; he understood the lacks and wants by which we know our needs and in which we move. Traherne discussed shadow in the context of painting (C, I, 41) as if he understood that the shadow is that which makes the round object globed, that takes a still life's floating vase and places it on a real table. He wrote of 'perfective needs' (C, I, 42) and of wants that confer value on our treasures. For Traherne, want is a rich and layered word. And yet want is the shadow side of felicity that we have largely ignored, or treated rather lightly, as if it meant nothing more than wishing – a vague yearning to match Traherne's rather vague optimism. Whereas want is the bedrock of joy, the spring of action, the shaping shadow, the force of the spiritual quest and the ground of all felicity. Without this shadow our depictions of felicity remain unrounded and unrooted, circles rather than spheres, routes without origins.

This wanting originates in the heart of God, according to Traherne, and is emulated in our own need to love and be beloved of God, others, ourselves. And all this loving occurs in a virtuous circle of loving and being beloved that is, as we shall see in the final chapter of this book, felicity itself. This cycle, says Traherne, in *The Kingdom of God*, is the beginning and end of felicity, against which no evil can prevail.

It is no surprise that felicity may be described as a circle. What Traherne is saying in style as well as in content, here in the newly published *The Kingdom of God* as in other works we have seen, is that felicity is not a fixed point towards which we make a linear progress. This is one reason why identifying felicity either in Traherne's memories of childhood or in naive optimism about the future will not do. His felicity is neither solely retrospective nor prospective. It is located in neither end point of destination or beginning but, like T. S. Eliot's arrival at a destination that discovers it to be in fact the place of departure known 'for the first time',[1] felicity occurs in the circle joined. That is not to say that in the pursuit of felicity nothing happens. Innocence and vision are lost and regained; the soul is stretched, beautified, humbled and enlarged as it comes to see its purpose and potential, the height from which it has fallen and the love that bids it rise. The entrances and exits to the felicitous path occur in the maelstrom of life and in the dynamic of change.

What is it that drives this change? Donald Bruce has noted that, in Traherne's writing, it is desire that keeps the will in motion.[2] For Bruce, desire is a wound, for which felicity is the easement; since by desire the will is kept in motion and the mind prevented from becoming static, desire is its own cure. But in *The Kingdom of God*, Traherne goes further: more than a wound that needs healing, desire is the moving force of the soul. He writes that the soul is 'like a Watch wound up' and that 'Appetite and Desire are the spring that urge it'.[3]

In a recent article the American theologian Belden Lane records his encounter with Traherne in the Ozark wilderness, and his ensuing awareness of desire as the moving force not only of the soul but of the universe. Everything is 'pulsing with want', writes Lane. 'We are incurably creatures of desire, "wanted" into being by the restless ardor of God's own heart.'[4]

Lane cites the physicist Brian Swimme, who asserts: 'the unity of the world rests on the pursuit of passion'. Drawing on human experience and the exploration of space alike, he writes that the same attraction 'that excites lovers into chasing each other through the night, that pulls the parent out of bed for the third time to comfort a sick child' is glimpsed in the Hubble Space Telescope's pictures of the Eagle Nebula, the birthplace of new stars where huge dark clouds containing hydrogen atoms rush together by gravitational attraction. They are stripped of electrons and fuse to form helium ions releasing massive amounts of

---

[1] T. S. Eliot, *Four Quartets*, London: Faber, 1969, p. 197.
[2] Donald Bruce, 'Thomas Traherne, 1637–1674', *Contemporary Review*, 226 (1975), pp. 19–24.
[3] *KOG*, Ch. 5, l. 11; cf C, II, 22.
[4] Lane, 'Thomas Traherne and the Awakening of Want', *The Anglican Theological Review*, 81, no. 4 (Fall 1999), pp. 651–64, **656** and **652**.

unseen energy in a brilliant lightburst.[5] Lane also quotes the cellular biologist Ursula Goodenough: 'The whole planet shimmers with desirability . . . Fireflies pulse, houseflies bat their wings, moths send out musk, fish dance, frogs croon, birds display feathers and song, mammals strut and preen.'[6]

As Lane asserts: 'Want is the universal, alluring activity that permeates the entire cosmos.'[7] He could not have chosen more relevant examples to illustrate his point in an article on Traherne: Traherne too was fascinated by the discoveries of microscope and telescope, and overwhelmingly convinced of the primacy of desire in the universe. In the recently published *The Kingdom of God*, 'Allure' is the very word he shares with Lane. According to Traherne all things allured God to make them:

> All the Pleasure of Life, all Worlds allured him to make them. all Angels and Men, all Beauties and perfections all Delights and Treasures, all Joys and Honors allured him to make them. All that he Saw his Omnipresence and Eternitie Capable of, Invited him unto them. His own Wisdom, and power allured him: So did the Hallelujahs, and praises of all his Creatures. (*KOG*, Ch. 15, ll. 144–8)

As Traherne reminds us in *Commentaries of Heaven*, the word allure has its origins in hunger, in the red, raw meat on the falconer's mitt, in the claims of beak and claw:

> The meat which falconers hold up to their Hawkes, when they are on high in the Air, or pearching upon some Tree to entice them to their hand is among Englishmen called a Lure: from whence the world Allurement seemeth to be derived.[8]

This chapter looks at this notion of desire that permeates Traherne's writing – first of all the layered word 'want', with its suggestion of both lack and longing; then at passion and prudence, at insatiability, infinity and finally what it might mean to 'want like a GOD' (*C*, I, 44).

---

[5] Brian Swimme, *The Universe is a Green Dragon: A Cosmic Creation Story*, Sante Fe, NM: Bear & Company, 1984, pp. 48–50; quoted in Lane, 'Thomas Traherne', pp. 656–7.
[6] Ursula Goodenough, *The Sacred Depths of Nature*, New York: Oxford University Press, 1998, pp. 132–3; quoted in Lane, 'Thomas Traherne', p. 657.
[7] Lane, 'Thomas Traherne', p. 656.
[8] 'Allurement', *COH*, folio 68v.

Desire and Sexuality

What exactly do I mean by desire in Traherne? The word 'want' with both its positive implication of stretching out towards an object and its negative connotation of lack seems to be a near synonym; however, 'want' has not always had this double meaning. Whereas desire has, from the start, been associated with longing – wish, need, covet, demand – the earliest entries in the *Oxford English Dictionary* for 'want' define wanting solely in terms of lack. 'Want' is used predicatively or quasi-adjectivally to denote shortage or deficiency – want of beauty, want of trees, want of milk or eggs; Hobbes so uses it in 1651 in his *Leviathan* (Part I, Ch. 8, l. 34): ''tis the want of Discretion that makes the difference'. Want may be a state of lack, the condition of penury, starvation or suffering as in Dryden's *Aeneis* (1697), in which he wrote of 'Rough Saticulans, inur'd to Wants' (Book VII, l. 1009). Want is also a fault, a gap, a hole, a hollow as used by Traherne's fellow theologian Richard Baxter in 1664: 'The wants in the wheels of your watch are as useful to the motion as the nucks or solid parts' (*Divine Life*, I, x). Like the adjectival and nominal forms of the word, the verb 'to want' also has its antecedents in lack. 'To be lacking or missing; not to exist' is the earliest verbal meaning given in the *OED*. 'To want' may also mean to be without, as in this domestic instruction from 1684: 'if you want Peaches, you may use Juice of soure Apples'; or to be deprived of or to lose, as in this domestic blunder: 'The Pot-hooks and Hanger were carried out of the Chimney, and being wanted four days, they found them at last in a Cockloft' (1695). These lack-based meanings were also used at this time in what was to become the United States. John Winthrop (1630) in his *Letter in New England* (I. 379) wrote: 'Though we have not beef and mutton, etc. yet (God be praised) we want them not; our Indian corn answers for all.' Deficiency, shortage, penury, a gap, a loss or a sense of absence – wherever you look in the seventeenth century and before, 'want' is transcribed as lack of one kind or another. The modern understanding of the word 'want' in its outward reach towards desire, longing or wish does not become normative until the beginning of the eighteenth century. For Traherne to describe God as wanting, then, may seem to challenge the notion of divine omnipotence; his God is a God who in some sense lacks. This construct of desire is one to which we shall return in the fourth chapter when we consider Traherne, lack and God in reference to the modern psychoanalyst and philosopher Jacques Lacan. For now, it is important merely to note the long history of lack in the word 'want'. Although there are indications that a more need-based or desire-based use of 'want' was evolving,[9] lack would have been the simplest meaning of want in Traherne's day. We can see this single meaning of 'want' in such lines as 'the want of Modesty is pernicious and destructive'(*CE*, p. 237).

A gradual change in the meaning of 'want', which soon gained momentum, seems to have begun sometime in the mid to late seventeenth century when a thing that was wanted (missing) was also wanted (desired, needed); this can be seen, for instance, in the practical 1695 example above of the lost 'Pot-hooks and Hanger' that were 'wanted' for four days. Dryden's 1697 'Make me but happy in his safe Return, Whose wanted Presence I can only mourn' (*Aeneis* IX 34) is the *OED*'s first use of 'want' that combines lack with desire or need. Just nine years later, a modern reading of desire is recorded in which lack has disappeared altogether – 'to want' means simply 'to desire' or 'to wish for'.[10] While lack-based meanings of want carried on in common parlance for many years, the newer meaning of 'want' as 'desire' had clearly arrived to run alongside it, a meaning that would, by the late nineteenth century, overtake the earlier one completely. Exactly when this transition started is not possible to say, but as early as 1630 Winthrop's use – 'Though we have not beef and mutton, etc. yet (God be praised) we want them not; our Indian corn answers for all' – suggests that wanting is not only a matter of lacking but also of apprehending the lack as need.

Etymologically, 'want' moved decidedly towards 'desire' through the elliptical use of 'wanted' in advertising. 'Wanted, a governess' and 'Experienced bookkeepers wanted' suggested both what was lacked and what was sought. But long before newspapers made such ads commonplace, 'want' suggested something sought or required. In 1593, Henry VI's cry 'Oh welcome Oxford, for we want thy helpe' (Shakespeare, *Henry VI*, V, i, 66) is just such an instance of need/want. By the time that 'desire, wish for' eventually occurred as a primary meaning of 'want' in the early eighteenth century, it had already been accompanying lack as an associated meaning for decades. Traherne's writing occurs early in this period of linguistic change, long before the want-ad and comfortably after Shakespeare; for Traherne, as for Shakespeare, Dryden and others, to want is not just to lack but to know our need of that which is lacking. Lack is still present, but the 'need' that will lead

---

9 A very early use of 'to want' as 'to seek' is recorded in a 1563 Rogation sermon, but this is designated as 'obsolete' and 'rare'.

10 'All such as want to ride in post-haste from one World to the other' (E. Ward, 1706).

to 'desire' is beginning to show itself in his word 'want': 'Were there no needs, wants would be wanting themselves, and supplies superfluous' (C, I, 41). Traherne writes of human wanting. Divine wanting is no less a mixture of need/desire and lack: 'He [God] wanted the communication of his divine essence, and persons to enjoy it. He wanted Worlds, He wanted Spectators, He wanted Joys, He wanted treasures. He wanted, yet He wanted not, for He had them' (C, I, 41).

While it would be a mistake to read Traherne's 'want' simply in modern terms of desire and wish, it would be equally misleading to read his 'want' in all cases as simple lack. Traherne often couples lack-want and desire as if the two ran in parallel, thus associating want with desire: 'No misery is greater than that of wanting in the midst of enjoyments, of seeing and desiring yet never possessing' (C, I, 48). He writes, 'Infinite Wants satisfied produce infinite Joys ... *The Desire Satisfied is a Tree of Life*' (C, I, 43), again running 'want' and 'desire' in tandem. Nowhere is this marriage of lack and desire more clearly stated than in this formidable description of 'Appetite' in *Commentaries of Heaven*, in which want that is lack also creates, and in which vacuity and capacity stir desire.

> The Objects of the Intelligible Appetite is all the GOOD the vacuitie & capacity of the Soul can Suggest to its Desire: Hunger in the Dark, supplying the place of Beauty in the Light: the meer Absence of Good things creating a sence, like the Knowledg of them. (*COH*, fol. 112r)

Absence creates a sense of that which is missing as strong as knowledge; hunger acts in the place of beauty, capacity awakens desire. This potent mixture of power and need, of wholeness and hunger as the primary business of the soul is what this book seeks to explore. What is the lack saying; what is it calling forth; where is it taking us? These are the questions that Traherne seeks to address.

Why not simply use the word 'desire'? It does not have such a highly evolved etymology: from its earliest occurrences in the English language, it meant pretty much what it does now – need, demand, wish, covet, crave. It is not a word that looks two ways. While want retains a double aspect of lack and longing, desire (though less complicated) can be even more misleading, not because of its ancient history but because of the strong identification with sex that has accrued to it in our current age. This strong identification with sex has occurred almost to the exclusion of other related meanings, so that desire is often used in a less nuanced sense than a word such as 'want', which exacerbates the problem of reading 'want' when 'want' = 'desire'. Not only is sex about wanting but wanting is also evidently now about sex. A great deal of contemporary advertising tells us this – that sex sells. It sells everything from novels to three-piece suites.[11] If we make something sexy people will want it. And so sexual desire, as well as being an expression of our want, has become a catalyst to it, leaving terms such as 'desire' and 'want' difficult to read in an unsexualized light.

Until recently there has been so little sex in Traherne that, although some scholars have noted sensuous imagery of feasting and treasure, discussing desire in terms of sexuality has not been an issue for Traherne scholars. The newest discoveries, however, include sensual imagery in which sexual allusion cannot be ignored. These discoveries invite a fresh interpretation of Traherne's imagery as a whole to include the impetus of eros, and we see that sprinkled through his writings are discernible echoes of Dionysius the Areopagite, who speaks of God as 'the fullness of erotic love'. It is He, says Dionysius, 'the creator of all . . . who out of extreme erotic love moves outside Himself . . . (and approaches humanity), burning with great goodness and love and eros'.[12]

The poem 'Love', for example, with its mixture of heterosexual and homosexual images, is clearly charged with erotic energy – heavenly blessings pour on the poet's head like Jove's 'golden rain' came to Danae's 'pleasing, fruitful womb' and the poet is gathered up as Ganymede to Olympus, a heavenly consort. But as the modern American theologian William Countryman notes, 'The eros that informs and animates this vision is not narrowly heterosexual or homosexual. It is not exclusively sexual at all.'[13] It is a poem above all about intimacy, in which the poet is, in the end, gendered and non-gendered, by physical allegory metaphysically related to God as 'His image, and His friend. / His son, bride, glory, temple, end.' The coming down of God and the gathering up of the human to be the companion and consort is what

---

11 Witness anything from the cover of a Jilly Cooper novel to a recent DFS furniture catalogue in which headings read 'how to fake it' (photo of alluring woman in low-cut, animal-skin print lounges seductively on leopard-skin couch), 'legs are in' (photo of curvy legs peeking from opened bathrobe) and 'feel me' (beautiful woman lounging luxuriantly on couch with ogling man standing above her).

12 Dionysius, *De Div. Nom.* IV, 12. Dionysius was a late-fifth-/early-sixth-century theologian and philosopher, whose manuscripts grew popular in the Middle Ages – Aquinas cites Dionysius over 1,700 times.

13 L. William Countryman, *Love Human and Divine: Reflections on Love, Sexuality and Friendship*, London: Morehouse, 2005, p. 64.

the poem is about, and through its eroticism, not despite it, it takes us into the outer reaches of what early Christian theologians called *theosis*, the notion that God became human so that humanity might become divine, a dominant theme in Traherne's theology to which we shall return in later chapters.

Erotically charged imagery also appears in the *Centuries* and *Commentaries of Heaven*, imagery of tasting and feasting and having and seizing with passion. In 'Allurement' (*COH*), for instance, Traherne, quoting the Psalms and Song of Songs, describes the soul as a bride and God as the lover who sends the sun and stars as emissaries to entice the beloved: 'The sun comes like a Bridegroom forth, to shew / The shining of his Love' and 'The Moons a Messenger that steals by Night / In to my Bedchamber', whose bright face enflames his soul with love. Even the earth 'clad in sweet and royal liveries / of curious flowers' joins in this allurement and the rivers in great and global seduction:

> The silver Strings and Streams my Soul inflame.
> While passing by they lick and kiss my feet . . .

Meanwhile gifts exotic, sweet and valuable are poured out like offerings:

> Milk Hony Gold Arabian Spices, sweet
> Perfumes Wines Oyls all these he from abov
> Doth send as Sacred Tokens of his Love.
> My very Body was his Gift.
>
> (ll. 40–60)

These references, though certainly sensual, even erotic, allude to rather than describe sexual union. Two works in the Lambeth Manuscript, however, move these sensual allusions into a more sexual setting – the bride and her bridegroom, the lover and the beloved.

In the final chapter of *The Kingdom of God*, there is a passage in which we see the bride/soul image developed more highly than anywhere else in all of Traherne's work.[14] The passage is some four folios

---

14 The image of the divine lover and the soul/bride is scattered throughout Traherne's work. See: 'O remember how all Thy Lov Terminates in me: How I am made thy Bride', (*SM*, I, 82); 'I am made His Bride to Delight Him' (*SM*, II, 5); also *SM*, I, 83; II, 16–18; II, 23; II, 40; II, 66; and *C*, V, 10; as well as poems such as 'Adultery' (*COH*). But most of these metaphors are not expanded beyond a few lines. In *Inducements to Retiredness* a

in length and is given entirely to outlining the role of the bride and the bridegroom, the reasons for their joy and the risks of their love. On the second folio we find a certain amount of sexual suggestion when the soul is described as the untouched virgin whose divine bridegroom is gratified with the greater pleasure because of the freshness of her experiences as he approaches.

> And as there are Pleasures peculiar to the Estate of Woers, and perhaps Sweeter than those of Marriage, but wholly different; So was She placed in the Estate of Trial, as a virgin untouched, that She might experience all the Approaches of So Beautiful a Suitor, and Gratifie his Affection with the Greater Pleasure.[15]

These euphemistic lines are few in the whole of the passage. What is more significant, to my mind, is the tension that runs throughout. Will she receive his approaches? Will satisfaction be attained? Will she conceive what he begets?[16] The passage as a whole participates in the sexual dynamic of power, consent and union, and these three themes reverberate repeatedly over the several pages. The specifically sexual lines cited above are the metaphor distilled, sexual consummation expressing the consummation of their whole life in union and communion with each other. Traherne makes it clear from the outset that this passage is about God and the soul,[17] whereas in his short treatise *Love*, also from the Lambeth Manuscript, he begins with an extended description of love that is purely human.

In this second passage, the language is more physical – there are caresses and embraces, the beloved surrendering herself up to be devoured by the love of her lover, whose glances, sighs and touches ravish her more than anything in the world. Notice how her exalted station

---

slightly longer passage on the soul as bride occurs (*ITR*, ll. 925–38) but its concern is to depict the honours conferred on God's bride rather than the joys of wooing and winning. In several places in *The Kingdom of God*, the soul/bride image is developed more fully to convey both the force of God's jealousy (*KOG*, Ch. 6, ll. 12–106) and God's joy in giving to us (*KOG*, Ch. 14, ll. 45–138).

15 *KOG*, Ch. 42, ll. 356–60.

16 These questions are posed by such lines as 'O what fear and compassion! what Expectation and Desire! what Agonie, what Weakness, Danger . . . But O what unspeakable Joy! . . . when all the Danger is over, and the satisfaction attained' (ll. 366–9) and by that cited in the text above. The word 'danger' itself appears no less than four times and is suggested many times over.

17 God is the bridegroom and the soul is the bride. Line 341 begins: 'But this is not all. His Bride must hav som thing peculiar to her sex, which God himself doth not Enjoy unless it be in her'.

heightens the pleasure of the lover, how it lends frisson to the merest touch and renders her favours 'more then celestial':

> It is a prodigious thing to contemplate the illimited sweetness of Tyrannical Love. Even here upon Earth it hath been seen somtimes so transcendent and endless, that a Majestie admired and adored by others, a Beauty scarce permitted to be seen afar off, desired by thousands, but by none to be familiarly approached not to be spoken to by the greatest Kings but upon the Knee, nor accosted but with Trembling, hath surrendered up it self to be devoured by the Love of one, and as greedily desired his Embraces as prodigaly bestowed her own. As if they were somthing more then celestial, a favorable Glance, a Sigh, a Touch, are able to enflame a loving Soul with Raptures, and inspire Delights which no Ravishments in the World can equal. All the Conversation is Extasie, feasts, Banquets, Victories, Triumphs, Crowns, Scepters, Jewels, Perfumes, Elixars, Spices, Treasures, Palaces, Temples, Pictures, Caresses, Songs, Musick, whatever can be thought of; all are nothing, compared to the Conversation the Lov and the Beauty of such a particular Person. What is the reason of all this high and Strange Esteem? It is Lov alone. This Lovly Empress hath conceived an Affection in her soul to such a person: and the most high and worthy souls are capable of the most high and violent Affections. This makes her Object so happy and glorious in the Conquest of such a rare and invincible Potentate. And in all this the Communicativ Humor of his Love is delighted. But this is not all. As He is more Enjoyable here then in other places, he has more to enjoy. His Eys are the Sun that enlighten her Soul, his Face is the Abridgment of heaven in her Esteem, his Arms the circle of felicitie, his Breath more Sweet then Arabian Airs, his soul a mysterious Abyss of Glory, his Accents more delightfull then the Musick of the Spheres, his existence the Lustre of the World, and his person more pleaseing then the same: She livs only for his sake, he is the only Life of all her Comforts, the Soul nay the very idol of her Soul. Thus it happeneth often in profane Loves. But (as we said) this is not all. There is an Avaricious humor likwise in Lov that desires to be satisfied: and to this she yeelds up herself a willing sacrifice. He passeth through all her Guards, is reverenced by her Nobles, enters her Closet, ransacks her Letters, Treasures, Jewels; ascends her Throne, plays with her Scepter, invades her Crown, reigns in her Kingdom; enjoys all her Gardens, Palaces, Revenues, nay her Beauties, Desires, Affections. Her Arms, her Heart is open to him; and all these are

esteemed only delightfull and glorious for his sake, because he alone is the truly Beloved, the Idol of her Soul, and her very soul. Were she able to do Millions of things more for him, she would: her very Eys and hands are his, as well as her Jewels. (*L*, 126r–v)

There is a sense here that real bodies are being referrred to – there are arms and eyes, faces and breath to Traherne's lovers. There is greed in their embraces and prodigality in the bestowal of their favours. 'There is an Avaricious humor' in their love that desires to be satisfied. Traherne stops just short of taking his reader into their bed. In fact, initially he did exactly that and thought the better of it, since he edited out 'her Bed' from the list of what was open to the lover: 'Her Arms, her Heart, is open to him'.[18] Similarly, a few lines later, 'Lips' were edited out of the manuscript, though hands and eyes remain to be given to the lover along with her jewels.[19] What he did not see the need to reduce was his description of the taking of her power or, one might say, the giving up of her power, since 'she yeelds up herself a willing sacrifice' to the one who passes 'through her Guards, is reverenced by her Nobles, . . .' The fact of this taking remains total despite Traherne's removal of two 'alls' ('all her Letters' and 'all her Beauties'). The lover is unchecked as he passes through her several layers of protection and privacy to the very highest symbols of her power: her throne, sceptre and crown. These he 'ascends', 'playes with' and 'invades'. His actions are the actions of conquest, described in language of sexual allusion both playful and violent.[20] The explicit sexual activity Traherne has edited out he has re-integrated metaphorically, and he has re-integrated it into that part of the account of their love that deals with the taking and relinquishing of power. Again the themes of power, consent and union, which appeared in the passage from *The Kingdom of God* above, resurface; this time with even greater force. Where, in *The Kingdom of God*, the beloved is initially a Queen, here she is experienced by her lover as a Tyrant, Empress and Potentate. In neither account is it fitting that she should be compelled. The importance of this power to choose becomes the theme of subsequent chapters; what is significant here is that in both accounts the power she has to deny the lover heightens the pleasure of their union.[21]

---

18 This initially read 'Her Arms, her Bed, her Heart, is open to him' (l. 68).

19 '& Lips' was edited from 'her very Eys and Hands & Lips are his, as well as her Jewels' (l. 71).

20 In these few lines the lover is also said to 'enter', 'ransack' and 'enjoy'.

21 Compare *KOG* (Ch. 42, l. 355): 'neither befits it the Estate of a queen to be compeld . . . What Praise, what Blessedness . . . when the satisfaction attained' with *L* (ll. 51–3):

In both the soul/bride metaphor of *The Kingdom of God* and the account of human love in *Love*, Traherne shows himself to be at home in the language of physical love, and we may see that he has no small knowledge of the dynamic of sexual desire. Yet in neither of these accounts is sexual desire his primary concern. It may be the image, but it is not the end. His purpose is always to show the desire that exists in God for the human soul and in the human soul for God and the process by which these two may be united in love. And so it is not surprising that, in *Love*, he shifts attention from the human lover to the divine:

> Let us ascend from temporal to Eternall Loves. If these Petite and finit Lovers can be thus ardent, and by meer Instinct understand their Interest . . . what may we think of God Almighty? By how much the more he loves, by so much the more doth he exceed in all.[22]

As with St Augustine, Gregory the Great, Gregory of Nyssa and many others who came before him, for Traherne the greatest loves are soul to soul, God to soul, and soul to God, for which all other binding loves serve as pictures. Thus his poem in *Commentaries of Heaven* entitled 'Adultery' is not about a husband and wife but about the soul's infidelity to God.[23] Similarly, in the *Centuries*, he admonishes his reader to see the beauty of the 'curious and fair woman'[24] and to see, moreover, that her greatest beauty is the image of God that she carries

---

'and the most high and worthy souls are capable of the most high and violent Affections. This makes her Object so happy and glorious in the Conquest of such a rare and invincible Potentate.'

22 *L*, ll. 79–80. Similar parallels are also made in *KOG* when, in his discussion of adultery of the soul/bride, Traherne writes: 'And by how much that more great and ardent Lov is, by so much that most is it grieved, if not chafed and enraged at the loss of its Object' (*KOG*, Ch. 6, ll. 33–5). Again, in a passage on the soul/bride that clearly echoes the Pauline model of husband and wife as Christ and the Church, Traherne reiterates: 'These [examples of earthly love] are Litle Hints of Infinit Mysteries' (*KOG*, Ch. 14, ll. 78–9).

23 Similarly, in his discussion of infidelity in *KOG* (Ch. 6), the most terrible aspect is the violation not of the body but of the relationship between the husband and the wife who represent the soul and God: 'The injury consists not so much in defiling the Body, as in Adulterating the Mind' (ll. 20–1).

24 *C*, II, 68: 'Suppose a curious and fair woman. Some have seen the beauties of Heaven in such a person. It is a vain thing to say they loved too much. I dare say there are ten thousand beauties in that creature which they have not seen. They loved it not too much, but on false causes. Not so much upon false ones, as only upon some little ones. They love a creature for sparkling eyes and curled hair, lily breasts and ruddy cheeks: which they should love moreover for being God's Image, Queen of the Universe, beloved of Angels, redeemed by Jesus Christ, and heiress of Heaven, and temple of the Holy Ghost: a mine and fountain of all virtues, a treasury of graces, and a child of God.'

within her, that spark of the divine that makes her both wholly human and tinged with heaven. He specifically does not say that to love the physicality of her is wrong, only that it is too little. They that love her eyes and hair and breasts and cheeks love too little, not too much.

The Passion Imperative

What are we then to say about excessive love in Traherne's understanding of desire? Can there be such a thing as too much love? It seems that, over and over again in his writings, excesses of love and desire are praised. In the *Centuries* Traherne writes of love: 'Love is infinitely delightful to its object, and the more violent the more glorious ... Excess is its true moderation: Activity its rest: and burning fervency its only refreshment.'[25] In his Poem 'Affection' (*COH*, fol. 31), a poem of 137 lines devoted entirely to the praise of the affections of the soul, the reader is reminded that the whole purpose of creation is love. The world is made by Love out of love. Love, by several names, is presented as not only the cause and end of creation but also that which sustains and redeems it.

Having been made by Love out of love, Traherne's world is the place where love is to be sought and found. And this seeking is not only human; for God, too, is loving and seeking to be loved. '[H]ow much he thee doth prize',[26] writes Traherne; 'All his Endeavors sanctified by Love / Do with his Passions thy Enjoyments prove.'[27] Here we see not only a God whose love abounds in a generously charitable sense but a God who loves as we love, a God who woos, whose passion dictates his action. This is a departure from the traditional image of God found in Christian theologians such as Thomas Aquinas and the long line of those who have followed in the Thomist tradition. For Aquinas writes,

> When love, joy, and the like, are attributed to God or the angels or man's intellectual orexis, they refer simply to acts of will which produce indeed the same sort of result as does action prompted by emotion, but are not in fact accompanied by emotion.[28]

---

[25] C, II, 54, n.
[26] *COH*, 'Affection', l. 70.
[27] Ibid., ll. 72-3.
[28] Ia2ae. 22. 3.

In other words, neither the human mind nor God nor the angels feel emotion when they act; we merely apply to them the terms for various emotions because we recognize the actions they perform as being like those we perform out of emotion. As Saint Augustine writes,

> The holy angels feel no emotion of anger when they inflict punishment, and feel no emotion of pity when they render help. But ordinary usage applies to them the terms for the various emotions because the actions which an angel performs are similar to those prompted in us by the emotions, although he himself is not subject to the weakness of those emotions.[29]

This is the logical conclusion of a hierarchical system that places the mind above the body and then seats the emotions in that body. Emotion can be nothing other than weakness.[30]

In terms of excessive love, Traherne's God is far removed from the Thomist model. His is a God whose passion is not a projection of our own human emotion but whose emotion is the original stuff out of which our souls' capacity for passion is formed. In the poem 'Allurement' we see a rare role reversal, in which God's love is likened not to Traherne's usual image of a king's love for his intended but a woman's love for her child or her lover, a love so powerful that it tyrannizes her:

> No Kind and tender Mother doth allure
> Her Child so Winningly, No virgin sure
> So loves her Lov, nor ever was there seen,
> A Proud, but tamd, enflamd, heart-wounded Queen
> Subdud by Love, whose Lov did tyrannize
> So much ore [sic] her, as his Above the Skies
> Doth him enflame. His Essence is all Love . . .
>
> (ll. 76–82)

For Traherne, God is love and we love in God's image. 'You must want like a God that you may be satisfied like God', he writes (C, I, 44), and 'He made us want like Gods' (C, I, 41).[31] We understand divine love in

---

29 *De civitate Dei*, IX, 5, PL 41, 261.

30 The implications of want in God, specifically what this might suggest about need and lack, will be explored in greater detail at the end of this chapter and in chaper four of this book.

31 The indefinite article in 'You must want like a God' and the plural in 'He made us

human terms because the pattern of divine love is in us. So it should be no surprise that Traherne's divine lover loves in a fashion that we recognize. He seeks to please; he sacrifices for and woos his beloved object. He offers Treasures, delights and bliss; he is singleminded, seeking nothing but the return of his love: 'pure Love / Aspires to nothing els, for nought doth move / But this, to be Beloved'.[32] And he is not immune from the anguish of loving: this aspect of divine love is so shocking to Traherne that he interjects 'My God!' at the very thought. It is at once terrible and wonderful to imagine God in anguish for the love of one human soul, and this is exactly what Traherne dares do:

> He woes, he grievs, he Fears, he doth lament
> He hopes he covets and is discontent
> My God! what are we that thou so shouldst strive
> To retriev Mortals . . .[33]

Moderation and decorum, elegance and poise are not the silks of this God's courtship. There is nothing classical[34] or courtly in Traherne's picture of God. Every word in the universe is his, whose only eloquence is ardour. For Traherne's God is a passionate God whose desire for the human soul is beautified by its own excess:

> Sweetness and Ardor, Zeal and Violence,
> Excess of Lov, joynd with an Excellence
> So great, might justly ravish and Enflame
> Us[35]

---

want like Gods' may raise some question concerning what kind of God Traherne is meaning. Is this 'god' *any* or *some various* gods, a notional deity, a pagan god? Clearly not, since in the very sentence following 'He made us want like Gods', Traherne goes on to distinguish between 'the heathen Deities' who 'wanted nothing, and were therefore unhappy, for they had no being' and 'the Lord God of Israel the Living and True God . . . from all eternity'. For Traherne, the God of our 'wanting' is clearly understood in the monotheistic tradition of a Judaeo-Christian God.

32 'Affection', ll. 56–8.
33 Ibid., ll. 104–6.
34 Compare Traherne's picture of God with, for example, Aristotle's notion of virtue as lying in the mean: 'So virtue is a purposive disposition, lying in the mean that is relative to us and determined by a rational principle, and by that which a prudent man would use to determine it. It is a mean between two kinds of vice, one of excess and the other of deficiency' (*NE*, 1107a1. 1–5; pp. 101–2 in the Thomson translation). If this is what he would expect of a virtuous man, what would he expect of the divine?
35 'Affection', ll. 96–9.

Far from being revolted, Traherne says we are simply to be ravished by this excessive display of divine passion. It is the very kind of thing John Donne also required of God when he wrote:

> Batter my heart, three-personed God; for You
> As yet but knock, breathe, shine, and seek to mend;
> That I may rise, and stand, o'erthrow me, and bend
> Your force, to break, blow, burn, and make me new.
> ... for I
> Except You enthral me never shall be free;
> Nor ever chaste, except You ravish me.
>
> (Holy Sonnet 14, ll. 1–4, 12–14)

In fact, a passionate God is what we human beings want most of all: 'Created Nature desires Lov no where more Severely, then in God',[36] Traherne reminds us in *The Kingdom of God*. And he urges his readers to offer in response a human heart utterly unbridled. Like Augustine, whose *Confessions* respond to God's loud cry with 'shattered deafness' that admits finally 'You were fragrant, and I drew in my breath and now pant after you. I tasted you, and I feel but hunger and thirst for you. You touched me, and I am set on fire', Traherne also confesses in his poem 'Affection' burning longing that does not expect to escape the pain of love.

This excessive emotion, far from barring us from the virtuous life, perfumes the air as we rise toward the divine. God's passion and our reciprocal love are that for which the world was made, according to Traherne:

> The World was made to be a Scene of Love,
> And all the Earth a Theatre doth prove
> Of those Affections, which we ought like Wise
> Obliged and Holy men to exercise.[37]

The 'wise, obliged and holy men' sound lost in this poem, like ancient thoughtful sages observing the excesses of youth. Sandwiched as they are between Traherne's preceding rash claim – 'Lov sanctifies all Passions'[38] – and his description of an ardent God, their presence invites

---

36 *KOG*, Ch. 6, title.
37 'Affection', ll. 84–7.
38 Ibid., l. 74.

a fresh reading of 'wisdom'. Could Traherne be suggesting that there is a kind of wisdom in excess? As he approaches the end of the poem, the beauty of passion sanctified by love is reiterated in unequivocal terms:

> ... Desire
> Hope, Covet, Languish, flie, persue, admire
> Open thy chaste extended Armes, prepare
> Thy Heart with Jealousy and Zeal and Care
> Love like a Spring doth all the Passions move
> And that which sanctifies them all is Love.[39]

Passion and Prudence

This fulsome praise of passion is all very well, but what are we then to do with Traherne's poems and exclamations of contrition, in which he begs to be released from the tyranny of passion, appetite, desire? Take for instance the poems 'Adultery' (*COH*), in which he cries: 'O mortify my fleshly Appetite ... make me to crucify / my Loathsom flesh', and 'Appetite' (*COH*), in which he would sacrifice his appetite as Abraham would have sacrificed Isaac. In both he uses the language of violence and death: 'mortify', 'subdue', 'eradicate', 'Suppress', 'Annihilate', 'sacrifice', 'Die', 'circumcise'.[40] What we are to make of these and other similarly impassioned pleas for the restraint of appetite and how we are to reconcile all of them with the more moderate but no less confident writing on prudence are the questions to which this study turns. For, while Traherne honours the passions and affections of the soul, he also recognizes the need for moderation, prudence and temperance. Without these he does not believe that he can lead a life that will enlighten others around him – a life both excellent and useful, a life of virtue. At the end of a meditation on the nature and effect of prudence, Traherne concludes, 'if I will enrich the world or my Selfe with Actions, Prudence must be my Companion, Light and shadow'.[41] Light and shadow, behind him and before; this guiding power of prudence is intimated in Traherne's words on prudence from *Select Meditations*,

---

39 Ibid., ll. 117–21.
40 See also his exclamations of contrition in *Select Meditations* such as 'O my God how infinite art thou in Goodness! How I in unworthyness! I loath and abhor my Selfe; who have Sinned a[gainst] the Light of thy countenance!' (*SM*, II, 34; also *SM*, II, 36; *SM*, III, 64; *SM*, III, 70.
41 *SM*, IV, 57.

'It [prudence] is of universal Benefit in Finding vertues, nay in Framing composing creating them.'[42]. Traherne's understanding of virtue is not primarily about maintaining upright habits, but about the good life in a broader sense. The virtuous life (*arete*) is rich and full, poised and balanced, a good life where good includes both pleasure and utility. It is not about merely living but about living well. Perhaps it is because he sees prudence as the virtue that leads to the flourishing of other virtues that he writes of it: 'Of all vertues in the whole world this is that which I most want.'[43]

Traherne is convinced not only of the beauty of prudence as a virtue, but also of its usefulness in every day life. Prudence is both 'Delightfull and of Daily use in every occurrence'.[44] This Prudence about which he writes is no tight-lipped twin-set librarian who shushes every outburst and counsels one to stifle enterprise, but a kind of practical wisdom, in the Greek, *phronesis*, that is more like moral savvy. The spiritual or ethical value of prudence is rooted in its temporality. Of all the virtues it is the most worldly. Traherne makes this plain in his discussion of prudence in *Christian Ethicks*. The title of the chapter itself sets the temporal tone, speaking of prosperity on earth (rather than heaven), of the subservience of virtue to temporal welfare and of the reconciliation of duty with convenience.[45] Traherne could not be more unashamedly honest: prudence is practical; it is about what works.[46] And it is about

---

42 Ibid.

43 Ibid. The high esteem in which Traherne holds prudence is underscored by his singling it out from among all the virtues, especially since his notion of virtue is itself high. Virtue is that by which a person may 'become Excellent and usefull'. By virtue the human is exalted almost to deity: 'Vertue of old hath been counted So Generous and noble a Thing, that it hath not onely made men Gentlemen, But Gods too in the Account of the Heathen . . . How therefore may a man become Excellent and usefull while He Liveth? . . . by Adorning Himself with all kind of vertues', among which Traherne lists 'Justice Prudence Temperance and courage' (*SM*, IV, 21).

44 *SM*, IV, 57.

45 The full title to chapter XX is: 'Of Prudence. Its Foundation is Charity, its End Tranquillity and Prosperity on Earth, its Office to reconcile Duty and Convenience, and to make Vertue subservient to Temporal Welfare. Of Prudence in Religion, Friendship, and Empire. The End of *Prudence is perfect Charity*' (*CE*, p. 152).

46 For Aristotle, too, prudence is practical. Prudence (*phronesis*) means 'practical common-sense' (see Hugh Tredennick's note 1, p. 209 in *NE*). By 'practical', Aristotle is referring to something that can be attained through action: 'the man who is capable of deliberation will be prudent. But nobody deliberates about things that are invariable, or about things that he cannot do himself.' (*NE* 1140a34–5). According to Aristotle, prudence is 'reasoned, and capable of action with regard to things that are good or bad for man.' (*NE* 1140b8–9). This reading of 'practical' and of 'prudence' coincides with Traherne's: in *SM*, IV, 57 he speaks of prudence in terms of choice, and this choice is choice for particular action 'attaining' a way and 'walking' in it.

what works for oneself; one's own welfare is at stake. Indeed, one's own welfare is the good that prudence seeks:

> PRUDENCE hath an eye to every Circumstance, and Emergence of our Lives. Its Designe is to make a mans self as Great and glorious as is possible, and in pleasing all the World, to order and improve all Advantages without incurring the least inconvenience.[47]

Traherne's prudent man does not view his own happiness and the life of virtue as being in any way in opposition, but is both personally prosperous and pleasing to the world without compromising his virtue. The world is not the enemy; rather, according to Traherne, the prudent man seeks to please the world and in pleasing it to increase the advantages and decrease the inconveniences of his own life. This is a very nicely feathered nest indeed. The express purpose of prudence, says Traherne, is 'To reconcile our Devotion, Obedience and Religion, to our Interest and Prosperity in the World . . . to surmount all Difficulties, to overrule all Disadvantages, to discern all Opportunities, and lay hold on all Occasions of doing Good to our selves'.[48]

There appears to be no hint of altruism in this pursuit of prudence: the good we seek appears not to be the common good at all, but 'Good to our selves'. And yet this good that we would, by prudence, do to ourselves contains within it the life of virtue. For any true good cannot, in Traherne's view, be a good outside virtue. And real prudence includes the good of others in one's own good. Centuries before Traherne, Aristotle asserted that, although prudence 'is concerned with the self and the individual, . . . it is impossible to secure one's own good independently of domestic and political science';[49] that is to say, independently of other people. Traherne, too, saw the application of prudence as primarily a personal matter but also as a virtue whose exercise would benefit friendship, family and kingdom.[50] For both men, there is an indissoluble tie between prudence and goodness. Where Aristotle asserts

---

47 *CE*, p. 152. Again his words echo the sentiment of Aristotle: 'Well, it is thought to be the mark of a prudent man to be able to deliberate rightly about what is good and advantageous *for himself*' (*NE* 1140a25–7; italics mine).

48 *CE*, pp. 152–3.

49 *NE* 1141b33,1142a8–9.

50 Cf. *CE*, pp. 156–60, in which Traherne outlines the benefits of prudence for friendship, empire and family: 'WHAT the efficacy of Prudence is may be seen in friendship . . .'; 'IN the Management of Empires, and Kingdomes Prudence hath a vast and Mighty Province to reign in . . .'; 'IN Families the force of Prudence is prodigious . . .'; etc.

'one cannot be prudent without being good',[51] Traherne insists, 'He that is not Good can never be Prudent: for he can never benefit himself, or others.'[52] And so one's own welfare, in the end, cannot be the enemy of another's good. We cannot 'effect our own Welfare' without virtue 'in the Execution of our Duties'.[53] And it is the task of prudence so to order those virtues that, as they 'mingle' in the execution of duty, they may cause each other to flourish.

Although each virtue may be beautiful in itself and every virtue contribute to the happy or blessed or good life of the one who practises those virtues, according to Traherne, virtues when held in isolation lead not to happiness but to 'Disgrace and Infamy'.[54] For, he claims, 'we are prone imprudently to expect more from any Vertue than it is able to perform'. Rightly admiring the beauty of a given virtue, we wrongly expect from it good effects beyond its powers alone to give. 'We are apt to believe that in every Vertue there is an infinite Excellency', and this, while it reflects a rightful good opinion of virtue, cannot but lead to disappointment.

Any one virtue, viewed in isolation and taken to its logical extreme, at best disappoints and at worst actually deters the viewer from pursuing the life of virtue. For each virtue also has its limits or insufficiencies, which seem defects to the one who has expected infinite good from that virtue. According to Traherne, the fault is not in the virtue's limitation, but in our too long gazing, our over-expectation (*CE*, p. 154). Expecting unlimited good in a virtue, we do not limit that virtue in our imagination. And so virtue's extreme is also imagined – an extreme that frightens and deters:

> we [are] deterred from Liberality for fear of the Poverty to which it exposeth us; from Meekness, because it encourageth all People to trample us under feet; from Holiness, because it is scorned and hated in the World; from Fortitude and Courage, because of the Perils and Hazzards, that attend it; from self-Denial, because of the Displeasures we do to our selves in crossing our Appetite.[55]

The problem, as Traherne sees it, is that each virtue can only answer the specific need for which it is designed. Together the virtues equip

---
51 *NE* 1144a25. He also says, 'it is not possible to be good in the true sense of the word without prudence, or to be prudent without moral goodness' (*NE* 1144b31–2).
52 *CE*, p. 152.
53 Ibid., p. 153.
54 Ibid. p. 154.
55 This and the two preceding quotes are from ibid., p. 153.

one for every eventuality where alone they may expose one to harm: 'For all these Vertues can answer but one exigence, for which they are prepared . . . and a mistake in one of them doth expose us to more Inconveniences, then its Benefit is worth.'[56] And so the virtues, like the various parts of the body, need each other.[57] In fact, Traherne goes so far as to claim, 'no Vertue is of any Value as cut off from the rest'.[58] This is where prudence comes into her own. For prudence is the virtue that unites and governs all the others; under her umbrella they flourish, attaining together more than could ever be possible separately:

> All the Vertues are United by Prudence like several Pieces in a Compleat armour, and disposed all like Souldiers in an Army, that have their several Postes and Charges, or like the several Orders and Degrees in a Kingdom, where . . . every Man has his Office assigned by the King, and knows his own work, and is fitted for the same.[59]

Prudence is that king, that governor, that overseer. In obedience to prudence all the virtues multiply and thrive: 'the Great End is attained by *all*, which no *one* of them alone, was able to Effect'.[60] And yet each remains distinct. There is no muddling of the virtues into a kind of general goodness – the harsh edge of self-denial is still sharp; the open arms of liberality as inviting as ever. And it is critical that such distinctions should remain since only in their difference can the distinct benefit of each virtue be felt. As Traherne attests:

> one Vertue supplies the Defects of another, and tho every one of them moves in his own Precincts, and does not at all intermeddle with anothers charge, yet the Work is done as effectually as if any one Vertue did all alone.[61]

---

56 Ibid.
57 This parallel between virtues and parts of the body is developed more fully by Traherne later in the same chapter on prudence (pp. 154–6). I quote only a small portion of that here – 'The Office of the Tongue is to Tast well, of the Nostril to smell well, etc. and there is no Defect in any of these, because they are every one sufficient for its own immediate end' – to reiterate that the interdependence of virtues is not seen by Traherne as a fault. He also uses the metaphor of an army to illustrate the same point (pp. 153–4).
58 CE, p. 154.
59 Ibid., p. 153.
60 Ibid. Similarly Aristotle claims that the one who has prudence also has all the other virtues: 'for the possession of the single virtue of prudence will carry with it the possession of them all' (NE 1145a14).
61 CE, p. 153. The importance of difference will be explored more fully in chapter four.

So it is that the final end of prudence is happiness – a harmony of virtues lived out in a full life. 'THE Last End of Prudence is Eternal Happiness and Glory', concludes Traherne, a lasting happiness that is the end of all of Traherne's questing.

Both Traherne and Aristotle see wisdom as higher than prudence,[62] since wisdom studies universal truths but prudence is concerned with particular goods. But, whereas Aristotle sees this distinction as marking out wisdom for particular reverence, Traherne seems to exult in the earthy particularities of prudence. Aristotle writes of wisdom and prudence that 'each is a virtue of a different part of the soul', concluding that prudence does not exercise authority over higher wisdom, but serves it.[63] But Traherne admires the 'crooked Meanders and windings out' by which prudence arrives at 'Eternal Happiness'. It is as if, for Traherne, the very crookedness of the prudent path is one of its charms. He acknowledges wisdom's superiority but paints prudence in more colourful terms:

> It is a strange Vertue, for its Conversant amongst Terrene and inferior Objects, and yet a far more Difficult Vertue then Wisdom it self. Wisdome is a more High and Heavenly Vertue, but its Rules are always fixed, and its objects Stable, where as Prudence hath no set and Stated Rules, but in all occasions, is to mould and shape it selfe, it knows not which way, till it comes to Action.[64]

Prudence keeps one guessing; it evolves, becomes, changes, adapts like magic. Perhaps this is what Traherne finds fascinating about prudence. The final words of his chapter on prudence read like an ancient rune: 'Its Paths are in the Deep and mighty Waters, among Storms and tempests.'[65]

And yet Traherne's prudence also seems so ordinary. It is a choice and a task; and the choice is a choice away from extremity and toward

---

62 *NE* 1141a20–b27; *CE*, p. 160. See also *SM*, IV, 56, in which Traherne begins with wisdom and praises its beauties first before entering into his discussion of prudence: 'Begin with wisdom. wisdom is the Light in which Happiness is Enjoyed . . . It is that which . . . makes us to Aime at the Best of Ends . . . is in all respects Better then Rubies . . .', etc.

63 *NE* 1143b16–17; see also *NE* 1145a20–23: 'At the same time, prudence does not exercise authority over wisdom or over the higher part of the soul, any more than the science of medicine exercises authority over health; for it does not use wisdom, but provides for its realization; and therefore issues orders not to it, but for its sake.'

64 *CE*, p. 160.

65 Ibid.

balance.[66] One of the designs of prudence, according to Traherne, is 'To shun all extreams',[67] and to find the mean. Prudence alone 'Applies the Rule, and Discerns the Golden mean where vertue Lieth'.[68] This is where Traherne's writing on prudence comes full circle to meet his earlier chapter on the affections of the soul. For in chapter four of *Christian Ethicks*, 'Of the Powers and Affections of the Soul', Traherne addresses the problem of excess. He concedes that, although with regard to the highest object (that is, supreme happiness) the affections of the soul cannot be excessive, with regard to inferior objects the soul may indeed default by excess.[69] He writes:

> if we look upon inferior Things, which are meerly Accidental to the nature of Felicity, such as the Favour of men, Injuries, Crosses, Temporal successes, the Beauty of the Body, the goods of Fortune, and such like; our affections and passions may be too excessive . . .[70]

Not many of these objects are unfelicitous in themselves. Indeed, with the exception of 'injuries' and 'crosses', they are all good things – gifts, beauties, bounties, rewards. Desirable or undesirable, they are all things which, each in their own way, could arouse strong passions – desire or aversion, gratitude or bitterness. Traherne's point in listing these examples is not to explore each object's value; he is not here concerned with the wholesomeness or unwholesomeness, the intrinsic goodness or evil of the object. The fault he finds with these 'inferior Things', both desirable and undesirable, is their finitude. That they are merely incidental to felicity is what makes them ultimately unimportant. The good or evil they can produce is limited. Our excess is excess because it is unequal to the finite nature of the given thing we desire (or abhor). Or, as Traherne puts it, 'our affections and passions may be too excessive, because the good or evil of these is but finite; whereas the Good of Sovereign Bliss is altogether infinite, and so is the evil of Eternal Misery'.[71]

---

66 Aristotle also sees choice and prudence as closely related: 'choice cannot be correct in default either of prudence or of goodness, since the one identifies the end and the other makes us perform the acts that are means towards it' (*NE* 1145a5). On Traherne and prudence as a choice, see *SM*, IV, 57.

67 *CE*, p. 152.

68 *SM*, IV, 57.

69 'THE Inclinations and affections of the Soul may be Defective or excessive in their exercise towards Objects. In relation to the Highest Object there is no danger of excess. We can never too violently either *love* or *desire* our Supream Happiness' (*CE*, p. 29).

70 *CE*, p. 30.

71 Ibid.

Excess, then, is about an imbalance or inequality between the infinite affection or emotion and its finite object or end. By implication, we cannot be excessive in our loathing of sin, since its end – 'Eternal Misery' – is of infinite proportions. And we cannot be excessive in our love of good or of eternal happiness since that end is also infinite. By this reckoning, Traherne's passion imperative is not imprudent because love of the divine is not love of a finite object but of the infinite. His poetry of contrition with its strong language of mortification and self-loathing is justly passionate when measured against the end it fears – eternal suffering. For Traherne, in his extremes, matches like for like and so achieves a kind of balance. When he writes in *Christian Ethicks* that, under prudence we should 'take heed that we do nothing out of season, nor be guilty of any Defect, or Excess, or Miscarriage',[72] he is not expecting us to live like mice, in tiny steps with morsels of emotion, but to be aware of the finitude or infinitude of the objects and ends that we long for or abhor and to measure our emotion accordingly. He would not see the affections of the soul amputated by prudence but marshalled so that, appropriately proportioned, they might most effectively be the soul's 'wings and nimble feet'.

Indeed, not only is extreme love permissible within Traherne's notion of prudence; it is also occasionally required. When the infinite divine loves or desires or hates, it is prudent and appropriate that he should do so extremely. Traherne records 'The Infinit Excessivness' of God's love, which perseveres despite our sinfulness,[73] as an example of appropriate excess. According to Traherne, to love an infinite soul or to love God less than excessively is worse than dishonourable; it is a sin of omission that makes one as culpable as if one had inflicted deliberate injury. '*Lukewarmness* is Profane, as well as *Malice*', he reminds us; 'to be beloved Lukewarmly is to be embraced with polluted and filthy Armes'.[74] In the affair of human and divine love, 'We cannot be at all Beloved by Almighty GOD unless we are infinitely Beloved', since that which is by nature infinite acts infinitely. And 'it is our duty to love him infinitely' in return.[75] The connection between this passion and holi-

---

72 Ibid., p. 153.
73 *SM*, III, 94.
74 *CE*, pp. 88–9. Cf. *The Kingdom of God*: 'He that can submit to an Inferior degree of Lov, or take up with a Smaller Measure in the Deitie, is a degenerat person ... Who infinitly desireth ... he only is a truly Sublime, and Generous Soul, that is Worthy of God.' (*KOG*, Ch. 6, ll. 128–34).
75 *CE*, p. 89. Similarly infinite goodness, like infinite love, must desire infinitely: 'For infinite Goodness must needs desire with an infinite violence, that all Goodness should be compleat and Perfect' (*CE*, p. 88).

ness is something to which we shall return; it may suffice to note here that this is true not only of loving God but of all infinite objects and even of the way in which we may speak of infinite objects. Traherne insists that 'In Divine Things there can be no Hyperbolie'.[76] The love of the soul must match its end or object. Once like is matched with like and the infinite love finds its infinite object there can be never be too much love.

For Traherne, prudence is the king of virtues, eminent and illustrious, the virtue he desires above all others. And I would venture, that this is so at least partly because of Traherne's belief in the possibility of and his pursuit of earthly happiness.[77] Prudence is for the earthbound;[78] in heaven, where there is no question of matching finite with finite and infinite with infinite since all is infinite, prudence will not be needed. When virtues perfectly regulate themselves and the affections of the soul are all focused on the infinite divine, prudence could seem like a dusty old hat at the back of the cupboard, a relic of earthly days. But heaven will see prudence rewarded, an old retainer honoured for its past service; no longer useful but remembered:

> The truth is there will be Little need of Prudence there among all Stable and Permanent Things, which will Shine there as Eternal Objects to perfect wisdom. But here upon Earth among such Lubricities, variety of Dispositions Apprehensions and occurrences, Prudence is a Thing so Eminent and Illustrous: that it will Shine in Heaven for the Sake of the Benefit it did on Earth, and be far more Bright then the morning Star.[79]

For Traherne, the passion imperative is about loving God and being loved by God with unlimited desire. It is about loving infinite souls with that same kind of passion. Prudence is about tasting something of that happiness now – felicity on earth where passion and prudence meet.

---

76 *SM*, III, 7. See also *C*, II, 52 and *KOG*, Ch. 15, ll. 105–7, in which he claims that the Truth is 'infinitly sublime, and far abov the Reach of all Hyperbolies: tho they be καθ υπερβολω εισ υπερβολω. Hyperbolies piled one upon another.'

77 Traherne's enthusiasm for present happiness is rooted in his belief that heaven is now as well as forever and that eternal happiness is a continuation and fulfilment of that happiness that begins on earth. His criticism of Aristotle's notion of happiness makes this clear: 'I do not see that Aristotle made the End of Vertue any other then a finite and temporal Felicity, which is infinitely short of that felicity which is here begun, and enjoyed for ever' (*CE*, p. 58).

78 Traherne describes prudence as 'this celestial vertue, which hath So much Place here upon Earth, as if it had none in Heaven' (*SM*, IV, 57).

79 *SM*, IV, 57.

The Infinite End

Just as passion and prudence at first seem to clash in Traherne's notion of desire, so too do infinity and finitude. This is true not just in terms of desire and object, as seen above, but also in terms of experience or perception. We perceive the infinite but often experience the finite in the working out of desire. And so I want to look at these two aspects of desire – infinity and finitude.

Infinity could occupy a whole volume in itself in a discussion of Traherne's work.[80] There is the infinity of God, which he assumes as a characteristic of God by definition; and there is the infinity of human beings, in God's image. There is absolute infinity and relative or partial infinity. The infinity of space becomes the subject of his final unfinished fifth *Century*,[81] a subject that occupied many of the best seventeenth-century minds.

In the fifth chapter of *The Kingdom of God*, Traherne explores the nature of infinity and its extent. For him, the inclinations and powers of the soul are very much tied up with infinity.[82] Properly understood, there are no degrees in Traherne's infinity. A thing either is or is not infinite. A finite thing cannot be made 'more infinite', nor can an infinite thing be made 'less infinite', since any loss makes it not infinite at all but finite. Infinity is infinite, then, not by addition but by the absence of subtraction. (In this respect, Traherne's 'infinity' is a bit like the words 'virginity' or 'unique'– there is no such thing as 'more' or 'less virgin' or 'more' or 'less unique'.) He writes:

> The Greatest And vastest, the most excessive Additions cannot make a finit Thing infinit, yet the least abatement and Substraction Imaginable, takes away Infinitly from that which is infinit. For the least

---

80 'To understand Traherne's concept of "infinity" is to understand his metaphysical and moral universe, always seen *sub specie infinitatis*, or, *sub specie Dei*' (Rosalie Colie, *Paradoxia Epidemica: The Renaissance Tradition of Paradox*, Princeton: Princeton University Press, 1966, p. 151). 'The word "infinity" might well be selected as the key to Traherne's total devotion' (Ibid., p. 146).

81 Colie notes (ibid., pp. 69–70) 'the expanding intellectual universe of the Rennaisance' and the 'infinite space suggested by the new science' as an environment in which poets and philosophers might see the 'real' manifestation of the theory of infinity. She suggests that the prevailing space theory model of the seventeenth century was the combined Platonic and Judaeo-Christian theory of absolute space.

82 The chapter title 'A Philosophical Account of Gods Kingdom drawn from the Inclinations and Powers of the Soul, and from the Nature of Infinitie. All which show his Kingdom to be Compleat and Perfect' (*KOG*, Ch. 5) makes this point by placing the two (inclination and power) in tandem. But the point has been made elsewhere many times over: see, for instance, the poems 'My Spirit', 'Sight', 'Insatiableness' and 'Thoughts IV'.

Diminution of what is possible; makes it finit... Finite we know is Infinitly short of Infinit perfection. so that a paradox breaketh forth, whether we will or no... An infinit Abundance receiveth Infinit loss by the least Substraction.[83]

The same is true of action as of object, since God's almighty and infinite power, unlike our limited power, 'can never exert it self by finit degrees... Nor will a finit procession tho proceeding to Eternity ever attain an infinit End'.[84]

Infinite virtues such as goodness, beauty or wisdom are not diminished by being spent. If all gifts of goodness were to be given, the goodness left behind would be 'Infinit still'.[85] Nevertheless, Traherne is able to conceive of a kind of infinity that is relative or partial. The infinity of a grain of sand is a 'Relativ Infinity',[86] and the infinite line, for instance, may be broken so that it becomes infinite in one direction only. 'But an Infinit Line, and Infinit Goodness are not alike', asserts Traherne, 'For Infinite Goodness cannot be divided, nor is it capable of a Partial Infinitie. There is a great difference between that which is Absolutely infinit, and in some respect.' This is so because, unlike the imagined line, the virtues are grounded in God's continuing gift of power. 'Infinit Goodness is founded in the willingness of Allmighty power, to do all the good that it is able. If it stops any where, it hath found a Period.'[87]

For Traherne, the infinity of God, of the soul and of space are absolute infinities. Divine infinity is absolute by definition, and the infinities of the soul and of space are absolute by derivation from the divine. What is more, for him all absolute infinities are infinite in every way. He makes this clear in several places. Here, in the fifth chapter of *The Kingdom of God*, he asserts that 'What is absolutely so, is evry way Infinit'.[88] Similarly, in the second *Century* he claims that Love is 'both ways infinite', filling all eternity and yet expressed in 'a finite room'.[89] This both/and of infinity is reiterated again in chapters 8 and 18 of *The Kingdom of God* when he describes divine goodness as 'that which is

---

83 *KOG*, Ch. 5, ll. 91–100.
84 Ibid., Ch. 15, ll. 47–9.
85 Ibid., Ch. 15, l. 113.
86 'The infinity we speak of in Good Works, is not an Absolute, but a Relativ Infinity: such as a sand is capable of' (Ibid., Ch. 15, ll. 170–1).
87 Ibid., Ch. 5, ll. 128–30.
88 Ibid., Ch. 5, l. 128.
89 C, II, 80.

Infinit', both 'remote yet near at hand within us and without us';[90] and when he describes the atom as evidence of divine power 'being infinitly great in things infinitly small, as well as great'.[91] Even when speaking metaphorically he insists on the same principle – the sun, an image of the infinite divine essence, shines both ways: 'His Beams are not one Way, but evry Way.'[92] Absolute infinity that reached infinitely in every direction fitted nicely with the new scientific discovery of infinite space.

Infinite space fascinated Traherne; he could see that its discovery had huge implications for poetry as well as for science.[93] Whereas for centuries poets had loved the perfect circle of earth and heaven, centre and circumference, the circle without beginning and without end, which symbolized eternity and man's place on earth, the new astronomy changed the place of the world. No longer was the earth the centre of the universe, nor was man the centre of the world; the macrocosm/microcosm model was grinding to a halt. As Marjorie Hope Nicolson has noted, the telescope broke that perfect circle and released human imagination to a 'spaciousness of thought'[94] hitherto unknown, but infinite space induced an erosion of certainty as much as it allowed infinite possibility. In an age when scientists often wrote their discoveries in the language of poets,[95] some of the century's poets lost their long-held images. 'The Sun is lost', wrote Donne in response to the

---

90 *KOG*, Ch. 8, l. 10.

91 Ibid., Ch. 18, ll. 86–7.

92 Here, in chapter 20 of *The Kingdom of God*, Traherne is using the sun as an image of divine essence and an emblem of the Holy Trinity as fountain, means and end. He admits that 'The Sun is not *Infinitios Infinitus*', that its sphere is limited to this world while God's sphere is eternity, but he still finds the sun a useful metaphor (*KOG*, Ch. 20, ll. 137, 141–2).

93 Traherne's fascination with the new sciences can be seen in works such as 'Ant' and 'Atom' (*COH*); C, III, 41; notes from his *Early Notebook* (see Carol Marks, 'Thomas Traherne's Early Studies', *PBSA*, 62 (1968), pp. 511–36); his *Commonplace Book* entry 'Cold'; and chapters 18–24 of *KOG*. For a greater exploration of Traherne's connections to scientific discoveries of his day see Stephen Clucas, 'Poetic atomism in seventeenth-century England: Henry More, Thomas Traherne and "scientific imagination"', *Renaissance Studies*, 5 (1991), pp. 327–40; Nabil Matar, 'Thomas Traherne's Solar Mysticism', *Studia Mystica*, VII, 3 (Fall 1984), pp. 52–63; S. Sandbank, 'Thomas Traherne on the Place of Man in the Universe', *Scripta Hierosolymitana*, 17 (1966), pp. 121–36.

94 See Marjorie Hope Nicolson, *The Breaking of the Circle: Studies in the Effect of the 'New Science' upon Seventeenth Century Poetry*, Evanston, IL: Northwestern University Press, 1950, p. 145.

95 See for instance William Harvey, who used poetic language, albeit sparingly; or, more abundantly, the writings of William Gilbert, whose discoveries in magnetic science read like mystical philosophy. See also Kepler, whose language is charged with poetry.

post-Copernican discoveries, 'and no mans wit / Can well direct him where to looke for it'. His was not just a loss of one image, but of a whole world-view: "Tis all in peces, all cohaerence gone',[96] he wrote in apparent bewilderment as he became one of the first English poets to assimilate the implications of the new heavens. Most did not find this change easy; where some foundered in search of a new metaphor, Traherne simply enlarged himself to include. His metaphors inhabited this new infinity; his circle became the circle whose circumference had no limit and whose centre was everywhere.[97] That is not to say that Traherne had no scepticism about the new discoveries. In *The Kingdom of God* he seems not quite to believe the reports of the existence of new and numberless stars when he writes:

> Then taking courage to sally out of all Bounds, and soar higher, they pretend new stars lately discovered by the Assistance of telescopes, higher then all the fixed stars that are known: so that for ought we can perceiv (say they) beyond those there may be other stars by no help of Instruments visible to us, by reason of their Distance: And more again beyond those, and so forth onward to everlasting spaces.[98]

But it is not clear whether it is the existence of these stars that is in doubt or the conclusions propounded by the 'Atheisticaly disposed' thinkers, who read into these findings an 'overthrow of religion'.[99] In contrast, Traherne's alterations to *Commentaries of Heaven* (noted in the appendix), suggest an assimilation of the new astronomy. If he found the new discoveries incredible he would not be alone; many of the seventeenth century's best thinkers record bouts of incredulity, a healthy scepticism, or inconsistencies of thought as new hypotheses are weighed and approved and old ideas not so much jettisoned as gradually released. What is clear is that, however swiftly or hesitantly Traherne assimilated the new discoveries, they were no threat to his faith. After

---

96 This and the preceding Donne quotation are from 'First Anniversary', ll. 207–8, 213.

97 Not a new image, of course, since its origins are in the ancient Hermetic writings. Nicholas of Cusa and Giordano Bruno also used the image before Traherne (see Colie, *Paradoxia Epidemica*, pp. 71–2).

98 *KOG*, Ch. 20, ll. 32–8. It would appear that it was primarily the potentially atheistic disposition of some scientists rather than their discoveries that Traherne opposed, since this criticism appears in the larger context of a defence of religion in the face of science and since the concept of everlasting space, as many of the other new ideas, is embraced elsewhere in his work.

99 Ibid., Ch. 20, ll. 16–17.

five pages of examining the claims of Hevelius' *Selenographia* and the assertions of other 'Wits of the Age', Traherne concludes:

> What if the Stars should be all inhabited, what would follow? May we conclude thence, that there is no GOD? no Religion? No Blessedness? verily it is more Apparent, that there is a God, a Religion, a Blessedness thereby. What if beyond the Heavens there were Infinit Numbers of Worlds at vast unspekable distances? ... Would that abolish Heaven? verily in my conceit, it enricheth it. For it is more answerable to Goodness, Wisdom, and Felicitie, and demonstrates visible that there is a GOD, and that Divines hav not in vain affirmed GOD to be all Act, since his Power is exerted in filling his Omnipresence with infinit Treasures.[100]

True to form, Traherne found, in this new and, for some, unlikely territory, an affirmation of his basic theological themes and structures and a source of blessedness. Not uncritically, then, he embraced the new sciences as food to his faith, since each new discovery opened a world of miracle and afforded new reaches of capacity. As we shall see in chapter four, Harvey's theory of the circulation of the blood, which Traherne discusses in *The Kingdom of God*, becomes a model of our relationship with God in the poem 'The Circulation', in which he writes, with double meaning: 'All Things to Circulation owe / Themselves; by which alone / They do exist'. In 'Sight' the inward eye of imaginative intuition is likened to the telescope. And discoveries such as infinite space are incorporated into his theology so that, in the words from *The Kingdom of God*, for example, infinite space becomes 'a consequent of Eternal Wisdom'.[101] Similarly, in his 'treatice of Atoms' (*KOG*, Ch. 18), Traherne sees spiritual truths and virtues – the atom being infinitely small and yet the most stable thing (as it was believed to be) is a model of humility. In the following chapter, a study on light becomes an allegory of divine nature: 'Should we now turn all those Realities into an Allegorie: God is Light'. An experiment with fire and an empty cup[102] becomes a lesson on the invisible agents that work to the benefit of men and to the praise and glory of God. Traherne's overwhelming reaction to the new scientific discoveries of his day was not despondency at the loss of the familiar but a sense of wonder and eager aspiration as one world-view was gradually replaced with another. Where 'infinite' had

---

100 Ibid., Ch. 20, ll. 154–66.
101 Ibid., Ch. 7, l. 132.
102 Ibid., Ch. 23. The quote 'God is light' comes from *KOG*, Ch. 19, l. 293.

for ages past been a word belonging only to God, it now belonged to the expanding universe of humankind, appropriated by hungry minds such as Traherne's.

Marjorie Hope Nicolson notes a divergence in the seventeenth century between the poets of limitation whose response to infinity was to confess that earth must end and hope that only heaven remain, and those poets of aspiration, whose imaginations raced into unmanageable realms beyond. She cites Herbert as the prime example of the poets of limitation who assert that happiness is found within limits and by restraint[103] and for whom 'contentment' is felicity, as Herbert writes:

> Content thee, greedie heart.
> Modest and moderate joyes to those, that have
> Title to more hereafter, when they part.
>   Are passing brave . . .
>   Wherefore sit down, good heart . . .
>
> ('The Size')

Similarly the theologian Richard Allestree's popular work, *The Art of Contentment* (1675), urged its readers to pull in their wings. Traherne's predispositions differed from Allestree's and Traherne warns his readers to be wary of a 'Negative Contentment' that 'mingles Nature and Vice in a confusion, and makes a man fight against Appetite and Reason' (*COH*, 'Appetite'). Unless contentment is based on satisfaction it is pernicious. Traherne asserts: 'Contentment is a sleepy thing!'[104] While Donne swings between the extremes of contentment and aspiration, urging sometimes one and then the other, Henry More stretches boldly towards aspiration and infinity. And Crashaw, his own insatiability writ large, cries: 'One little world or two, Alas! will never doe. We must have store', while Abraham Cowley calls us to plunder the orchard gathering our fill of the new philosophy.[105] There is a note of triumphant freedom in the tone of these aspiring poets, whose imaginations seemed to expand with the universe, vaster in a new vastness. Nicolson's view is of Traherne as the climax of these seventeenth-century poets of aspiration. This may be in part because the new discoveries,

---

103 Nicolson, *The Breaking of the Circle*, p. 177.
104 284 l.1, 'Contentment is a sleepy thing!' (*CE*, Ch. 27).
105 'The orchard's open now and free; / Bacon has broke that scarecrow deity [the old philosophy]; / Come, enter, all that will; / Behold the ripened fruit; / Come gather now your fill' ('To the Royal Society', ll. 58–61). For similar sentiments see also John Norris and William Drummond of Hawthornden.

rather than upending Traherne's ready notions of the world, coincided with his infant intuitions as he sometimes 'soar[ed] above the stars' to 'enquire how the Heavens ended, and what was beyond them'.[106] 'Infinite is the first thing which is naturally known', he wrote in the second *Century*, having sensed infinity within himself even before its scientific debut. The infinity within him was met by an infinity without: the science that thrilled him was confirming what he already wanted to believe about himself, the world and his creator.

> That things are finite therefore we learn by our senses. But infinity we know and feel by our souls: and feel it so naturally as if it were the very essence and being of the soul. The truth of it is, it is individually in the soul: for God is there, and more near to us than we are to ourselves. So that we cannot feel our souls, but we must feel Him, in that first of properties, infinite space.[107]

Rosalie Colie also sees Traherne as a poet of infinite aspiration. In fact, for Colie infinity is 'the key to his metaphysical and moral universe',[108] a universe in which it is only by infinitized aspiration that a true understanding of the infinitely infinite God can be reached. For Colie infinite space is primarily about what is out there, and 'infinite aspiration' is the zenith of Traherne's ethic. This gloss engages with Traherne's call to ascend from temporal to eternal but in this 'outward' reading of Traherne's infinity, the 'internal infinity' of the fourth *Century*, that infinity which is 'both ways infinite' is lost. What the new sciences gave Traherne was as much to do with the microscope as with the telescope. As Nicolson notes: 'When he saw eternity in a grain of sand, he was speaking not only mystically but microscopically.'[109] What both of these valuable studies miss is the absolute centrality of infinity to Traherne's other theme of felicity and desire.

For Traherne, infinite space is not tangential, a subject of pleasant speculation extraneous to his great theme of felicity. It is an integral part of his doctrine of enjoyment; it is absolutely necessary if joy is to be endless. In *The Kingdom of God* he reasons that just as it would be a foolish thing to choose transitory joys when one could choose eternal ones, so it is foolish to choose small joys when one could choose

---

106 C, III, 18.
107 C, II, 81.
108 Rosalie Colie, 'Thomas Traherne and the Infinite: The Ethical Compromise', *Huntington Library Quarterly*, 21 (1957), pp. 69–82, 71.
109 Nicolson, *The Breaking of the Circle*, p. 173.

expansive ones.[110] Since these expansive joys are also eternal, they are ever expanding and so they require infinite space, not just a world of joy but Immensity itself.[111] So it is that infinite space is the fruit of eternal wisdom 'being prepared to be the Repositorie of its endless Enjoyments'.[112] The image cited here of infinite space as a repository or storeroom is not unique in Traherne. In several places in the *Centuries* infinity is 'the room and place of our treasures, the repository of joys ... a cabinet, a receptacle, and a storehouse'.[113] Because infinite space is boundless, there is always room for more in this storeroom, yet infinite space is not empty. Infinite space is always being filled; it was designed expressly for that purpose:

> Infinity of space is like a painter's table prepared for the ground and field of those colours that are to be laid thereon. Look how great he intends the picture, so great doth he make the table. It would be an absurdity to leave it unfinished, or not to fill it. To leave any part of it naked and bare, and void of beauty, would render the whole ungrateful to the eye.[114]

The fact that there is always more room in Traherne's infinite space speaks not of emptiness then, but of capacity – a capacity that, despite being always filled, is never spent.[115] This is where Traherne, unique

---

110 *KOG*, Ch. 7. Traherne writes similarly about the foolishness of other choices for the inferior: 'He is Evil, and not Good, that is less Good, then he may be. Truly it is a Foolish Thing to be less Wise, then one may be' (ibid., Ch. 5, ll. 107–9).

111 He writes: 'As it would be a foolish thing to chuse Momentary Shadows, or Transitory Joys, that perish in the using, when we may acquire those that are Eternal so it is a vain and foolish thing, to make Diminutiv and feeble Joys, when Almighty and Infinit may be created Is it not folly in a man that may enjoy the Glory of the Whole World, to confine his fruitions to a Miserable Cottage? ... So in like Manner to creat a World, and a World of Joys, is Wise, if we compare it to the Palace of a King, because it is far more August, and Magnificent. But a limited World, tho never so Great, is a Beggars Cottage compared to Immensitie' (ibid., Ch. 7, ll. 115–30).

112 Ibid., Ch. 7, ll. 131–2.

113 C, V, 2; C, V, 3; C, V, 4. Infinity 'without us is the chamber of our infinite treasures, and within us the repository and recipient of them' (C, II, 81). See also *SM*, I, 93, in which eternity is a bottle wherein the tears of the penitent are stored. Traherne's overlapping of Eternity and Infinity will be discussed below.

114 C, V, 5. See also 'Felicitie', in which felicity is 'No empty Space' but full of sight and soul and life.

115 The link between infinite space and capacity is an important one in Traherne because it is in exercising our capacity that the soul becomes like the Deity. See 'Silence': 'A vast and Infinit Capacitie, / Did make my Bosom like the Deitie, / In Whose Mysterious and Celestial Mind / All Ages and all Worlds together shind'; and 'My Spirit', in which, in early innocence, 'My Essence was Capacitie'. Infinite space and our capacity to receive the Deity by receiving it is also the subject of *A Serious and Pathetical Contemplation of the Mercies*

among his peers, has something to say that relates intimately to a desiring God. Many of the poets of aspiration were enamoured of the new theories of infinity, but none saw so clearly as Traherne that infinity led straight to the notions of capacity in God – a capacity he saw exhibited in the exercise of divine desire. Not only is infinite space the receptacle for our ever-expanding joys but also the place where almighty power may be exercised. Here Traherne's image shifts from storehouse to theatre, from accommodating objects to accommodating action. Except for infinite space, God's almighty power would be straitened, Traherne writes, 'for lack of a theatre magnificent enough ... there must of necessity be an infinite capacity to answer that power'.[116]

It is when Traherne moves his discussion of infinite space from objects to action in the *Centuries* that he begins to overlay Infinity and Eternity. He has described what infinite space is; now he ventures to describe where we may perceive it. Just as the present moment is in some sense the only moment, so for Traherne the present space is the only space; the two are tied together for him. The present moment 'exhibits infinite space' because, in the space that is here now in front of us, we see the only space that is. And yet there are other moments and other spaces. For just as there must be an infinite place for infinite treasures and joys, so there must be an infinite duration of time in which infinite moments may be held. He explains as follows:

> This is the space that is this moment only present before our eye, the only space that was, or that will be, from everlasting to everlasting. This moment exhibits infinite space, but there is a space also wherein all moments are infinitely exhibited, and the everlasting duration of infinite space is another region and room of joys. Wherein all ages appear together, all occurrences stand up at once, and the innumerable and endless myriads of years that were before creation, and will be after the world is ended, are objected as a clear and stable object, whose several parts extended out at length, give an inward infinity

---

of God, in which Traherne urges his reader to 'Measure all the Spaces beyond the Heavens. / Receive the Deity of the eternal God, / and those Spaces / By him unto thee' (*A Serious and Pathetical Contemplation of the Mercies of God*, ed. Roy Daniells, University of Toronto Studies, No. 12, Toronto: University of Toronto Press, 1941, p. 29).

116 C, V, 4. That God's power should be exerted infinitely is important to Traherne not because it shows his might but because it shows his love. 'For we could never believe that He loved us infinitely unless He exerted all His power', he writes. 'For κατα Δυναμιν is one of the principal properties of Love: as well as εκαινου ενεκα. To the utmost of its power, as well as for His sake' (C, II, 82).

to this moment, and compose an eternity that is seen by all comprehensors and enjoyers.[117]

Thus eternity is born and duration (time) becomes another room (place). What matters is the endlessness of both. Both capacious and full, the present moment becomes a metaphor for infinite space; it is filled and yet beyond the present moment there is more to come.

Infinite space then, for Traherne, is important because it is the repository of our joys, because it is the field of almighty power, because in it the infinite duration of moments may be held; but also because it is in infinite space that we come to know the nature of God and of ourselves.

Traherne's infinite space is full of God. It is the theatre not only of God's power but also of his omnipresence:

His Omnipresence is an Endless Sphere,
Wherin all Worlds as his Delights appear.
His Beauty is the Spring of all Delight,
Our Blessedness, like His, is infinit.
His Glory Endless is and doth Surround
And fill all Worlds, without or End or Bound.

('Thoughts. IV', ll. 29–32)

The 'endless sphere' of God's omnipresence is like the other 'Endless Sphere' of the soul, described in 'My Spirit', a sphere with its own centre, whose boundary is everywhere.[118] This image echoes the well-known hermetic image of the circle whose centre is everywhere and whose circumference is nowhere. Traherne writes, 'my Soul is an infinite sphere in a centre';[119] and God is in that centre: 'For being wholly everywhere, His omnipresence was wholly in every centre: and He could do no more than that would bear: Communicate Himself wholly in every centre.'[120]

Here Traherne sees the human spirit as full. It is 'a centre in eternity comprehending all, and filled all about . . . in an endless manner with infinite riches'.[121] But the same human spirit experiences grave lack and loss. A. L. Clements attempts to tackle this by discussing the

---

117 C, V, 6.
118 The soul, 'being Simple like the Deitie / In its own Centre is a Sphere / Not shut up here, but evry Where . . . an Endless Sphere, / Like God Himself' ('My Spirit', ll. 15–18, 30–1).
119 C, II, 80.
120 C, II, 82.
121 C, II, 80.

psyche and *pneuma* as separate categories of the self. He notes that 'I am God' does not mean 'I am God Almighty', 'For the "I" psyche, or ego ... is one's conception of himself. The known created object, not the knowing, creative Act.' As an illusion, the psyche prevents one realizing one's full nature: 'The condition of the fallen man, then, is the sin, the error, of misapprehending his psyche as his essential being and of behaving, or rather misbehaving, accordingly'.[122] Perhaps we call ourselves by the name of our psyche because it is easier to hold and catch than is the shape of our soul. Traherne's figure of the soul as the circle whose centre is everywhere and whose circumference is nowhere suggests that the soul is not easily apprehended. The soul is infinite, without *fin*. As Clements puts it, it cannot be circumscribed or de*fin*ed: 'It will not sit for its photograph'.[123]

In this sense the soul is perhaps most accurately described by what it is not, by its lacks rather than its fullnesses: 'the soul is a miraculous abyss of infinite abysses' (C, II, 83), a 'Naked Simple Life ... Not shut up here, but evey Where. A Deep Abyss' ('My Spirit', ll. 2, 17, 77). Here what we read from Traherne seems to contradict the earlier assertion that the infinity of God (and the soul within that infinity) is essentially full. I think a way of understanding this is to distinguish between what is the human soul's experience and its origin and destiny. This can be glimpsed in the spiritual journey that Traherne outlines in the *Centuries*, where we find skirmishes on the edge of nothingness. Against the claims of the likes of Itrat-Husain and Robert Ellrodt, who assert that Traherne never trod the *via negativa*,[124] Clements and Colie assert that, in matters of infinity and the essence of the soul, he is very much in tune with a negative theology.[125] Where Clements notes the soul as abyss, Colie notes the *horror vacui* that is present in the third *Century* when Traherne writes:

---

122 A. L. Clements, *The Mystical Poetry of Thomas Traherne*, Cambridge, MA: Harvard University Press, 1969, pp. 22–3.

123 Ibid., pp. 25–6.

124 See for instance, Itrat-Husain, *The Mystical Element in the Metaphysical Poets of the Seventeenth Century*, Edinburgh: Oliver & Boyd, 1948, p. 292. Here the author cites Underhill (who also asserted Traherne's lack of purgation as the thing that ultimately prevented him from being classed as a mystic): 'The two aspects of the purification of the self which Underhill calls "the Negative Purification or self-stripping" and "the Postivie Purification," or "Mortification," "a deliberate recourse to painful experience and difficult tasks", are not to be found in the life of Traherne.' This asertion is expanded on pp. 292–5. See also Robert Ellrodt, *L'Inspiration personelle et l'esprit du temps chez les poètes métaphysiques Anglais*, Paris: Librairie J. Corti, 1960.

125 See Clements, *The Mystical Poetry*, p. 27 and Ch. one, n. 18. See also Colie, *Paradoxia Epidemica*, pp. 145–68.

Another time, in a lowering and sad evening, being alone in the field, when all things were dead and quiet, a certain want and horror fell upon me, beyond imagination. The unprofitableness and silence of the place dissatisfied me; its wideness terrified me: from the utmost ends of the earth fears surrounded me. How did I know but dangers might suddenly arise from the East, and invade me from the unknown regions beyond the seas? I was a weak and little child, and had forgotten there was a man alive in the earth. (C, III, 23)

In the *Thanksgivings*, the soul is 'An infinite Abyss';[126] as such it may experience the vastness of infinite space naturally and with horror as well as with joy. This experience of total loneliness is also recorded in 'Solitude':

>How desolate!
>Ah! How forlorn, how sadly did I stand
>   When in the field my woful State
>   I felt![127]

In neither of these accounts is the horror without hope. In the third *Century* he continues 'Yet something also of hope and expectation comforted me from every border.' And in 'Solitude', the 'Silence', 'Sorrow' and 'Want' that grieve him are the result of his own blindness rather than experiences of ultimate reality. Nevertheless, his immediate experience of loss and of lostness is vivid:

>   Ye Sullen things!
>Ye dumb, ye silent Creatures, and unkind! . . .
>   Will ye not speak
>What 'tis I want, nor Silence break? . . .
>   They silent stood;
>Nor Earth, nor Woods, nor Hills, nor Brooks, nor Skies,
>   Would tell me where the hidden Good,
>   Which I did long for, lies:
>   The shady Trees,
>   The Ev'ning dark, the humming Bees,
>The chirping Birds, mute Springs and Fords, conspire,
>   To giv no answer unto my Desire.[128]

---

126 'Thanksgivings for the Soul', l. 175.
127 'Solitude', ll. 1–4.
128 'Solitude', ll. 41–2, 45–6, 49–56.

The *horror vacui* is real, though the ultimate void it signals is not.

In moments of self-consciousness, in which the self is a subject separate from its object, infinity is a lack. In moments of communion between a subject and its object, it is experienced as capacity.[129] The infinity of God is full, argues Traherne; that it is also always capable of more is what we are sensing when we experience the horror of infinite lack. And so the soul's experience of lack may be read as a signal of promised fullness as much as it may be read as a signal of promised vacuity. To some extent, the difference between these two readings may be a matter of choice. What is unassailable, says Traherne, in both the expectation of nothing and the expectation of everything, is that the soul has sensed a sliver of the possibility of infinity within itself.

Infinity is basic to being human, infinite space is 'that first of properties', 'the first thing which is naturally known'.[130] And it is as essentially God as it is essentially us. We feel and know infinity by our souls, and feel it as naturally as if it were our very essence. It is in the soul because God is also in the soul and where God is there is God's infinity. So it is, Traherne believes, that we live and move and have our being in God. As we have seen, Traherne's experiences of lack were not without hope and they led him to the conclusion that God's infinity, far from making him unknown and remote, implies immediate proximity. He writes, 'I am made . . . an Infinit Sphere in which thou Dwellest forevermore'.[131] The hopeful human soul therefore experiences God's infinity not as void but as presence. In his *Thanksgivings for the Soul*, Traherne tries to explain this soul, full of God's infinity, in the oxymoron of a full abyss:

> Unsatiable is my Soul,
>   Because nothing can fill it.
> A living Centre, wider than the Heavens.
>   An infinite Abyss,
> So made by the perfection of the Presence.[132]

The human soul, at once full and capacious, is the home of God's infinity as much as is limitless space.

---

129 Compare for instance, C, III, 23 (*horror vacui*) with C, III, 3 ('the corn was orient and immortal wheat') – in the first he experiences lostness, in the second, both fullness and capacity. In both meditations the author observes and recounts the world of his childhood, though they seem quite different worlds.
130 C, II, 81.
131 SM, I, 82.
132 'Thanksgivings for the Soul', ll. 172–6, Denise Inge, *Thomas Traherne: Poery and Prose*, London: SPCK, 2002, p. 60.

It is this basic struggle of the infinite soul in a finite human life that is at the heart of much of Traherne's work.[133] His image of the white-page infant whose spirit still remembers eternity and infinity, a stranger in the world of 'custom' who is frustrated and alien, is, in part, a picture of this uncomfortable infinite/finite union.[134] There is in Traherne's infant, almost from the very beginnings of consciousness or of self-consciousness, a capacity for union with the divine – a capacity the use of which it will take him the rest of his life to recover.[135]

The Finite Means

Traherne believes that infinity is our home and that this concept is not just something that our wishful imagination conceives but a reality that our deepest self acknowledges, that it is a kind of first principle, the first thing naturally known.[136] He describes how in his infancy 'something infinite behind everything appeared: which talked with my expectation and moved my desire'.[137] God's infinity is 'the peculiar possession of evry Soul . . . the Secret Right and private Estate of evry person',[138] we sense our right to participate in it as we are, from infancy, 'drawn with the expectation and desire of some Great Thing'.[139] It is our beginning and it is the end towards which we move. How can it be then, that human experience is so often experience of the finite? We may be on a journey into the infinite but it is our finite feet that

---

133 See *SM*, II, 92: 'There is in a man a Double selfe, according as He is in God, or in the world. In the world He is confined, and walketh up and Down, in Little Roome: but in God He is evry where.'

134 'An empty book is like an Infant's Soul' (C, I, 1); 'the divine light wherewith I was born' (C, II, 1); 'Innocence', 'Eden', the child's innocence corrupted by custom (C, III, 2, 7); the infant as stranger to this world; 'The Salutation'; to name only a few.

135 In my view this may explain Traherne's philosophical acceptance of the 'estate of trial', which, in *The Kingdom of God* and elsewhere, is part of what beautifies the Bride and raises her to be a fit companion for the divine. Perhaps the struggles that the soul undergoes as an essentially infinite being housed in a finite frame are the makings of the soul; the particularity of human loves and pleasures being part of what makes the soul able to enjoy eternity not as an amorphous void but as a collection of specific and eternal fulnesses.

136 C, II, 81: 'Infinitie is the first thing which is naturally known . . . And this we know so naturally, that it is the only *primo et necessario cognitum in rerum natura*: of all thing the only first and most necessarily known.'

137 C, III, 3.

138 *KOG*, Ch. 16, ll. 14, 16. Here the particular quality of God's infinte nature to which Traherne refers is infinite goodness. In the *Centuries*, infinity is 'individually in the soul: for God is there' (C, II, 81).

139 C, I, 2. The 'some Great Thing' of the *Centuries* has been understood in several ways – usually as some form of blessedness or felicity, but always as something eternal and infinite.

do much of the walking. We hunger, we thirst, we want and need, we experience lack and discontent – all manifestations of the limited or finite nature of things. What is more, because we are creatures of infinite capacity we experience these things infinitely. This is where our infinite capacity clashes with the disappointment of the finite. This is, if you like, the dark side of desire – not the bright stars of heavenly aspiration but the sting of human insatiability. The 'Reason of all our Ambition, curiositie, Desire, and Insatiable Avarice' hangs on the disparity between the unlimited capacity we sense in our selves and the limited nature of our experience. 'We feel our Right by a tacit Instinct, and our want of it by open Experience.'[140]

Traherne is aware of the burning possibilities of insatiability and throughout his work insatiability is seen as a good. The praise of insatiablilty is a powerful characteristic of his distinct voice. Where other Christian authors and spiritual writers of other religions may recommend a paring down of appetite, Traherne insists: 'It is of the nobility of man's soul that he is insatiable. Insatiability is good.'[141] It is good for two reasons: first, because it leads the desiring human to seek and to carry on seeking; and second, because it is a divine quality.

In his poem 'Desire', Traherne praises God for giving him that 'Eager Thirst', which, by never being satisfied, 'did incessantly a Paradice / Unknown suggest, and som thing undescribed / Discern'.[142] Similarly, in 'Dissatisfaction', the questing soul is the endlessly unsatisfied soul. Here we see insatiability as a driving force of the spiritual journey. Whatever we have, we always seek something more, and that more, for Traherne, is no less than the divine. In this reading of desire, even her customarily ugly sisters, covetousness and avarice, are redeemed. '*Ambition* and *Covetousness*' are described in *Christian Ethicks* as 'Inclinations of the soul, by the one of which we are carried to *Glory*, by the other to *Treasure*'.[143] And in the poetry, desire is not ashamed to be called 'Heavenly Avarice', that 'Soaring Sacred Thirst,/ Ambassador of Bliss' that brings him to 'the true and real Joys' precisely *because* it makes him 'apt to Prize, and Taste, and See'.[144] In this way the pursuit of one's desired object becomes a heavenly path or a 'way to Blessedness'. And the one who attends to desire's insatiable demands is not necessarily on the road to perdition.

---

140 *KOG*, Ch. 16, ll. 10, 17.
141 C, I, 21, 22.
142 'Desire', ll. 2–11.
143 *CE*, p. 29.
144 'Desire', ll. 8, 53–61.

Traherne is not alone in understanding insatiableness as a dynamic feature of the spiritual life. As Nabil Matar notes, there were several mid-seventeenth-century theologians who, like the poets of aspiration noted earlier, shared Traherne's imagery of insatiableness and infinite desire.[145] John Smith, Nathaniel Culverwell and Peter Sterry, drawing in part on the mysticism of Gregory of Nyssa, as well as of Gregory the Great, whose God was limitless and therefore continually sought and never entirely found, used images of expansion and journey and of infinite proportion similar to the images used by Traherne.[146] When Gregory of Nyssa writes: 'We can conceive of no limitation in an infinite nature; and that which is limitless cannot by its nature be understood',[147] we hear not only echoes of Augustine's 'What then are we to say of God?'[148] but also a bass note over which, thirteen centuries later, Sterry would blend: 'God is . . . Being it self in its absoluteness, undivided, unrestrained, unconfined . . . in All, thro' All, on every Side, beneath, above, beyond All, every where the same . . . nowhere Bounded'.[149] And 'God cannot be bounded, or limited . . . Will you limit the Holy one of Israel?'[150] For Smith, as for Traherne, the infinity of God is the ultimate object of our 'restless appetite': 'We alwaies find a *restless appetite* within our selves which craves for some *Supreme and Chief good*, and will not be satisfied with any thing less then *Infinity* it self.'[151] Indeed, it would seem that not only is the object – God – infinite, but that the subject – the soul and her craving – must likewise remain unlimited in her quest for the infinite other. In the Nyssan tradition the soul remains insatiable

---

145 'Mysticism and Sectarianism in Mid-17th Century England', *Studia Mystica*, 11 (1988), pp. 55–65. Carol Marks had already established the link between Traherne and the Cambridge Neo-Platonists who feature in Matar's article. For further discussion see: Carol Marks, 'Thomas Traherne and Cambridge Platonism', *Proceedings of the Modern Language Association*, 81 (1966), pp. 521–34.

146 We know that Traherne read Gregory of Nyssa: he quotes him in several places in the *Centuries* and mentions Gregory's famed conversations with his sister Macrina in *Seeds of Eternity*.

147 *Patrologia Graeca* (hereafter *PG*), 44, col. 941; trans. by Herbert Mursurillo, as *From Glory to Glory* (hereafter *FGTG*), New York: Scribner's, 1961, p. 213.

148 'What, then, brethren, are we to say of God? For if you have understood what you want to say, it is not God. If you have been able to understand, you have understood something other than God' (Sermon 52, section 6.16). 'To reach out a little towards God with the mind is great blessedness but to understand is wholly impossible' (Sermon 117, section 3.5).

149 Sterry, quoted in Vivian de Sola Pinto, *Peter Sterry, Platonist and Puritan*, Cambridge: Cambridge University Press, 1934, p. 90.

150 Peter Sterry, *The Appearance of God in the Soul of Man*, London, 1710, pp. 121, 388.

151 John Smith, *Select Discourses*, London, 1660, Discourse V, p. 135.

partly because her object remains to some extent unknowable. To continue the quote from Gregory:

> We can conceive then of no limitation in an infinite nature; and that which is limitless cannot by its nature be understood. And so every desire for the Beautiful which draws us on in this ascent is intensified by the soul's very progress towards it. And this is the real meaning of seeing God: never to have this desire satisfied [κορον].[152]

For Gregory, this infinite desire without satisfaction does not tire the soul on its spiritual journey but gives it a force that drives the soul towards God. Each step nearer to God intensifies desire and every new desire heightens anticipation in the journey's next step. As Matar writes, 'For Gregory, the experience of God consists in a continual progress from one level of divine knowledge to another: it is a ceaseless dialectic of participation in and distance from an infinite God.' He continues: 'The mystical progress in God, the movement "from glory to glory", represented for them [Culverwell, Smith, Sterry, Traherne] the height of the Christian faith.' Their experience of seeking God was an experience of 'perpetual and unlimited progress, an insatiable stretching forth'.[153] As Gregory put it:

> The soul that looks up towards God, and conceives that good desire for His eternal beauty, constantly experiences an ever new yearning for that which lies ahead, and her desire is never given its full satisfaction. Hence she never ceases to 'stretch forth [επεκτεινομενοσ] to those things that are before,' ever passing from her present stage to enter more deeply into the interior, into the stage which lies ahead.[154]

Spiritual maturity consists of constant seeking. In his *Great Catechism*, Gregory wrote of the soul in journey, 'ever making one discovery a stepping-stone to another, ever reaching forth'.[155] As the soul journeys, it is as if each discovery opens another door but does so without ever finding the final room. And yet there is more of a sense of

---

152 *PG*, 44, col. 405 A, trans. in *FGTG*, pp. 147–8.
153 Matar, 'Mysticism and Sectarianism', p. 57.
154 *PG*, 44, col. 1305 A; trans. in *FGTG*, p. 268; referring to Phil. 3.1–14.
155 *The Great Catechism*, in Philip Schaff and Henry Wace (eds), *A Select Library of Nicene and Post-Nicene Fathers of the Christian Church*, New York, 1890–1900, reprinted Grand Rapids, MI: Eerdmans, 1972, vol. V, p. 492.

progress than frustration in Gregory's tone: 'For those who are rising in perfection, the limit of the good that is attained becomes the beginning of the discovery of higher goods. Thus they never stop rising, moving from one new beginning to the next.'[156] Writing just before Traherne, the Cambridge Platonist John Smith described the progress of the soul in similar terms of upward movement towards an infinite God, although his imagery exchanges feet for wings: the soul

> finds then no more ends nor bounds to stop its swift and restless motion. It may then fly upwards from one heaven to another, till it be beyond all orb of finit being, swallowed up in the boundless abyss of divinity.[157]

The soul in 'swift and restless motion', the soul 'ever reaching forth'; a soul that is never given 'its full satisfaction'. These are the images of Gregory and of Smith. Culverwell, too, wrote of the necessity of continual effort:

> one must nowhere relax the tension of the toil nor stand aside from the struggles lying before him nor pay attention to things of the past if any good thing has been done, but one must forget those things according to the apostle, stretch oneself [επεκτεινεζσαι] out to what lies before and shatter the heart with thoughts of toil, holding the desire of righteousness without satiety [ακορεζτον].[158]

Again, continual effort is required, though final satisfaction is not to be expected by the 'panting soul'. In his better known *The Light of Nature*, Culverwell included a short treatise, *The Panting Soul*, in which he wrote:

> though this may seem very wearisome and tedious, to be alwaies a panting: yet the Christian soul findes far more incomparable sweetness ... he findes more of this in very panting after God, then any worldling can, when with the greatest complacency he takes his fil of his choicest delights.[159]

---

156 *PG*, 44, col. 914 C; trans. in *FGTG*, p. 213.

157 *Select Discourses*, Edinburgh, 1756, p. 102.

158 Quoted in Rondal E. Heine, *Perfection in the Virtuous Life*, Cambridge, MA: Philadelphia Patristic Foundation, 1975, p. 88.

159 Nathaniel Culverwell, *The Panting Soul*, London, 1652, p. 71.

At first all of this may sound similar to Traherne's thought; and in some ways it is. He too writes of the thirsty soul, 'panting and faint' in its pursuit of felicity.[160] His poem 'Insatiableness' is one of his works that conveys something of the desperation of the seeking soul:

> ... Can I no Rest nor Satisfaction find?
>   ... Till I what lies
>   In Time's beginning find;
> Must I till then for ever burn?
>
> Not all the Crowns; not all the heaps of Gold
> On Earth; not all the Tales that can be told,
>   Will Satisfaction yield to me:
> ... Till I what was before all Time descry,
> The World's Beginning seems but Vanity.
>
>   ('Insatiableness', ll. 2, 8–13, 21–2)

Here we see a soul in an agony of desire, craving knowledge of its origins, knowledge of an elusive divine, craving meaning. It would *seem* then that Traherne does follow Gregory's model – infinite appetite for the infinite divine being at the heart of the Nyssan tradition.

But whereas Gregory, and to some extent Smith and Culverwell, suggest an essential divine unknowableness as necessary for the sustenance of insatiability in the soul's quest, there is no such necessity in Traherne. For him, as we have seen, the infinity of God is not something remote. Neither is it wholly out of his reach. There is an unlimited 'stretching forth', as there is in Gregory, Smith and Culverwell. But it is not a movement towards the exterior unknown.[161] In fact, the infinity of God is, for Traherne, as much a present reality as a distant one; so much already in the human soul that eventual consummation seems hardly necessary.

'The Infinity of God is our enjoyment', he writes, 'the ground and foundations of all our satisfactions . . . It surroundeth us continually on every side, it fills us, and inspires us. It is so mysterious that it is wholly within us, and even then it wholly seems and is without us.'[162]

---

[160] 'Dissatisfaction', l. 29; see also 'Desire'.

[161] For Traherne, it is more of a stretching towards something internal and essential: 'When I retire first I seem to com in my selfe to a centre, in that centre I find Eternitie and all its Riches' (*SM*, I, 81).

[162] C, V, 2. This is part of Traherne's larger claim that we are in God and he in us: see *SM*, I, 82; *SM*, III,14; C, IV, 72; etc.

For Traherne there is no escape from the infinity of God, no place where his infinity is not. Where Gregory sees the infinity of God as making God ultimately beyond our grasp, Traherne sees that same infinity as indicating God's immediacy. His infinity is where we live; and we are where God's infinity dwells: 'It [God's infinity] is more inevitably and constantly, more nearly and immediately our dwelling place, than our cities and kingdoms and houses. Our bodies themselves are not so much ours, or within us as that is.'[163]

Such immediate contact with the infinity of God is neither optional nor temporary. Traherne admonishes his readers to be sensible of this fact, not because such assent would gain them greater proximity to the divine but because the immediacy of God's infinity is simply true and so not to see it is to live away from a clear vision of oneself and of the world.

> The immensity of God is an eternal tabernacle. Why then we should not be sensible of that as much as of our dwellings, I cannot tell, unless our corruption and sensuality destroy us. We ought always to feel, admire, and walk in it. It is more clearly objected to the eye of the soul, than our castles and palaces to the eye of the body. Those accidental buildings may be thrown down, or we may be taken from them, but this can never be removed, it abideth for ever. It is impossible not to be within it, nay, to be so surrounded as evermore to be in the centre and midst of it, wherever we can possibly remove, is inevitably fatal to every being.[164]

That we do not sense our closeness to this infinity but feel rather our distance from God reflects a division deep within the self – the self divided from its original, looking outward for an answer that is in fact to come from within. As Augustine's famous lines describe it: 'Too late I loved you. O Beauty ever ancient and ever new! Too late I loved you! And, Behold you were within me, and I out of myself, and there I searched for you' (*Confessions*, X, 27).

Our infinite aspirations and questions, our insatiability, Traherne suggests, are unavoidable because to be human is also to share in this divine quality – infinity. We desire infinitely not because God is so completely other and unknowable in his infinity but because his infinity is in us. This notion, that we contain a divine infinity within us, which is asserted again and again in Traherne, resonates with the teachings

---

163 C, V, 2.
164 Ibid.

on eternal life that we find in St John's Gospel.[165] 'I have come that you might have eternal life' proclaims Jesus Christ, and for Traherne that is not a vague promise for the future but a statement of God's initial intention from the beginning, an intention that we should live the infinite life of eternity now. The idea of a divine infinity within each woman and man is an idea Traherne refined over time, submitting it to scrutiny and clarifying it when necessary. The Lambeth Manuscript gives us some evidence of this process. In *Inducements to Retiredness*, the first work in the manuscript, against Traherne's bold claim 'for Man is such a Wonderfull Creature that Infinity & Eternity is within Him'[166] there appears a marginal comment from his 'critical reader', which warns 'Infinity and Eternity is in man by Derivation from God; not as it is in God, for in him it is his very essence in us by communication from him Only.' It appears that Traherne took this correction to heart since, by the time he came to write the most highly developed work in the manuscript, *The Kingdom of God*, his description of man as wonderful admits that any excellency in the soul is that 'which it deriveth from the Nature and power of GOD'.[167]

Being made in the divine image, by derivation blessed with infinity and by nature largely limited to the finite, our experience of insatiability is often tinged with discomfort. But even this discomfort is seen by Traherne as a cause for praise. In his poem 'Desire', for instance, Traherne can praise God for the 'eager thirst' and 'restlesse longing' that, from his birth, disallowed any rest until he should find 'the true and real Joys'. In this poem he calls desire by many names: 'a burning Ardent fire, A virgin Infant Flame', 'An Inward Hidden Heavenly Love', 'soaring Sacred Thirst', 'restlesse longing' and 'famine', as well as the

---

165 I am grateful to David Ford, whose attention to the Gospel of John has affirmed and energized my reading of Traherne.

166 *ITR*, ll. 26-7. This claim comes in the larger context of his claims about the importance of retirement from the world: 'For in Retirement alone can a Man approach to that wch is Infinit & Eternal. Infinity & Eternity are only to bee seen by the Inward Ey. By Expanding the Understanding, & by the Introversion of the Soul, do we approach unto those: namely by observing & noting what is within. for Man is such a Wonderfull Creature that Infinity & Eternity is within Him. And if those are within Him, all ye Things they contain, are within Him likewise. For it is as Easy, for a Cabinet to be in a Palace & yet those Treasures wth wch it is replenished to be out of the Palace; as for the Eternity of God to be in the Soul of Man, while the Things contained in Eternity are out of the soul, in wch Eternity is contained (*ITR*, ll. 22-31).

167 *KOG*, Ch. 24, ll. 1-2. Here the infinite that man has by derivation is God's infinite goodness, his omnipresence, his divine spark. In *The Kingdom of God*, that these qualities should be derived is important to Traherne's developed notion of communication, since he believes that 'Evry thing therfore receiveth from all and communicateth to all, after its Kind and mannner'.

unexpected 'Heavenly Avarice' and 'Ambassador of Bliss'. In his description of desire, Traherne offers a kind of collection of images rather than a definition; in fact, he seems to be not so much concerned about defining the thing at all as he is in conveying the power of its working in him. He writes of his experience of desire in the first person; it is

> A Love with which into the World I came,
> . . . Which in my Soul did Work and move,
> And ever ever me Enflame,
> With restlesse longing . . .

He is approached and inhabited by desire:

> This Soaring Sacred Thirst,
> Ambassador of Bliss, approached me first,
> Making a Place in me,
> That made me apt to Prize, and Taste, and See . . .
>
> ('Desire', ll. 4, 6–8, 53–6)

In all of this he is initially acted upon, and he therefore acts. His questing is the result of a gift received, for which he gives thanks: 'For giving me Desire . . . be Thy Name for ever praisd by me.'[168] Here we see desiring as, in a strange way, an act of fulness – it is an exercise of capacity bestowed rather than a manifestation of lack. The contrast here between Traherne's thought and the previously noted Herbert's (whose work we know Traherne read[169]) is interesting. According to Herbert's 'The Pulley', our human restlessness is not the result of a gift bestowed but a gift withheld. At the creation of man the Trinity, having bestowed strength, beauty, wisdom, honour and pleasure, decide to withhold 'rest':

> 'For if I should', said He,
> 'Bestow this jewel also on My creature,
> He would adore My gifts instead of Me
> And rest in nature, not the God of nature;
> So both should losers be.'
>
> ('The Pulley', ll. 11–15)

---

168 'Desire', ll. 1, 13.
169 In *KOG*, Traherne quotes the following lines from one of Herbert's poems, 'Longing': 'Mothers are kind, becaus Thou art (saies the Divine poet) And dost dispose to them a part; Their children them, and they suck thee, more free!' He refers to Herbert at several other points.

The result is 'repining restlessness', wealth and weariness. We are tossed at last to God's breast, if not by goodness then by sheer exhaustion. This may resonate at certain stages with one's experience of life but lacks the energy and passion of Traherne's 'prizing and tasting and seeing'. Where Herbert's restlessness repines, Traherne's restlessness thirsts and tastes and has.

Restless longing in Traherne, like hunger and thirst and all the other lacks and needs, is the springboard of infinite joys, for the limitations of the finite serve as a continual reminder to our forgetful selves that we are creatures of infinity. Our insatiability, grounded in God's infinity, which is by direct image our own, is good, true and unavoidable. What is more, according to Traherne, insatiable desire is at the heart of God.

Wanting Like a God

'You must want like a God that you may be satisfied like God', 'He is from eternity full of want', 'He made us to want like Gods', claims Traherne.[170] This wanting in God is the foundation of all desiring in Traherne. The sexual imagery of *Love* and *The Kingdom of God* is a picture of the Divine lover in pursuit of the beloved, the soul. The passion of this desiring God is the model of our passion; God's prudence in desiring an eternal and infinite soul is an example of the prudence that we should exercise. The infinite aspiration with which we reach infinitely towards the infinite end – that is the love of God – is mirrored in God's infinite reaching towards us. And the insatiability of our hungers and thirsts echoes the great hunger for souls in the heart of God. All of this is implied in Traherne's simple phrases above. Traherne's notions of desire have daring implications for his theology. Desire in Traherne means we must want like a God who is from eternity full of want.

What terms can one use to understand this wanting God? Certainly 'need' is one of the words that Traherne uses alongside 'want'. In meditation 42 of the first *Century*, when he writes 'Want in God is treasure to us. For had there been no need He would not have created the World, nor made us', 'want' and 'need' seem to be used synonymously. Yet in the preceding meditation 'need' is something more concrete than 'want'; 'needs' lending an external reality to 'wants' that are, in this case, an internal action of the mind: 'Were there no needs, wants

---

[170] C, I, 44; C, I, 42; C, I, 41.

would be wanting themselves, and supplies superfluous'.[171] And if these apparent contradictions were not enough, in the same meditation Traherne plays further with the word 'want', listing the many things God wanted 'from all eternity' and concluding in both a pun and a paradox: 'He wanted, yet He wanted not, for He had them.' This playing with 'want' leads me to believe that Traherne was aware of the ambiguities of the word he had chosen; that, in fact, the ambiguity of 'want' was deliberate. In *The Shadow of Eternity*, Sharon Seelig refers to the wit of the metaphysical poets, among whom Traherne is often grouped, as a wit that represents a world-view – 'the metaphysical cast of mind . . . that saw in a single . . . event several kinds or levels of meaning'.[172] This is undoubtedly true of Traherne's playful use of the word 'want', but there is also a deeply functional side to his ambiguous 'want'. The ambiguity creates space for the competing claims of his paradoxical concepts – the empty soul that is full of infinity, the abundant God who is full of want can only be accommodated by the quirky oxymoron in an open frame. Playful, ambiguous, witty or clever, Traherne's use of the simple word 'want' is meant to surprise and delight us, as well as to raise important questions about capacity, plenitude, desire and deity.

Then there is, in the phrase 'want like a God', that little indefinite article that may be troublesome. 'You must want like *a* God' – perhaps Traherne is not identifying our wanting with the wanting of 'the one' God at all. After all, just three meditations previously he has also written 'You must want like *Gods*' in the plural.[173] But no, despite the variant forms of the term 'God' that Traherne employs, it is not *any* or *some various* gods to which Traherne likens the desiring human, since in the very next sentence he deliberately distinguishes between 'the heathen Deities' who 'wanted nothing, and were therefore unhappy, for they had no being' and 'the Lord God of Israel the Living and True God . . . from all eternity'.[174] Clearly then, for Traherne the God of our 'wanting' is understood in the monotheistic tradition of a Judaeo-Christian God. The indefinite article and the plural are attached to the desiring human, not the god whose wanting they replicate.

And what about this action or state of God *wanting*? As William Countryman's recent reflections on desire note, there is in the Christian

---

171 In *Select Meditations* this view is also expressed using some of the same words: 'For without want there Could be no Enjoyments, but all Redundancies and Superfluities' (*SM*, III, 79).

172 Sharon Seelig, *The Shadow of Eternity: Belief and Structure in Herbert, Vaughan and Traherne*, Lexington, KY: The University of Kentucky Press, 1981, Introduction, i.

173 C, I, 44; C, I, 41.

174 C, I, 41.

tradition a tension between the notion of a passionate God that runs through all of Scripture and the doctrine that God lives above any kind of need. Countryman writes, 'This portrayal [of a passionate God] collides with the later theological dictum that God is "without body, parts or passions".' Neither Scripture nor tradition are wrong, he suggests, but they are making different points about God.[175] For Traherne, too, the notion of a wanting God is 'very strange' since 'in Him is the fulness of all Blessedness'.[176] And yet it is in the same meditation in which Traherne writes 'For in Him is the fulness of all Blessedness: He overflowed eternally' that he also claims 'He is from *eternity full* of want'.[177] Not only is God's wanting full and eternal, it is also glorious. For Traherne, God's wanting is the source of his joy because 'infinite want is the very ground and cause of infinite treasure' and 'Infinite Wants satisfied produce infinite Joys'.[178] It is this very 'wanting' in the heart of God that instigated creation: 'he wanted the communication of His divine essence, and persons to enjoy it. He wanted Worlds, He wanted Spectators, He wanted Joys, He wanted Treasures.'[179] Ultimately, he wanted us – creatures and the created world.[180] And so God's wanting is the source of our existence and therefore not only the root of God's treasure and joy but also a 'treasure' to us.[181]

All of these assertions are underpinned by two beliefs that Traherne held concerning God's wanting. The first is that God's wanting is essentially passionate, that is to say that God's passion is an expression of God's essence. The second is that need in God is always about capacity.

In the long line of theologians from Aquinas to the present, Traherne sees God's nature and God's acts as inextricably linked. The best does the best. The infinite acts infinitely. And God's infinite life, which is infinite in fervour as well as extent, results in action that is likewise infinite in both extent and fervour.[182] When thinking of the fervour of God's act, one is not only reminded of the perfection of his action in

---

175 William Countryman, *Love Human and Divine: Reflections on Love, Sexuality and Friendship*, London: Morehouse, 2005, p. 25.
176 C, I, 42; cf. SM, III, 82: 'God is a Fulness in all Extremes'.
177 C, I, 42 (italics mine; to be *full* of *want* is itself something of a paradox).
178 C, I, 42–3.
179 C, I, 41.
180 C, IV, 75. Having created the world, 'He desired some one that might weigh and reason, love the beauty, and admire the vastness of so great a work.'
181 'Want in God is a treasure to us' (C, IV, 75).
182 Interestingly, the human soul is also described as being two ways infinite – infinite in extent and excellency (C, II, 83).

creation as set out in *The Kingdom of God*[183] but also of the passionate God described in 'Affection' and mentioned earlier, whose 'Sweetness and Ardor, Zeal and Violence, Excess of Lov' is the reason why he 'Woes, grievs, Fears and doth lament, hopes, covets and is discontent'. In both the human soul and in God an abatement of passion is seen as polluting. As we have seen in *Christian Ethicks*, 'Lukewarmness is Profane' and to be loved lukewarmly is to be embraced with polluted arms (*CE*, p. 89). For Traherne, the link between passion and perfection means that did God love us any less, that abatement of ardour would be as damaging to his purity as actual evil. He writes:

> The fervor of his Lov, and the extrem Ardor of his desire, wherwith he is carried to Infinit perfection, is his real puritie ... the Abatement of his Affection to the Best of things, or the slackness of his endeavor and Desire, any of these had been like Dross in his Brightness; Admixtures of unprofitable Dirt.[184]

So it is that the human soul too is considered sullied by any inferior expression of love. 'He that can submit to an Inferior degree of Lov, or take up with a Smaller Measure in the Deitie, is a degenerat person', Traherne writes. 'Who infinitely desireth ... he only is a truly Sublime, and Generous Soul, that is Worthy of God'.[185]

Not only should we desire God ardently but we should also ardently expect perfection in God. To expect less is not modesty but cowardice, according to Traherne:

> Neither will any pretence serve the turn to cover our cowardice, which we call modesty, in not daring to say or expect this [perfection] of the Deity. Unless we expect this with infinite ardency, we are a lazy kind of creatures good for nothing. 'Tis man's holiness and glory to desire absolute perfection in God.[186]

---

183 See *KOG*, Chs 3, 5, 8 and 6; but in this last, Traherne also asserts that creation, however perfect, is empty – a nest without a bird, a temple without a deity – without the omnipresence of God (*KOG*, fol. 167r–v). The wonder of creation is also, of course, a major theme of the *Centuries*, and appears in most of Traherne's works.

184 *KOG*, Ch. 15, ll. 115–19. Traherne makes a similar link between passion and perfection in his chapter on holiness in *Christian Ethicks*: 'For infinite Goodness must needs desire with an infinite violence, that all Goodness should be compleat and Perfect: and that Desire, which makes to the Perfection of all Goodness, must infinitely avoid every slur and Miscarriage as unclean ... It cannot desire less then infinite Perfection, nor less then hate all Imperfection, in an infinite Manner' (*CE*, p. 88).

185 *KOG*, Ch. 6, ll. 128–34.

186 *C*, II, 83.

Just as man's holiness is here identified by the ardency of his desire, so also God's holiness is seen in the ardency of his hatred of profaneness and love of righteousness.[187] These are, for Traherne, a perfection in his action.

In chapter 12 of *Christian Ethicks*, Traherne argues that the reason why the angels in heaven do continually cry 'Holy, Holy, Holy' is not because they wish to emphasize God's purity or aloofness but because they are stunned again and again by the excess and violence of his love, the zeal that carries him to perfect Blessedness, which they see and feel everywhere brought about by 'the irresistible strength of his Eternal Ardor'. The holy fire that touched the prophet's lips, the burning coal, is this: a passionate love for God's ways, a share of divine zeal, a sliver of ardour. This is what equips the prophet Isaiah for ministry. Whatever else Traherne has to say about divine holiness, he is quite clear that in God holiness and passion are inextricably linked. This connection between holiness and passion is why passion matters to Traherne.

God's fervour, then, is an expression of his essential perfection. By desire he is carried to glory; without his zeal his holiness would be hollow. Traherne goes further. What is true of divine holiness is also true of divine blessedness and goodness and love. Every way you look, God's essence requires an infinite expression: 'look upon his Blessedness, it must hav Infinit Treasures; upon his Goodness, it must be infinitly communicated; upon his Lov, it must be infinit in fervor'.[188]

Likewise his actions must be infinite in extent. The infinite extent of God's action has been alluded to earlier in this chapter – that realm of infinite space that is the theatre of divine action, having an infinite capacity to answer his power. For although God's omnipresence and omnipotence, when they are exercised, are always exercised fully, they are also always full of greater capacity. Like infinite space God's act is at once full and capacious – at once effecting and leaving room for all things.[189] A divine act that leaves room may seem like a contradiction in terms, since it seems not like a 'perfect act' at all but like an imperfect or incompleted act. Yet, for Traherne, God's exercise of capacity

---

187 'The infinite Excess of his Eternal Goodness is its own Holiness . . . FOR infinite Goodness must needs desire with an infinite violence' (*CE*, pp. 87, 88). The passionate nature of God's holiness is suggested in the title of this twelfth chapter in *Christian Ethicks*: 'Of Holiness: Its Nature, and Violence, and Pleasure. Its Beauty consistent in the infinite Love of Righteousness and Perfection.'
188 *KOG*, Ch. 15, ll. 31–4.
189 'He leaveth room for and effecteth all things' (*C*, II, 19). Here Traherne is referring to the physical presence of God but since, in doing so, he is arguing from God's nature, the point remains.

is not about emptiness but action. Capacity is a 'Passive Power' and so to exercise capacity is to act. Traherne asserts: 'he made capacities for his Essence, and Passive Powers, that might answer his Activ Omnipotence'.[190] I believe that this issue of capacity keeps recurring in Traherne because of the centrality of desire in his scheme of things. However perfectly in extent or fervour God or the human acts, there is always potential for more, and where there is potential there is desire. Traherne says of God:

> All that he saw his Omnipresence and eternitie capable of, invited him unto them. His own Wisdom and Power allured him: So did the Hallelujahs, and Praises of all his Creatures. His own Goodness pricked him on: and the utmost Heights being most desirable, were most pleasing.[191]

Here it is God's own capacity that urges creation. This echoes those meditations in the *Centuries* in which Traherne claims that God needed to create the world. All that he wanted he had from eternity and so we may see God's wanting as a choice, his needing as an expression of chosen desire. According to Traherne, it was of God's wisdom that this should be for there must be innumerable means for the satisfaction of innumerable capacities.

God's wants are always satisfied. 'His wants are as glorious as infinite', writes Traherne, 'ever Blessed, because always satisfied'.[192] Since 'all Eternity is at once in Him', he wants and has concurrently. From all eternity he 'wanted like a God'. Traherne continues, 'He wanted, yet He wanted not, for He had them.'[193] His wants and enjoyments being always present together, each perfect the other:

> His wants are as lively as his enjoyments: and always present with Him . . . He feels them both. His wants put a lustre upon His enjoyments and make them infinite. His enjoyments being infinite crown His wants, and make them beautiful even to God Himself. His wants and enjoyments being always present are delightful to each other, stable, immutable, perfective of each other, and delightful to Him.[194]

---

190 *KOG*, Ch. 30, ll. 188–9.
191 *KOG*, Ch. 15, ll. 146–9.
192 C, I, 42.
193 C, I, 41.
194 C, I, 44.

The 'lustre' added to his enjoyments may sound superficial but God's wants are really the root of his treasure. 'He is from eternity full of want, or else He would not be full of Treasure. Infinite want is the very ground and cause of infinite treasure', insists Traherne. 'Want is the fountain of all His fulness.'[195] To God it is natural to know his treasures; for us it is something we must learn: 'This is a lesson long enough: which you may be all your life in learning, and to all Eternity in practising. *Be sensible of your wants, that you may be sensible of your treasures.*'[196]

What does it mean then for us to want like God? God wants perfectly in extent and fervour but this wanting occurs out of fulness into infinity. We want out of a need that, while it may remind us of our infinite origin and end, is also rooted in the unchosen but given needs of our finite frames. As Traherne writes in the *Centuries*:

> Here upon Earth, it [the soul] is under many disadvantages and impediments that maim it in its exercise, but in Heaven it is most glorious. And it is my happiness that I can see it on both sides the veil or screen. There it appeareth in all its advantages, for every soul being full and fully satisfied, at ease, in rest, and wanting nothing, easily overflows and shines upon all. It is its perfect interest so to do, and nothing hinders it . . . But here it is pinched and straitened by wants: here it is awakened and put in mind of itself: here it is divided and distracted between two. It has a body to provide for, necessities to relieve, and a person to supply. Therefore is it in this world the more glorious, if in the midst of these disadvantages it exert itself in its operations.[197]

And yet our needing and wanting can be passionate and prudent, as God's is; it can be perfective and satisfied. That Traherne intends satisfaction for the human soul is in no doubt. This is the very reason why we have been given desire in such generous measure: 'You must want like a God *that you may be satisfied like God.*'[198] And our wanting can be, in a sense, even more profoundly perfective than God's. For, whereas God's wants perfect his pleasures, our wants can perfect our selves. Traherne follows his injunction to '*Be sensible of your wants,*

---
[195] C, I, 42.
[196] C, I, 45.
[197] C, III, 60.
[198] C, I, 44 (italics mine). See also 'He made us to want like Gods, that like Gods we might be satisfied.' (C, I, 41).

that you may be sensible of your treasures' with the assurance that 'He is most like God that is sensible of everything'.[199] It would seem, then, that learning to want as God wants involves the soul in a profound change – refined by fire, we become like him and live in his likeness. 'Wants are the bands and cements between God and us', Traherne asserts. 'Wants are the ligatures between God and us, the sinews that convey senses from Him into us, whereby we live in Him, and feel His enjoyments' (C, I, 51). It is in this sense that wanting like a God is truly transforming.

We may want then, passionately and prudently, in imitation of God; knowing, by our wants, both our need of him and the joy of treasure that we receive. We may, like God, experience want as perfective and satisfying. By knowing our wants we may come to know our treasures and enjoy them in full extent and fervour. As Traherne describes it:

> To enjoy therefore the treasures of God after the similitude of God is to enjoy the most perfect treasures in the most perfect manner. Upon which I was infinitely satisfied in God, and knew there was a Deity because I was satisfied. For in exerting himself wholly in achieving thus an infinite Felicity He was infinitely delightful, great and glorious, and my desires so august and insatiable that nothing less than the Deity could satisfy them. (C, II, 59)

Traherne's desire, it seems, increased with every satisfaction until, by desires 'august and insatiable', he was led to the chief treasure, which is God himself. This is why he proclaims the virtue of desire – partly because it is itself a divine quality, but perhaps even more significantly because it is in the often painful but inescapably compelling dynamic of desiring that the human soul finds its home and its happiness.

The purpose of this chapter has been to explore the notion of desire in Traherne. As we have seen, desire in Traherne is not only about sexual desire (although sexual imagery plays a significant role in his discussion of power, consent and union in the dynamic of God and the soul, and passion is an important part of that dynamic). Desire in Traherne is at its best when it is both excessively passionate and prudent – that is to say, when the infinite love is matched to an infinite object. Infinity and infinite space are places in which this infinite desire may grow, infinite space being the first thing naturally known along with the desire of 'some Great Thing'. Desire is about stretching into this

---

199 C, I, 45.

space with 'infinite aspiration', and so by desiring infinitely we exercise the soul's capacity made in the image of God. Gregory of Nyssa's 'ever reaching forth' and the 'insatiable stretching forth' of Matar speak eloquently of Trahernean desire's insatiability. They suggest illimited desire – unbounded, unquenchable, divine in proportion and human in its experience of hunger and of thirst. This experience of the darker side of desire – want, need, hunger, thirst, dissatisfaction – is embraced by Traherne because it is out of this intersection of the finite and the infinite that human insatiability arises, a good that, like infinite space, is an exercise in infinite capacity. Traherne has given us many terms with which to discuss the workings of desire – hunger, thirst, restless longing, heavenly avarice, prizing, wanting, affection, need, ardour, fervour, among others. The simple word 'want' is the word I favour because its ambiguities seem to have been appreciated and employed by Traherne and because it implies both sides of desire – the side that looks out towards the infinite and the side that feels the limitations of the finite. Most of all, desire is divine: we are to desire as God desires – with full fervour and extent, experiencing satisfaction and perfection as wants become 'Sacred Occasions and Means of Felicity'(C, I, 43).

2

Discerning Treasure

> By Prizing I am all things to Posess,
> My Duty is to giv the Sun its Due
>
> (*COH*, 'Avarice I')

It is all very well to advocate want but what is it exactly that we are to be wanting? This chapter attempts to address that question by considering Traherne's many references to treasure. Prominent in this discussion is the king as the chief accumulator and distributor of treasures, and I consider briefly Traherne's attitude to the king, the king's role in regard to wealth and honours and the greater treasure of social stability, and the related issues of wealth creation and inheritance. Traherne's objects of desire are many – physical and spiritual – and the criterion for discerning real treasure from false treasure is described. The trust he places in 'highest reason' and its echoes in the Cambridge Platonists are set out, as is his belief that one of the most valuable treasures we have is the divine light within. Prizing is discussed as an activity of the heart as well as of the intellect, the point where discerned treasure meets hot-headed desire. Finally, as the relationship between need, treasure and the value of things in their place is explored, we see that Traherne's notion of treasure is intimately linked with his whole concept not only of value and worth but also of reality.

What is Treasure?

For most of us 'treasure' is a flippant word – the province of pirate-playing children or of the 'memories' and 'moments' so guarded by sentimental greetings cards. For Traherne, 'treasure' was nothing of the sort. Perhaps living through days of iconoclasm and restoration in which tangible treasures were hidden, destroyed, forgotten, replaced or lost, made a difference to his use of the word; for Traherne's word carries meanings that are lost to us, and none of them are about things imaginary or elusive or sentimental. To speak of 'treasure' in

Traherne's work is to raise serious questions of want and worth. It is to have a means of ascribing value.

Traherne is unashamed of his apparently insatiable desire for treasure. So familiar is the theme that some readers have become embarrassed by his catalogues of booty – the thrones, sceptres, crowns, gold, silver, kingdoms that are the toys of his happy men and women. The whole of the third chapter of *The Kingdom of God* is about the treasures in the world. Traherne's man 'cannot rest without a Clear and apparent Treasure' (*KOG*, Ch. 3, ll. 20–1), since where there is no 'desire of Treasure there can be no Sence of felicitie' (*SE*, l. 55). All of this reiterates the famous sentiment of the *Centuries*: 'You are never truly great till all the world is yours' (*C*, II, 14) and he praises the 'avaricious humour' by which we desire that treasure be wholly ours.[1] In his poem 'Desire', when Feasts, Honours, Imperial Treasures and living pleasures are the things for which Traherne yearns, it would seem that he takes for his own the biblical text 'In thy presence there is fulness of Joy, and at thy right hand there are pleasures forever more'.[2] In one instance Traherne turns even fasting into pleasure because the faster's increased desire heightens the pleasure of treasure attained so that fasters may be the greatest epicures.[3] This may seem a picture of Traherne the greedy, the glutton, the sensualist, the gourmand, until one considers that his 'treasures' are less straightforward than they seem.

Although his images of treasure are often framed in royal terms, they are never exclusively the king's. For Traherne, treasure is wholly one's own while at the same time being everyone else's too.[4] His 'Thrones', 'sceptres', 'crowns', 'feasts', 'palaces' and 'pleasure' may be images of false or true treasure. When they are gifts bestowed by God rather than treasures sought from a temporal power, they speak of divine authority and benevolence. God is king; humankind is royal; the heavens and the earth are the endless expanse of his kingdom filled with infinite treasure. This is not only the first principle of *The Kingdom of God*, in which Traherne repeatedly refers to Christians as 'subjects', but the underlying supposition of all of his work, and the phrase itself is a common one in the Gospels. And yet the same 'sceptres' and 'crowns'

---

1 *C*, II, 79. Here the avaricious humour and the communicative humour go hand in hand – see below, note 4.

2 Ps. 16.11. Cf. 'Thoughts IV', which begins with these very words; see also *C*, II, 100.

3 'A Vertuous man is more covetous, more Ambitious, more prone to Celestial Epicurisme, if I may so speak, than all the World besides' (*CE*, p. 285). See also *ITR*, ll. 353–5.

4 Thus, by 'the most delightful accident imaginable' (*C*, II, 79) his treasures satisfy two opposite humours at once – the avaricious humour and the communicative humour – in an economy of gift and receipt that will be explored more fully in subsequent chapters.

associated with a kingdom can be among those things that are false treasures: 'The Inventions of Sin are now becom our only Treasures: Houses and Lands, and Monies, and Cloaths, and Enclosures, a few Crowns and Scepters are all we can Admire' writes Traherne in *The Kingdom of God*, in a fierce criticism of rising notions of property and ownership. Do the subsequent lines 'and the God of this World, is the Deitie we Adore because upon Earth he hath power to giv and distribute these' (*KOG*, Ch. 7, ll. 16–19) also veil a criticism of the king or are they purely a reference to Satan? Nabil Matar has made a strong case for the Davidic imagery of the *Centuries* to be seen as implied criticism of Charles II[5] – could *The Kingdom of God* be seen in similar terms?

The case is not as clear cut as that. Two chapters later in *The Kingdom of God*, the self-sacrificing love and loyalty that would call subjects to lay down their lives for the king and the king to lay down his life for his subjects is, like the loyalty of husbands and wives, of lovers and their objects, a spark of 'Eternal Goodness' (*KOG*, Ch. 9, l. 69). Here the relationship between king and subject appears in a catalogue of acts of self-giving generosity that are 'natural' expressions of goodness:

> These little Creatures we before spake of [ants],will Expose themsels in Battel to the Death for the preservation their king. Even feeble Hens forgetfull of their Weakness will flie into the Paws of a Lion to sav their Chickens from being devoured; the Pellican will feed her yong ones with her Blood, Tygres tho ravenous, almost Starv themselves to Death while they cary the Prey to their Cubs. A Lioness or a Bear bereaved of her Whelps, as if her Heart and Soul were stoln from her, runs upon all Dangers, and Death to recover them. Will not a Mother step upon a Naked Sword to save her child from a Bloody Ruffian? Hath not many a father adventurd into a Burning house to fetch out his son, and lost his Armes, or Legs in Exchange? How many Kings hav died for the honor and prosperity of their Kingdoms, How many Subjects for their Kings, how many wives with their Husbands, how many Lovers for their objects, how many hav pined away to Death after the Loss of their Beloved. The Generous principles of Nature, are Seeds and Sparks as it were of Eternal Goodness. And the contemplation of this goodness is the fuel and food of faith. (*KOG*, ch. 9, ll. 55–70)

---

[5] Nabil Matar, 'The Political Views of Thomas Traherne', *The Huntington Library Quarterly*, 57, 3 (Summer, 1994), pp. 241–53.

For a writer who had seen a king beheaded, a kingless commonwealth and a king restored, whose intellectual world included the works of anti-monarchists and absolute monarchists alike, and who devoted an entire work (arguably among his most sophisticated) configuring the world as a kingdom with God as its king, the king image is one that it is important to unpack: where treasure and kingship are linked, the ambiguities of one are reflected in similar ambiguities about the other.

On the one hand the king is seen as lofty and inviolate, occupying a unique position as emblem of authority and giver of gifts and blessing. In this model, the ownership and accumulation of treasure is one of the hallmarks of kingship.[6] On the other hand Traherne insists that the high estate to which all humanity is lifted by the act of the incarnation of God as a human being in Christ and by Adam's having been made caretaker of creation makes every person higher than a king. 'Lord what is a Thousand Kingdoms, compared to mans Dominion over the world?' Traherne asks. 'Can hats and knees, and Thrones and sceptres and Silver and Gold and Splendid Palaces, appear any other than Shells and Patches, and Tinsell vanities, when they are put in Competition with all the Gloryes of Heaven and Earth!' (*SM*, III, 10). This is the real greatness of kings: the height of their subjects.

> And if kings did understand this, and see the Grandure of their Subjects, so as to know over whom they reigned, Did they reign in all their Hearts and Triumph in the affections of such Glorious Creatures, were they exalted in the Throne of their Immortall soul, and did they liv like God sincerely Honoured and Admird in their Temple; as by His laws and Statutes every son and freind of his ought to doe; this were somewhat. (*SM*, III, 10)

The implication here is that many or at least some kings do not so live (possibly that Charles II did not so live). Without this understanding of the height of every subject, 'all the other tinsell vanities are shews without substance and Beggerly Elements without Significations'.

Clearly Traherne longs for the exterior show of authority and pomp attached to a king to be matched with an interior appreciation of the worth of each subject. Yet even without this quickening spirit the trappings of authority are not dead things to be discarded. They remain necessary since

---

[6] For the symbolic significance of this image see Alison Sherrington, *Mystical Symbolism in the Poetry of Thomas Traherne*, St Lucia: University of Queensland Press, 1970.

they restrain the Inordinat vulgar, and Breed a Reverance in Dull Spectators. For the person of a King and the Benefit of His office ought to prevail. Whoe is most Beautiful in His Naked Authority: But a Blinded people that see noe Truth would tread upon Authority without some Ensigns Exhibiting it to them. (SM, III, 10)

Whether the monarch be virtuous or dissolute there are practical benefits of monarchy that Traherne is loath to discard. These practical benefits, rather like the 'harsh and sour' virtues of *Christian Ethicks*, are accidental, a result of the fall. In an estate of innocence, Traherne argues, there is no need of a king. It is only after the advent of sin that governance is necessary:

Then did Citties need a Governor, societies a Gardiner, Kingdoms a Phisitian to Pluck up those noysom weeds, to Heal those Diseased, to Terrifie with punishments, to Alure with Rewards, to here the cry of orphans, to plead the caus of the needy, to Strengthen the hands of the weak, and to be an impartial judge of Right and wrong, Banishing and suppressing those Dreadfull poysons that sin introduced. So that the office of kings is exceeding Glorious wheather they be Beloved or no: Provided they understand and Discharge their Duty. (*SM*, III, 11).

In Traherne's writings the king may be seen variously as grand and glorious or misguided and misguiding, or perhaps most diminishingly as merely a practical benefit, a kind of beneficent accident. Part of this ambiguity rests in the fact that Traherne rarely names the distinction his thoughts have taken between monarchy and kingship, between the political and social order complete with splendour and pomp and the interior state of greatness, virtue, ambition, courage, dignity, benevolence, faithfulness and deep belonging. The fact that these two could be conceived as separate may in itself reflect dissatisfaction with the current monarch, Charles II; certainly they indicate a thoughtful stance that neither accepts the notion of kingship unquestioningly nor prepares to abolish historical precedent on the basis of temporary or current dissatisfaction.

Over and over again Traherne's favoured king is the Old Testament king David, the king in whose likeness (brave in battle, loved by his people, harp-playing, psalm-composing) Charles I was said by his followers to have reigned. But this same David is the king with whom

Charles II aligned himself on his return from exile,[7] which, as Matar notes, was a theme taken up not only by Traherne but by seventeenth-century poets, clergymen and court wits as diverse as John Dryden, Gilbert Sheldon, Isaac Barrow and Henry Glover. Though damaged by politics, Traherne nevertheless, as Carol Ann Johnston notes, 'fashions his whole interior world after a quintessentially political form' of a kingdom.[8] The ideology of monarchy remains despite the implied criticism of the monarch that may be found in some parts of his work, and the model for all humanity is that of kingship. When he writes:

> If I live truly in the Divine Image I shall appear among kings a Greater king. For to be a King like God is a thing more Divine then to Reign like a Man, unless that Man Reign like a God (*SM*, III, 15)

Traherne is talking about desiring a kingly life, not undermining the notion of monarchy. He continues:

> To be a King like God is all mens hopes, some men[s] fruition. If it be mine, O let me Liv with kingly manners. God that made and ordained Thee for his Throne, made thee for himselfe. Despaire not, Forgett not, Be not careless, but Liv always at this Height. (*SM*, III, 15)

Similarly the poem 'Misapprehension' asserts:

> For did [men] know their Reall Interest
> No doubt they'd all be Kings.
>
> There's no a Man but covets and desires
> A Kingdom, yea a World; nay, he aspires
> To all the Regions he can see
> Beyond the Hev'ns Infinity
>
> ('Misapprehension', ll. 12–17)

---

7 Charles II, 1660 speech cited in Richard F. Jones, 'The Originality of "Absalom and Achitophel"', *Modern Languages Notes*, 46 (1931), p. 215. See Matar, 'The Political Views of Thomas Traherne'.

8 Johnston, 'Masquing/Unmasquing: Lambeth MS. 1860 and a Reconsideration of Traherne's "Curious" Visual Language', in Jacob Blevins (ed.), *Re-reading Traherne: A Collection of New Critical Essays*, Tempe, AZ: Arizona Center for Medieval and Renaissance Studies, 2007, pp. 177–220, 220.

Kingship is simultaneously natural to us and out of our reach. Yet it is incipient in the heart of every person. The task is to realize one's high estate, receive the world as gift, reign in it and take the initiative in offering it back observed and loved, transformed, to God.

The desire to be rich in possessions and the desire to be a king are intimately linked. To be kingly is to be rich and generous, to live bountifully, nobly, virtuously, to have an abundance of treasure. In all of this inheritance plays a significant role, not only as a means of passing on bounty but also as a signifier of relationship. It is inheritance that makes an heir. One of the distinctive features of Traherne's thinking is that inheritance is multiplied rather than divided. Thus he claims:

> That all we see is ours, and evry One
> Possessor of the Whole;
> That evry Man Is like a God Incarnat on the Throne ...
>
> ('Ease!', ll. 17–19)

God is King, the world is his kingdom, we are his heirs. It has been noted that Traherne has a definite taste for wealth and magnificence. And yet repeatedly in the *Centuries* as elsewhere he speaks of treasures belonging to him as if to him alone while at the same time they belong just as much to everyone in the same manner. The world is made for him alone and for his neighbour; echoing the Augustinian notion that God loves each of us as if there were only one of us, Traherne's world serves him in serving his neighbour and it serves his neighbour in serving him, as if each person were the divine favourite. This suggests that Traherne's desire for treasure, his delight in thrones and sceptres, is as much about corporate good as it is about individual power or pleasure. He longs for a resplendent king because he wants to be heir to and a subject of such a kingdom, and because, as we have seen, the notion of a king's approval (or disapproval) not only tempers the malcontent but also gives an ideal to aspiring humanity and feeds its desire. One example of this is in his writing on patience in *Christian Ethicks*, where the most valiant soldier fights the good fight with alacrity, at last succeeding, through a life that has been trained in the hard school of patience. And the reward of this virtuous life? The blessing of God, described as attaining 'the Crown of Righteousness, and the Kings favour' (*CE*, Ch. 24, p. 193). Like his desire for a nation united, his love of kingship is about where he wants to belong more than it is about what treasures might belong to him. Where elsewhere they divide, this is where his notions of kingship and monarchy conjoin, in the good of the people. The good of kingship is that it models nobility, generosity, benevolence, virtue; the good of monarchy is that it provides, for Traherne, the carrot and stick, the rewards, punishments and authority that lead to social order (*SM*, III, 10; *CE*, p. 45; *COH*, 'Adam'). Though untinselled and ungilded, social order is perhaps one of the greatest treasures the king can offer.

This sounds in some respects not unlike the ideas of the seventeenth-century arch-secularist Thomas Hobbes, since for Hobbes society was held together by contracts enforced by a sovereign. The notion of social contract, however, is alien to Traherne; life is gift, human relations involve gift and receipt – covenants perhaps, if one has to speak in terms of agreements, but not contracts. Differences between the two men go further. For Hobbes, 'Imagination is nothing but decaying sense' (*Leviathan*, part 1) and memory is faded image. This seems to deny both the creative power of imagination and the poignancy of memory that can pierce the present with pungent desire. For Traherne, memory is a warehouse of material for the imagination and imagination is a fertile womb.

There were other social theorists, however, whose models more nearly resemble Traherne's. Traherne's notion of an inheritance-bequeathing king who is also father, for instance, brings to mind the anti-Hobbesian work of Robert Filmer, whose *Patriarcha*, when it finally appeared, was one of the most widely read books in England. Written at about the time of Traherne's birth but not published until several years after his death, *Patriarcha* could not have been read by Traherne, though Filmer's numerous pamphlets, derived from the earlier unpublished work and in circulation as early as 1648, may well have been. For Filmer, society was structured along familial lines. Political authority existed, as in a family, from the father downwards. The child accepts the authority of its parents because they exercise power with love. The deference to a benevolent power is extended from family to society.[9] The authority of the king is like the authority of the father and can be traced back to the original father, Adam. For Filmer social contract theories are figments of the imagination: no one is born totally free, we are all in relationship. The male dominance of Filmer's patriarchy might ring alarm bells in the minds of modern readers but Traherne may well have seen in it a more humane face to social theory than Hobbes's fierce and ultimately isolating individualism. Traherne

---

9 I am indebted to George Steiner for directing me to the work of Filmer.

insists that we are creatures created for and to each other. And Traherne's pleasure at the restoration of the king and the recommencement of peacetime pastimes – cultivation, navigation, commerce, art, society, culture, education – is cast in tones much closer to Filmer's benevolent authority model than to Hobbes's utilitarian one. As we have seen above, Traherne draws clear parallels between familial love (in both animals for their young and humans for each other), and the love of king for subject and subject for king (*KOG*, Ch. 9, ll. 53–70).

Traherne uses the medieval term 'vassal' to describe our relationship to God as king: 'As he gives us the Elements and the World it self, or as the Apostle phraseth it, Life and Breath, and all things, we owe our Bodies and souls unto him, and are his obliged Vassels' (*KOG*, Ch. 14, ll. 42–3). In an extended illustration of gift and receipt in which what is given increases the estate of the giver, this vassal image occurs between this paradox:

> By Receiving more is added to our Estate, yet our Condition is less then before. By giving, a Part of our Estate is taken away, yet our whole estate is Increased therby. For we are made higher by the Benefits we do, and our Interest in the Person, that receives at our hands, is Increased; he himself becomes part of our Estate (*KOG*, Ch. 14, ll. 35–9)

and the assertion that, just as a husband does not really give away what he gives to his wife, so the father enjoys his estate more in his son. These, claims Traherne, 'are Litle Hints of Infinit Mysteries' (*KOG*, Ch. 14, ll. 51–2, 64–5). The king, like the father or the husband of traditional models, is holder of authority and giver of gift, and these are all images for Traherne of a benevolent God.

Traherne's king, therefore, is plentiful in treasure, is bequeather of an inheritance, is a father; there are some clear parallels when the king about which he is speaking is not the king of England, but the king of heaven. In *The Kingdom of God* Traherne's God-king is first of all 'God the Father Almighty, creator of heaven and earth' – an absolute monarch, creator of all; that being established, he is also sustainer, redeemer – a benevolent, generous, hopeful, desiring king in search of a bride, whose longing for his creation and whose gift of human freedom makes him vulnerable as well as absolute, a king who writes when all else fails, in his own blood, the letters of love to his creation (*KOG*, Ch. 41). This is, for Traherne, what it means 'To be a King like God' (kingly self-restraint is a subject to which we return in chapter three).

It is in the sometimes uncomfortable tension between the vagaries of his historical place and his visionary understanding of human potential that the richest meanings occur; the meaning of kingship in Traherne can no more be divorced from this divine king of *The Kingdom of God* than it can be from his comments on seventeenth-century monarchy in the *Select Meditations* and elsewhere throughout his work. This interdependence is perhaps most poignant in Traherne's expressions of his hope of salvation. Just as the king stands as father of a household (à la Filmer), so he stands as a door of salvation for the nation. The New Testament story of the jailer who was baptized 'and all his house'[10] is just such a case, and Traherne makes it plain that his concept of salvation is as much about salvation of the people as it is about the belief and salvation of a person:

> The Anabaptists deny the Being of a National church. Wheras our Savior deals with nations in their National Capacitie, threatens cities that reject his Disciples, as well as nations, baptizing them in the Name of the Father, & of the Son, & of the H. Ghost. And if there be a National Church, it is one of the Greatest Impieties in the World to destroy it. (*COH*, 'Baptism')

Traherne is a person in the cusp of change standing at the beginning of a notion of the individual but still loudly proclaiming the importance of the nation. Whether the treasures are spiritual or temporal they are inextricably connected, in theory and in practice, to the role of a king.

Traherne's constant references to 'worth', 'value', 'use' and their cognates, to notions of boundaries and boundlessness, and to his fascination with possession and inheritance reflect his interest in the emerging political economy and changes to land laws, as we will see in subsequent chapters. But the single most important context of that possession and bequest is that of the king, the kingdom and the king's heir. In a kingdom in which the king is eternal there may be generous gifts but there is no concern about succession. Traherne makes all men kings not to undermine the notion of monarchy but because in so doing he makes all people inheritors of untold treasure, thus freeing them up from the pursuit of empty riches. They are inheritors of the whole world.

Such ownership is quite different from the exclusive ownership that

---

10 Acts 16.29–34.

appears among the 'barbarous inventions' (C, III, 13) of 'custom' in the *Centuries*. And yet even private ownership is not completely denigrated by Traherne. In fact, it is ownership that allows certain kinds of prosperity and stability that Traherne recognizes as valuable to society. Ownership itself is not vilified by Traherne: in *The Kingdom of God* he writes, 'One of those Causes that made my Father Delightfull to me upon Earth was the Convenient House and Estate I did inherit by descending from him' (*KOG*, Ch. 34, ll. 11–14).

Out of such stability and prosperity benevolence may spring, as it did in Traherne's case when he became a benefactor of Brasenose College and offered assistance at various times to the poor, or left several houses that became almshouses on his death. The hope of inheritance is cherished in the Judaeo-Christian tradition, with God portrayed throughout Scripture as father and his children as heirs. In fact, to destroy the inheritance is seen as a sin.[11] Traherne refers directly to the custom of primogeniture when he writes 'And for this it is that the Church is called, *The Assembly of the First-born*, because all her Children are the perfect Heirs, and Kings and Bridegrooms, every one compleatly, and more to his satisfaction, than if he were so alone' (*CE*, p. 250).

Traherne has a balanced view of wealth. If you have it, it is to be enjoyed and well-employed; if you do not have it, you may still be happy:

> THAT which I desire to teach a man is, How to make a Good use of all the Advantages of his Birth and Breeding; How in the Increase of Riches and Honors, to be Happy in their Enjoyment: How to secure himself in the temptations of Affluence, and to make a man glorious in himself, and delightful to others in Abundance; or else if Affliction should arise, and the State of Affairs change, how to triumph over *adverse* Fortune, and to be Happy notwithstanding his Calamities. How to govern himself in all Estates so as to turn them to his own advantage.
>
> FOR tho felicitie be not absolutely perfect in this World, nor so compleat in Poverty, as in a great and plentiful Estate; you are not to believe that wealth is absolutely necessary; because sometimes it is requisite to forfeit all for the sake of Felicity. Nothing is absolutely necessary to Bliss, but Grace and vertue. (*CE*, p. 17)

---

11 See the story of Naboth's vineyard in 1 Kings 21.

And sometimes it is necessary to abandon wealth altogether, since 'RATHER then make Shipwreck of a good Conscience, we must do as Mariners in a storm, cast our riches over board for our *own* Preservation. It is better losing *them*, then *our selves*' (CE, p. 17). The unlosable treasure is the soul and its virtues.

Riches, the treasures perhaps most commonly sought, are discussed in the fourth *Century* in which Traherne makes it clear that riches are only useful as the servant of happiness.[12] 'It more concerns me to be Divine than to have a purse of gold', he insists; therefore we should dig for wisdom and mine happiness (C, II, 7). Later in the same *Century* he considers the value of desiring riches for the sake of others – either that they should have riches themselves or that he should have them to give away – and concludes that, for himself, it is as well not to have them in the first place and for his friends: 'He desired no other riches for his friends but those which cannot be abused; to wit the true treasures, God and Heaven and Earth and Angels and Men, &c, with the riches of wisdom and grace to enjoy them.'[13] Perhaps this is because Traherne has discerned that wealth makes men vulnerable. In the *Select Meditations* he writes: 'The costly Delicate[s] we have invented have made us miserable. we must needs be as Gods, and by creating Riches of our own devising made work for Robbors.'[14]

The clear implication here is that heavenly treasures will not so disappoint. In *The Kingdom of God* Traherne admonishes his reader to

> See the difference between pure, Intelligent, spotless pleasures, and those Sordid, foul Abominations that allure the Wicked; between Angelicall and Swinish Delights, feeble Enjoyments, and Eternal rewards; Hypocritical Embroyderies, and Solid Realities; fading transitory Joys, and everlasting possessions; Earthly and Heavenly Treasures. (*KOG*, Ch. 3, ll. 44–9)

One may imagine these heavenly treasures to be invisible and infinite, and indeed some of them are. The second *Century* tells us that God

---

12 'Riches are but servants unto happiness: when they are impediments to it they cease to be riches', he writes. 'When we see the pursuit of riches destructive to Felicity, to desire them is of all things in nature the most absurd and the most foolish' (C, IV, 10).

13 C, II, 35; see also C, II, 32–7.

14 SM, III, 12. Similarly in the *Centuries*, the 'riches of darkness', 'those which men have made, during their ignorance of God Almighty's treasures', are the things that 'lead us from the love of all, to . . . false proprieties, insatiable longings, fraud, emulation, murmurings and dissension . . . theft and pride and danger, and cousenage, envy and contention' (C, I, 33).

has made treasures for us infinite in both extent and excellency *(C,* II, 83). Eternity and infinity are two examples of such infinite treasure.[15] In *Select Meditations* he speaks of the virtues as invisible treasures: 'Consider, and well understand, that Among invisible Things vertues are the fairest . . . becaus they are the Interiour Treasures of the Soul' (*SM*, IV, 55). He goes on to discuss wisdom, prudence, courage, justice, temperance and the theological virtues of faith, righteousness, holiness and humility as invisible treasures (*SM*, IV, 54–68). And in the third *Century* 'common, but invisible' treasures are 'The Laws of God, the Soul of Man, Jesus Christ and His Passion on the Cross, with the ways of God in all Ages' (*C*, III, 54).

However, heavenly virtues are not necessarily so completely otherworldly. The human is made 'to Enjoy By his Soul the Eternity of God, with all the invisible Treasures of his spiritual kingdom' (*SM*, III, 95) but, at the same time, 'This visible World is wonderfully to be delighted in, and highly to be esteemed' (*C*, II, 97). Man is 'by his Body meet to Enjoy all the Materials of the created world' (*SM*, III, 95). In *The Kingdom of God* the human body is 'the Darling of the Whole Creation', a vessel fit for treasure,[16] and many times human bodiliness is praised over and above the bodilessness of angels.[17] Traherne continually writes of the beauty of the earthly treasures of this physical world:

> The Skies and the Rivers, the sun and the stars, the Beauty of the world, their Dominion over Beasts and Fowls and Fishes, the Dignity of their Nature and the Image of God which none could Deface, but each man Himselfe; these were permanent and stable Treasures . . .[18]

Here, as elsewhere, it is the world in its prelapsarian state to which Traherne is referring.[19] And yet that paradise, though lost, may again be found. All who will may enjoy the earth as treasure still: 'To return to the Living waters, and leave sophisticat puddles, is to Returne to the simple Treasures of Eden . . . The Treasures of Eden are Simple and

---

15 See Traherne's discussion of eternity and infinity in the fifth *Century*.

16 *KOG*, Ch. 16, ll. 2, 133. The importance of the body and its being made for pleasures on earth and in heaven is emphasized many times in Chs 15 and 16.

17 See, for instance, Ch. 41.

18 *SM*, III, 12. The earth as a stable treasure and creation as treasure are also found in 'Thoughts IV'.

19 Or the world seen through innocent eyes – see, for example, the famous 'The corn was orient and immortal wheat' of *C*, III, 3, as well as *KOG*, Ch. 25, ll. 142–81.

Divine: Simple, but Illust[r]ious; Necessary; magnificent, Great; and Glorious' (*SM*, III, 13).

These simple, great and illustrious treasures of Eden are not just elemental treasures of earth and air and water, of sun and sky – they are skin too, and tissue and all living things, energies and organisms from atom to Adam. Traherne is aware that, in praising such treasures, he is calling his reader to a reading of the word that ran contrary to much of the thinking of his day. In his poem 'The Person' he first suggests the conventional treasures of crown, scarlet and gold and then promises to 'glorify by taking all away'. He asserts 'The Naked Things. Are most Sublime'.[20] Then, in gruesome detail, Traherne goes on:

> Survey the Skin, cut up the Flesh, the Veins
>   Unfold: The Glory there remains.
> The Muscles, Fibres, Arteries and Bones
>
>   ('The Person', ll. 28–30)

So it is that the simple thing is the most valued, the functional is beautiful, the fundamental and elemental is glorious. 'The Naked Things / Are most Sublime' he has claimed; taking pleasure in the bare necessities is praised in the *Centuries* as well: 'A naked man is the richest creature in all worlds, and can never be happy till he sees the riches of his nakedness.'[21] Nature, too, like humankind, is best undressed: 'The air is better being a living miracle as it now is than if it were crammed and filled with crowns and sceptres. The mountains are better than solid diamonds'.[22] Here in the *Centuries*, as in *The Kingdom of God*, Traherne presages so much of our contemporary concern with conservation and preservation of the natural world. Where in the *Centuries* living air is better than diamonds, in *The Kingdom of God* earth – which is 'generally reputed to be a Globe of Dirt, the very Dregs of

---

20 'The Person', ll. 16, 17–18.
21 C, IV, 36. In this context Traherne is considering the riches of Adam in paradise. See also C, III, 12 in which 'They that go naked and drink water and live upon roots are like Adam, or Angels in comparison of us . . . But we pass them in barbarous opinions, and monstrous apprehensions, which we nick-name civility and the mode, amongst us. I am sure those barbarous people that go naked, come nearer to Adam, God, and Angels in the simplicity of their wealth'.
22 C, II, 12. See also *KOG*, Ch. 25, ll. 144–8: 'I knew a Stranger upon Earth that in his Infancy thought the Heavens more sublime then saphires, and the Stones in the streets more pleasant then fine Gold. The fields laden with delights, more rich then Carbuncles, and the meadows more divine then if covered with Emeralds'. Here Traherne's reflections mirror the well-known meditations from the third *Century* (C, III, 1–3).

Nature' – is better than gold.[23] In many other similar expressions the conventional treasures of crowns, sceptres, jewels and gold are superseded as Traherne turns on its head the received wisdom of what is real treasure and what is not. 'Happy is the People whose God is the Lord' he asserts; 'Gold and Silver are Beggary to their Wealth.' When he speaks of their prosperity 'There is no End of their Silver and Gold', not because they have it locked in ample trunks but because they have the earth out of which it comes and because 'They are conceived with Pleasure, and come forth of the Womb to Innumerable Blessings.'[24]

This task of discerning real from imagined treasure is a serious concern for Traherne. It is the principal question behind his writings on 'custom' in the *Centuries* and in his poems[25] and it occurs again in many of his other works. If real treasures may be things here on earth or things heavenly, things finite or infinite, visible or invisible, what is the criterion for discerning real treasure? Traherne gives us a clue when he writes that the best things are misunderstood because they are 'great, common, and simple' (C, II, 16). As he explains further in the third *Century*:

> it is most consonant and agreeable with His nature, that the best things should be most common. For nothing is more natural to infinite goodness, than to make the best things most frequent; and only things worthless scarce. Then I began to enquire what things were most common: Air, Light, Heaven and Earth, Water, the Sun, Trees, Men and Women, Cities, Temples etc. These I found common and obvious to all: Rubies, Pearls, Diamonds, Gold and Silver; these I found scarce, and to the most denied. Then began I to consider and compare the value of them which I measure by their serviceableness, and by the excellencies which would be found in them, should they be taken away. And in conclusion, I saw clearly, that there was a real valuableness in all the common things, in the scarce a feigned. (C, III, 53)

This idea is explored further in *The Kingdom of God*. When he writes that it befits God's goodness 'to make the best things most common:

---

23 'The Earth is generally reputed to be a Globe of Dirt, the very Dregs of Nature, and the basest of all the elements, yet is it comparable to the fine Gold, if not a Work incomparably more Divine, and excellent' (*KOG*, Ch. 25, ll. 142–4). The first words of the title of chapter 25 (from which this is taken) suggest both the baseness and the beauty of the earth: 'Of the Globe of the Earth. Its baseness, its litleness, its Dignity, its Glory . . .'.

24 *KOG*, Ch. 25, ll. 58–9, 84–6.

25 See, for instance, C, III, 7–13; 'Innocence'; 'Right'; 'Silence'; 'Apostacy'; 'Dissatisfaction'. False treasures are discussed in 'Infant-ey', 'Adam', 'Inference I' and 'Eden'.

And those are best, that are most serviceable',[26] we can see a clear pattern or principle emerging in which real treasure is judged to be so by its ubiquity, its utility and its simplicity.

In *The Kingdom of God* a drop of water is seen to be the fruit of earth's labour. Melted, distilled, presented in abundance to match our need, drops of water are 'transparent and living gems' (*KOG*, Ch. 26, ll. 112), which we despise because we have them. Justly, says Traherne, may we be 'cast into the lake, where we shall prize them eternaly becaus we have them not' (*KOG*, Ch. 26, ll. 113–14).

> You have seen heaven and Earth, and Sea, conspiring together to make a Drop of Water. It is not the less precious, because there is so much of it, it is more to be esteemed. The most excellent things, are the most common. (*KOG*, Ch. 26, ll. 115–17)

Simple and common, water is also a treasure because is 'serviceable' and 'satisfies Necessitie' (*KOG*, Ch. 26, ll. 215, 126). Just as the useful, common and simple things are the highest treasures, so also the small is great: 'For GOD, that is Great in all things, and not small in any, is infinitly great in the smallest Thing' (*KOG*, Ch. 24, ll. 68–9).

Let us go to that smallest of Traherne's treasures, the atom. In 'Atom', the longest poem in *Commentaries of Heaven* (at 431 lines, it is four times the length of other 'longer' poems), the usefulness of atoms is praised 'for the Truth is / Atoms are the first Elements of Bliss' (ll. 183–4). Here the soul is like an atom, seeming nothing but very real; the atom is 'a firm Material Thing', though it, like the soul, may 'delude a Solid Touch' (ll. 424, 415). So prized is the atom that Traherne's atomic discussion spans more than ten pages of *The Kingdom of God* (*KOG*, fols 217r–222v); the atom is described as 'an infinit work ... a sacred and ineffable mysterie ... a temple of his omnipresence ... a gift of his Lov, a work of his wisdom, a means of our happiness, and engine of his Glory' (*KOG*, fol. 218r–v). Among other features, he admires its smallness, beauty, power, weakness, its ubiquitous nature, and what the cutting edge of seventeenth-century science had revealed about its incorruption, volatility and capabilities. The atom is described as 'being infinitly small and simple' (*KOG*, fol. 218), something that 'notwithstanding its commonness, ought to be infinitly esteemed' (*KOG*, fol. 218r), since 'The Glory of all these Atoms is, that they are infin-

---

26 *KOG*, Ch. 26, ll. 196–7. See also *SM*, II, 88 in which treasures are ' soe freely Given, so Reall, common, near' and 'necessary yet common, Divine and Glorious, yet freely surrounding us'.

itly usefull' (*KOG*, fol. 221r). Once again, Traherne's three defining qualities of treasure – simplicity, commonness or ubiquity, and utility – appear.

Traherne's world is full of given treasure, but there is also a treasure that becomes treasure through the process of redemption. Traherne writes of his happy man: 'Thus he was possessor of the whole world, and held it his treasure, not only as the gift of God, but as the theatre of virtues' (C, IV, 39) – a place in which the human soul may discover its worth and the worth of others. As Traherne writes, 'They are our true treasures about whom we are wisely employed' (C, IV, 39). In this sense, even 'disorders' or troubles and trials may be treasure to us since they are the crucibles of change (SM, IV, 5). We may become God's treasures by living in virtue and, when we fail, 'Yet he returneth, and maketh up his Treasures by a Surmounting wisdom'.[27] So we ourselves become living treasure.[28]

In a chapter in *The Kingdom of God* devoted to the discussion of treasure, the distinctions between possession and use, and the means and end of treasure, Traherne directs us by a marginal note towards a definition. On folio 309v the marginal note reads: 'What Treasures are'. A philosophical consideration of the word 'treasure' follows in the text, drawing his reader through practical applications to the striking end that, while all things in heaven and on earth may be treasures for humankind, for Christians in particular the concept of 'treasure' is turned on its head:

> Whether *Treasure* be a Word so Comprehensiv, as to Include all objects of Delight, as well the final End, as the Means of gaining it, I shall not determine: it is Sufficient for me that the Means are Treasures, be the End what it will; which if you please, shall undergoe the Name of Blessedness; or if you pleas, of Glory. Riches are Means by which we acquire Pleasure, and the Means by which we acquire Glory. And if Socrates his Definition of Riches be true, all those things wherby a man may acquire Blessedness, are his Treasures: for *Treasures are* (saith he) *those things wherby a Man may be Benefited*. Be they Living, or be they dead, in his opinion, if a man

---

27 SM, III, 51. We become treasures to God by our actions in C, IV, 95 as well. Conversely in the second *Century* (II, 30) we become 'an unlovely object' by our sin. This seems to contradict Traherne's principle of the inestimable worth of the human soul, which would suggest that we are treasures regardless of our actions.

28 On being oneself a treasure see SM, II, 23–9. We are treasures to him and to other souls: see SM, IV, 50; C, IV, 53.

may be Benefited by them; they are his Riches; be they within, or be they without, be they for the Body, or for the Soul: for the Increas of Power, or Honor, Authority, or friendship; Health or Beauty, security or pleasure: be they Sweet, or Sour; Leight or Heavy, Bright or obscure, if they are conducive to his Desires, and Ends, they may be stiled Treasures: Chymical Drugs, and bitter Ingredients, Purges and Vomits, oyle and Playsters, may be a Sick Mans Treasures, perhaps a physicians; and an Apothecaries; as Swords and Darts and Lances may be the Treasures of a Soldier; friends and servants, the Treasures of a Prince; Implements of Husbandry and Instruments of Labor, the Plough Man's Treasures; flocks of Sheep and Herds of Cattle, the Shepherds, and the Herds Man's: All things in Heaven and in Earth are the Treasures of a Man, that are conducive to his felicitie; Afflictions and persecutions, and Death it self, the Treasures of a Christian. (*KOG*, Ch. 33, ll. 78–99)

Once again the notion of 'treasure' is turned upside down. Not only are treasures those things that are the most common, and useful and simple; Traherne's theology insists, along with so many before him for whom God was not merely a philosophical notion but a daily reality, that for Christians the eventual treasure, though we do not seek it, is death. Counter-cultural as this may seem to many modern readers and severe as it sounds alongside Traherne's more familiar life-affirming strains, the simple fact is that for him mortality is a promise not a threat. If desire is the dark side of felicity, treasure has its shadow too. Death may be the eventual, unsought treasure for Christians; meanwhile one is to seek intervening treasures with care and discernment.

Spiritual Discernment

'I must lead you out of this, into another World, to learn your wants. For till you find them you will never be happy: Wants themselves being Sacred Occasions and Means of Felicity' (*C*, I, 43), wrote Traherne to his 'friend' of the *Centuries*. What does it mean to learn our wants? If desire is the force of all creation, if we live in desire as God does, are we not already wanting without having to learn it? Of course we are. Traherne is admonishing us not just to a life of amorphous wanting but to a life of educated wanting – desiring that is based on a considered understanding of our own lacks and needs. A life in which we know what it is we really want and what that want signifies; a life in which wants are not merely temporary pleasures or objects of desire but also indicators on a spiritual path.

It is when we move the discussion from temporal treasure to spiritual or eternal treasure that the question of discernment becomes more complicated. Do Traherne's three guidelines for discerning treasure – ubiquity, utility and simplicity – hold true in the quest for spiritual treasure as they do in the quest for earthly treasure? If other souls and we ourselves may become living treasure, isn't treasure something altogether bigger and broader? These and other questions call for something different from the kind of truth revealed in the elemental tugs of bald desire.

When it comes to spiritual discernment, Traherne most often relies on what he calls 'highest reason' – largely a combination of intellection and experience. Traherne's great respect for reason can be traced in his debt, mentioned in the introduction, to the Cambridge Platonists, those 'men of Cambridge who naturalized Plato an Englishman'.[29] Although himself an Oxford man at a time when the curriculum consisted of much more Aristotle and Aquinas than Plato, and situated, as we have seen, in a most Puritan college,[30] when Traherne read his Plotinus, Ficino and Hermes Trismegistus, as well as Plato, he was being drawn to the same texts that attracted the attention of the Cambridge Platonists.[31] They all shared a belief in a 'natural light' placed within every person by God and which did not disagree with the light of reason.

Nathanael Culverwell, writing about the capacity of man's reason to grasp the natural law refers to 'cleare and undelible Principles, some first and Alphabetical Notions', which 'are stampt and printed upon the being of man'.[32] And in Traherne's *Commonplace Book* we find the following:

> And indeed these common seeds of naturall Light are a private Law, which God has deeply engraven on mens consciences, and

---

29 Marks, 'Thomas Traherne and Cambridge Platonism', p. 521. Marks lists them as Benjamin Whichcote, John Smith, Peter Sterry, Ralph Cudworth, Nathanael Culverwell and John Worthington, students and Fellows of Emmanuel College, and Henry More of Christ's.

30 See above, p. 19.

31 Certainly Sterry read Plato, Plotinus, and Ficino, these texts being cited among others in his possession by Vivian de Sola Pinto (*Peter Sterry: Platonist and Puritan*, Cambridge: Cambridge University Press, 1934, p. 57). For a fuller account of the literary diet of More and the other Platonists see Marks, 'Traherne and Cambridge Platonism', pp. 521–23. We know that Traherne read from all the above writers' works from the notes in the *Early Notebook* (Bodl.Ms.Lat.Misc.f.45) and the *Commonplace Book* (Bodl.MS.Eng.Poet.c.42).

32 Nathanael Culverwell, *An Elegant and Learned Discourse of the Light of Nature, With Several Other Treatises*, ed. William Dillingham, London, 1652, p. 54.

is universally extensive unto all, though with a latitude of Degrees; it being in some more, in some Lesse, but in all in great measure obliterated, and defaced since the *fall*. It is also by Divines generally termed the *Light*, or *Law of Nature*, because it flows in, and with, and from Human Nature.[33]

Such is Traherne's confidence in this Light of Nature that he asserts that all things except the doctrine of Redemption 'are evident in themselves by the Light of Nature, because they may either be clearly deduced from the principles of Reason, or certainly discerned by plain Experience'.[34] Reason, experience and the natural or divine light work together to reveal God's truth. What the natural light intuits, reason and experience confirm; and those truths that lie buried 'under the Rubbish of our Fall'[35] may be found again.[36] Traherne claims that the truths he 'knew by intuition' in his infancy he regained, after his 'Apostacy', 'by the highest reason'(C, III, 2). And in *Christian Ethicks* he reaffirms the interconnectedness of faith and reason: '*Faith* is by *Reason* confirmed, and *Reason* is by *Faith* Perfected.'[37] For Traherne there was no disparity between revealed truth and reasoned truth. He was confident in the unity of all truth, although, as we can see from *The Kingdom of God*, he sometimes felt the need to explain his position, as did others, such as the Cambridge Platonist Benjamin Whichcote, who wrote:

> I find that some men take offence ... to hear *reason* spoken of out of a pulpit, or to hear those great words of *natural light*, of *principles of reason, and conscience*. They are doubtless in a mighty mistake ... there is no inconsistency between the *Grace of God*, and the calling upon men carefully to use, improve and employ *the principles of God's creation*.[38]

---

33 CB, s.v. 'Reason', fol. 83, col. 1. quoted from Theophilus Gale, *Court of the Gentiles*, vol. I, part II.
34 CE, p. 119.
35 Ibid.
36 This view that truth lies waiting to be uncovered, rather than that it has been utterly forsaken, that the human intelligence has been disused rather than abandoned, corresponds with a similar stance taken by Trouillard: 'Vice is not a perversion of intelligence, but a condition in which this activity is absent or dormant. Wrongdoing is not so much a rebellion and defiance as bewilderment and weariness' (Jean Trouillard, 'L'Impeccabilité de l'esprit selon Plotin', *Revue de l'Histoire des Religions*, 143 (1953), pp. 19–28). There are shades of this kind of thinking in Traherne, although Traherne also admits rebellion or apostasy.
37 CE, p. 112.
38 Benjamin Whichcote, *Works*, London, 1751, vol. I, Discourse XXIII, p. 370.

To Culverwell, reason and the divine light or 'Law of Nature', written in the heart of man and in the natural world around him, work together, reason like a hen incubating the egg of natural law: 'Reason thus . . . by warming and brooding upon these first and oval Principles of her own laying, it being itself quicken'd with an heavenly vigour, does thus hatch the Law of Nature.'[39] To the Platonists, as to Traherne, women and men, in the image of God, are at their best and fully human when exercising those divine faculties such as reason and intuition.

Because for Traherne, as for the Cambridge Platonists, the divine light and the contemporary revelation of the new philosophy or of science point to and originate in the same truth, which is God, there is a theological freedom to explore the capacity of the human mind. Traherne's study of the natural sciences increased his faith in the providence of God. Of his time at Oxford he writes:

> I saw into the nature of the Sea, the Heavens, the Sun, the Moon and Stars, the Elements, Minerals, and Vegetables. All which appeared like the King's Daughter, all glorious within; and those things [divine truths] which my nurses, and parents, should have talked of there were taught unto me.[40]

Clearly his study of science and the new philosophy was reaffirming his infant intuitions. Whereas some Puritans suspected the new discoveries of science, the Neo-Platonists (and Traherne alongside them) apprehended God 'in and through nature, not in spite of or beyond it', the latitude of their approach enabling them 'to bring together the new knowledge and the old faith'.[41] So great was Traherne's faith in the

---

39 Culverwell, *Discourse of the Light of Nature*, p. 82. Interestingly, the same image of the brooding hen is used by Theophilus Gale in *Court of the Gentiles* to describe God's creation of the universe: 'In this description of *Moses* Gen. 1. 2. we have the Spirit's *Motion, Fomentation,* and *Formation* of all things out of this *Chaos,* or *watery mixture* in these words, [*and the Spirit of God moved etc.*] P. Fagius explains here, by *motion* and *agitation;* or by *Fomentation* of an *Hen,* that sets a brood' (Discourse II, Ch. III, pp. 323–4). Both pictures – man's reason and God's creation – are of a mind ordering substance out of disparity or out of chaos. Yet the image chosen to depict this is distinctly female; we are called to imagine brooding, incubating, nursing, hatching qualities, the creative force happening in the womb and in the nest. Ultimately, then, the mind's bringing order out of chaos is depicted as a kind of birth; and reason as a participation in God's act of creation. This corresponds with the Neo-Platonic notion that to use one's reason is to act in the image of God. Hence, also, the appropriateness of Traherne's claim that new birth is necessary to renewal of vision.

40 C, III, 36. There are also many references to Traherne's range of subjects, particularly the new sciences, in *The Kingdom of God*, Ch. 23.

41 G. R. Cragg, *From Puritanism to the Age of Reason*, Cambridge: Cambridge University Press, 1950, p. 53. Inasmuch as Cragg discusses the Cambridge Platonists over against

revelatory power of the natural world that he wondered how the heathens could have missed the truth it tells. In the *Centuries* he muses:

> I wonder much, (the World being so Beautiful and Glorious in every Eye, so really deep and valuable in Worth, so peculiarly applied to the use and service of every person;) that the Heathens did miss the fruition of it, and fail to measure themselves and their Felicity, by the Greatness of its Beauty ... For the Earth is really better than if all its Globe were of beaten Gold, the Seas are better than if all their Abysses were full of Diamonds, ... and the Sun alone a greater Treasure then all the wealthy Mines in the Indies: every man is surrounded with all the Light of their Advantages, and so much served by them, as if no man but himself were alive in the World.[42]

The divine light then, according to Traherne is to be found in the created world of nature as well as in the heart of the individual. Here he diverges most significantly from the Neo-Platonic model and has more in common with the Eastern Christian tradition, which sees the whole creation charged with the life of God. Maximus the Confessor (c. 580–662) is one such Church Father who saw the word of creation speaking the Word of God. Traherne cites Maximus in *A Sober View* (folio 40v) which suggests he had obtained a Greek copy since Maximus' writings were not published in English until after Traherne's death. Like Maximus, Traherne saw the whole creation speaking the word of God but for Maximus this divine utterance could only be heard via meditation. Like the Cambridge Platonists who championed highest reason, Maximus perceived that a particular and unusual kind

---

the Puritans, he is right. But when the Platonists come up against 'the new knowledge' in the form of the materialistic determinism of Hobbes, their recourse to reason fails them. As T. O. Beachcroft puts it, 'They [the Cambridge Platonists] wrote to give a "reason for the hope that is in us". Hobbes wrote to give "a reason for the hope that is not in us"' ('Traherne and the Doctrine of Felicity', *Criterion*, 9 (1930), pp. 291–307). Over this dividing line the two camps' assertions of reason became simply one declaration hurled against another.

42 *CE*, p. 59. Indeed, thought Traherne, despite our learning, by our despising the worth of the natural world, we are less wise than the heathen: 'By this you may see who are the rude and barbarous Indians: For verily there is no savage nation under the cope of Heaven, that is more absurdly barbarous than the Christian World. They that go naked and drink water and live upon roots are like Adam, or Angels in comparison of us ... I am sure those barbarous people that go naked, come nearer to Adam, God, and Angels in the simplicity of their wealth, though not in knowledge' (*C*, III, 12). Culverwell, too, in his *Discourse of the Light of Nature* quotes Salmasius: 'the famous Salmasius ... tells us that he had rather search for nature's law in a naked Indian, than in a spruce Athenian; in a meer Pagan, rather than in a Jew or Christian' (p. 118).

of knowing was required. As John Stewart Allitt notes in his recent study of Traherne:

> St Maximus the Confessor explains in his precious writings that all logoi (archetypes) of creation are tied to the Christ Logos. Accordingly, one could say that all of creation sings a hymn of exaltation to Him, our Lord . . .
>
> Traherne saw himself in a similar vision, and was with St Maximus when he writes that it is only through contemplation that the eye of the heart sees the Christ Logos in the logoi of creation. 'See how the lilies grow in the fields.' Our souls are nothing other than [specche] mirrors that should reflect this mystery.

Allitt continues: 'Traherne invites the reader to fervent meditation, because only in this way does the eye of the heart open, through the intervention of the Holy Spirit, allowing the Divine intellect to "see" through us. Obviously this requires true repentance.'[43]

Allitt's theory for perceiving the divine in creation presupposes a level of religious commitment on the part of the viewer that not every reader may share. Whether they do or not, it is clear that for Traherne the whole of *The Kingdom of God* is predicated on this thought: that God is revealed and discovered, sensed and perceived profoundly in the created world, a predication that, as we have noted, puts him outside the traditional bounds of Neo-Platonism. Unlike Peter Sterry, for whom the created world is a veil upon the face of the divine that reveals only obscurely, Traherne sees the world as a revelation of the divine as full as if it were God's own body. Where Sterry writes:

> The Creation of the World was a Vail cast upon the Face of God, with a figure of the Godhead wrought upon this vail, and God Himself seen through it by a dim transparency; as Sun in a morning, or Mist, is seen by a refracted Light through the thick medium of earthly Vapours[44]

---

43 John Stewart Allitt, *Thomas Traherne: Il Poeta-Teologo*, Milan: Edizioni Villadiseriane, 2007, p. 238 (trans. into English by Thomas Willet). I am indebted to Sam Wells, who first pointed me in the direction of Maximus the Confessor.

44 Pinto, *Peter Sterry*, p. 95. According to Pinto, the first creation is called by Sterry 'a kind of Incarnation; for in that the Image of God was made Flesh' (p. 98). Sterry writes of the manifestation of God in nature using vivid images of root, blood and body: 'The natural Being of every person hath his Root in the Grave of Christ, and is watered with his blood . . . He is the Root out of which every natural . . . Plant springs, which brings forth himself through every natural existence, and brings forth himself out of it as the flower,

Traherne asserts: 'how do we know, but the world is that body, which the Deity hath assumed to manifest His Beauty and by which He maketh Himself as visible, as it is possible He should?'[45] And this disclosure of the divine through 'The brightness and magnificence of this world' (C, I, 38) is plainly visible to all.

According to this understanding of divine light, its manifestation supersedes the boundaries between Christian and pagan, speaking of eternal truth, which, however partial, predates the revelation of Christ. If the divine light is not exclusive to Christians, the wisdom writing of pre-Christian writers may benefit the Christian apprehension of eternal truth. So, where 'True Philosophy' is the convergence of divine light, reason and experience,[46] Traherne could have confidence to say with Simon Patrick that 'True *Philosophy* can never hurt sound *Divinity*'.[47] Along with Plato, he could be convinced of the importance of human reason. Indeed, we may come to see that the religious life and the life of reason are one. This, according to his early biographer Gladys Wade, is the greatest debt Traherne owes to Plato and his followers, not the ideas he borrowed but 'the support their philosophy afforded to his own experience that the religious life is the reasonable life: indeed, the only reasonable life; and that reason will guide a man right to the top of the ladder that leads to communion with God.' That this very communion with the divine should sometimes involve the human in irrational or 'unreasonable' experiences causes Wade no concern whatsoever:

---

the brightness of the Glory of God. He is the Root and Truth of all things' (*A Discourse on the Freedom of the Will*, London, 1675, pp. 27–39). Clearly Sterry holds a high view of the image of God in the natural world but, for him, this image is lost in Adam's fall. For Traherne, however, the image of God in creation remains full; it is the sight of humanity that is faulty.

45 C, II, 20. See also *SM*, IV, 34, in which Traherne argues that God is invisible and yet has manifested himself in the world as an assumed body to shew his divine attributes; and *KOG*, Ch. 27: 'God therefore being Incorporeal is seen in his Works: and the World is the Glorious Body, which he hath assumed to make himself famous' (ll. 31–2). In each case God does this to satisfy the atheist or sceptic.

46 While the body of the Platonic tradition would support Traherne's combination of divine light, reason and experience, it would not on the whole give as much weight to experience as Traherne does. Traherne's insistence on the primacy of what instinct and intuition taught him in his early experiences of childhood is unique among the writers of the period and the genre. Something similar is seen again much later in the imagination of Wordsworth – a connection noted in William Ralph Inge, *The Platonic Tradition in English Religious Thought*, London: Longmans, 1926, pp. 66, 73; and by Hilda Vaughan in her introduction to the *Centuries* (London: Faith Press, 1975, p. xii), among others.

47 Simon Patrick, *A Brief Account of the New Sect of Latitude-Men*, London, 1662, p. 24.

If at the top there come experiences that are unutterable, these are not contrary to reason; reason is at its highest pitch when it merges with all the rest into a mode of awareness for which language has no name. That harmonizing of the whole personality into a unity no longer conscious of its multiplicity is something all the great mystics have known. It is, they tell us, a mode of being akin to the divine, it is to be love: it is to be mind. 'We shall be Mentes as he is Mens, we being of the some mind with Him who is an infinite, eternal Mind,' as Traherne expresses it once.[48]

This is not 'reason' as we are used to recognizing it. Certainly there is logic, the application of deduction to a collection of facts. But the 'true reason' of Traherne and of the Platonists,[49] like the 'True *Philosophy*' defended by Simon Patrick above, is of a particular kind. It is not just pure logic, which More disparagingly refers to as '*dry Reason*',[50] but a kind of quest and a resolve 'to follow truth whenever it may appear',[51] which is described in the language of sensory experience.

Traherne's constant references to sight are mirrored in the writings of Peter Sterry who also frequently used the imagery of 'spiritual senses' and particularly of 'the spiritual eye'.[52] For him as for Traherne, truest vision comes from reaching through sense to a world beyond sense. We apply what we already practise of the body's way of knowing to the action of our souls, and are led from what we know physically to a way of knowing that is spiritual. This comes near to the Plotinian concept of religion as essentially instinctive rather than dogmatic, in which, for example, the musician, the lover and the metaphysician are all led on their journey to the Good by what they already instinctively love.[53] However, where Plotinus denies the essential enduring reality of the physical world, Traherne affirms the physical with his whole heart. The world is where God is. Thus it is that, although spiritual treasure is discerned by a process of 'highest reason', the criteria for discerning such treasure are much the same as that by which earthly treasure is discerned: ubiquity, utility and simplicity. Traherne would see the treasure of Eternity, for instance, as being everywhere, useful and

---

48 Gladys Wade, *Thomas Traherne*, Princeton: Princeton University Press, 1944, pp. 220–1.
49 Derivative from Plato's νους.
50 Henry More, *Divine Dialogues ... The Two Last Dialogues*, London, 1668, Dialogue 5, p. 403.
51 Whichcote, *Works*, I, Discourse 22, p. 355.
52 Pinto, *Peter Sterry*, p. 115.
53 Plotinus, *The Enneads*, Tractate III, 2.

simple. In turning the whole notion of treasure on its head from rare to common, from luxurious to useful and from extravagant to simple, Traherne ultimately shows his apprehension of spiritual treasure to be more practical and less idealistic than we might have expected.

Traherne's love must have its objects and treasures. While having much in common with the Cambridge Platonists in their search for renewed vision and their faith in the divine light and in highest reason, while asserting, like them, that our 'mistakes are occular' (*C*, IV, 15), Traherne is not quite of their number. Traherne's vision is always set not on transcendence into intelligibility but on the treasures immediately in front of him. Even when the objects of his desire are absent, the desire itself conjures a sense of those objects that makes them real (*COH*, 'Appetite').

Traherne's treasures, those prized objects that are frequently the subject of Traherne's pen, are ultimately necessary because they are so much more than riches. More importantly, they are his clearest expression of want and worth. In them we see the usefulness and beauty that make his treasures objects of desire. In them we may find our wants – what we need and what we desire – met by the bounty of divine providence. In the service of treasure, want may be creative and enabling: God found it 'requisite to multiply our Wants, that our Treasures might be multiplied' (*KOG*, Ch. 42, ll. 148–9). To seek true treasure, then, is to enter into the heart of desiring, where what we prize is what we have righteously apprehended and esteemed and what we will rightly choose and do. This is why treasure can be seen as both means and end.[54] Traherne's treasures are not mere baubles and gewgaws, not even the finest works of cloth and gold. To speak of treasure in Traherne is to speak seriously about questions of worth and value, questions that go deep into the heart of what we are, what we desire and what we may become as human beings. With this high view of treasure in mind, Traherne may be justified in admonishing his reader to 'Be serious in enjoying Treasure as Christ was in Redeeming the World' (*SM*, II, 97).

Prizing

Having a clear vision of want and worth is exactly what prizing is about. Knowing a thing and knowing its value may seem to be an act

---

54 Traherne describes treasure as 'by nature those precious Things,which are Means whereby we acquire our Ends, or those Things which we most Esteem, as the Sovereign Objects of our Joy' (*CE*, p. 68).

of intellection and discernment and, as we have seen above, it is so. But prizing is also about yearning. It is, if you like, where intellectually discerned treasure meets hot-hearted desire. To prize involves both the intellect and the affections in an act of knowledge and love. It is in this way that prizing makes objective treasure real treasure to the individual. Prizing is also, in some sense, a public affair – it is about upholding as desired and desirable the things that we know to be real treasure.

Prizing is perhaps the first place where the full implications of Traherne's theology of desire are intimated because it is in his discussion of prizing that we see desire not just as that which indicates or locates treasure, or that which awakes in us the infinite, but as a force that purifies our sight and transforms our actions. Here is where we begin not only to know our need of God but to be made capable of the life of heaven.

The importance of Traherne's 'prizing' may be better understood by considering his writing on righteousness. In chapter ten of *Christian Ethicks* he writes: 'there is a Righteousness of Apprehension, a Righteousness of Esteem, a Righteousness of Choise, and a Righteousness of Action'. Right apprehension,

> tho it be the First and smallest part of Righteousness, is of Great importance ... He that mistakes his Hand for his Meat, will rise hungry from the Table. He that mistakes a Fiddle for an Axe, will neither cut Wood well, nor make good Musick. The Misapprehension of Great and Transcendent Objects, whether visible or Spiritual, is not perhaps so Gross, but more pernicious and Destructive.[55]

From this right apprehension, right esteem may follow and this right esteem, in its correct appreciation of worth, is very like the discernment of real treasure discussed above – it gives value according to merit and accords everything its right place. Righteousness of esteem is

> that Habit, by Vertue of which we value all things according as their Worth or Merit requires. It presupposes a right Apprehension of their Goodness, a clear Knowledge of all their excellencies. It is a Virtue by which we give to every thing that place in our Soul which they hold in Nature.[56]

---

55 *CE*, p. 71. See also C, V, 15: 'Mornay's simile of the saw is admirable: If a man would cut with a saw, he must not apprehend it to be a knife, but a thing with teeth, otherwise he cannot use it. He that mistakes his knife to be an auger, or his hand to be his meat, confounds himself by misapplications.' Right apprehension is the subject of C, IV, 14–17.

56 *CE*, p. 72. That there should be enough capacity in the soul for all of this is not

Traherne makes bold claims for right esteem, seeing it not only as honouring but also as perfecting its objects. In so doing he gives esteem an active role, so that esteeming becomes more than a purely intellectual exercise but an action whose results, though unquantifiable, are real. This, he admits, is 'a little Misterious'.[57] The significant thing to this study is that Traherne seems to be locating action prior to the later two types of righteousness, 'Righteousness of Choise' and 'Righteousness of Action'. It is as if the right esteem out of which right choice and right action flow is inseparable from that choice and action. In fact, in *A Sober View*, prizing is itself is described as 'a Righteous Act'.[58]

We must know an object before desiring it, as Stanley Stewart reminds us in *The Expanded Voice*, 'for what a man knows he naturally loves'.[59] This principle is perhaps most profoundly true when applied to the notion of self.[60] 'ΓΝΟΘΙ ΣΕΑΥΤΟΝ [sic]' (know thyself), Traherne reminds us in *Seeds of Eternity*, 'becaus in the knowledge of one self, the knowledg of God and all things appeareth.'[61] Repeatedly, in *Seeds of Eternity* as in the *Centuries,* Traherne urges his readers to know the greatness of their own souls[62] and to love the image of God that is written there. 'Be venerable to thy Selfe, and Let thy Person be Sacred in thine one Esteem. O Prize thy selfe as thy God prizeth Thee', Traherne writes, so may one be 'a Sacred Treasure unto many Thousand others'

---

doubted by Traherne: 'There is a Room in the Knowledge for all Intelligible Objects: A Room in our Esteem for all that is worthy of our Care and Desire. I confess this Room is strange and Mysterious. It is the Greatest miracle perhaps in Nature. For it is an infinite Sphere in a Point, an Immensity in a centre, an Eternity in a Moment. We feel it, tho we cannot understand it' (CE, p. 73).

57 CE, p. 72. The context reads as follows: 'How the Creatures are honoured by esteem, needeth not to be unfolded: but how they are perfected by it, is a little Misterious. A thing is then perfected when it attains its End. Now the end for which all things were made is that they may be seen and enjoyed. They are seen that they may be esteemed, and by an intelligent and right esteem are all enjoyed. In our esteem therefore they find and attain their end, and by attaining that are consequently perfected.'

58 'To prize God in all his Attributes Works and Ways is to do a Righteous Act for it is to render unto him his Just Esteem' (SV, fol. 28v). Similarly, in *Select Meditations* Traherne says of those actions of apprehension, esteem and love that make up prizing 'By Doing this I become Righteous and Holy' (SM, III, 43).

59 Stanley Stewart, *The Expanded Voice: The Art of Thomas Traherne*, San Marino, CA: Huntington Library, 1970, p. 63.

60 'The Knowledge of a Mans self is highly conducive to his Happiness', writes Traherne (CE, p. 42); and 'The principal objects of our Knowledge are GOD, and a Mans self'. There follows a list of secondary objects, which 'in relation to GOD and a Mans self, are of great Importance' (CE, p. 41).

61 SE, ll. 299–300. Traherne cites the oracle of Delphi on both fol. 138v and fol. 140v (using O in place of Ω).

62 'Remember always the unsearchable extent and illimited greatness of your own soul' (C, II, 92). See also C, IV, 48, 50, 51, 77, 81.

(*SM*, IV, 50). Once again we are back at that pool that must first be filled before it can overflow, with self-love as the basis of all love 'so that God by satisfying my self-love, hath enabled and engaged me to love others'.[63] Knowing who we are and what we have is the foundation of our righteous esteem of ourself and of others. Sometimes knowing what we have lost is as effective: 'A Tasted Joy thats lost we more Desire' Traherne reminds us in *The Ceremonial Law* ('Elim', l. 86). Nowhere is this more evident than in our appreciation of the full effect of the fall. Traherne admonishes his reader to

> *Remember from whence thou art fallen, and repent*, Which intimates our duty of remembering our happiness in the estate of innocence. For without this we can never prize our Redeemer's love: He that knows not to what he is redeemed cannot prize the work of redemption.[64]

Inversely, in *Seeds of Eternity* it is the realization of the greatness of the soul's capacity for companionship with God that Traherne hopes will inspire his reader not to sin in the first place.

Perhaps it is because prizing has its roots in knowledge that it is something that can be taught. Traherne certainly believed that misprizing was a learned fault. 'Before I learned to be poor, / I always did thy Riches see', he writes in 'The Return' (ll. 14–15).[65] And on many other occasions, especially in the third *Century*, he recounts, sometimes with sorrow and sometimes as an admonition, his own lessons in misapprehension and misesteem.[66] But he never loses hope in the possibility of and belief in the necessity of prizing rightly, describing it as something difficult to learn in life yet 'almost the only lessons necessary to its enjoyment' (*C*, IV, 55). Learning to prize rightly is so important to Traherne because prizing is inextricably tied up with treasure. And when he writes:

> I will prize all I have, and nothing shall with me be less esteemed, because it is excellent. A daily joy shall be more my joy, because it is

---

[63] *C*, IV, 55. How this love serves others, including how God's self-love overspills to his creatures, is explored at greater length in the subsequent meditations: 56–65.

[64] *C*, II, 5. In the *Kingdom of God* also, what is lost is valued: 'It is a strange thing that a Blind man should see the valu of his eys, better then one that has sight' (*KOG*, Ch. 16, ll. 46–7).

[65] Similarly, in *Select Meditations* he writes: 'Till custom and Education had bred the Difference: it was as obvious to me to see all within us, as It was without' (*SM*, III, 27).

[66] *C*, III, 7, 8, 9, 11, 12, 13.

continual. A common joy is more my delight because it is common. For all mankind are my friends, and everything is enriched in serving them. (C, IV, 17)

we can see once again the characteristics of treasure – simplicity, commonness and utility – represented in his prized things.

However, spiritual discernment or knowledge – that is right apprehension – is not only gained by right intellection. It is also gained by the actual experience of want. In *The Ceremonial Law*, Traherne describes the raging thirst of the Israelites in the desert and the blissful relief they found in Elim as an example of how all people may be taught to 'Prize and so Enjoy their Bliss'.[67] It is largely prizing that makes heaven and hell. 'To have blessings and to prize them is to be in Heaven; to have them and not to prize them is to be in Hell, I would say upon Earth; To prize them and not to have them is to be in Hell.'[68] And so prizing has eternal significance. To prize rightly is to prize righteously, to prize righteously is to be involved in the business of righteous choices and righteous action. It is to live in heaven even now and to see, esteem and desire the highest and the best.

An Economy of Need and Treasure

As we have seen in the preceding sections, Traherne's understanding of worth has important theological implications, since appreciating worth or right prizing leads to just actions, but his assertions about knowing a thing's value, about the right prizing that leads to just action, also occur in a particular economic and political context. In his treatment of wealth and treasure, Traherne is giving his reader advice on happy and holy living within the particular political and social trends emerging in a 1670s economy: of all the new sciences that he so openly explored, political economy was not the least burgeoning. When Traherne employs the language of the rising market economy such as 'use', 'worth', 'value', 'price', 'prize', 'possess' and their cognates, he not only explores the origins and working of desire but also, as the recent work

---

67 TCL, 'Elim', l. 130. Earlier, Traherne writes '*Joys Possest but Tasteless prov*: / Unless we prize them' (ll. 124–5).
68 C, I, 47. See also the preceeding meditation: 'For they in Heaven do prize blessings when they have them. They in Earth when they have them prize them not, they in Hell prize them when they have them not.' and the subsequent meditation: 'They that would not upon earth see their wants from all Eternity, shall in Hell see their treasures to all Eternity.' For more regarding heaven on earth see also C, I, 83; SM, IV, 27.

of David Hawkes suggests, critiques the assumptions and values of that same system that would exchange intrinsic value for commercial value and worth for marketability.[69] Here his theology of desire spills over into a theology of social responsibility and both are linked by his understanding of 'use' or 'usefulness' to questions about ultimate reality.

The *Centuries* and the poems are sprinkled with mercantile language. His poems ' The Odour' and 'Right Apprehension', peppered with 'price', 'prize', 'use' and 'Valu', are much concerned with the cost, value, worth and use of things. In the *Commentaries of Heaven* Traherne devotes six columns to 'Accounts'.[70] Here merchants, kings, generals, publicans are all among those who must keep and give accounts. Alluding to the parable of the talents (Luke 19.11–27), Traherne discusses God as a merchant:

> GOD as He is a Merchant Distributing His Talents, keepeth a Book of Accounts for Angels & Men. In the counterpart of which they lay down an Accounts [sic] of their Receits Expenses & Gains. To Neglect which maketh them Bankrupts, but to do it faithfully – crowneth them with Glory. (*COH*, 'Account')

We are 'Good Accountants' when we account the value of God's gifts rendering 'past finding out' at the bottom of the page. The account we live matters most of all, since this is the account given before God, not made 'with Ink & Paper after the maner of Men, in Books; but in a living Maner in their Realities & Places' (*COH*, 'Account').

Traherne's 'accounting' involves not just listing, adding and justifying numbers but also ascribing a certain worth or value – counting one thing in relation to another. It is in this second sense that lines from the concluding poem of the 'Accounts' entry urge the reader to make a true account:

> . . . O how Sublime a Thing
> Would Man becom! Did he but truly count
> Himself and Glory, He would all surmount!
>
> (*COH*, 'Account')

---

69 David Hawkes, 'Thomas Traherne: A Critique of Political Economy', *Huntington Library Quarterly*, 62, 3 & 4 (1999), pp. 369–88.

70 He promises to liberate the word 'account' from its narrow use and apply it also to the work of angels.

And

> Let others Count their Gold, my Holy Eys
> The Stars shall number in the Highest Skies
> I will endeavour with a Curious Sence
> To measure Angels, and their Excellence.

Right through the poem an account is both a record kept and a particular way of telling a story; and Traherne's final rhyming couplet, as a double pun, turns on these meanings:

> But abov all My Saviors Drops of Blood
> In my Account hav don the chiefest Good

Christ's blood is held to account against our sin in God's account of things.

Despite the apparent playfulness of a pun, there is a deep seriousness in Traherne's interest in the political economy of his day. Early seventeenth-century thinkers such as Gerard de Malynes in *The Maintenance of Free Trade* (London, 1622) and Edward Misselden in *Free Trade* (London, 1622) had concentrated on the ethical questions of trade and usury, on the whole staying well within the bounds of the Old Testament and Aristotle, but the Restoration afforded the perfect impetus for change.[71] The nation was to be enriched, policies that enabled that to happen were to be embraced and conventional moral philosophy was about to be swallowed up in the practical theories that spoke to the mercantile interests. By the 1690s discourse had shifted: a blind eye was turned to usury; the arguments were largely instrumental rather than ethical, with writers such as William Petty in *Discourse on Political Arithmatic* (London, 1690) arguing for a 'political arithmatick' that would provide a precise way of determining policy; and Locke was concerned about the rates of interest.[72] As David Hawkes notes in his study of Traherne and the political economy, 'ancient ethical strictures against the everyday practices of the marketplace quickly came to appear anachronistic impediments'.[73]

---

[71] For an account of these changes, see Hawkes, 'Thomas Traherne: A Critique of Political Economy'.

[72] See John Locke, *Some Considerations of the Consequences of the Lowering of Interest* (London, 1691); William Petty, *Discourse on Political Arithmatic* (London, 1690); see also Nicholas Barbon, *A Discourse of Trade* (London, 1690). These are all cited in Hawkes, 'Thomas Traherne: A Critique of Political Economy'.

[73] Hawkes, 'Thomas Traherne: A Critique of Political Economy', p. 369.

DISCERNING TREASURE

It is during this period of rapid change that Traherne raises his not exclusively theological questions of worth and value, questions that we are once again faced with in the financial crises of our own day. He was not the only theological writer to be concerned about the changes in practice and theory in the marketplace. John Bunyan's *The Life and Death of Mr Badman*, an anti-market polemic published six years after Traherne's death, ineffective in the face of the by then unstoppable surge of new economic science, was nevertheless an earnest attempt to challenge the new assumptions of the rising free-market economy. That is not to suggest that such criticism was the province of Puritans; indeed Puritanism gained a stronghold in the mercantile classes of the sixteenth and early seventeenth centuries for whom wealth was a sign of divine benediction. Hawkes cites Shakespeare, Donne and Milton among the many writers who were uneasy about what the changes to political economy might mean.[74] I would argue, with Hawkes, that Traherne was among those impassioned few, from varying philosophical and theological backgrounds, who raised an alarm against the unconsidered moral and philosophical implications of an unbridled market economy.[75] The England of Traherne's day may have been in the process of jettisoning the notion of usefulness as the basis of value but, for Traherne, worth remained connected with usefulness, each thing valued in its role, its use, its operations:

> That anything may be found to be an infinite treasure, its place must be found in Eternity and in God's esteem. For as there is a time, so there is a place for all things. Everything in its place is admirable, deep, and glorious: out of its place like a wandering bird, is desolate and good for nothing. How therefore it relateth to God and all creatures must be seen before it can be enjoyed . . . Divest it of these operations, and divide it from these objects, it is useless and good for nothing and therfore worthless, because worthless and useless go together.[76]

The object's capacity for answering a specific need is what ascribes worth. In these terms only, the traditional 'treasures' of gold, silver and

---

74 See Donne's reflections on alchemy in the *Anniversaries*, Shakespeare's meditations on usury in the *Sonnets* and *The Merchant of Venice*, Milton's characterization of Mammon in *Paradise Lost*, and the anti-theatrical campaigners such as William Prynne. See Hawkes, 'Thomas Traherne', p. 370.

75 For Bacon also, practical use equals real use. In his essay *Of Riches*, the value of money itself is 'feigned' because there is no 'solid use' in riches themselves (*The Essays*, London, 1895, p. 47).

76 C, II, 55. See also, among the poems, 'The Odour' and 'Right Apprehension'.

precious stones may have real, though limited, value – these 'false' treasures may be deemed real treasures because their abundance is in proportion to their use. In a typically paradoxical twist, in which they are valued and devalued at the same time, it is their very scarcity rather than their commonness that makes these particular things treasures, scarcity limiting their availability since their usefulness is likewise limited:

> The Wisdom of God is exceeding marvellous, that made these [minerals, metals, precious stones and jewels] so secure: the Abundance and Plenty of them being proportionable to their use. For had he made them common, he had made them vile, which are now made Treasure by their scarcity ... because their Abundance would exceed the uses to which they are capable of being applied.[77]

It is because everything has a place, however limited, that everything may ultimately be a treasure.[78]

When Traherne writes of the value of the sun as more than gold or the moon as more than silver, when he insists that the value of precious stones lies not in their scarcity but in the perfect balance between their scarcity and their limited usefulness, that everything is a treasure in its place, he is challenging the new assumptions that would place exchange-value above use-value. His love of things common, simple and useful, amply noted above, is not merely a romantic gesture away from the flashy and brash to the quiet and serene: it is a clarion call to consider seriously the philosophical implications of the economic changes that were happening around him. This makes him a fascinating partner in dialogue with modern theologians such as Peter Selby who would take issue with a tyrannical market. In his study of debt Selby writes:

> The political rhetoric of recent decades has all been about an increase of choice; not surprisingly that leads to the idea that we choose what standards to apply in the whole of life. But in fact we have become more and more obsessed with the cash nexus and with the power of money as the criterion of value.[79]

---

77 *KOG*, Ch. 26, ll. 190–6. These things may be treasure, but they are still more limited, by their relative uselessness, than the common treasure of air, water, sunlight, etc.

78 That it is possible for anything to be a treasure is affirmed in the third *Century*, where Traherne's study of the common invisible treasures led him back to everything else: 'But to my unspeakable wonder, they brought me to all the things in Heaven and in Earth, in Time and Eternity, possible and impossible, great and little, common and scarce; and discovered them all to be infinite treasure' (C, III, 54).

79 Peter Selby, *Grace and Mortgage: Language of Faith and the Debt of the World*, London: Darton, Longman & Todd, 2009, pp. 105–6.

In the twenty-first century money forms the primary basis of our understanding of worth: not only personal worth but also the worth or worthwhileness of actions and ideas. Money is the primary determining factor in the viability of projects and in the formation of policies, and is the driving force of politics. Selby argues that money has become a god that is 'exacting its own demands, presenting itself as credible beyond question, objectively verifiable, and utterly totalitarian'.[80] We see this in the phrase that is more often implied than stated: 'there is no alternative'. As Selby notes, 'money with its promise of freedom, is itself given such freedom that it destroys the very freedom it pretends to offer'.[81] Or as sociologist Nigel Dodd writes:

> In the mature money economy, money's empowering features have compromised that very freedom which money itself promises to embrace. Monetary freedom has in this sense been alienating. It is a freedom which is empty of content, having only negative connotations linked to the removal of constraint.[82]

The freedom offered in this new market became not freedom to but freedom from. As the philosopher Georg Simmel in *The Philosophy of Money* wrote of market freedom: 'In itself, freedom is an empty form which becomes effective, alive and valuable only through the developments of other life-contents.'[83] Devoid of other models of ascribing worth besides the value of money itself, monetary wealth becomes its own end. Part of its appeal is that it promises a freedom that carries with it no concomitant responsibilities or duties. Houses must be painted, land maintained, animals fed and housed, vehicles serviced, jewels stored; monetary wealth however, rarely held or seen, grows and diminishes in a line of zeros existing only in the moment that holds it as potential or as risk, vanishing as quickly as it came.

The collapse of Barings bank in the 1990s, sparked by the trading of Nick Leeson in Singapore, who borrowed money and invested it in the hope of the Tokyo stock market rising, and then, when this did not happen, tried to raise it himself; the dot-com bubble of the late 1990s; and more recently the global banking collapses of 2008: each in its

---

80 Ibid., p. 106.

81 Ibid., p. 108.

82 Nigel Dodd, *The Sociology of Money: economics, reason and contemporary society*, New York: Continuum, 1994, p. 49, quoted in Selby, *Grace and Mortgage*, p. 108.

83 Georg Simmel, *The Philosophy of Money*, London: Routledge & Kegan Paul, 1978, p. 236, cited in Selby, *Grace and Mortgage*, p. 108.

way resulted from the commodification of money and reliance on a virtual economy – one in which money works for and by itself without any clear connection between it and the world of trade and industry. That we keep repeating similar scenarios indicates something of our devotion to the unbridled market model that Traherne so much feared and resisted. 'Be not a Bubble, be solid like God, and let all thy worth be within' (*COH*, 'Attire'), Traherne wrote as a critique of fashion; but his words might just as well apply to an economic model that is as unattached to the exchange of real goods and services as the fashion of his day was to serviceability.

When Traherne writes of 'invented wants' and 'illusory riches' he is not just suggesting that riches ultimately let you down but critiquing the whole ascendant market philosophy. We take interest, debt, exchange of money, and money as the medium of exchange as axiomatic. For Traherne it was not so. Standing in a long line of thinking, from patristic and scholastic traditions through to Calvin and Luther, that felt a profound unease towards money as a medium of exchange, Traherne's argument for ascribing value to things also has clear secular antecedents; he owes as much to Aristotle as to the tradition and Scripture.

This can be seen clearly in his use of the term 'custom'. Traherne is much concerned with nature and custom in *Christian Ethicks*. The 'powers of the soul' are ours by nature but they are not virtues till they 'put on a habit', are clothed by many acts of vice or virtue. Virtue is a habit we acquire by study, choice, desire, pursuit and labour (*CE*, p. 25). The virtuous habit, 'by long Custome', says Traherne, 'turns to a second Nature'(*CE*, p. 26). Here he is clearly following Aristotle: 'the reason why custom is held to be so strong is that it turns things into nature'.[84] Traherne's 'custom' right through his poetry and particularly in the *Centuries* is laden with ethical and moral implications. When by 'custom' we acquire virtue the word is used neutrally but the word is not most commonly so used. More often he rails against 'custom', not only because to follow custom is to be corrupted but also because to follow custom is to be led down a blind alley. Custom is artifice. Traherne saw and feared this in the political economy of his day: exchange-value was just such a form of custom.

Going back to Aristotle:

> every possession has a double use. Both of these uses belong to it as such, but not in the same way, the one being proper and the other

---

[84] Aristotle, *Magna Moralia*, II, 1203b30–1, quoted in Hawkes, 'Thomas Traherne', p. 374.

not proper to the thing. In the case for footwear, for example, one can wear it or one can exchange it.[85]

The use-value is natural to the thing; the exchange-value is not. As Traherne writes in *Commentaries of Heaven*: 'Abuse, if we consider the Importance of the Word, is a Turning away from the Use of Things' (*COH*, 12v). For him as for Aristotle, to see an item primarily in terms of its exchange-value is a perversion. Early seventeenth-century writers might have agreed[86] but, among the scientists of the new political economy, as Hawkes notes, 'the polemic was going in the opposite direction: not only was exchange-value equal in status and authenticity to use-value, but exchange-value was also beginning to displace use-value altogether.'[87] And so it has. It did not take long. The arguments differentiating between the 'natural and 'intrinsic' value and the 'artificial' and 'extrinsic' value of money had lost sway by the early 1690s, a few decades after Traherne's death. Coins were no longer worth their weight in gold; money had become pure exchange-value. What was considered 'real' had little to do with its ancient antecedent reality.

Traherne's discussion of reality is intimately linked with his ascription of worth. The 'child' of the *Centuries* who again and again bewails the intrusion of custom is almost always concerned with questions of worth and value in his discussion of seeming and reality:

> It was a difficult matter to persuade me that the tinselled ware upon a hobby-horse was a fine thing. They did impose upon me, and obtrude

---

85 Aristotle, *Politics*, 1257a1, 7–10.

86 It is not clear that Traherne read Misselden's *Free Trade* but he would have agreed with the sentiment: 'The natural matter of Commerce is Merchandize: which Merchants from the end of Trade have stiled Commodities. The Artificiall matter of Commerce is Money'.

87 Hawkes, 'Thomas Traherne', p. 376. The progression of this debate is traced in the writings of Bernardo Davanzati, whose *Discourse upon Coins* (trans. John Toland, London, 1696; originally published 1588) holds that making gold and silver the price and measure of all is a kind of idolatry (*A Discourse Upon Coins by Bernardo Davanzati, A Gentleman of Florence; Being publickly spoken in the Academy there, Anno 1588*, trans. John Toland, London, 1696, pl.1) and Bacon who describes the 'feigned prices set upon little stones and rarities' riches that give 'no solid use to the owner' (Of Riches, *Essays, or Councils, Civil and Moral*, Folio Society, London, 2002, p. 126); however, within a few decades the voices shifted as in for instance, the writings of William Petty (*A Treatise of Taxes*, 1662, *Quantulumcunque*, 1682) where he moves from insisting that gold and silver were the best metals to use for money since the value of the weight of the metal in the coins could equal its exchange value to admitting that money had become a commodity in its own right (see *The Economic Writing of Sir William Petty*, ed. Charles Henry Hull, 2 vols. Cambridge, 1899). A fuller outline of these changes can be found in Hawkes, pp. 277–9.

their gifts that made me believe a ribbon or a feather curious. I could not see where was the curiousness or fineness: And to teach me that a purse of gold was of any value seemed impossible, the art by which it becomes so, and the reasons for which it is accounted so, were so deep and hidden to my inexperience ... Nature knows no such riches: but art and error makes them.[88]

Art, artifice; exchange-value may have become axiomatic for adults but the 'value' of money must still be taught to children (any child knows that, regardless of its denomination, the only coin worth having is the one that usefully fits the bubblegum machine). It is the adult, Traherne would argue, who has become fully versed in the art of exchange-value, who needs to unlearn. For Traherne, in matters of political economy as much as in anything else, 'our misery proceedeth ten thousand times more from the outward bondage of opinion and custom, than from any inward corruption' (C, III, 8).

This is because there is an ontological inauthenticity about custom; it is about what is not rather than what truly is. It is a system that leads perversely to valuing scarcity above plenty and ornament above utility.

> Their Opinion is that themselves are the only Makers of Riches, and that Gods Works are to be Despised for Trifles, either because they be Common, or freely given. That Clothes are to be regarded more then the Body, and Ornaments to be preferd abov the Members. That Scarcity, not Service maketh Jewels ... that Men who have nothing but the Wide World are poor and miserable, and that a Twenty Shillings piece is a greater Caus of Joy then the Sun: that nothing is ours, but what we have under lock and Key, or at least within a Ring-Hedge; and that He is Great who hath many Revenues ... All these Opinions are fals in the World.[89]

So writes Traherne in *Inducements to Retiredness*: as long as scarcity rather than plenty is connected to value, need is exacerbated rather than answered. When money itself becomes a commodity we can never

---

[88] C, III, 9; see also C, III, 5, C, III, 7, C, III, 8, C, III, 11.

[89] *ITR*, ll. 840–51. Traherne speaks clearly to the concerns of those affected by new property law. See Lynne A Greenberg, '"Cursd and Devised Proprieties": Traherne and the Laws of Property', in Jacob Blevins (ed.), *Re-reading Thomas Traherne: A Collection of New Critical Essays*, Tempe, AZ: Arizona Center for Medieval and Renaissance Studies, 2007, pp. 21–36.

have enough. Such misguided thinking leads to 'Servitude and Dangers' (*ITR*, ll. 838–9) he argues presciently; 'we are to grow Rich, not by seeking what we Want, but by Enjoying what we have' (*ITR*, ll. 859–60).

Approaching the truth – this is where Traherne's arguments in favour of utility have a powerful voice, as an answer to skewed vision. His high estimation of utility is not just an anthropomorphic glance backwards to the Rennaisance humanist ideal of man as the centre of creation, or to the patristic intimations of incarnational theology, pertinent as these glances are; utility is a real good in Traherne because it operates as a protection against illusion. It is in terms of sight that we are to become 'as it were, a child again'(*C*, III, 3). This has often been interpreted in rather airy-fairy terms as becoming a child in imagination or regaining an unstained innocence, but having 'infant-like and clear' vision may be as much about being able to tell what is true and what is falsely valued. Consider when he writes:

> Our Saviour's meaning, when He said, *He must be born again and become a little child that will enter into the Kingdom of Heaven*, is deeper far than is generally believed. It is not only in a careless reliance upon Divine Providence, that we are to become little children, or in the feebleness and shortness of our anger and simplicity of our passions, but in the peace and purity of all our soul. Which purity also is a deeper thing than is commonly apprehended. For we must disrobe ourselves of all false colours ... all our thoughts must be infant-like and clear ... and disentagled from men's conceits and customs. Grit in the eye or yellow jaundice will not let a man see those objects truly that are before it ... Ambitions, trades, inordinate affections, casual and accidental riches invented since the fall, would be gone. (*C*, III, 5)

Could the 'casual and accidental riches invented since the fall' be, in part, a result of the emerging system of exchange-value that separates an object from any notion of 'real' value and makes all value relative to the accidents of the market? For Traherne use-value is a philosophical anchor against these and other unrealities and illusions. Its concreteness is its tonnage; we are to be pitied without it. When Traherne writes:

> Had any man spoken of it, it had been the most easy thing in the world, to have taught me, and to have made me believe that ... the

> Earth was better than gold, and that water, every drop of it, was a precious jewel. And that these were great and living treasures: and that all riches whatsoever else was dross in comparison (C, III, 8)

he is not only bewailing a personal loss of innocence but speaking prophetically of the essential emptiness of a market model of worth. The child's clarity being swallowed up by custom may also be read as a warning of servitudes and dangers to come.[90] In the rise of exchange-value, Traherne was witnessing what had hitherto been ontologically illusory and ethically dubious becoming, through practical necessity, common practice. For Traherne what is ontologically false is morally corrupting; what is practised and taught as 'custom' becomes second nature. What he is arguing against is the notion that the ontologically illusory, if empirically real, might become the ontological and empirical – the only – reality. Too late to stop the changes of his own day, he is like the dog who barks at the passing train, impotent yet full of integrity, and perhaps proven right in saying what he says about choices that lead to emptiness. 'Even a child can see' and 'only a child can see' are perhaps equally damning to the adult reader.

Once again we are thrown back to the importance of right apprehension, right esteem, right prizing, since the choices and actions that follow for a nation or a culture, as for a person, derive from these. The joint theme of freedom and desire is a blade that cuts both ways – it not only suggests the importance of freedom in our choices but also reminds us that our choices may lead to freedom or to bondage. For Traherne mis-desire leads to bondage, and authentic or well-prized desire to freedom. Usefulness or use-value is a kind of lens through which we may attempt to discern real from illusory treasure and so well-aimed or mis-aimed desire.

Use-value as the 'real' estimation of worth implies an economy of need and treasure that is essentially relational. Traherne describes this kind of double economy as 'valu and interest', or 'worth and interest', or 'interest and treasure'. By the one, we long to see the excellency of a thing (its value); by the other, we long to see it as our own (our interest). By the one we see the simplicity, commonness and utility of a thing; by the other, we feel its usefulness to us. The first seems dis-

---

90 The dot-com bubble of the late 1990s, where companies with a low 'use-value' had a high market value, might be seen as one modern example of a failure to value things according to some real sense of usefulness; but Traherne's concerns are philosophical rather than economic – the emotional and sociological poverty resulting from a life spent valuing what is essentially empty.

interested, the second covetous, and yet the two are tied together for Traherne. Consider that greatest of treasures, the soul, as discussed in *Seeds of Eternity*:

> Two things ther are concurring [together] to make the Contemplation of the Soul delightful; its own Worth, and our Interest. for as we naturaly desire to see Things excellent, and most violently long for things infinitly so; [so] we likewise ardently covet to have them ours ... we could wish our Interest as infinit as their Excellency. And tho these two Desires are inclinations generaly suppresst, either through fear, or some tacite Neglect yet when we remove the impediment that covers them ... we cannot chuse but feel them, becaus they are parts of our very selves. (*SE*, ll. 41–8)

This desiring, which is at once disinterested and covetous, is a necessary part of felicity and without it nothing can be truly apprehended (*SM*, III, 6); and

> Things are never profitably apprehended, till they are apprehended under the [Double] Notion of Interest & Treasure. Did God apprehend them to be of no valu, & to be none of his; they would be uselesse before him. As they are meer Objects of Speculation, they are Air: but as they are Enjoyments & possessions they feed us with Pleasure, increas our Grandure, unite us unto God.[91]

I have used the term 'economy' to describe this balance of need and treasure in Traherne. Richard Jordan calls Traherne's fascination with the uses and services of objects a 'logic of relationships'. That treasure is dependent upon communication and relation is absolutely fitting in Traherne's scheme of things, and we shall consider communication in greater detail in chapter four. Here it may suffice to note, with Jordan, that, in this logic of relationship, a balance is always maintained 'between wants and supplies within God's creation, the relationships of men to God and to each other, and the harmonious nature of the universe.'[92] And yet there is more than balance in the dynamic of need and treasure; there is generation and regeneration as well. For God

---

91 *ITR*, ll. 1140, 1145. Note again that treasure becomes treasure as it is enjoyed and used and that there is no disparity between our enjoying the pleasure of this treasure and our being united with God.

92 Richard Douglas Jordan, 'Thomas Traherne and the Art of Meditation', *Journal of the History of Ideas*, 46 (1985), pp. 381–403, 400.

would not make 'nor create any thing but to answer some Exigent and necessity conceived by Him' (*SM*, III, 8). The need is conceived and then the treasure created; thus the economy of need and treasure underlies all of creation, and by it new treasures are continually made. God did

> multiply the Treasures of his Eternal Kingdom by wants and supplies. Had there been noe creatures made that could need the sun, the sun could never hav been made a Treasure: nor could God frame a sea, but first he must conceive a Person needing it: Air to them that need no breath, nor open liberty, nor Bodily Refreshment, would be superfluous and made in vain . . . (*SM*, III, 9)

The implication is that wherever a new need arises a new treasure is waiting to be formed. So may treasure multiply as need produces fresh outlets for divine bounty. Treasure satisfies want – that is to say a desire or a need – and the loftier and larger the want, the greater the treasure. So it is that Traherne could say, 'whatsoever satisfied the goodness of Nature, was the greatest treasure'.[93] Divine goodness is surrounded by treasure, God's wants and treasures perfecting each other and delighting him. 'The sense of His wants, as it enlargeth His life, so it infuseth a value, and continual sweetness into the treasures He enjoyeth.'[94]

Since Traherne's greatest treasures are not conventional riches but the things that are most simple, common and useful, they may be finite or infinite, earthly or heavenly; but, as we have seen, their value is linked to their ability to answer a need rather than their rarity. In this economy of need and treasure each treasure has its place and false treasures cease to have value. The pursuit of true treasure both requires and sustains a clear vision of want and worth; and Traherne's call to prize rightly is not only about having one's mind turned towards heaven but also about apprehending what is real and what is illusory in the value system of the world in which we live. The whole notion of 'treasure' in Traherne is a deep exploration into the value of things, so

---

[93] *C*, IV, 44. Traherne claims that this is a principle at the bottom of nature, the misunderstanding of which causes men to err, since all inclinations and desires flow from and towards the satisfaction of goodness. Taken to its logical conclusion, God is his own best treasure. This Traherne states in *CE*, p. 68 – 'God is his own best and most perfect treasure.'

[94] *C*, I, 44. As stated earlier, God's wants are chosen rather than given as are ours. Thus Traherne can also say: 'he Knows how to enjoy, what he never needed, and to improve his Enjoyments by giving them away' (*CE*, p. 68).

that when he asserts that 'the true treasures, those rivers of pleasure that flow at his right hand for evermore, are by all to be sought and by all to be desired' (C, II, 100), he is less the epicure and more the prophet than we may have imagined.

3

Choice

> Let evry Thought and Wish and Choise of mine,
> Proceed from Thee
>
> (*COH*, 'Affairs II', ll. 53–4)

Just as the subject of treasure in Traherne touches upon profound questions of worth and value, so the subject of choice raises questions of liberty and grace. As we have seen in chapter one, Traherne's picture of the divine lover and the soul as bride raises particular issues of power, consent and union. Desire, as the moving force of the universe, is that which powers the soul as a watch is powered by its spring. In this chapter we will consider power in another sense – the soul's power to choose, and to consent or to act. The chapter begins with *Roman Forgeries* as a defence of liberty and proceeds to consider human freedom as part of the image of God in humanity and to explore the notion of humankind as 'the golden link'. Who we are as humans and what we may become is bound up with choice, the freedom to make choices and the kinds of choices we make. And so the chapter moves on to consider power and act, potentiality and actuality. Traherne's debate on election and free will in *A Sober View* is a part of this discussion, as is his work in *Christian Ethicks* and *The Kingdom of God*, where questions of moral goodness and virtue arise. That these questions surrounding human liberty were being raised in the particular climate of seventeenth-century church politics means that they are loaded with specific social and political implications. In this chapter we will see Traherne at his most vociferous as he engages with the controversies over church authority and with Calvinism and Arminianism. The choices Traherne advocates and, more importantly, the power to choose that he protects are not just matters of ideology but also of friendship and loyalty. In times of conflict what tells us most about a person is not only what they thought or said but what they did, who they hated and liked, and the words they used for their enemies and their friends. Concomitant with all of these political and ethical choices runs desire. 'The deliberate refusal to allow desire and choice to be separate was one of the main inspirations of seventeenth-century religious art and poetry', writes Staley. 'But it seems to be clear to Traherne that as soon as the separation is sanctioned, the beauty begins to go out of religion and the certitude out of art.'[1] Where desire is the moving force of the universe, choice is that desire's manifestation. It is in our choices that we exercise desire, that desire becomes in some sense visible. And so the chapter ends with hope – that 'Vertue mixt of Belief and Desire' by which we both choose and are stirred up to action, a virtue that stands in the cusp of potential and actual, linking what is envisioned with what is enjoyed.

In Defence of Liberty

In his chapter on holiness in *Christian Ethicks* Traherne writes: 'To make Creatures infinitely free and leave them to their Liberty is one of the Best of all Possible Things; and so necessary that no Kingdome of Righteousness could be without it' (*CE*, pp. 90–1). In *The Kingdom of God* he paints a picture of a God who is fully aware of the possible advent of evil into his perfect kingdom but whose desire for creatures like Godself – free agents whose liberty is a necessary part of their volition – is greater than his wish to maintain the purity of his creation. 'To constrain them, was to dishonor them' (*KOG*, Ch. 8, l. 71), writes Traherne, so God adventured the possibility of sin (*KOG*, Ch. 8, ll. 80–1). So that they might become wise 'and be the Authors of Actions, which God doth Infinitly prize, and without which all his other Works would be insignificant' (*KOG*, Ch. 8, ll. 83–5), infinite goodness 'put the Gate of Fate into the hand of its Creature' (*KOG*, Ch. 8, ll. 87–8). 'He Cheerfully committed the World to his Creatures Ingenuitie, hoping and expecting a Return of Glorious Delights and Thanksgivings' (*KOG*, Ch. 8, ll. 114–15). In this chapter of *The Kingdom of God*, God is the gardener whose trees may bear or forbear and can frustrate the hand of the gardener.

This is just one of many similar images of God's chosen vulnerability. 'Oh Lord!' he prays in *Thanksgivings for the Soul*,

> Thou so loved'st us,
> That for our perfect glory,

---

[1] Thomas F. Staley, 'The Theocentric Vision of Thomas Traherne', *Cithara*, 4 (November 1964), pp. 43–8, 44. Staley sees this as Traherne's 'normal and considered position, and examples of his adherence to this view of the inseparability of choice and desire occur again and again in his poetry and prose'.

Thou didst adventure into our hands
A Power of displeasing thee.[2]

The importance of human liberty is a theme to which Traherne returns again and again at various stages in his work. Words such as 'liberty', 'free will' and 'voluntary' are not, for him, tied up with righteousness alone but with his whole concept of humanity. Who we are and what we may become is intimately connected with freedom. It is entirely consistent, then, that his understanding of church – both its history and its practice – should concern itself, in part, with freedom. And so this chapter begins in a somewhat unlikely place, with *Roman Forgeries*.

I use the term 'unlikely' because it is not immediately apparent how *Roman Forgeries* is concerned with freedom, and because *Roman Forgeries* has often been considered an outside text:[3] its style is polemical, its arguments are technical, its content highly specialized. Apart from the biographical interest in his encounter with a papist in its introduction, it has been largely regarded as unapproachable. At best it represents a Traherne with whom we are not familiar.[4] Something has been made, by Stanley Stewart and Gladys Wade, of the text as evidence of Traherne's scholarliness, but for the most part we have not known what to do with it. In it Traherne seeks to prove that certain records of Church Councils[5] have been falsified and that the authority of the Roman Church is therefore flawed. Undergirding all this scholarly digging is his belief that 'The Supremacy of the Roman Church was a meer usurpation, begun by Ambition, advanced by Forgery, and defended by Cruelty'.[6] *Roman Forgeries* is a work with a particular and unashamed aim.

---

2 ll. 459–63, in Denise Inge, *Thomas Traherne: Poetry and Prose*, London: SPCK, 2002, p. 61.

3 'It is impossible not to feel that Traherne was wasting his genius in its composition', declares Bertram Dobell ('Introduction', *The Poetical Works of Thomas Traherne*, London: by the editor, 1903, p. xlvii) and that, or something similar, has been the view of the majority of critics in the twentieth century. In its own day, however, the text may have enjoyed a certain amount of popularity. It is a more common book than *Christian Ethicks*, and at the time it captured sufficient attention to earn Traherne a place amongst the distinguished graduates of Oxford.

4 As Stanley Stewart, who has made the most complete study of *Roman Forgeries* to date, admits, it reveals 'a stridency of character not at all consistent with the current stereotype of Traherne' (*The Expanded Voice: The Art of Thomas Traherne*, San Marino, CA: Huntington Library, 1970, p. 17).

5 Traherne lists in his 'Advertisement to the Reader', '*Apostles Canons, Decretal Epistles*, and *Ancient Councils*' as those things 'which they have either depraved by altering the Text, or falsified, as it were, by Whole-Sale, in intire Lump' (*RF*, fol. B6v).

6 *RF*, 'A Premonition', fol. A7v. Here Traherne is quoting Edward Stillingfleet: authorial marginalia notes 'Dr. Stil sermon on Acts 24.17 p.45'. As Malcolm Day notes (*Thomas*

CHOICE

Traherne begins the work by discussing 'the Nature, Degrees, and Kinds of Forgery', beginning with the beggar who forges 'only to satisfie his Hunger' and moving through the 'Leafe, Bond, Will or Deed', which is 'the greater', on to the forging of an instrument 'in the *Kings* Name' or his seal, which is high treason. According to Traherne, 'The Highest degree of Forgery is that of altering the *Holy Scriptures*; because the Majesty offended being Infinite, as well as the Concernment, the Crime is the more heinous'.[7] Second only to that is the forging of rules and councils or the putting of words into the mouths of the apostles, martyrs and fathers (an act that Traherne calls 'fathering upon'[8]). He writes:

> The highest, next under that, is to counterfeit *Rules* in the Names of the *Apostles*, *Oecumenical Councils*, most glorious *Martyrs*, and Primitive *Fathers*, that is, to make *Canons, Letters, Books,* and *Decrees* in their Names, of which they were not the Authors.[9]

This goes to the heart of the matter since, 'If the Church of *Rome* be guilty of this Crime, her *Antiquity* and *Tradition*, the two great Pillars upon which she standeth, are very rotten, and will moulder into nothing.'[10]

For Traherne, the authority of the Church and the authority of the state are intimately related; and the usurpation of the liberty of one taints the freedom of the other. As Stewart points out, 'Comparison between legal and theological procedures suggests the religious constraints on a parishioner amount to invasion of his rights as a citizen.'[11] In a sense Traherne's claims to theological liberty suggest an appeal to civic liberty as well. The Church, just as the individual, must find that its freedom comes from within. As Traherne so clearly states: 'no force of External Power can make us free; whatever it is invades our Liberty, destroys it' (*CE*, p. 93).

Traherne saw the centralization of power in Rome as just such an invasion. Whereas at the time of the Nicene Council the bishop of Rome

---

Traherne, Boston, MA: Twayne, 1982, p. 89 and note 3), this sermon was actually on Acts 24.14 and, more importantly, was preached on 21 September 1673, which dates *Roman Forgeries* later than has been posited by Wade, Margoliouth and others.

7 This and the preceding quotations in this paragraph are from *RF* pp. 1–3 (fols C3r–C4r).
8 This term is used in *RF*, Chs 13, 15, 18, 24.
9 *RF*, p. 3 (fol. C4r).
10 Ibid.
11 Stewart, *The Expanded Voice*, p. 28.

was 'expressly noted to be equal to that of the other Patriarchs' (*RF*, p. 8), he later 'invaded the Jurisdiction of his Fellow-Patriarchs'.[12] Both Protestant and Catholic Christians view the Council of Nicea as speaking with lasting authority so it is not surprising that it is this council that is most powerfully represented in *Roman Forgeries*. Traherne had great faith in the early councils; what he so strongly objected to were the later alterations and additions, those things that were 'fathered upon' the councils, which turned the workings of a council into the decrees from on high. The early councils are his reference point, not because he is harking back to, as Stewart suggests, a time of primitive unity in which all members agreed[13] but because he is looking back to a time of primitive co-operation in which all members discussed. The truth of the Church was Scripture interpreted by a council of equals who had reached a consensus. According to this means of government, each member of the council exercised reason and choice in the taking of their decision; and when this system was overridden something of that choice was lost. Take, for instance, the case of the outcast member – the excommunicate – dealt with in the fifth canon of the Council of Nicea. As Stewart points out, the outcast member had the right of appeal twice a year (once before Quadragesima and once about the middle of Autumn).[14] According to Stewart, 'In the early church, bishops gathered to assure by their common voice that any eccentric judgment of a local church official could not bar a member of the congregation from Easter communion. Ideally, such decisions represented not secular power but communal judgment: the reasoned opinion of the congregation',[15] and it was this consensus that gave the councils their authority. It is perhaps this communality of reasoned voice that appealed to Traherne as much as the Council's antiquity. Certainly it was the overthrow of this fifth canon, when the pope received appeals from excommunicated members of other dioceses, and in so doing exchanged the communal voice for the personal one, that riled Traherne.[16] To Traherne, the voice of the Council had been supplanted by

---

12 *RF*, p. 10. The second chapter of *Roman Forgeries* deals with the falsification of the gift of Constantine, which Traherne sees as the 'The first Popish Encroachment upon ... The Primitive Order and Government of the Church' (see title of chapter 2, p. 7).

13 Stewart, *The Expanded Voice*, p. 19: 'the primitive condition of the church was one of utopian unity and order'.

14 Ibid., pp. 32–3, where he cites sigs A4v–A5 of the Council.

15 Ibid., p. 33. Stewart recognizes the importance of consensus in the process of truth-finding when he writes 'The value of the councils rested in their recognition of human frailty and in their abiding humility' (ibid.).

16 The pope did not receive appeals from laity alone, as Traherne outlines: 'Yet when persons were Immorigerous, if any Bishop were censured by his Metropolitan, or Priest ex-

the voice of the one and consensus had been replaced with mandate. This power of excommunication is made most ridiculous to Traherne at the Sixth Council of Carthage, when all of Africa was excommunicated. From then on to the Reformation, church history is, for him, 'the unfolding drama of a developing tyranny, perpetuating itself by the bondage of the people's ignorance, by intimidating, silencing, or burning all dissenters'.[17] Again the issues are ones of that liberty that is necessary to choice, and again the theological and civic boundaries are blurred. When he writes of the evils done by 'Jesuitical Souls' he lists among their practices

> Poysoning Emperours, Murdering Kings, attempting on Queens, their Massacre at *Paris*, the Gunpowder-Treason, &c. The *Instruments* of which Acts, are by such Records rather favoured than discouraged; and some of them Canonized, rather than punished in the See of *Rome*.[18]

To Traherne, the centralization of ecclesiastical power was no less than theological and cultural invasion and his defence against Rome is an attempt to claim back a voice, and with that voice the liberty of choice. If his argument is about authority it is also about freedom. He would contend that the freedom to discuss, and free access to accurate texts are central avenues to discovering theological truth. The forgeries and falsifications against which he rails are not just fabrications; they are restrictions. They are about records lost, records forged, texts 'chained

---

communicated by his Bishop, or Deacon offended with his Superior, who chastised him for his guilt; though the Canon of the Church was trampled under foot thereby (which forbad such irregular and disorderly flights) the manner was, for those turbulent persons to flee to *Rome* . . . and the Roman Bishop trampling the Rule under foot, as well as others, did (as is confessed) frequently receive them' (*RF*, p. 10). His outrage at this seems to increase as he writes '*Rome* became an *Asylum*, or City of *Refuge*, for discontented persons; disturbing the Order of the Church, spoiling the Discipline of other Provinces, and hindering the Course of Justice; while her Bishop usurped an Authority, which neither *Scripture* nor *Canon* gave unto him' (p. 11). It is interesting to note that among his grievances listed above he notes the perversion of justice, again drawing parallels between theological and legal disputes. His anger continues on until he likens the rise of the pope's supremacy to the legend of Sappho who, wanting to be a god, trained birds 'to say Μεγας Θεος ο Σαφω: Sappho *is a great God*', before letting them loose to teach all the other birds the same. According to Traherne the pope's birds are his priests, and seminaries the captivity in which they are taught to sing. The story serves 'for an *Embleme* of the Pope's Atchievement', writes Traherne, 'who by this means has made the World to ring of a Doctrine which makes him a God; or if not that, at least Lord of all *Councils*, greater than Emperors, Head of the Church &c' (p. 38).

17 Stewart, *The Expanded Voice*, p. 39.
18 *RF*, p. 316 (appendix).

up' and expurgated, bought up and burned.[19] They are about his own ecclesiastical history rewritten and the authority of his church invaded – intellectual and ecclesiastical bondage.

It is precisely in its defence of intellectual and ecclesiastical freedom in the pursuit of truth that we may see *Roman Forgeries* not as a text isolated from the rest of the canon by its polemical voice but as a text that is linked to all the rest by its fundamental assertions. Like desire as the moving force of creation, and like the pursuit of felicity, this defence of freedom is fundamental in Traherne. For without the intellectual and ecclesiastical freedom that *Roman Forgeries* seeks to defend, Traherne's other themes could find no home. In its tone, *Roman Forgeries* heeds the admonition of *Christian Ethicks* that passion be prudent by matching vehemence with degree of importance of its subject matter. In its quest for right knowledge and his assumption that knowledge liberates, it affirms what he also explores in various forms in his poetry and his poetic prose. Even his polemical tone is not unique. The kind of language he uses in *Roman Forgeries* appears again in the *Centuries*[20] and in *A Sober View*,[21] and it should be no surprise that the situations in which we find Traherne's most vehement language are these three. As he rails in *Roman Forgeries* against the bondage of the mind by the falsification of records, so he rails in *A Sober View* against the poison of lies, and in The *Centuries* against the bondage of 'custom' – also a bondage of mind by the falsification of evident truth.

A Sober View of Dr Twisse and *Roman Forgeries* not only connect Traherne with the political events and discussions of his day but are also connected to each other by their fundamental explorations of freedom and authority. Questions of freedom and authority also surface at vari-

---

19 See, for example, the *Advertisement to the Reader* (*RF*, fols B5v–B6r), in which they 'buy up the Editions' and 'endeavored to corrupt' by 'their Indices Expurgaturii'.

20 In *RF* he calls the council of Carthage 'audacious *Guesses*' (p. 129), claiming 'The more you stir this business, the more it stinks' (p. 130). Ch. 18 ends 'Surely the feet upon which this Peacock stands, are very Black' (p. 214) and he concludes his final chapter by suggesting that the Roman Church, a 'Mother of Lyes . . . espoused to the Father of Lies', has produced an 'adulterate brood' and so is 'defiled with so great an Off-spring of notorious *Impostures*' (p. 297). Similarly strong language is used against custom, those 'barbarous opinions, and monstrous apprehensions, which we nick-name civility and the mode' (*C*, III,12), which 'put grubs and worms in men's heads that eat out all their happiness' (*C*, III, 13); by custom he is swallowed up 'in the miserable gulf of idle talk and worthless vanities' (*C*, III, 14).

21 '[T]hat Doctine which some suck from this [Romans] Text, That God from all Eternity simply and without Caus hateth any, and that there are Multitudes of Reprobates so hated, is as Damnable poison as can that way be put into the mouth of a Christian' (*SV*, XXVIII, ll. 142–5).

ous points with the same kind of zeal and even anger in *Commentaries of Heaven*, another text that shows Traherne to be very much engaged in the anti-papist controversy. The long entry 'Antichrist',[22] intent on proving that the pope is the antichrist, reads as inflammatory as any of the many millenarian texts obsessed with interpreting the Book of Revelation, even propounding the zany theory that the name of antichrist may be deduced by calculating the number values for the letters in the latin name λατεινος, the appellation of the Romans according to Virgil, to equal the sum 666, thus proving that the antichrist must be a Roman. This, Traherne has the grace to admit, is frivolous as a naked conjecture but he argues that, in the context of other strong prophetic indicators, it is 'full and weighty' (*COH*, 'Antichrist').

Passionate, even angry writing, at times uncharacteristic of his writing elsewhere appears here, where these central questions of authority and freedom occur. They are at the heart of Traherne's understanding of himself, his God and his nation.

The human being's power to act is reliant upon the power to choose. It is part of the Imago Dei that humanity should have this freedom and so, in defending the liberty of text and the authority of several voices rather than a dictum from on high, Traherne is not only defending the authority of his church but the image of God in all humanity as well.

The Golden Link

The image of God in humanity is, of course, one of Traherne's well-known themes. Adhering as it does to the Renaissance tradition of man as the centre of the universe and the pinnacle of creation, Traherne's high view of humanity is, in one sense, nothing new. But for Traherne this doctrine is more than a humanist ideal; it is the pivotal point of redemption, for it is in the incarnation – in which God becomes a man that humanity may become divine – that Traherne's redemption finds its roots. His redemption theology will prove a rich resource, particularly for theologians who are interested in the doctrine of *theosis*,

---

[22] 'Antichrist' cites Bishop George Downham's response to Bellarmine as a model argument. *Treatise Concerning Antichrist: divided into two bookes, the former, proving that the Pope is antichrist: the latter, maintaining the same assertion, against all the objections of Robert Bellarmine, Jesuit and cardinall of the Church of Rome* appeared in 1603 in English, and in Latin in 1620, under the name George Downame, though Traherne uses the spelling Downham. George Downham (d. 1634) was the Bishop of Derry. Traherne had also read the other side: he cites Dr Bayly's challenge to Protestantism, 'It is a great Brag among the Papists that none of the fathers or ancient Councils ever condemned the Pope of Apostasie'; but he cites only to refute.

prevalent among seventeenth-century divines, that drew on the incarnational theology of the Early Fathers and the Eastern Church. Traherne was not alone in his championing of the doctrine of *theosis*. The great reforming Thomas Cranmer describes how

> the Son of God, taking unto him our human nature, and making us partakers of his divine nature, giving unto us immortality and everlasting life, doth so dwell naturally and corporally in us, and maketh us to dwell naturally and corporally in him.[23]

Ralph Cudworth, who framed his interpretation of *theosis* in more Platonic terms, claimed that 'Salvation it self cannot save us, as long as it is onely without us' and 'the Gospel is nothing else but God descending into the World in our Form . . . that he might allure, and draw us up to God, and make us partakers of his Divine Form'.[24] Lancelot Andrewes, Richard Hooker and Jeremy Taylor (all of whom Traherne read and/or copied) pondered the wonder of humanity becoming a partaker of the divine. Traherne shares their exploration of the doctrine of *theosis* but, more explicitly than theirs, his writings provide a coherent and critical link between this Early Christian teaching and modern Christian humanism via the Rennaissance humanism of Ficino and Pico della Mirandola, and the hermetical writings before them.

In Traherne's writings, the universe is the theatre of redemption, and each person is a player with an unwritten script, capable of choices, whose thoughts and actions have eternal significance. What the human does matters to others and to God and to the proper or improper employment of all creation:

> By this you may see that the works or actions flowing from your own liberty are of greater concernment to you than all that could possibly happen besides . . . Should God give Himself and all worlds to you, and you refuse them, it would be to no purpose. Should He love you and magnify you, should He give His Son to die for you, and command all Angels and Men to love you, should He exalt you in His Throne, and give you dominion over all His works, and you neglect

---

[23] In C. W. Dugmore, *The Mass and the English Reformers*, London: Macmillan, 1958, pp. 184–5. I am grateful to Edmund Newey for pointing me in the direction of this and the following quotation: see his '"Ascend downward and descend upward": Returning to the Anglican Divines', unpublished paper given at the conference 'Returning to the Church', St Stephen's House, Oxford, January 2009.

[24] In C. A. Patrides, *The Cambridge Platonists*, London: Edward Arnold, 1969, pp. 109, 101.

them it would be to no purpose. Should He make you in His image, and employ all His wisdom and power to fill Eternity with treasures, and you despise them, it would be in vain. In all these things you have to do; and therefore your actions are great and magnificent... while all creatures stand in expectation what will be the result of your liberty. (C, IV, 48)

All creatures stand in expectation of our liberty. It is in this sense that human liberty gives its weight to the redemption drama. For without liberty no action could be righteous and no actor useful. As Traherne describes it:

For in every Kingdome there are subjects capable of Laws, and Rewards, and Punishments. And these must be free Agents. There is no Kingdome of Stones nor of Trees, nor of Stars; only a Kingdome of Men and Angels. Who were they divested of their Liberty would be reduced to the estate of Stones and Trees; neither capable of Righteous Actions, nor able to Honor, or to Love, or praise: without which Operations all inferior Creatures and meer Natural Agents would be totally Useless. (CE, p. 91)

But Traherne takes his praise of liberty further. Not only does human liberty exalt the individual human to the realms of righteous action but human liberty also has divine ends. Human liberty glorifies God. It does so because, as a free agent, the human can return (or withhold) obedience and praise. This occasions the possibility of a perfected creation reflected or returned by creatures who become themselves creative, and in so doing introduces a dynamic of mutuality into creation.[25] Thus, through the liberty of men and women, God may attain more than he attained by the use of his own liberty alone. By his own liberty, writes Traherne, he could create worlds and give himself to his creatures,

But to see them obedient, or to enjoy the pleasure of their amity and praises, to make them fountains of actions like His own (without which indeed they could not be glorious) or to enjoy the beauty of their free imitation, this could by no means be, without the liberty of His creatures intervening... In creating liberty therefore and giving it to His creatures, He glorified all things; himself, His word, and the subjects of His Kingdom. (C, IV, 46)

---

25 This notion of mutuality is discussed more fully in chapter four under the heading 'Circulation and Communication'.

The enjoyment of creation and the giving of praise that Traherne mentions above is a theme to which he returns many times. And it is enjoyment of the world that is humanity's unique employment. Traherne's angels may choose, they may obey or disobey, but they cannot enjoy the physical world as the human can. As Traherne writes in *Select Meditations*:

> Now Angels can Adore, Giv Thanks and lov. Yet without the Interposure and mediation of man cannot enjoy this Adspectable world, for haveing no Bodies, no smell, no feeling, sight, Eys or Eares, no need of Aire meat or Drink, all is Superflous to the Selves, as it is to God. Till man be made. (*SM*, III, 9)

The importance of the human body for the enjoying of creation is emphasized again and again in Traherne's writings, as is (in *The Kingdom of God*) the superiority of human bodiliness over angelic bodilessness.[26] With the psalmist David, Traherne sees the human as 'a little lower than the angels';[27] that is to say, a not quite entirely spiritual being and yet exalted high above the beasts. Neither extreme, the angel nor the beast, the creature that is either wholly spiritual or wholly physical, can achieve what the human can achieve.[28] Neither is able to perfect creation or to return to God the praise that he desires. And it is in fulfilling this unique role that the human surpasses an angel. As Traherne puts it:

---

26 In praise of the human body see day six of *Meditations on the Six Days of Creation*, in which, among many other praises of the body, the author asserts that God super-added something to his Image in creating it. See also 'Our bodies are not, as som Imagine them, enemies to be used, with all Kind of Rigor. They are vessels worthy the Treasures they inclose ... since he hath left there as in a cage, the Greatest of all his Miracles, The [Human Soul]' (*KOG*, Ch. 41. ll. 1–4); 'But Certainly the Body shall enjoy as much in Heaven, as In Hell it endureth, for it was made for pleasure, not for pain, and is most Apt and capable of that, for which it was first designed' (*KOG*, Ch. 40, ll. 302–4); and 'our Humane Nature is more then Angelical, because we have one Way more then they, to feel, and enjoy all Objects' (*KOG*, Ch. 41, ll. 86–8). See further 'This Body is not the cloud, but a pillar assumed to manifest His love unto us. In these shades doth this sun break forth most oriently ... God never shewed Himself more a God than when He appeared man' (*C*, 1, 90). The fact that bodiliness matters is, moreover, reiterated in Traherne's interest in the embodiment of God himself in creation in *C*, II, 20; *SM*, IV, 34 and *KOG*, Ch. 27.

27 Psalm 8.5. Man is 'made as David witnesseth a little lower than the Angels' (*C*, IV, 74). What Traherne is emphasizing here is not man's position in a hierarchy but the unique ambiguity of his nature – spiritual and physical.

28 'Since therfore neither Angels, nor Bruits can Enjoy the World, or make it so perfect as it ought to be without the Interventions of Man', writes Traherne, man was created (*KOG*, Ch. 40, ll. 86–7).

> IF you look in to the *Nature* of Angels and Men you will find this mighty Difference between them, Angels are more Simple Spirits, Men are Images of GOD carefully put into a Beautiful Case ... the visible World was made for the sake of these Bodies, and without such persons as men are, it would be utterly useless ... .[29]

And so the image of God in a body is a great mystery. Rooted in both the practical usefulness and the glorification of the world, the human body has both physical and spiritual significance. Traherne is fascinated by the implications of this unique position. Using the image of a case once again, in the *Select Meditations* Traherne calls the human position a great mystery of all eternity – 'Gods picture in a curious Case, besett with stars insted of Jewels'.[30]

This mystery of the double nature of the human person is aptly expressed in the mystery of birth, for in it the human stands between the physical and the spiritual, creating a body and giving home to a soul. In birth the human is 'able to beget the Divine Image, and to multiply [herself or] himself into Millions'.[31] And it is in the human body, we are reminded, that God himself chose to dwell.[32] This great mystery of the double nature in the human race is a theme to which Traherne frequently returns, and which never ceases to amaze him. The governor of all beneath him and dear to all that is above, the human is an inhabitant of both worlds, a messenger between created things and an interpreter of all of the natural world. Neither wholly in time nor wholly out of time, the human stands between the two as pause or, as Traherne writes, 'an interval'. And so the human is, as Traherne describes in the *Centuries*, a golden link:

> A messenger between the creatures. Lord of inferior things, and familiar to those above; by the keenness of his senses, the piercing of

---

29 *CE*, p.104; cf. 'For our Bodies therefore was all this glorious World made, and all things therein' (*MSD*, p. 71).

30 *SM*, III, 9; cf. 'and as we put fair and curious Pictures, which we much value, into rich and costly Cases, so God implanted his Image in this Body, the Richness of the Workmanship adding to the Magnificence of the Jewel: The Beauty of the Body adorning and commending the Image which it contains' (*MSD*, pp. 3–4). In the beauty of the case Traherne reads a significance because 'if the Case be so rich, how glorious must the Jewel be?' (*MSD*, p. 80).

31 *CE*, p. 104. In *MSD* the author writes that in Eden 'it was lawful and blessed to beget their Similitude; forasmuch as it was part of the divine Image conceded to them abov the Angels' (*MSD*, p. 73).

32 'His Body may be the Temple of GOD, and when it pleased GOD to become a Creature, he assumed the Nature of Man' (*CE*, p. 104).

his reason, and the light of knowledge, the interpreter of nature, a seeming interval between time and eternity, and the inhabitant of both, the golden link or tie of the world, yea, the Hymenaeus marrying the Creator and His creatures together . . .[33]

He is 'the Head of all Things visible, and invisible, and the Golden clasp whereby Things Material and Spiritual are United' (*CE*, p. 104).

This image of the golden link or clasp, beloved by many seventeenth-century poets and recurrent in Traherne, has its origins in the hermetical writings. In the *Kingdom of God*, Traherne cites Hermes when he writes of man again as a golden clasp in which the material and spiritual unite: 'wherin all Visibles, & Invisibles are fitly concentred, & meet together' (*KOG*, Ch. 40, l. 1).

It is just one of many ideas and images that Traherne borrows from *Corpus Hermeticum*, the hermetical writings once thought to have originated about the time of Moses, and the link between Hermes and Traherne has been ably traced by Carol Marks and commented on by several others.[34] Traherne's debt to Hermes is evident in completed works and notebooks alike, cropping up both in full quotes and in marginal notes, cited overtly and infused in Traherne's themes and motifs, like that of the golden clasp above. We know that Traherne gleaned his Hermes from several sources. He read Everard's 1657 translation and Ficino's *Argumentum* to his translation of Hermes, and he cites Ficino's description of Hermes as 'Primus . . . Theologiae Autor'.[35] It seems that he was aware of the questions of authority and authorship raised by Casaubon's 1614 debunking of the Hermes myth:[36] in his

---

33 C, IV, 74; quoting Pico.

34 See Carol Marks, 'Thomas Traherne and Hermes Trismegistus', *Renaissance News*, 19 (1966), pp. 118–31; S. Sandbank, 'Thomas Traherne and the Place of Man in the Universe', *Scripta Hierosolymitana*, 17 (1966), p. 135 and n. 28.

35 Ficino, *Opera*, II, Basel, 1576, p. 1836. This appears in Traherne's *Ficino Notebook* on folio 58 (BL.MS.Burney 126), which also contains notes from the *Argumentum*. According to Sandbank, Traherne read the 1650 Everard translation, which is what he follows in his long quotations from Hermes in *Christian Ethicks*, Ch. 28. For evidence that Traherne also read the second edition of the Everard translation (1657) of Hermes see Carol Marks, 'Thomas Traherne's *Commonplace Book*', *Papers of the Bibliographic Society of America*, 60 (1966), p. 464, n. 12.

36 The scholar Isaac Casaubon unearthed evidence that the hermetical texts were far younger than had first been thought and that they were likely to have been a compilation of the work of several writers. In *The Kingdom of God* Traherne refers to Hermes in the singular person 'he' and seems to affirm the pre-Casaubon notion of Hermes as more ancient than Moses (*KOG*, fol. 332r). Though most common, this reading of Hermes is not universal in Traherne since, in *CE* (p. 230), Traherne suggests the possibility of multiple or diverse authorship when he writes 'Trismegistus (or whoever else was the Author of that Book)'.

Commonplace Book he questions 'Whether this Author bearing the Name of Tris. Be that ancient Heathen, the Egyptian Hermes that was contemporary with Moses' or indeed 'whether there were any such Hermes or no' but he is loath to discard what has been regarded, by 'common consent of all learned men',[37] as venerable. Traherne uses several names for Hermes Trismegistus – sometimes he is 'Hermes' and sometimes 'Mercurius Trismegistus'.[38] Attribution in many places in the *Commonplace Book* is indicated by a simple 'Tris' at the end of the relevant passage.

What interests Traherne are the fascinating questions of self and soul that the hermetic writings raise. For Traherne, the knowledge of oneself is of central importance. It is the foundation of virtue and the beginning of wisdom.[39] Much of what Traherne believes about the self can be traced to Hermes, who went so far as to say that the soul, if it would commune with God, must be in some ways like God:

> If therefore thou wilt not equal thy self to God, thou canst not understand GOD. For the like is intelligible by the like. Increase thy self to an immeasurable Greatness, leaping beyond every Body, and transcending all Time, become ETERNITY; And thou shalt understand GOD.[40]

Traherne admits that this is dangerous territory – the desire to be like gods was the destruction of the world. And yet, he insists, it was not in the desire but in the means of attaining it that Adam and Eve sinned: 'to aspire to the Perfection in a forbidden way, was unlawful . . . but to know our selves, and in *the strait and divine Way* to come immediately to GOD'[41] is right and good. It was by disobedience, by following their own inventions, that our first parents sinned.

---

37 'However it be it is a venerable & learned Author of great esteem & Authority in the World, & by the Common Consent of all learned men, many grave & venerable Mysteries are contained in it: for the sake of which also the Work has so many Ages been esteemed Hermes.' This and the previous quote are taken from *CB*, under the heading 'Generation', fols 48bv, col. 2–49, col. 2.

38 Or 'Hermes Thrice-Great', see for example *KOG*, fol. 348r and C, IV, 74.

39 Cf. 'in the knowledg of one self, the knowledg of God, and all things appeareth' (*SE*, fol. 140v); and 'the knowledge of a Mans self the Foundation of Magnanimity' (*CE*, p. 225).

40 Traherne citing Hermes in *CE*, p. 226. Extended quotations from Hermes appear throughout this chapter, many of them reappearing again in *The Kingdom of God* (cf. *KOG*, fol. 333r).

41 *CE*, p. 228; that in italics is a quote from Hermes previously cited on the preceding page in *CE*.

Traherne's reliance on Hermes is clear. With the Early Church Fathers, Hermes shares a profound vision of the human person as a link between the spiritual and physical. From Hermes Traherne gleaned not just the metaphor of the Golden Clasp but also a vision of the human as the pinnacle of creation – fascinating terms by which to explore the doctrine of the incarnation and the doctrine of *theosis*. And yet Traherne does not take on board the hermetical tradition without discrimination and there are points upon which Traherne differs from Hermes. Hermes praises the body and yet denigrates the physical. As Carol Marks has noted there are, throughout Hermes' *Pymander*, two strains in juxtaposition – a 'dogmatic *contemptus mundi*, utterly foreign to Traherne; and an equally powerful ecstatic praise of the world and of man which agrees perfectly with Traherne's philosophy.'[42] The incarnation is one of the most important of all Christian doctrines for Traherne and it is in this doctrine that his understanding of the high position of humanity originates. Where Hermes is positive in his doctrine of man, Traherne applauds him. Whatever contradicts this view is ignored or marginalized. This may be because he finds too many contradictions within the hermetic writings or because he is simply doing with these writings as he does with most – borrowing what is useful and in some cases even glossing it to suit his argument. Traherne uses Hermes to second Pico (C, IV, 74) or to underscore a point made by one of the wise pagans such as Plato or Aristotle. The hermetic writings function as a synthesis of ideas and Hermes stands in a kind of twilight between pagan and Christian,[43] a position that is often useful to Traherne, who would himself like to synthesize the works of many of the same men. From Hermes he gleaned the important notion of the omnipresence of the soul, its power to be present, by a thought, with its object that appears in his poetry and in the *Centuries*. He is quoting Hermes when he writes:

> I conceiv, and understand not by the Sight of my eys, but by the Intellectual Operation &c. I am in Heaven, in the Earth, in the Water, in the Air, in the Living Creatures, in the plants, in the womb, evry where. (*KOG*, fol. 332r–v)

---

42 Marks, 'Thomas Traherne and Hermes Trismegistus', p. 121.

43 Traherne says of Hermes: 'This is Trismegistus that sublime and Mysterious Oracle among the Gentiles, who if he were a Heathen, was the strangest Heathen that ever the world produced', and that he is 'the most ancient Writer of the World ... the most venerable of all the Magi' (*KOG*, fols 332r, 333v). In *CE* (p. 226) he refers to Hermes simply as 'the ancient Heathen' and yet asserts that what Hermes professes is 'countenanced here and there in the Holy Scripture'.

and

> He understood himself to be where his Thought was . . . with Adam in Paradice, with Christ upon the Cross, with God in the Creation, with Moses in the Wilderness, with Noah in the Ark, with Solomon in the Temple . . . If it pleas, it can contract it self to the Litleness of a Sand, to a centre, and in a Moment dilate like a Flash of Lightning over all the heavens, nay full Eternity . . . *(KOG, fol. 333v)*

He takes from Hermes what will feed into the doctrine of *theosis*, exploring the notion that God became human so that humanity might participate in God or, as Athanasius wrote, God 'was made man that we might be made God' (*De Incarnatione*, LIV). We may see that the Christian doctrine of the incarnation was brought to life in a new way for Traherne by his reading of Hermes, and so the whole expression of his understanding of the human person owes a significant debt to Hermes. This is so not just because of his direct readings of the hermetic writings but also because these same writings so influenced those two later heroes of Traherne's – Ficino and Pico. To read Traherne on Hermes, Ficino and Pico is to sense an unbroken continuity in their conception of the position of man.[44]

After Hermes, Ficino held that the human stood between two worlds. Humanity is 'the mean between temporal and eternal things, since it receives the eternal and commands the temporal',[45] asserted Ficino. This could be so because, to Ficino, 'there was an ontological connection between the two spheres'.[46] God was in all things because

---

[44] Witness, for instance, the seamlessness with which he moves from Pico to Hermes in the *Centuries*: 'Picus Mirandula admirably saith, in his tract *De Dignitate Hominis*, I have read in the monuments of Arabia, that Abdala, the Saracen, being asked, *Quid in hac quasi mundana Scena admirandum maxime spectaretur?* What in this world was most admirable? answered, MAN: That whom he was nothing more to be admired. Which sentence of his is seconded by that of Mercurius Trismegistus, Magnum, O Asclepiades, Miraculum, Homo; man is a great and wonderful miracle. Ruminating upon the reason of these sayings, those things did not satisfy me, which many have spoken concerning the excellency of Human Nature. As that man was Creaturarum Internuncius; Superis familiaris, Inferiorum Rex; sensuum perspicaciâ, Rationis Indagine, Intelligentiae Lumine, Naturae Interpres, Stabilis Aevi et fluxi Temporis Interstitium, et (qd. Persae dicunt) Mundi Copula immo Hymenoeus' (C, IV, 74).

[45] Marsilio Ficino, *Theologia Platonica* (Bologna: Zanichelli, 1965), Bk. II, p. 276, translated in Charles Trinkaus, 'Marsilio Ficino and the Ideal of Human Autonomy', in Konrad Eisenbichler and Olga Zorzi Pugliese (eds), *Ficino and Renaissance Neoplatonism*, Ottawa: Dovehouse, 1986, p.142.

[46] Karen-Claire Voss, 'Imagination in Mysticism and Esotericism: Marsilio Ficino, Ignatius de Loyola, and Alchemy', *Studies in Spirituality*, 6 (1996), pp. 103–30, 108.

all things were in Him, the divine goodness so overflowing that it left no particle devoid of itself: 'Si ergo in uno mundi corpore vivente una quodam vita unique est quod alias ostendimus multo magis unum ipsum bonum est ubique etiam extra mundum.'[47] For Ficino's concept of man this meant that the human person, too, participated in the divine. The human mind could not be satisfied with the finite because it contained a ray of divine light. In this view of humanity, God transcends our faculties, though he is none the less a part of them – 'the Absolute is within us, and God became man in order that man might become God'.[48] Being in this sense 'god-like', the human person participates in the divine actions of love, knowledge and creative activity, always doing in lesser form what God may do in perfection. Repeatedly it is the fact not just that the human may so act but that the human may so act freely that interests Ficino. He says of divine action that God is not led to action by necessity of nature but by a purpose of will and that 'what is done by freedom of the will is more excellent than what is dragged into action' by necessity: 'That action is happiest in which the author is in command of his own actions'.[49] This is as true of the human as it is of God for Ficino. He reiterates that the free action is the highest action: choice is the evidence of both volition and freedom; and decision is exactly the peculiar office of the human. Ficino says of deliberation and decision that 'this is the property of man in so far as he is man'. Trinkhaus concludes, 'All men, always and everywhere engage in deliberation and choice; those who are above men do not need deliberation; those who are below are unable to choose.'[50] Freedom, volition and choice in Ficino are, it would seem, inextricably linked. And so they are in Traherne. Like Ficino, Traherne affirms the importance of actions done voluntarily or freely and that such actions are peculiarly human.

That elements of Ficino should appear in Traherne is no surprise. Among his other works, Ficino was responsible for translating Plotinus, the *Corpus Hermeticum* and Plato's dialogues from Greek into Latin. It is these very Platonic dialogues of Ficino's that occupy most of Traherne's *Ficino Notebook*. Not only does the existence of the *Ficino Notebook* give evidence of the importance of Ficino to Traherne (who

---

47 Ficino, *Theologia Platonica*, Bk. I, Ch. VI, p. 91.
48 Nesca A. Robb, *Neoplatonism of the Italian Renaissance*, London: G. Allen & Unwin, 1935, p. 67. See Ficino, *Theologia Platonica*, Bk. XIV, Ch. VIII, p. 137: 'Deus agitat mens humana quotidie, deo ardet cor, Deum suspirat pectus.'
49 Marsilio Ficino, *Disputatio*, 12; translated in Trinkaus, 'Marsilio Ficino', pp. 142–3.
50 This and the preceding quotation are from Trinkaus, 'Marsilio Ficino', p. 144.

wrote almost the whole of the notebook in his own hand, using an amanuensis only for two excerpts from Theophilus Gale's *Court of the Gentiles*[51]), and not only do Ficinan notions run as undercurrents in the Neo-Platonic tones that colour much of Traherne's work, but Ficino also appears explicitly in several of his texts. For example, Traherne's citation of Plato in *Century* III, 60 comes directly from fol. 48 of the *Ficino Notebook*;[52] and in chapter 13 of *Christian Ethicks*, 'Of Justice', he also cites Plato, this time the *Republic*, but again from the *Notebook*.[53] Carol Marks has drawn some parallels between Ficino and *Christian Ethicks*, the *Centuries* and the *Commonplace Book*,[54] and Diane Dreher has also noted Traherne's indebtedness to Ficino in the *Centuries*.[55] Catherine Owen has noted elements of Ficino in *Christian Ethicks*, but she asserts that what Traherne omits of Ficino is as important as what he includes. She analyses Traherne's notes on the *Charmides* and concludes that, in these notes,

> Ficino is drastically simplified, for Traherne jettisons abstruse comparison with Moses, Adam, Enoch and Elijah. More significant is the omission of a passage which spiritualizes Socrates' praise of beauty, limiting its application to the mind, and including the body only in

---

51 On the significance of the use of Traherne's own hand versus the hand of an amanuensis in his note-taking and composition of works see Carol Marks, 'Traherne's *Church's Year-Book*', *PBSA*, 60 (1966), pp. 44–66.

52 C, III, 60 reads: 'I no sooner discerned this but I was (as Plato saith, *In summa Rationis arce quies habitat*) seated in a throne of repose and perfect rest.' And on fol. 48 of the Notebook he remarks: '*Ex ipsius vitae Archivis dimanavit divina ista sententia, qua utebatur Plato – In summa rationis arce, Quies habitat.*' For further evidence of specific links between the *Centuries* and the *Ficino Notebook* and for links with the *Commonplace Book* see Carol Marks, 'Traherne's *Ficino Notebook*', *Papers of the Bibliographic Society of America*, 63 (1969), pp. 77–8.

53 The passage from *Christian Ethicks* (p. 95), which reads: 'IT was a notable Observation of *Plato*, that by reason of our Dim Eyes we are not able to see immediately what Vertue does in Secret in the Soul. And therefore he says, that as an Old man that is bleary'd if he hath something given him to read in little Characters, finds it necessary first to see the same in Capital Letters; so to observe first what Vertue doth in a Commonwealth, is expedient to him, that would understand what it doth in his own Soul', is derived from the *Ficino Notebook* (fol. 37v), which reads: 'idque eleganti ad modum [Plato] facit similitudine sc. proinde investigandam esse justitiam, ac si quis non acute cernentibus literas parvas (proculque positas) legendas mandasset; deinde animadvertisset aliquis essent alibi in majori quodam loco majores & eas inde primo legens, ita demum minores (quae eadem sunt) consideraret.' I am indebted to Carol Marks for this observation.

54 Marks, 'Traherne's *Ficino Notebook*'.

55 See Diane Dreher, 'Traherne's Second *Century*: A Source in Ficino', *Notes and Queries*, 224 (1979), pp. 434–6. Here she notes Ficino's *De Amore* as a source for Traherne's threefold process of love – 'love begetting, love begotten, and love proceeding' – of C, II, 40.

so far as it images intellectual beauty, for in this omission we may trace Traherne's own conviction of the intrinsic value of the physical body, and indeed of the whole material world. The only two aspects of Ficino's summary of the 'Charmides' which Traherne records are themes which constantly recur in *Christian Ethicks*; in his abstract Traherne stresses the need for an active temperance as opposed to mere passive abstinence, and the essential unity of the virtues, temperance being inseparable from prudence and wisdom.[56]

Traherne's note-taking, in the *Ficino Notebook* as in the *Commonplace Book* and in the *Church's Year-Book*, was personal and practical: he freely altered the passages he copied, entirely omitting what did not interest him. Nor is there any hesitation in inserting editorial comments of his own. In places Ficino is reworded and rearranged.[57] Traherne uses Ficino with respect; but he does not always follow him. Like Hermes and Pico, as well as his other sources, Ficino is the material not the master.

Alongside Ficino stands Giovanni Pico della Mirandola, that other great fifteenth-century Italian, thirty years younger than Ficino and of the same school,[58] famous for his proclamation of human freedom and, like Ficino, a source for Traherne's concept of humanity. Traherne's assertions in the fourth *Century* that man may shape himself into whatever nature he pleases, that he may have what he desires and be what he wishes, is pure Pico. Traherne himself identifies C, IV, 76–7 and part of 74 as belonging to Pico, calling it alternately *De Dignitate Hominis* and 'an oration'.[59] But Pico is also present elsewhere, in Traherne's notion of seed and crop, in his all-pervasive belief that the human has power to change and become. This is the essence of what he takes from Pico, the notion of interior power, his insistence that 'The deformity or excellency is within' (C, IV, 78).

It is to Pico that the birth of the modern concept of man as a self-actualizing agent is often credited. Eugenio Garin's 1963 address, which

---

56 Catherine Owen, 'The Thought and Art of Thomas Traherne', unpublished MA thesis, University of London, 1957, pp. 29–30.

57 This is particularly the case with regard to Traherne's notes on the *Republic*. See Marks' observations in 'Traherne's *Ficino Notebook*', p. 80.

58 Ficino was born in 1433, Pico in 1463. They were the leading figures of the Platonic Academy of Florence, which was a group of friends and disciples gathered around Marsilio Ficino and dedicated to his teachings.

59 See C, IV, 74: 'For which cause Picus Mirandula admirably saith, in his tract *De Dignitate Hominis*' and C, IV, 78: 'This Picus Mirandula spake in an oration made before a most learned assembly in a famous university'.

CHOICE

identified Pico's *De Dignitate Hominis* as a proclamation of radical human freedom, stated that 'The conscious image of man, which is characteristic of the modern world, was born here [in *De Dignitate*]: man exists in the act that constitutes him, he exists in the possibility of liberating himself.'[60] And this is a view of Pico still commonly held by many scholars, who take Pico's account of the creation myth as his central statement on man.[61] Garin, in common with others, saw in Pico's work a view of man as scarcely distinct from God: 'Human knowledge had the cosmic function of actuating reality, uniting it and leading it to perfection. Only through man could it attain its end, reunited and integrated in knowledge'.[62] Echoes of this may be traced in Traherne's notion, previously stated, that God can achieve more through man's liberty than by his own; though, unlike Garin, Traherne's reading of Pico sees the human as already free, existent not 'in the possibility of liberating himself' but in an already given freedom. The view of Pico that sees him as a spokesman for radical freedom has unavoidable implications for the distinction between God and humanity. If man is self-creating activity, actuating and unifying reality in his knowledge, then he is scarcely distinguishable from God.[63] Taken to its extreme, man creates himself by his own choices, he is father of himself; the only condition to which he is subject is that there is no condition – liberty. In this interpretation of Pico there is no need for grace; and Pico has been seen by some as Pelagian, his faith in free will so strong as to absolutely preclude predestination and his belief in man as creator of his own destiny making him anthropocentric. Pico's man is himself a god.[64]

---

60 An address by Garin cited in William G. Craven, *Giovanni Pico della Mirandola: Symbol of His Age*, Geneva: Librairie Droz, 1981, pp. 26–7.

61 Craven asserts that ' Modern accounts of Pico's philosophy of man are based almost exclusively on this passage' (Craven, *Giovanni Pico della Mirandola*, p. 22). See, for instance, André Chastel, who called God's words to Adam 'the most famous passage in all Renaissance anthropology' (*The Age of Humanism*, London: Thames & Hudson, 1963, p. 228).

62 Craven on Garin (Craven, *Giovanni Pico della Mirandola*, p. 25).

63 In fact Pico makes the difference between God and the human quite clear: 'The difference between God and man is that God contains all things in himself as their origin [*principium*] and man contains all things in himself as their center [*medium*]. Hence in God all things are of better stamp than in themselves, whereas in man inferior things are of noble mark and the superior are degenerate.' In man, inferior things existed in a better form and superior things in a less worthy form. (Eugenio Garin, *Giovanni Pico della Mirandola*, Florence, 1937, p. 202; cited in Craven, *Giovanni Pico della Mirandola*, p. 85).

64 See Craven, *Giovanni Pico della Mirandola*, pp. 77–81, in which he outlines this view, starting with the criticisms levelled by Semprini (in 1936) and Pusino (in 1925) and tracing that line of thinking into the 1950s and '60s. See Philip Hughes's comment that Pico's sentiments in the *Oratio* are 'simply those of noble paganism' ('Pico della Mirandola', *Philosophia Reformata*, 23–4 (1958–59), p. 133).

These are similar to some of the criticisms also levelled at Traherne; and, as in Traherne's case, they too arise from incomplete readings of his texts. If the *Oratio* is taken to be the best and clearest statement of Pico's philosophy (and it has been so read by the majority of critics), one may indeed find that the criticisms above have some justification. But, as Craven's study has made clear, the *Oratio* may not be such a statement at all.[65] Even if it were, it would have to be balanced against Pico's man in *Heptaplus*, whose statuesque stance is more passive and recipient than the man of *Oratio*.

There is a tension in Traherne between the human whose greatness is a greatness of being, the man or woman in microcosm whose greatness simply *is* by virtue of his or her other place in creation, and the human whose greatness is a greatness of potential – what he or she may become. In the microcosm model, man is all; in the radical freedom model, he can become all. Craven sees the same tension in Pico's different portrayals of humankind in the *Oratio* and *Heptaplus*. His man of the *Oratio* is radically free, his man of the *Heptaplus* 'surprisingly non-operative, extraordinarily passive, almost statuesque'.[66] 'The contrast remains', writes Craven, 'between a dynamic view of man who is potentially all and a static view of man who is actually all.'[67] That Pico does not conclude for one or the other is another similarity with Traherne, whose man also stands in the tension between potential and the actual, most fully human at the crossroads where choice is to be exercised, where power is to be converted into act.

Craven sees the bold statement to Adam of the *Oratio* as a kind of rhetorical device. Traherne sees the same passage in similar terms – as poetically exaggerated but deeply serious at the same time. He writes of *De Dignitate Hominis*: 'Any man may perceive that he [Pico] permitteth his fancy to wander a little wantonly after the manner of a poet: but most deep and serious things are secretly hidden under his free and luxuriant language' (C, IV, 78). To Craven, Pico's lines on the human freedom to choose one's own nature in the *Oratio* is a moral

---

65 Craven contends that the *Oratio* was intended not as a bold statement of human dignity, but as a moral spur to his listeners. He writes: 'Once the intention of the *Oratio* is appreciated, it can be seen how misleading it has been to depict Pico as the typical Renaissance enthusiast for human freedom and dignity. His lines about man's freedom to choose his own nature are not a metaphysical but a moral statement, and they function as part of an inflated, rhetorical argument for the educational effectiveness of philosophy and theology' (Craven, *Giovanni Pico della Mirandola*, p. 45).
66 Charles Trinkaus, *In Our Image and Likeness: Humanity and Divinity in Italian Humanist Thought*, Chicago: Univesity of Chicago Press, vol. II, p. 519.
67 Craven, *Giovanni Pico della Mirandola*, p. 31.

rather than metaphysical statement. It is about what a person ought to do as much as it is about what he or she is capable of (and it has more to do with Pico's desire to establish himself in the minds of his fellows as a serious philosopher than with a statement of radical freedom). It is in this light that Traherne cites the *Oratio* because for Traherne the central concern is always a moral one – ultimately we choose to live in the image of God or we do not.

Garin and many others have emphasized the empowering nature of Pico's writings and, while the picture of radical freedom they have portrayed may be only a part of Pico, what they have to say about power and act is relevant to this study of Traherne. Traherne's human, like Pico's, is both/and – potentially and actually great. His human's power to act is not radically free and fatherless, self-generated and perpetuated, but power to act an act transformed by grace into something resembling the divine. Ficino's concept of the centrality of man in the universe was transformed by Pico's doctrine of human freedom into the idea that all the universe and all reality are concentrated in human knowledge. However, because of the superiority of the will over abstract knowledge, it is in choice that man's greatness resides.[68] This is something Pico shares with Traherne who described the liberty of human will as 'the foundation of his Glory'.[69] But where modern humanism has read Pico's man existing in the act that constitutes him, existing in the possibility of liberating himself, Traherne's human already has liberty within, is born free in the image of God – the choice of Traherne's human is towards conversion into love.[70] Where modern humanism sees the human person as dehumanized and degraded in the absence of choice, Traherne's human, given dignity by right, simply by being alive and made in the image of God, remains fully human even when choice is denied. The importance of choice then, for Traherne, is not that by it we are made human but that in its exercise what kind of human we are is made evident. In our choices we show whether we are tuned to greed or to generosity, to hope or to despair, to life or to death; this is what makes choice so important to Traherne. We seem to be back on the territory of *A Sober View* in its urgencies of choice, and we see that, for all his much-noted connections with Renaissance humanism, the most pressing choice is this one – whether or not to be converted into love. What is 'radical' about Traherne's humanism is its bold claim that the human body has, in the incarnation, become the

---

68 Ibid., p.26.
69 *SV*, fol. 45v.
70 See C, IV, 80.

house of God; that the human heart may become God's home and the human soul God's bride.

Power and Act

In *The Kingdom of God* Traherne discusses the greatness of the human by beginning with the Image of God as the highest thing that God could create. He then considers this image in a body, and that humans are greater than the angels, and concludes the entire work with an exposition of why man is greater in an Estate of Trial than he would be in any other state.[71] In this model the human person is the means and the end, the user, enjoyer, perfecter and co-creator. By this double nature, men and women are not only 'Lord[s] and Heir[s] of the world',[72] head of all creatures, but also hold in common with the angels a life of the spirit. In *The Kingdom of God*, Traherne's 'Man' is both/and, by his physicality making useful the things of the earth and by his spirituality seeing into the end and causes of all things he has made useful:

> For neither can immaterial Spirits enjoy the Glory of the Day, or use the Light, or need the Sun, or feed upon Air, or Eat, or Drink. Nor can Dust & Ashes see into the cause and End of Things, or Weigh the Lov & Goodness of the Donor, or Sing, or celebrat his Everlasting prayses. Therfore by a Miracle of Eternal Wisdom, the Way was found to Joyn, & unite these two together, that as the one did reap the Benefit, the other might return the Glory. (*KOG*, fol. 348r–v)

In this way he is both the means and the end of the world's perfection:

> For as a Marriner is the Assistent form of his Boat & a Master of his Ship, that stears, & governs, and makes it usefull: so is Man in the World the Assistent form or εντελnχια, that makes it usefull, & give[s] it its perfection ... The use & perfection of the World depends upon Man as much as that of the Body does upon the Soul; or that of a Ship, on its Governor, & Master.[73]

---

[71] This is outlined by the chapter titles of chapters 36, 40, 41 and 42.
[72] *SM*, I, 82. Man is also 'head of all the Creatures' (*SM*, III, 95).
[73] *KOG*, fol. 348v; cf. 'Men being Angels by their Souls, have Bodies besides, that they may be united as the Angels are, and in another manner *make use of the World*' (*MSD*, p. 74, italics mine).

That a person 'makes useful' the world is more than a statement of utility. It is a statement of worth. As we have seen in chapter two, what is useful is valuable; and so, in being made the εντελησια, man is given power to make all things treasure. The human is needed as the perceiver of treasure without whom there could be no treasure. Does this make Traherne, as Dobell and others have suggested, a Berkeleian before Berkeley was born?[74] Not at all. Despite the apparently idealistic tenor of those much quoted lines from the third stanza of 'My Spirit':

> ... I could not tell,
>   Whether the Things did there
>   Themselvs appear,
> Which in my spirit truly seemd to dwell;
>   Or whether my conforming mind
>   Were not alone even all that shind[75]

Traherne does not doubt the reality of the 'objective world' independent of the perceiver's mind. In fact, as Sandbank notes, 'The resemblance, discredited by Berkeley, between the outer world and our own perceptions and ideas, is, to Traherne, the central miracle of human knowledge.'[76] Traherne's 'things' are 'remote, yet felt even here', 'The utmost Star, / Tho seen from far' is present to his eye. The perceiving soul and its object are united by the soul's act of perception that, rather than giving the object its reality, lifts the already real object to its true usefulness. By this being present with 'the Being it doth note' the soul's 'Essence [Capacitie] is transform'd into a tru / and perfect Act'. Aristotle's account of the process of thinking as a transition from power to act, from capacity to actuality, is married to the Neo-Platonic notion of the spiritualization of the material – or, as Traherne often describes, making 'thoughts' of 'things'. This returning of the world to the creator will be discussed at greater length in chapter four.

That Traherne's human inhabits this place between power and act, between the potential and the actual is, as I have hinted earlier, a unique privilege. The human is the golden mean whose role and whose power is the exercise of liberty through choice. Traherne writes that 'there

---

74 See Dobell, 'Introduction', pp. lxxxii–lxxxiv and Wade pp. 173–4. See also Stewart, *The Expanded Voice*, p. 62; and A. L. Clements 'On the Mode and Meaning of Traherne's Mystical Poetry: "The Preparative"', *Studies in Philology*, 61 (1964), p. 515.

75 'My Spirit', ll. 46–51. I concur with Sandbank that these lines should be regarded as a hyperbolic expression of wonder rather than as an indication of an underlying philosphical idealism (see Sandbank, 'Thomas Traherne', p. 128).

76 Sandbank, 'Thomas Traherne', p. 128.

are three Distinct Classes of being, Matter, Power and Act. Matter is the Worst, or vilest in it self, Act the best or most highly perfect. and Power as it were a mean between them both' (*KOG*, fol. 331). It is this position of power, between pure matter and pure act, that Traherne sees as decisive. It is in this sense that the human position as the golden clasp comes into its fullness. Yes, the human is beautiful as the image of God, God's picture in a curious case 'beset with stars', a messenger between the creatures, the interval between time and eternity, the Hymanaeus marrying the creator and his creatures. All of these things, writes Traherne, are great, but they are not the principal reason for human greatness. The excellency of humanity resides in one's ability to weigh and reason, love and admire,[77] ultimately to desire and choose. As, in the *Centuries*, Traherne quotes from Pico, in the voice of God:

> 'O Adam, we have given thee neither a certain seat, nor a private face, nor a peculiar office, that whatsoever seat or face or office thou dost desire thou mayest enjoy. All other things have a nature bounded within certain laws; thou only art loose from all, and according to thy own council in the hand of which I have put thee, may'st choose and prescribe what nature thou wilt thyself. I have placed thee in the middle of the world, that from thence thou mayest behold on every side more commodiously everything in the whole world. We have made thee neither heavenly nor earthly, neither mortal nor immortal, that being the honoured former and framer of thyself, thou mayest shape thyself into what nature thyself pleasest!'[78]

And these choices have eternal significance for the soul. They are not just about choosing what one may become here on earth but what one will become in eternity, since:

> As by the seed we conjecture what plant will arise, and know by the acorn what tree will grow forth, or by the eagle's egg, what kind of bird; so do we by the powers of the soul upon Earth, know what kind of Being, Person and Glory it will be in the Heavens.[79]

---

77 See C, IV, 75: 'He desired some one that might weigh and reason, love the beauty, and admire the vastness of so great a work [as creation].'

78 C, IV, 76. Here Traherne is quoting from Pico's *Oratio* which Traherne refers to by the commonly known title *De Dignitate Hominis* (C, IV, 75). As Craven points out (*Giovanni Pico della Mirandola*, p. 34), Pico's concern is with the use that the human may make of freedom rather than a proclamation of that freedom as absolute.

79 C, IV, 70. Here Traherne is very like Pico, whom he quotes in C, IV, 77.

Traherne is equally enthralled by what humanity is and by what humanity may become. Just as we may see in Pico the man whose greatness is actual (Pico's man of the *Oratio*) and the man whose greatness is potential (Pico's man of *Heptaplus*), so Traherne's high esteem of humanity is founded in both our potential and actual greatness. In fact, it is in the very interplay of these two models of man that the full weight of human greatness may be perceived. We spring from greatness into greatness; made in the divine image, we yearn for divinity. What is more, we are given the power to choose, to see, to act. We are 'Astonishing and Stupendous' creatures who 'can See Eternity, and Possess infinity' (*SM*, III, 90). Furthermore, the human may become God's 'voluntary work-man' (*SM*, III, 45) imitating God in blessing and giving.

And yet Traherne also says that human nature is 'Nauseating and weary' and that man is 'confined' (*SM*, III, 65–6). 'There is in man a Double selfe, according as He is in God, or the world. In the world He is confined . . . but in God he is evry where.'[80] There is a nothingness to Traherne's soul that is, paradoxically, also part of its greatness. In the *Select Meditatons* he insists:

> From all Eternity to my First Conception I was Nothing, from my first Conception to all Eternity I am a Being. From all Eternity my Being was with God Almighty. to all Eternity my Nothing will be before my Face. From all eternity to all Eternity my nothing and my Being Endless are unmovable: and I in both infinitly Greater . . . Gods fulness in Mans Emptiness Best Appearing. (*SM*, III, 78)

This 'nothing' or 'emptiness' is the other side of Traherne's great theme of 'Capacitie' and it is one of the features that makes the soul less than divine – Traherne's human soul lacks spontaneity. Its rich inner life depends completely upon outside forms lent by the creator. It is capable of infinity, but it is nothing until recipient.[81] This is an essentially Aristotelian notion: 'The mind', says Aristotle, 'is in a manner potentially all objects of thought, but is actually none of them until it thinks.'[82]

---

80 *SM*, II, 92. Here Traherne refers specifically to man's capacity for infinity and eternity – how his thoughts can touch eternity.

81 See, for instance, 'Thoughts III', in which thoughts – those things without which the soul is 'useless' (l. 16) – turn 'From nothing to Infinitie . . . Even in a Moment' (ll. 37–38). See also 'O Lord, of myself I am nothing, and therfore all that I am more I receive from thee' (*MSD*, p. 75).

82 *De anima*, 429b30–1; trans. R. D. Hicks, Cambridge: Cambridge University Press, 1907, p. 135; cited in Sandbank, 'Thomas Traherne', p. 123.

To Traherne these potentialities or capacities are 'Pure Empty Powers' ('The Preparative', l. 51). The mind is 'Changeable, Capacious, Easy, free' ('Thoughts III', l. 35). The soul is 'naturally very dark, and deformed and empty' until filled by the world with 'amiable ideas', for 'God and all things must be contained in our souls, that we may become glorious personages' (C, II, 84).

In this portrayal of the soul, the soul is similar to the child of Traherne's early innocence, and it is a measure of the coherence of Traherne's thought that his consideration of one theme should lead so easily to the other. As he writes at the very beginning of the *Centuries*: 'An empty book is like an Infant's Soul, in which any thing may be written. It is capable of all Things, but containeth nothing.'[83] Traherne's *tabula rasa* is more than a clean slate; it is a stage of both capacity and receptivity. The pre-knowledge emptiness of Traherne's child is the best condition for ideal knowledge, which is why Traherne writes that he 'must becom a Child again',[84] must 'retire' and 'get free'.[85] With this infant clarity, we would 'naturally see those things to the enjoyment of which' we are 'naturally born'[86] as does the child of the third *Century*, for whom 'The corn was orient and immortal wheat, which never should be reaped, nor was ever sown', for whom 'Boys and girls tumbling in the street, and playing, were moving jewels' (C, III, 3). The child's mind is 'disengaged'[87] and perfectly receptive and nearer to happiness. But disentanglement requires change. 'Unlearning' is one expression of the beginning of such a change: 'now I unlearn, and become as it were a little child again, that I may enter into the Kingdom of God'.[88] Yet 'unlearning' as simply a kind of re-education is insufficient. As with Nicodemus in the third chapter of the Gospel of John, new birth is requisite. 'My early tutor is the womb', writes Traherne; he flies 'to the womb' that he 'may yet new-born become'.[89] Again the image is of a return to nothingness, to a starting point of emptiness and void:

---

83 C, I, 1. In this case Traherne promises to take on the role of creator, filling the empty book with 'profitable wonders' for his reader as God filled the world and infinity with objects for the soul's capacity.

84 'Innocence', l. 60; see also C, III, 5.

85 'The Preparative', ll. 69–70. Notice also his invitation in *Inducements to Retiredness* to retire from the world for the betterment of the soul.

86 Ibid.

87 Ibid. l. 63.

88 Ibid.

89 'The Return', ll. 3, 11–12.

God Hath don more for us then we could find out How to Imagine. All the world is in his Infinity, and His Infinity within us. yet hath He made the Soul Empty, as if there were noe Such Infinity within us, no such world, no God, no Being. nay not a Soul till we meditate upon it . . . (SM, IV, 13)

The 'Infant-Ey' may be a perfect instrument of reception; it cannot, however, act upon the world and restore it back to God. That can only be achieved by the mind renewed. The pure and empty receptivity of the soul, typified in the child's mind, is the venue for cognition; it is the active mind of the adult, however, that can perform that particular task that Traherne assigns to humanity – the re-creation and exaltation of the physical world.[90]

That the human role as exalter of creation involves transition is exactly appropriate since human beings are themselves in transition between power and act. Unlike God, who is 'Power from all Eternity transformed into Act', the soul is pure power. It is actually nothing – derived, dependent and subject to accident, it is primarily great by virtue of its potential. As Traherne explains in *The Kingdom of God*:

Admitting the Soul to be meer and naked Power, being Divested of all Substance beside, it is next to Nothing, and yet it is the most Glorious Being in the whole World, It differs from God inevitably in these folowing things, it had a beginning, it received its being from another, it was made out of nothing, it dependeth on another, it is Mutable, it may be turnd into Nothing, it is compounded of power and Act, wheras God is all Act, it is obliged, and owes all it has to its Author, it is compounded of essence and existence, and is a substance subject of Accidents. (KOG, fol. 330r)

The soul is partial. It is in transition, one part of it moving towards act while the rest remains unexerted. It may seem to be 'in a long swoon, or a Dead Sleep', or

---

90 The divine light that was ours by birth and lost by the advent of custom into our lives, remaining latent in us can, according to Traherne, fed by experience and the application of reason, re-emerge as our guiding principle – our way of seeing, which is at the same time our way of life. And this new form of sight is even better than the first. 'I remember the time', writes Traherne, 'when the dust of the streets were as precious as Gold to my infant eyes, and now they are more precious to the eye of reason' (C, I, 25). Whereas the first light was purely intuitive, the second light is illuminated by reason and valued more highly because it is so hard won.

It may be compounded of Power and Act, as it is when the Soul having power to think and desire Innumerable Things, thinks of one, or desires this or that in Particular without thinking or desiring the residue: for then its Power is in Part exerted, and so it is partly Act, and partly Power.[91]

The desiring soul, the soul exerted, the soul extended: this is the soul in progress towards the divine. This is the soul moving from nothingness to substance, from potential to actual. The soul in motion is the soul at its most quintessentially human, at its most alive.

'Life is an Abilitie to Apprehend, and Move', says Traherne in a statement that he found it necessary to underscore in his manuscript. This is where the spiritual discernment or right apprehension discussed in chapter two meets the power to choose of this chapter. We apprehend, value, desire and move in one fluid movement. This is, for Traherne, the essence of what it is to be alive: 'for whatosever liveth is able to conceiv, and move in like manner: at least inwardly, by its very conception of Desire'. The inward movement or sense of desire is as significant as the realization or satisfaction of that desire. He goes so far as to claim that 'all that is in it [the soul] is power and Desire', and then he clarifies in a statement that exalts human desire from the level of a gut reaction to an act of will: 'or rather simple power, power to perceiv, or power to desire. Desire is an Act without which Life may be. But Power to desire is in it of Necessitie.'[92]

It is desire that is the engine of the extending soul. By desire the soul extends itself to all its objects; by exercising the power to desire the soul chooses and its power is poured out into act. When it sees as God sees and loves as he loves, desires all that he desires and extends itself to all objects, reaching at once to all things, 'then is its power poured out, and Transformed; and the Act wherin it appeareth will be so like God, that the Sun in a mirror will not more resemble the Sun in the Heavens ... For God will be the Soul of the Soul it self' (*KOG*, fol. 330v).

Here in *The Kingdom of God*, as so many times elsewhere, we may see how much the greatness of the human soul is linked with its ability to desire. In its essence the soul is nothing; in its capacity it is infinite. And the motor of its movement from potential towards actual is its desire. Inasmuch as it reflects the divine image, the soul is glorious.

---

[91] This and the immediately preceding quotation are from *KOG*, fol. 330v.

[92] This and all the quotations in this paragraph are from *KOG*, fol. 276v. Cf. *KOG*, fol. 334v, in which the power to enjoy is extolled. The power to enjoy is 'desirable' and 'blesssed' but always seondary to the power to desire.

CHOICE

With Hermes, Pico and Ficino, Traherne proclaims that the human is the golden clasp, the greatest miracle and the wonder of the world. And what we may become, and the very fact that we may *choose* to become at all, is the expression of that greatness. It is this that makes the human creature a link between two worlds. What one may become is a question of how one lives. 'If I live truely in the Divine Image I shall appear among kings a Greater king', Traherne reminds us, stretching himself to his fullest height:

> He made Thee for Himselfe in makeing Thee Like Himselfe. Despaire not, Forgett not, Be not careless, but Liv always at this Height. He made Thee for Himselfe, by makeing Thee Like God. when He made Thee His Image He Intended that thou shouldst Live Like a God . . . *(SM, IV, 15)*

It is in this most profound sense that what we are and what we may become is intimately linked to the issue of choice.

Free Agency

Despite what one might imagine, given Traherne's reputation as a poet of original innocence, for him all virtue is an acquired habit, not a natural gift. In *Christian Ethicks*, Traherne's study of the virtues, it is the will intending, the soul exerting itself in power: in other words, it is choice that converts natural gift into virtue. Love, for instance, that primary virtue, is bound by choice.

The extent to which we as humans are free to choose is the compelling question to which, as we have seen, Traherne devotes the entire newly discovered work *A Sober View of Dr Twisse*. In it he writes: 'Now Love is a free Affection which cannot be compeled, nor be without freedom' (*SV*, fol. 26r). And no other actions can be good unless they spring from love, performed willingly and with desire. Traherne insists that

> unless they are Willingly performed and with Desire God doth them instead of the Soul; if the soul be forced to do them whether it will or no; they are not fruits of Righteousness; but servile and Inanimate, their Beauty is Destroyed. (*SV*, fol. 26r)

In his chapter in *Christian Ethicks* on the virtue of magnanimity, Traherne contrasts the greatness of those who are born to greatness with the greatness of those who choose it against all odds. Of these he writes:

> others consider what they have to do, and make an election, and though they are born in a poor and despicable estate, are not Magnanimous by nature, or Fortune, but by *Choice* and voluntary Election ... and this is the Off-spring of the *Will*, the true and genuine *Vertue*. (CE, p. 232)

Over and over again, moral goodness is linked with freedom of choice. Although his Puritan background might lead one to expect him to take a strong Calvinist line, the doctrines of election and free will are held in balance in *A Sober View*. Traherne will deny neither, and yet the tension in which election and free will are held is an uncomfortable one.

This is not surprising given the immense strife that surrounded the debate as it was raging all around him. The Calvinist/Arminian debate about election and free will – do we choose God or does God choose us – seems to most modern readers largely philosophical, a kind of metaphysical conundrum, interesting in its way but hardly likely to raise the temperature of debate; certainly not of any international or national importance. In Traherne's day, of course, it was just the opposite: a hugely significant political/social/theological question, which concerned not only the way humankind in emerging enlightenment terms might see itself but also what the shape of government and the future of the monarchy might be. By the Calvinist or Arminian flag one nailed one's political colours to the mast. Careers, livelihoods – indeed, many believed, national sovereignty – were at stake.

In *A Sober View*, Traherne's indentification with fellow clergyman Robert Sanderson is plain. Sanderson, who did not want to lose his living lest his congregation be left in the hands of those

> as will be sure to misteach them one way or other ... either by instilling into them puritanical and superstitious principles that they may the more securely exercise their Presbyterian tyranny over their judgements, consciences, persons and estates; or else by setting up new lights before them to lead them into a maze of Anabaptistical confusion and frenzy[93]

---

[93] Sanderson, 'The Case of the Liturgy' in *The Works of Robert Sanderson, D. D.*, ed. W. Jacobson, Oxford, 1854, vol. 5, pp. 36–57; cited in Peter Lake, 'Serving God and the

is echoed in Traherne's recorded view of Anabaptists in *Commentaries of Heaven*.[94]

Sanderson had been an ardent Calvinist, a preacher of sermons as zealous as any Puritan,[95] who repudiated Puritanism, its proud non-conformity, its holier-than-thou attitude to those outside the Church, its tendency to denounce things that were in themselves (according to Scripture) indifferent, and the fact that this brought all religion into disrepute. He hated the way that Puritanism played on the fears and insecurities of honest seekers, and the 'world of base and unworthy pamphlets that like the frogs of Egypt croak in every corner of the land'.[96] Here we may see some temperamental similarities with Traherne, who also abjured false piety, writing in *Christian Ethicks* against those who confuse the heart of religion and the form of religion:

> IT is a great Error to mistake the *Vizor* for the *Face* . . . mistaking the Alterations and Additions that are made upon the Fall of Man, for the whole Business of Religion. And yet this new constellation of Vertues, that appeareth aboveboard, is almost the only thing talked of and understood in the World. Whence it is that the other Duties, which are the *Soul* of Piety, being unknown . . . Religion appears like a sour and ungratefull Thing to the World, impertinent to bliss, and void of Reason; Whereopon GOD is suspected and hated, Enmity against GOD and *Atheism* being brought into and entertained in the World. (CE, p. 34)

In 1657 Sanderson had what Peter Lake describes as 'a brief flirtation' with Presbyterianism, after which his friend Henry Hammond pulled him back into line.[97] In his 1657 edition of *Thirty-four Sermons*, which was the fifth edition, comments from the 1620s that had been anti-Pelagian and anti-Arminian were rewritten as solely anti-Pelagian and some vociferous marginal notes such as one that described 'our

---

Times: The Calvinist Conformity of Robert Sanderson', *Journal of British Studies*, 27, 2 (April 1988), pp. 81–116.

94 'The Opinion of the Anabaptists seems the most innocent, & is one of the most thorney & difficult opinions in the World: yet by a strange & (almost) unsearchable fate, it is the seed plot of Heresies, & the grand Nursery of Schismes & Disordrs. No man is an Anabaptist long but he sucks in some other horrible Opinion soon after' (*COH*, 'Baptism').

95 See C. H. George and K. George, *The Protestant Mind of the English Reformation, 1570–1640*, Princeton: Princeton University Press, 1961, who make the point that Sanderson in many ways covered the same ideological territory as the Puritans.

96 From a visitation sermon preached at Grantham in 1641: Sanderson, *Thirty-four Sermons*, 5th edition of the 1657 collection of his sermons, London, 1671, pt 1, p. 6.

97 Peter Lake, 'Serving God and the Times', p. 112.

English Arminians' as promulgating 'semi-pelagian subtleties on purpose to make sound truth odious and their own corrupt novelties more passable and plausible' were omitted altogether.[98] The letter from Sanderson to Hammond that forms the basis of much of Traherne's *A Sober View* was the result of a campaign on Hammond's part to get Sanderson to conform to more Arminian views.

Not only did Sanderson object to the individuality of (sometimes erroneous) opinon that Puritanism fostered, he also objected to the Puritan division between the 'godly' and the 'ungodly', arguing that no one but God could know the human heart and that therefore it was unethical to judge a person's spiritual state by his or her habits. God kept 'this royalty unto himself to be the only searcher of the hearts and reynes of others'.[99] To Sanderson, Puritans, like papists, attempted to take unto themselves the authority that remains only with God.

By proclaiming the doctrine of election – that God did the choosing – the Calvinist movement intended to wrest authority from the Catholic Church, its ordinances and indulgences, and restore it to God alone. However, thought Sanderson, they had instead replaced the Roman magisterium with a Puritan ideology every bit as authoritative as the system they had sought to abolish. The doctrine of election had evolved into complicated systems – the supralapsarians, who believed that God planned the doctrine of election before the creation of the world, and the sublapsarians, who saw Election as a result of the fall, a kind of plan B after plan A had failed – that excluded and included as rigorously as the practices of excommunication and indulgence had done before.

Significantly, in the section of the letter between Sanderson and Hammond that Traherne quotes in *A Sober View*, Sanderson locates the decree of election subsequent to Adam's fall so that 'so noble a creature' as humanity 'might not perish everlastingly'. And reprobation is restricted to the absence of election. In other words, God did not plan the processes of election and reprobation from before creation (the supralapsarian view). They were not 'written in' to the original plan for humanity but a necessary result of the Fall (the sublapsarian view). They are therefore, for Traherne, not part of an ideal construct. Like the offices of government and king, and the 'harsh and sour vir-

---

98 From a visitation sermon of 1619, p. 34 in *Twelve Sermons*, London, 1637. For a more detailed account of the alterations to Sanderson's sermons see Lake, 'Serving God and the Times', p. 85, n. 12 and pp. 112–16.

99 A sermon preached in the church of Grantham in 1620; cited in Lake, 'Serving God and the Times', p. 97.

CHOICE

tues' of patience, forbearance and the like, Traherne sees these decrees of election and reprobation as necessary and practical answers to the advent of sin.

If such were the similarities between Sanderson and Traherne, Traherne had as much in common with Henry Hammond, to whom Sanderson's letter was addressed. In Hammond, whom Traherne described in *Christian Ethicks* as 'a Great Divine of our English Zion', Traherne found support for his notion of heaven here as well as hereafter: '*The greater part of our eternal happiness will consist in a grateful Recognition* (not of our Joyes to come, but) *of Benefits already received.*'[100] The title *A Sober View of Dr Twisse* would lead one to expect the following 28 chapters to be devoted to the writings of Dr Twisse; in fact Traherne dispatches William Twisse and Samuel Hoard fairly early on in the work and concentrates instead on fine tuning his views to the views of Hammond and Sanderson, with whom, as we have seen, he has more in common. That is not to say, however, that Traherne abandons Calvinism; the first three sections of *A Sober View* make it clear that faith is a gift in which God takes the initiative, and Traherne's repeated reminder that 'all things work together for good', that 'even the Wicked and Rebellious hav' glorious duties to perform is not mere positive thinking but an affirmation of central Calvinist tenets. At the same time Traherne argues for the importance of human freedom, freedom to choose: in the same chapter, a few pages on he writes, 'no Action [is] Glorious that is not free' (*SV*, III, ll. 221–2). An apparent contradiction occurs here only if we read the freedom assertions out of their context. For this is not a proclamation of radical humanism but a testament to the wisdom of almighty power in ordaining human freedom. His Almighty God wants free and glorious companions. The king seeks a noble bride. 'For all these Causes God made Man free that by chusing Voluntarily to prize and love, he might do that of his own Accord, which was infinitly delightful to God Almighty: and therin be infinitly Glorious' (*SV*, III, ll. 243–5).

It is this matter of choice that fascinates Traherne and becomes the focus of the rest of the work. The fourth section considers the reprobate, that is the un-elect. Traherne claims that the reprobate is passed over so that he or she might be good of his or her own accord. The reason, therefore, of reprobation is not God's hatred of the sinner but his love of righteous action. The sinner is not converted irresistibly; but that is not to say that he or she is damned (*SV*, IV, ll. 150–70). Free

---

100 *CE*, p. 213. The words in brackets are Traherne's addition, which glosses the meaning towards present happiness.

grace is given to the elect, free will to the reprobate (*SV*, IV, ll. 233–4). This is why, Traherne argues, 'many are called but few are chosen';[101] it is because what God most desires is the freely chosen repentance of those who are not the elect. In Traherne's hands, rather than being a stamp of approval, a mark of distinction that secures membership of an exclusive band of holy brothers and sisters, election becomes rather a dull way of being a Christian. He seems more interested in the reprobate than in the elect, not out of charity, because they are the pitiful ones knocking on the door, but out of fascination, because they are the dynamic ones with real choices to make. While never denying God's almighty power, he delights most in the limitation of its use. Like the king in *The Merchant of Venice*, whose mercy becomes him better than his throne and crown, Traherne's God is magnified in the restraint of his power.

The very fact that he discusses the doctrine of election in such detail indicates that it is a hugely important doctrine to him, and the many internal inconsistencies that arise in his working out suggest that it was also a difficult one. In all this, the issue to which he consistently returns is the issue of free will. Over and over again he asserts the importance of actions done of one's own accord.[102] Traherne agrees with Twisse's restricting election to the giving or forbearing to give grace since, for him, damnation or salvation as an everlasting condition of humankind dehumanizes the person.[103]

And yet he never seems to resolve the difficult question 'Just how free are we?' in this work. If God's dealing with the elect is 'irresistible' are they not thereby compelled rather than voluntary? With a violence reminiscent of that in Donne's 'Batter my Heart three-personed God', Traherne describes the conversion of the elect in terms that sound almost like a kind of spiritual rape. The 'immortal Seed' is 'implanted in them' and 'tho in the Instant of recieving it they are meerly passive, are wrought upon by violence'. They are 'Invaded' that they may be

---

101 Traherne is quoting Matt. 22.14 when he writes 'O that there were such a Heart in them! This is that which God chiefly desires, this answereth all his Longings, and this filleth yea Crowneth his Endeavors. And for this Caus is it that so few are Elected, so many Reprobated, so many are called, so few are chosen' (*SV*, IV, ll. 241–5).

102 '[H]e requireth them all to repent and believ and make themselves a clean Heart, and this he desireth infinitly that they would do, but do it freely of their own Accord' (*SV*, fol. 25r.) Here he is referring to the prophet Ezekiel's admonition to Israel (Ezek. 18.30, 31).

103 'In restraining the Decrees of Election and Reprobation purely to the Act of giving or forbearing to give Grace he [Twisse] hath Done very Accurately, and Wisely' (*SV*, fol. 23v).

after it voluntary and Righteous Agents . . . For it is easy to observe, that above all things in the World God Desires that men should turn of themselves and that having all Means and Motives therunto, Should repent and believ of their own Accord.[104]

It is at this point that his 'critical reader' finds it necessary to comment in the marginalia: 'this seems contradictory to the last lines & to me is so in itself for graunting all have prevening Grace it is Impossible but it [the soul] must cooperate in the conversion, not [be] wholly passive' (*SV*, fol. 35r). Traherne manoeuvres around the question of passivity, suggesting that in the moment of conversion the elect soul is both passive and active at once, just as it is rebellious and righteous at once – rebellious in its passivity and righteous in its action of conforming to and complying with the work of God.[105] He continues, 'For there is no Instant of time wherin a Living Soul Is meerly Passive'[106] and 'But at the Instant of its Conversion it is Active. For it is never converted till it doth voluntarily turn from Sin to Righteousness' (*SV*, fol. 35r). He then struggles to maintain the simultaneity of this passive/active position by claiming that the soul is these things simultaneously in time which it cannot be simultaneously in nature, and that the soul is passive as it is inspired and active as it consents. Nevertheless, 'Just how free are we really?' is a question with which Traherne is not comfortable and which he never really resolves satisfactorily in this work, though all his efforts do lead him inexorably back to his basic premise that all righteousness is founded upon freedom of choice. Under this umbrella both the elect and the reprobate huddle, each given a different kind of chance to do good works 'of their own accord'. 'For that they may herafter do Good Works of their own Accord are the one now Invaded: and that in this Act the other might be righteous of their own Accord are the other emitted' (*SV*, fol. 35v).

---

104 *SV*, fol. 35r. On the next page he restates: 'For that they may herafter do Good Works of their own Accord are the one now Invaded: and that in this Act the other might be righteous of their own Accord are the other emmited' (*SV*, fol. 35v). A few folios later he again speaks of this 'invasion' as distasteful to God: 'For to convert . . . in a way so uncouth and unacceptable to God, as that is of invading many Wills is altogether as much if not more than the redeeming of Sinners while there was a Hope they would be righteous' (*SV*, fol. 39v).
105 'The Act of Conversion therfore being Instantaneous, it seemeth they were Righteous and Rebellious together. They are rebellious in being meerly passive, they are Righteous in Being Active: that is in Conforming to, and complying with the Work of God in a voluntary maner' (*SV*, fol. 35r).
106 *SV*, fol. 35r, followed by 'Or if it be in that Instant it is truly Rebelling. For it is its Duty to be vigorous and Active, and therfore in being Passive is being Rebellious; were it possible it could be purely and meerly Passive.'

I think that what Traherne is striving towards in his contradictions between freedom and election is a resolution between interior and exterior freedom. Not forgetting the particular and influential political context to Traherne's writings on Calvinism and Arminianism, alongside this runs a larger, timeless debate about human freedom in general. Is freedom something that is given to us; does it come to us from the outside, by the removal of exterior restraint? Or is it primarily an interior matter, a case of what we feel ourselves to be, something you keep rather than gain, like integrity or dignity? This he deals with rather more satisfactorily in *Christian Ethicks*. In chapter 12, 'Of Holiness', he describes human liberty as a quality that is as necessary to the whole creation as it is to individuals, since it is this liberty, this power to love, praise, honour and act that separates a man from a stone, a woman from a star:

> To make Creatures infinitely free and leave them to their Liberty is one of the Best of all Possible Things; and so necessary that no Kingdome of Righteousness could be without it . . . There is no Kingdome of Stones nor of Trees, nor of Stars; only a Kingdome of Men and Angels. Who were they divested of their Liberty would be reduced to the Estate of Stones and Trees, neither capable of Righteous Actions, nor able to Honor, or to Love, or praise . . . So that all the Glory of the world depends on the Liberty of Men and Angels . . . Either to refuse to give the Power, or Having given it, to interpose and determine it without their Consent, was alike detrimental to the whole Creation. (CE, pp. 90–1)

In the following lines he again confronts the problem of divine imposition that we saw in *A Sober View*. If God imposes his goodness or love or will upon his creatures what good can that do? Any imposition of a good, such as dignity or freedom with which a human is born, is only good in as much as it allowed to be used, or sadly neglected, at the behest of the recipient:

> There is as much difference between a Willing Act of the Soul it self, and an Action forced on the Will, determined by another, as there is between a man that is dragged to the Altar, whether he will or no, and the man that comes with all his Heart with musick and Dancing to offer sacrifice. That GOD should not be able to deserve our Love, unless he himself made us to Love him by violence, is the Greatest Dishonour to him in the World. (CE, pp. 91–2)

But all of these considerations of freedom move towards the fundamental assertion from which they also spring: that 'no force of external Power can make us free; whatever it is that invades our Liberty, destroys it' (*CE*, p. 93).

Whatever *invades* our liberty destroys it. This then is not freedom from but freedom to. Just as choice, in Traherne, is not primarily about gaining radical and fatherless freedom so that we may call ourselves human but rather about how the choices we exercise show the kind of human we are, so freedom is not about raising ourselves out of a lower state of bondage but about living in the freedom that is already ours by birthright. We may or may not live as free. We may or may not choose to be converted into love. Because every choice, every action, every thing is connected, Traherne claims that the loss of human freedom is detrimental to the whole creation. As a new Adam or a new Eve, in the exercise of choice and liberty we take the world with us. Redemption of the person and redemption of the world are inextricably linked.

In *A Sober View*, Traherne seems more interested in the reprobate than in the elect whose destiny is already sealed. It is the reprobate whose greater freedom of choice offers the greater glimpse of glory, whose eventual repentance and return to the fold causes more joy in Heaven than the just 99 who rest secure.[107] And we are reminded that it is the reprobate who has been forgiven most who loves the most (*SV*, fol. 39v). It is characteristic of Traherne that his imagination fixes on the only two redeeming features of evil – that it affords the possibility of forgiveness and restoration, and that it is evidence of human freedom.[108] He writes that 'mans Power to sin proceeded from the Excessive Greatness of Gods Love, the Liberty of his Will being the foundation of his Glory' (*SV*, fol. 45v) with real conviction. For him reprobation is never forever because choice is such a fundamental part of being human. Where there is liberty of will, there may be repentance. Better still, there may be obedience. And so, in *A Sober View*, the purity or impurity of the soul is determined by its own choices, choices that constantly exercise our liberty and God's grace:

---

107 'Nay they trample on his Bowels and tread underfoot the H. blood of their Redeemer and yet they exceed Angels for there is more Joy in Heaven over one Sinner that repenteth than over 99 just men that need no repentence' (*SV*, fol. 39v). Here Traherne refers to the parable of the lost sheep from Luke 15.3–7.

108 See, for instance, *KOG*, fol. 176r–v in which the Fall, though a crime as 'The Blood of Dragons, and the Venom of Aspes' unto God, is disaster turned into 'Delights and Victories' – a wonder greater than the original creation of the world.

A pure and Holy soul is the vessel which God expecteth to com out of the fire Bright and pure: Pure and Holy it cannot be unless it be Willingly When therfore it useth its Liberty to Obedience it is Holy; but when to Rebellion it is impure. (*SV*, fol. 26v)

Liberty and Grace

Liberty exercised to obedience or to rebellion – either is a backdrop for grace. For Traherne, it is by grace that one may be obedient; it is by grace that one's rebellion may be recovered. And it is to the consideration of grace that this chapter now turns. Properly understood, there are four estates in Traherne – the estate of innocence, the estate of misery, the estate of grace and the estate of glory.[109] The third estate, grace, far from being an easy option, is also the estate of trial since it is in trial that grace is often most keenly felt. Traherne makes this clear at the beginning of chapter 24 of *Christian Ethicks* when he writes:

> PATIENCE is a Vertue of the Third estate; it belongs not to the estate of Innocence, because in it there was no Affliction; nor to the estate of Misery, because in it there is no Vertue: but to the estate of Grace it appertains, because it is an estate of Reconciliation, and an estate of Trial: wherin Affliction and Vertue meet together. In the estate of Glory there is no Patience. (*CE*, fol. 185)

In the first and fourth estates of innocence and glory grace is not necessary. In the second estate of misery grace is not found. But in the third estate grace is essential. The estate of grace is an estate of progress, of reconciliation and of trial. It is a mixed estate, the estate in which we live the vast majority of our lives – the place where virtue may grow out of affliction. It is not where we were, nor what we hope for, but where we are.

Much has been written about Traherne and innocence and about

---

109 The estates may be viewed as three or four depending on whether or not one sees misery and grace as separate or combined. Richard Jordan's study (*The Temple of Eternity: Thomas Traherne's Philosophy of Time*, Port Washington, NY: Kennikat Press, 1972) saw three estates – innocence, misery-grace and glory. In *CE* (Chs 14, 23, 24) and in *KOG* (Ch. 17), Traherne speaks of an Estate of Trial, which is a state in which the soul experiences both affliction and virtue mixed, and this seems to blur the distinction between the estates of misery and grace. However, for Traherne, although being in the estate of grace may mean a move away from abject misery, it does not imply an absence of affliction. It is this very mixture that is seen as the working of grace – grace is only grace when worked through difficulty. Misery and grace are most correctly understood as two separate estates.

Traherne and glory, and yet it is to this neglected third estate that almost all of his work in some way refers. Since what has been said of patience above is true of the other virtues as well, all of his work on virtue resides here. Anything that purports to be of practical service must pertain to this estate, since it is particularly in this estate that the working out of our lives occurs. His memory of innocence, however bright, is essentially a memory lost, the regaining of which occurs here. His apprehension of final glory refers back to and includes the virtues won in the estate of grace. When it comes to desire and the working out of redemption, it is the estate of grace that matters most.

So close is Traherne's understanding of grace and trial that he uses the two terms interchangeably. The estate of grace is the estate of trial; to be in one is to also be in the other. In fact, it is at the lowest point of trial, with the soul 'incurable and Incourageable' refusing mercy and defying love, that 'Free Grace is exalted to the utmost Zenith' (*SV*, fol. 39v). However, since grace is present not only in the estate of trial but also in the divine acts of creation and consumption,[110] it may be clearer to refer to this particular third, in-between state simply as the estate of trial.

Without an estate of trial there could be no righteous kingdom. In *The Kingdom of God* Traherne writes: 'Now without an estate of Trial, there could be no Righteous Kingdom no Libertie of Action, no Ingenuitie, and fidelitie of Lov in a weak estate, no occasion of Reward at all' *(KOG,* fol. 362v). Similarly, in *Christian Ethicks* Traherne asserts 'that the state of Trial, and the state of Glory are so mysterious in their Relation, that neither without the other could be absolutely perfect' (*CE*, p. 184).

One of the important features of the estate of trial is that it is a process and that it is a process requiring liberty. We have seen the importance of liberty to the Renaissance humanist notion of Man; and we have noted the traces of this template in Traherne's appropriation of the doctrine of election. Here we consider the significance of human liberty as a key element in what we become. The question here is not whether we have been given liberty or what having it means in philosophical terms, but what we may do with it and into what kind

---

[110] 'And as free Grace was the fountain of the Creation, and of the Redemption, so we see it the fountain of the Sanctification of the world; and richer and more Sublime at last then at the first' (*SV*, fol. 40r). On the need for grace see *SV*, fol. 42v: 'My Good Child Know this, that thou art not able to do those things of thyself, nor to walk in the Commandments of God and to serv him without his Special Grace, which thou must learn at all times to call for by Diligent Prayer.'

of persons that makes us – particularly how our liberty and its exercise interacts with the desire of God. In *The Kingdom of God* Traherne makes it clear that, were we to bypass the process and advance immediately to glory, we would miss the debate, the choice; something of our liberty would be lost. We would, in fact, be imposed upon (*KOG*, fols 362v–363r).

The problem with that, as Traherne sees it, is not the end result, which would be union, but what is destroyed in the process. He concludes, 'Now for the soul to Act by necessity destroys its Glory' (*KOG*, fol. 363r). Traherne continues with an image of the soul at a pinnacle of liberty – the vertical point, the very zenith of our utmost height – that is having the power to choose. On either side – powerlessness or being compelled to use our power – is a direct descent. The utmost height is in 'the Top of Libertie . . . To decline from which on either hand, is to debase us' (*KOG*, fol. 363r).

This question of status matters to God, according to Traherne, because the dignity of the human is the dignity of his bride. God desires a bride whose power to choose is similar to his own, who is free to act, to desire and to become. God himself is a free agent, acting without compulsion but with desire; desire is seen by Traherne as an expression of God's freedom. 'It is the Glory of God, that he is a free, and eternal Agent'; had God acted 'without Desire, and Delight', he had been less honourable (*KOG*, fol. 363r). To be without desire is to be dishonourably passive. God wants the bride to be free to act with desire and delight, just as God does: 'Willingness in its operation is the Beauty of the Soul, and its Honour founded in the freedom of its Desire' (*CE*, p. 149). And so:

> He adventured to make high Creatures like himself, that might Act freely. That they might be Divine and Holy too, the springs and fountains of excellent Action, Admirers Honorers, Adorers, and Praisers, Lords, and Lovers, friends, and Sons, most high and Admirable persons abov the reach of Fate after the Similitude of the Deitie . . .[111]

---

[111] *KOG*, fol. 174v. '[F]or God desired that Good Works should spring from Ingenuitie not necessity; from Good Will and Pleasure, not from Fate; from Love and Obedience, not from Bondage, from inward Desire, and not from outward force', he reiterates (*KOG*, fol. 175v). See also 'Man is made to appear in Glory, as well as to inherit all Treasure. And therfore is Endued with Liberty of will as well as comprehension . . . But God would have Him Glorious in Himselfe in respect of His own Actions works and operation. He would have Him voluntary as God is' (*SM*, II, 32).

Several times in *Christian Ethicks*, in the *Thanksgivings* and in *The Kingdom of God*, Traherne uses the word 'adventured' of God.[112] He 'adventured' to do or to make, as if to suggest risk in God's loving. Traherne seems intrigued by this, and notes the paradox of divine goodness making possible the advent of evil: 'Thus his infinit Goodness, by the utmost excess of its perfection, made evil possible ... For it put the Gate of Fate into the Hand of its Creature'.[113] It is as if the risk attached to God's action in making his creatures free is part of his joy as a lover.[114] Where 'all is easy, safe, and secure', the beloved is 'meerly Passiv' (*KOG*, fol. 363v), but

> GOD intended more then this for his Bride; she must hav features and Graces more Delightfull, ornaments more Amiable, and Beautifull; so Divine, that the very Memory of them should be sweeter, then all that in a solitary state of stiffe, and passive Glory can be devised. (*KOG*, fol. 363v)

The implication is that God wants a bride who is not merely recipient, stiff and passive, but one who, graced by her power to choose, participates in a dynamic of gift and receipt as in the lovers' dynamic of power, consent and union. God desires our 'Naked Lov' generous and free, a love that can be neither bought nor sold (*KOG*, Ch. 32, ll. 151–63).

Just as 'Nothing but freedom and desire' (*KOG*, fol. 363r) carried God to his act, so he wishes it to be for his bride. He wishes this not just because his joy as a lover is increased by the free response of his bride but because, as we have seen, the freedom of her action signals the height of her estate. In the epic poem *The Ceremonial Law*, Traherne claims that God's wooing of us as a 'Heavenly Queen' is 'a Signe, we Equal objects are / Even with the Angels' of his love and

---

112 In the previous quotation he adventured to make us high creatures. In *CE*, p. 92 'God adventured the possibility of sinning into our hands'. In *Thanksgivings for the Soul* God 'didst adventure into our hands / A Power of displeasing thee'. Later in *KOG*, fol. 174v he also 'adventured the Possibilitie of a Sin into his Creatures Hands'. This part of *KOG*, fol. 174v almost exactly parallels that cited above from *CE*.

113 *KOG*, fols 174v–175r. Traherne notes that God made provision that we should use our liberty well and then 'cheerfully commited the World to his Creatures Godliness, hoping and expectin a Return of glorious Delights' (*KOG*, fol. 175r–v). He then immediately returns to the element of risk: 'Souls indeed are not like trees, that must flourish of Necessity.' They can bear or forbear and frustrate the labour of the husbandman.

114 See also above, p. 33, n. 16, where the word 'danger' with regard to God's risk in loving is considered.

care.[115] As we saw in chapter one, in both *Love* and *The Kingdom of God* the Bride is described as being royal. She is queen, empress, potentate; and, as Traherne reminds us, it does not befit 'the estate of a Queen to be compeld'.

Although the freedom of the bride is given to the soul by right, that is to say by virtue of her being created in the image of God, the virtues and graces that adorn the soul as queen and bride are won in the estate of trial. In *The Kingdom of God* Traherne describes the estate of trial as having five benefits:

1 Multiplication of our wants (that our treasures may be multiplied).
2 Whetting of the appetite, enflaming of desire.
3 The establishment of rewards and dispensations by which government and empire are framed.
4 The glory of actions by which virtue is won and felicity is gained.
5 The possibility of danger, which affords delight to the spectator and a crown of triumph to the actor.

This estate benefits either God or the human or God's kingdom, or, as Traherne goes on to confess, all of them together, God, angels and men: 'For they all are in a twofold Capacitie, either as Actors or spectators: and in either Relation have a double Happiness.'[116]

In *A Sober View* Traherne speaks of the estate of trial as being an expression of divine wisdom. The first scene of divine wisdom was innocence, in which God's glory and man's happiness were united. The second scene is the estate of trial. This is a scene in which 'Wisdom Discerned a Means without destroying the Subjects to renew the Kingdom'.[117] In this estate evil is turned into good: 'Sin itself enflamed unto Love, and Hatred unto Zeal and Guilt unto Holiness, . . . Despair added Wings to Endeavor. . . all were cemented by the Blood of Christ and made greater Treasures to God and each other'.[118]

---

115 The full quotation reads: 'That He should Woo, and treat His Heavenly Queen / On Earth, that she His GLORY here might see,/ And be Espoused to the DIETY [*sic*]: / It is a Signe, we Equal objects are / Even with the Angels of His Lov and Care' (*TCL*, introduction, ll. 32–6).
116 *KOG*, fol. 361v.
117 *SV*, fol. 38v.
118 *SV*, fol. 39r. Traherne goes on to describe election as a third scene, in which the Holy Spirit acts upon the reprobate in an overwhelming act of grace: 'Wisdom displayeth it best, in making the Depth of incurable Rebellion the Greater occasion of a Righteous Kingdom and the Basis or foundation of more exalted Righteousness . . . Free Grace is exalted to the utmost Zenith. For to convert such worthless and Horrid creatures in a way so uncouth and unacceptable to God as that is of invading many Wills is altogether as much as if not

So we may see that not only does the estate of trial beautify the bride and make plain her status as a free agent but it also allows the restoration of righteousness. This is so most importantly because it is in the estate of trial that the soul makes its choices.

As we have seen, all virtue, moral goodness or righteousness is tied to this principle of freedom.[119] Moral goodness differs from natural goodness chiefly in this: that it has a life of its own by virtue of the liberty and ingenuity that underlies it. It is more than natural goodness, hard won and ardently desired.[120]

Moral goodness is never accidental. And although it benefits all, its real value lies in the soul of the one whose will and understanding have become good; the greatest good of moral goodness is in the will of the one who exercises it. In his chapter on goodness in *Christian Ethicks* Traherne writes:

> A mad man, or a fool, may by accident save a mans Life, or preserve an Empire, yet be far from that Goodness which is seated in the Will and Understanding ... And the Truth is that the *External Benefit*, tho it saves the Lives, and Souls, and Estates, and Liberties, and Riches, and Pleasures, and Honors, of all mankind, acts but *Physically* by a Dead or Passive Application, the root of its influence and value is seated in another place, in the Soul of him whose Goodness was so Great as to sacrifice his Honor, and Felicity for the Preservation and Welfare of those whom he intended to save. It is seated in the *Counsel* and *Design* of the Actor. (CE, p. 79)

Wherever Traherne discusses moral goodness, freedom is not far behind. In fact freedom and goodness are inseparable: 'Their freedom is

---

more then the redeeming of Sinners while there was a Hope they would be righteous. Here likewise Election is the Fountain of Comon Salvation. Election of a few is the benefit of all' (SV, fols 39r–40v). His 'critical reader' admonishes him not to make a distinction between the work of Christ that makes possible the estate of trial (Traherne's 'second scene') and the work of the Holy Spirit by which the reprobate is elected (Traherne's 'third scene').

119 Traherne asserts in *Christian Ethicks* that, unless we do excellent actions of our own accord, 'no External Power whatsoever can make us, Good, or Holy, or Righteous' (CE, p. 93) and in *A Sober View* nothing is morally good but that which flows from a person 'purely from his Love to virtue ... freely, without compulsion or Constraint' (SV, p. 58, sect III, ll. 21–4).

120 See CE, p. 78. Similarly, in SV (fol. 27r) Traherne states: 'That a Work may be Good, it must be suitable to the End for which it is ordained. It must proceed from a right principle, in a right manner, be according to Rule, directed to a Good end, and freely performed.' And again, 'Nothing is Moraly Good but what is Righteous. That is, which floweth ... freely, without compulsion or Constraint; having a desire of doing [what is] Beautifull' (fol. 27v).

their Goodness, for unless they [fruits] Spring from Love which is the only fountain of Good Works, they are Despoyled of all their Glory';[121] 'GOD therefore may be infinitely Holy, and infinitely desire our Righteous Actions, tho he doth not intermeddle with our Liberty, but leaves us to our selves' (CE, p. 93). The purpose of the estate of trial is the improvement and adornment of the soul but also the possibility of pleasure for God. It is God's gamble – the possibility of what he infinitely hates for the chance of enjoying what he infinitely desires. And in all of this he has given us a free hand. This is the astonishing fact that captures Traherne's imagination – that actions of piety freely wrought, those objects so desired by God that for their sake he created angels and souls and all worlds, are left to the liberty of human beings. And this liberty is not the perfect liberty of heaven, where all is irresistibly drawn by divine love, but the imperfect liberty of Eden, that liberty of absolute and very corruptible power by which the human soul may choose to do exactly as it pleases. As Traherne explains:

> GOD adventured the possibility of sinning into our hands, which he infinitely hated, that he might have the Possibility of Righteous Actions, which he infinitely Loved ... The very utmost Excellence of the most noble Created Beings, consisted in Actions of piety freely wrought: which GOD so Loved, that for their sake alone, he made Angels and Souls, and all Worlds ... That we might do these in a Righteous Manner he place us in a mean Estate of Liberty and Tryal, not like that of Liberty in Heaven where the Object will determine our Wills by its Amiableness, but in the Liberty of Eden, where we had absolute Power to do as we pleased, and might determine our Wills our selves infinitely ... (CE, p. 92)

The unenviable position of God in this risk-taking is a point to which Traherne returns again and again. In *The Kingdom of God*, even as Traherne points to God as eternal Act, he notes God's self-limiting power:

> Alas he is able to make innumerable Myriads in a Moment. But he cannot make us to be, what we ought to be, Amiable, and Gratefull, Obedient, and Pious, Loving and Holy, Wise, and Voluntary, freely delighting, and well pleasing; unless we are willing to be what we

---

[121] SV, fol. 26r. That virtue and free will are inextricably linked is a ubiquitous notion in Traherne. As well as the quotations given above see also: CE, pp. 25, 31–5, 78–9, 85, 90–3, 148–50; the Fourth *Century*; SM and KOG. See also MSD, pp. 23, 78, 83–4.

ought. For to be Willing is to Will of our own accord . . . He would have us willing and willingly obedient. (*KOG*, Ch. 38, ll. 85–91)

All the glory of the world, Traherne says, depends on the liberty of men and angels and God gave it to them 'because he delighted in the Perfection of his Creatures: tho he very well knew there would be the Hazzard of their abusing it, (and of Sin in that abuse) when they had received it'.[122] It would seem that God has tied his own hands behind his back and made human liberty greater than his own.[123]

It is not only God who waits to see what we humans will make of our liberty. According to Traherne 'all creatures stand in expectation what will result of our liberty' (*C*, IV, 48). This is a salutary thought indeed and one that, because of the interconnectedness of global consumption and global destruction, is becoming true in ways that Traherne could never have predicted.

What are we then to think of ourselves as human beings? We are creatures of immense power and liberty – power to frustrate or to fulfil the very design of God, power to change ourselves and be changed. We are in a positition where our desires matter more to each other globally than ever before. By the dignity of the high position we already inhabit as free agents, we have the power to become even greater. Already eternal beings, we may, by our desires and choices, become persons of virtue and moral goodness, fit for divine company. We have been granted the freedom to choose and the power to act, and our highest and simplest choice is love; we may choose to love or not to love. In such a position we are neither wise nor holy, though we may become both.[124] And so we are in a position of potential, of possibility and of hope.

Hope

This freedom of choice and ability to act, when married to desire, occasions the virtue of hope. Traherne writes, 'Hope is a Vertue mixt of Belief and Desire, by which we conceive the Possibility of

---

122 *CE*, p. 91.

123 And yet Traherne holds that God gives us power without lessening his own: 'all Power was put into many Hands without any Diminution of Power in his own' (*SV*, fol. 38v). This is so, according to Traherne, because God augments his power through his response to our choices – either enjoying or punishing them (cf. *SV*, fol. 38v).

124 'Power to Lov is subject to Miscarriages; it is neither Wise nor Holy. But the Act of Loving, in a most Wise and Holy manner, casteth out all fear' (*Love*, fol. 127v).

attaining the Ends we would enjoy, and are stirred up to endeavour after them'.[125]

Apart from his chapter on hope in *Christian Ethicks*, Traherne does not often mention hope as a virtue, though its origins and its qualities are much discussed by other names. His hope is a hunger and a thirst, a mixture of love of things unknown and dissatisfaction with what is known. In the opening meditations of the *Centuries* he describes the hope phenomenon as the violent attraction of an unknown love:

> for though it be a maxim in the schools that there is no Love of a thing unknown, yet I have found that things unknown have a secret influence on the soul, and like the centre of that earth unseen violently attract it. We love we know not what, and therefore everything allures us. As iron at a distance is drawn by the loadstone, there being some invisible communications between them, so is there in us a world of Love to somewhat, though we know not what in the world that should be. There are invisible ways of conveyance by which some great thing doth touch our soul, and by which we tend to it. Do you not feel yourself drawn with the expectation and desire of some Great Thing?[126]

In his poem 'Dissatisfaction', Traherne recounts the other side of this expectation of 'some Great Thing' – the despair of the one who senses such a pull but who cannot find its source. The disappointed searcher finds 'nothing more than empty Space' in heaven above, and on earth is confronted with dirt, toil, dens of thieves, complaints and tears. 'The Oaths of Roaring Boys, Their Gold', their wines, their lies, 'Their gawdy Trifles' and 'mistaken Joys' disgust him no less, and even books do not satisfy. He cries:

> But then, where is? What is, Felicity?
>   Here all men are in doubt,
>   And unresolv'd, they cannot speak,
> What 'tis; and all or most that Silence break
>   Discover nothing but their Throat.[127]

---

[125] CE, p. 117. Similarly in Ch. 4 of CE he writes of seeing and attaining: 'The *Understanding* was made to see the value of our Treasure; and the freedome of *Will*, to Atcheive Glory to our actions' (p. 29).
[126] C, I, 2.
[127] 'Dissatisfaction', ll. 66–70. See also ll. 23, 37–47.

In *Seeds of Eternity*, this inquisitiveness and restlessness are a natural part of being human; for man, Traherne claims, 'is an inquisitive and restless Creature' and, knowing that there is an origin and an end to everything, 'he is not contented to see the surface or colour of things', to taste and smell them or take in their brightnesss or beauty, 'but feeleth an Instinct strongly moving him to know from whence this Creature came, and whither it tendeth'.[128] Where does everything come from and where does it go? From infancy to old age, this question never leaves us.

Even when the human moves beyond the most superficial to higher things 'yet he is dissatisfied in the midst of all the splendor of Heaven and Earth and immediately enquires whither it began and what was the original of so Divine a Being, and to what end and purpose was it created' (*SE*, fol. 144r). 'Contentment is a sleepy thing', cries Traherne, as we have seen in his poem by the same name. One is reminded by such restlessness of the 'repining restlessness' in Herbert's poem 'The Pulley', in which, at creation, God withheld the gift of 'rest' so that humanity might when all else fails be tossed to God's breast by sheer weariness – but where for Herbert restlestness is the result of a gift withheld, for Traherne restless longing is the gift itself.

In the poem 'Desire', Traherne praises God for giving him 'An Eager Thirst, a burning Ardent fire . . . An Inward Hidden Heavenly Love' that enflamed him 'With restlesse longing Heavenly Avarice, That never could be satisfied, That did incessantly a Paradice unknown suggest, and som thing undescried Discern'.[129] Like this 'Heavenly Avarice', in *Christian Ethicks* ambition and covetousness are two sisters who may carry the soul to glory and treasure (*CE*, p. 29).

That hope is natural to the human soul Traherne recognizes as part of its destiny. But he also admits that shaped hope is problematic. Dissatisfaction does not rest easily with Christian virtues such as gratitude and contentment and peace any more than do ambition and avarice. And for this reason hope is often at best neglected, at times denied by Christians. It is perhaps because we sense the gnarled roots of dissatisfaction twisted in with our shining hopes that we cut off our hopes and cast them aside as things deformed. And yet in so doing, Traherne asserts, we miss the chance to discover what is at the root of these desires; we resign our liberty and have the temerity to do so with pride. In *The Kingdom of God* he describes this casting off of hope:

---

128 *SE*, fol. 143v.
129 'Desire', ll. 2–11.

Our hopes are nipt in the Bud for fear of presumption, our Desires crusht in the Growth with pretended Pietie. We silence our dissatisfactions and suppress their Clamour, we resign our Libertie and giv up ourselvs to an implicit Bondage, we see not the root of our Discontent and yet in the midst of all this corruption we are as confident and Dogmatical; as if we had all the Light of Holy Angels. (*KOG*, fol. 208r)

And yet it is the very earthiness of hope, its tangled roots of dissatisfaction and ambition, that give it something of its value. To be hope at all, rather than a projection or fantasy, hope must have one foot in the mud. Just as the human is the golden clasp between physical and spiritual, so hope is virtue's golden clasp between spiritual and temporal. It is a gritty mixture of faith and desire.[130]

It is the purpose of hope to elevate the soul by focusing it on ever higher ends. The soul extends itself by hope imagining itself higher and better and by so imagining reaching new possibilities. The higher the hope, the greater the growth of the soul, and it is perhaps with this in mind that the author of *Meditations on the Six Days of Creation* writes 'O my God, give me *Perfection* in my Desires at least, and make me grow from *Grace* to *Grace*, from *Strength* to *Strength*, until I atttain such *Perfection* in *Act*, as thou wilt in thy Son accept.'[131] For Traherne, the perfect marriage is humility of spirit with greatness of desire; by this we may 'aspire unto' God.[132] But even lesser hopes may also be of value. Reaffirming the potential good in ambition and avarice, Traherne writes:

All that Ambition or Avarice can desire, all that Appetite and Self-Love can pursue, all that Fancy can imagine Possible and Delightful; Nay more than we are able to ask or think; we are able to desire, and aspire after . . . And the more Sublime its Objects are, the more Eagerly & violently does our Hope pursue them, because there is more Goodness in them to ravish our Desire.[133]

---

130 'HOPE presupposes a Belief of the Certainty of what we desire' (*CE*, p. 117).
131 *MSD*, p. 23.
132 Ibid., p. 75.
133 *CE*, p. 122. Later in the same work he writes: 'I do not look upon Ambition and Avarice . . . as things that are evil in their root and fountain' (*CE*, p. 173). '*Avarice* and *Ambition* may pass for Counsellors. They may do will to put a man in mind of his Interest, byt when they depose Right Reason, and usurp the Throne, Ruine must follow in the soul' (*CE*, p. 96).

CHOICE

Lesser hopes, appetites and pleasures may adorn superior desires, lesser hope being sanctified by highest hope:

> Our very Appetites also being ravished with Sensible Pleasures in all our Members, not inconsistent with, but springing from these high and Superior Delights, not distracting or confounding our Spiritual Joys, but purely Superadded, and increasing the same ... and the Hope that is exercised about these Things is a Vertue so great, that all inferior Hopes, which this doth Sanctifie, are made Vertues by it.[134]

This is the high calling of hope. A right hope is a great virtue because its objects really do surpass all imagining. Among hope's objects Traherne lists our perfection and transformation from glory to glory, communion with God as a bride who possesses his throne, and the sweetness of the bridegroom, the resurrection of the body, life eternal and all the pleasures and treasures of an eternity that begins now, a world in which all objects in all worlds visible and infinitely rich are 'Beautiful, and OURS!'[135]

As with treasure, so with hope: right and proportionate matching of object and desire make for true hope, disproportionate or misplaced desire turns hope into false hope. And Traherne gives stern warnings about the importance of keeping our hopes fixed on superior objects:

> I Know very well that Presumption and Despair are generally accounted the Extreams of Hope ... But I Know as well, that there may be many Kinds and Degrees of Hope, of which some may be vicious, and some Vertuous: and that some sorts of Hope themselves are Vices. When ever we make an inferior Desire the Sovereign Object of our Hope, our Hope is abominable, Idolatrous and Atheistical. We forget GOD. and magnifie an inferior Object above all that is Divine. To Sacrifice all our Hopes to Things unworthy of them ... is vicious. (CE, pp. 123-4)

And yet Traherne's regard for hope remains high. While 'drowsy hope' makes no impression on the mind (CE, p. 122), to follow hope with passion is to be carried to perfect virtue; and 'to be Remiss and sluggish in Hoping for Things of infinite Importance' is as bad as hoping

---

134 CE, p. 123. Traherne goes on 'but without this all other hopes are Debasements and Abuses of the Soul, meer Distractions and delusions, and therefore *Vices*'.
135 Ibid., for this and the preceeding quote

for unworthy things (*CE*, p. 123). Without hope we are neither great nor noble; we are not fit for the life of virtue. We should lift up our eyes in hope of bounty because 'to desire the most high and perfect Proofs of his Love, is the Property of a most Great and Noble Soul, by which it is carried above all the World, and fitted for the Life of the most high and perfect Vertue' (*CE*, p. 124).

4

Difference

> His face the Patern is, being one in Three,
> Who without being Three, One cannot be.
>
> (*COH*, 'Act II')

There is a line of thinking that sees Traherne within a basic framework of unity – that for him all things come from and refer back to one end, and that the soul's progress is a kind of Neo-Platonic quest for union with the One. Studies in this unity model generally emphasize Traherne's imagery of unboundedness, his love of infinity and Neo-Platonic interpretations of the soul and God. This chapter begins by briefly outlining the unity model, and considers his boundary aversion in the context of changes to land and inheritance laws, as well as his emphasis on interior ownership, before asserting that the dynamic of his unified cosmos is a dynamic of gift and receipt that relies inextricably on the existence of subject and object. The importance of an 'other' to Traherne's whole project is explored. Similarities and differences between Lacan's model of self-knowledge and Traherne's, which both rely on the interplay of desire and the 'other', are discussed, as are the importance of subject and object in the process of creation and re-creation. The necessity of an 'other' in Traherne's philosophy and the tension that exists in his writings between the competing claims of unity and difference make this chapter particularly relevant to those theologians interested in exploring relationship in God and the doctrine of the Trinity. For Traherne this doctrine has vital significance not just because it insists that Jesus, the Son, was both fully human and fully divine (which has, as we have seen, particular relevance to his high view of humankind) but also because it places relationship at the heart of divinity and suggests that the tension of unity and difference is one that should not be seen as a problem to solve but a paradox to explore.

Traherne's theory of communication and circulation – that all things that give do first receive – is laid out in detail; it is a theory that was fed from the latest advances of philosophical, astronomical and medical science alike, and that had its root in his Trinitarian concept of God.

Felicity as Unity

The *Centuries* and much of Traherne's poetry, particularly the best-known poems of the Dobell Sequence, suggest that Traherne's quest for a type of unitive knowledge is a fundamental influence on his style. Several critics have noted this. For Malcolm Day (in *Thomas Traherne*), the central reality undergirding all of Traherne's thought is the Neo-Platonic notion of everything united in the single undivided One. For A. L. Clements, who writes about Traherne as a mystical poet in *Mystical Poetry*, Traherne is unitive almost by default because the mystical mind is dialectic rather than logical or dualistic.[1] Stewart, who sees Traherne's style as 'open', 'additive' and 'expansive', eroding distinctions and collapsing boundaries of style, time, person, author and audience, and character into one great flexibility guided by 'a process of association, like reverie',[2] suggests a Traherne who is not so much united as unbounded. It is true that Traherne rails against boundaries, walls, confinement in his poetry. 'No walls confine! Can nothing hold my mind?' and

> This busy, vast, enquiring Soul
> Brooks no Controul.
> No Limits will endure,

he writes in 'Insatiableness I' and 'Insatiableness II'.

Just as Traherne's consideration of treasure is rooted in the material and social donations of the king and his notions of worth are tied up with understandings of exchange value that appeared in the seventeenth-century emerging market economy, so his theories of boundarilessness may be seen to be connected with both the new scientific explorations of infinity and the alterations to property and inheritance laws of his day. It may be that Traherne's poetry of the unbounded has as much to do with these social changes as with his metaphysical understanding of the self. Certainly any full discussion of unboundedness must consider the volatile seventeenth-century social context of boundary and border.

As noted in chapter two, *The Kingdom of God* lists 'enclosures' among the false treasures that are a direct result of the Fall. Much of Traherne's poetry of innocence and of nature features Edenic, un-

---

[1] A. L. Clements, *The Mystical Poetry of Thomas Traherne*, Cambridge, MA: Harvard University Press, 1969, p. 501.

[2] Stanley Stewart, *The Expanded Voice: The Art of Thomas Traherne*, San Marino, CA: Huntington Library, 1970, p. 209–10.

claimed landscapes that the poet possesses deeply while never having to own materially. The world is completely his while also completely his neighbour's; he is the sole heir and every person is the soul heir of the same kingdom. So strong is his affinity for interior ownership and mutually shared possession that the historian Christopher Hill has placed him with the radical Digger Gerrard Winstanley as an ideal communist.[3] It is inviting to see Traherne's poetry of the unbounded, then, as a reaction to the changes in property law that saw in many parts of the country new intrusions of fence and hedge, curtilage and rights of private ownership; but we can only do so by overlooking his writings that have to do with inheritance.

As Lynne Greenberg notes in her recent study on Traherne and property laws, the seventeenth century was a time of particular change in terms not only of property ownership but also of patronage and inheritance. When in 1646 the Long Parliament abolished the Court of Wards and military tenures, they disturbed the Crown's hitherto-held rights to intrude on individual property rights. In effect the whole of the land no longer belonged to the monarch, a principle that was confirmed at the Restoration in 1660 and led to the eventual commoditization of land because it could now be freely bought and sold, enclosed, mortgaged and bequeathed.[4] In fact, despite Traherne's omission of his own five houses in Hereford in his nuncupative will, his interest in bequest and inheritance is clear at many points in his writing in which to be an 'heir' is to be a son or daughter, to be loved and blessed. This echoes not only the Old Testament tradition in which blessing went inextricably with inheritance, but also the Pauline notion of co-inheritance with Christ. Those who are born of God's spirit are children of God, 'and if children heirs – heirs of God and co-heirs with Christ' (Rom. 8.16–17). This inheritance, it should be added, is not only about inheriting the earth but also about inheriting the sufferings of Christ as well as his glory. Inheritance and ownership are tied up, in Traherne's mind, with blessing, status and spiritual vitality.

---

3 Christopher Hill, *Collected Essays: Writing and Revolution in Seventeenth-century England*, Amherst, MA: University of Massachusetts Press, 1985, pp. 226-46; and *The World Turned Upside Down: Radical Ideas During the English Revolution*, London: Maurice Temple Smith, 1972, p. 414.

4 For the fullest available exposition of how this is relevant to Traherne see Lynne Greenberg, 'Curs'd and Devised Proprieties: Traherne and the Laws of Property' in Jacob Blevins (ed.), *Re-reading Thomas Traherne: A Collection of New Critical Essays*, Tempe, AZ: Arizona Center for Medieval and Renaissance Studies, 2007, pp. 21–35. See also Christopher Hill, *Liberty Against the Law: Some Seventeenth-century Controversies*, London: Allen Lane, 1996; Alan Macfarlane, *The Origins of English Individualism: The Family, Property, and Social Transition*, Cambridge: Cambridge University Press, 1979.

Traherne takes a daring step further – ownership is a route to pleasing God. By receiving the gift of creation, by taking up one's place as heir to a kingdom, owning, prizing the gift and making it part of one's very self before returning it again in adoration, one fulfils the divine intent. Refusal to so reign frustrates divine intention. As he writes in *Commentaries of Heaven*:

> The Glorious Sun doth run His Race for Thee
> For Thee the Seasons by the Deitie
> Were made: for Thee the Rain descends: the Seas
> And Rivers flow with Living Streams to pleas,
> And Honor Thee. They all are made in vain,
> If being made thou dost not ever Reigne.
> If Thou dost not return them back again,
> Tho nere so Glorious, they are made in vain.
> . . . He all Created by His Endless Might
> For Thee; for Thee alone: and small Delight
> Small Pleasure can He take in any Thing.
> Till it from Thee a Second Time doth Spring
>
> (*COH*, 'Adoration', ll. 75–90)

All of this seems to contradict Traherne's frequent admonitions in the *Centuries* to eschew material possession and ownership. When he writes that 'to say this Hous is yours, and these Lands are another Mans . . . is deadly Barbarous and uncouth to a little Child' (*C*, III, 11), or that the 'false proprieties' of houses and lands, fields, gold and wealth are to be scorned as we 'do as Adam did' ('Blisse', l. 3) and live unfettered and free, is he not railing against the very laws of enclosure, bequest and propriety that were transforming not just the social and psychological landscape of his day but the physical landscape as well? I think this is unlikely. Traherne's arguments against boundaries are metaphors for his stretch towards infinity. Inheritance may be a sign of blessing, ownership may be a way of enjoying and exclusive ownership may be thought by many to be desirable, but the real issue is about interior ownership, developing the ability to live like a king without the burdens that exclusive ownership entails. This is not achieved by the exchange of documents but by a change of vision. In an image that suggests at once intimate and exclusive possession and a spaciousness or largesse, he writes of the world:

> Of it I am th'inclusive Sphere,
> It doth entire in me appear
> As well as I in it: It gives me Room,
> Yet lies within my Womb.
>
> ('Misapprehension', ll. 62–5)

The world is outside him and inside him at the same time, a home and an outpost, its literal possession the beginning of interior possession.

Hedges and fences became commonplace in Herefordshire prior to enclosure in other parts of the country, and protest against the new legislation seems to have met with less resistance there, possibly because the practice was already customary. Traherne would have grown up with views of fields patched and pieced. In light of this, I suggest that Traherne's boundary aversion is less a protest against new land laws and more a feature of his fascination with infinity and his conviction of the human soul's capacity for infinite reach. In *Select Meditations* he reminds his readers that the limitless life is the life attuned to interior perceptions of infinity, tuned to one's relatedness to all things:

> The Reason why man is a Feeble worm is because he DeSpiseth his understanding, and lives onely by His Fleshly Body: wou[ld] He live by His understanding he Should Soone perceiv Himselfe an infinite creature. All Sight, and Love: the Nature of which are both Infini[t]. All! all! all the souls in Heaven and earth Shall Dwell in Him. And He in them, and they in God, and God in Him, and He in God forevermo[re]: they limmit not each other. (*SM*, II, 27.)

It is in this sense of limitlessness that Stewart discusses Traherne's radical unboundedness. Souls 'limit not each other', neither should a soul limit itself by stifling its imaginative reach. When Traherne cries: 'No more shall Walls, no more shall Walls confine' in his poem 'Hosanna' (l. 1), he is crying down the barriers that keep people from each other, that keep him from union with God, the psychological, emotional and spiritual barriers that station the soul in isolation. Critics such as Day, Stewart and Clements are right to note the unitive urge in Traherne's writings. Like E. M. Forster, whose motto 'only connect' reminds his readers of the interrelatedness of persons, Traherne, too, urges his readers to see the deep belonging that already binds them one to one and each to God, to creation, to the reaches of infinite space.

The danger, however, of such a loose understanding of oneness in Traherne is that it can easily slip into a kind of fusing of all things into one indistinguishable sameness; God and the great oneness become synonymous. God is not a person at all but a kind of overarching unity, a concept. In such a model the central quest is not essentially about the soul relating to God or for that matter to any 'other', since being related presupposes a certain degree of separateness, a divide across which relationship becomes a bridge. In the unitive model, the central quest in Traherne is essentially a Neo-Platonic quest for the transformation of the Mind into its original condition as Soul and thereby to union with the divine. At a glance this seems similar to the doctrine of *theosis*; however, the Neo-Platonic quest never fully embraces the incarnation. It is concerned with what man is becoming at the expense of what God became in the person of Jesus. Essentially it leaves the earth behind as a lower form.

Whether the quest is described in Neo-Platonic terms or not, there is much in Traherne's poetry that seems to stand in favour of this unity argument. His prelapsarian spirit knows no boundaries and his soul lives in a state in which to be with and to see are one. And this is not just so in the poetry of childhood. 'For not to be, and not to appear, are the same thing to the understanding',[5] Traherne writes in *Christian Ethicks*, sounding like both Meister Eckhart and Plotinus at once.[6] In the *Select Meditations* Traherne writes that we are so much a part of God that he could not even want us: 'From all Eternity God included us, and therefore He could not at all want us ... we could not be superadded to him, becaus we were in Him' (*SM*, III, 79). And yet in the same passage Traherne admits that God does want us, by his goodness, and in an image of overflowing, uncontainable goodness he describes that divine abundance that desires a recipient as breast milk that must be given or spoil. For:

> Blessednes Naturaly Loveth to be seen, and is Like milk in a womans Breasts more Delightfull in being Distributed, then in Lying Still in it own Fountaine. It curdleth there and recoyling upon it selfe; in

---

[5] *CE*, p. 37.
[6] 'The eye by which I see God', wrote Eckhart, 'is the same as the eye by which God sees me. My eye and God's eye are one and the same – one in seeing, one in knowing, and one in loving' (*Meister Eckhart: A ModernTranslation*, trans. R. B. Blakney, New York: Harper & Row, 1957, p. 206). 'He who then sees himself, when he sees will see himself a simple being, will be united to himself as such, will feel himself become such. We ought not even to say that he will see, but he will be that which he sees' (Plotinus, *The Sixth Ennead*, IX, 10, trans. W. R. Inge, *The Philosophy of Plotinus*, 3rd edition, New York: Longmans, Green & Co., 1929, vol. II, p. 141). These are also cited in A. L. Clements, 'The Mode and Meaning of Thomas Traherne's Mystical Poetry: "The Preparative"', *Studies in Philology*, 61 (1964), p. 506, where he notes the emphasis on the oneness of all things in both of these writers.

flowing from the mother it feedeth a nother and becometh usefull. Delightfull to the mother while it is usefull. (*SM*, III, 79)

Even as he insists on the unity of all things in God, Traherne cannot escape the dynamic of need and treasure, of gift and receipt that marks the soul's relationship with the divine. Everything may be a unity inasmuch as Traherne's subject matter is the unified life of a dynamic cosmos, a world of time and eternity in one continuous motion of love from God to creation and from creation to God. And yet to say this without exploring the nature of that dynamic, its cycles and circles, the otherness implied in its objects and subjects and in its communication is to miss the vital movement of that unified life.

The Importance of Difference

That an 'other' is necessary to Traherne's whole project is evident. It is implied by the very existence of desire, since the action of desire necessitates an object; more importantly though, an object or other is necessary to the meaning as well as to the mechanics of Traherne's desire. It is primarily desire of an authentic other that keeps him from falling into the danger, often noted by critics of his Dobell poems in particular, of solipsism. This is where Traherne's erotically informed poetry and prose noted in the first chapter have a particular role to play; an important function of the erotic and sometimes sexual imagery in Traherne, apart from its usefulness as accessible allegory, is that it reinforces the need of a concrete other. Those objects and treasures that inspire Traherne's desire lift his written self away from the image of an isolated ego steering its own solipsistic course, towards an enlarged self stretching towards an infinite end; and it is the existence of this 'other' separate from the self, whether sexually allegorized or not, that distinguishes between insatiable desire that energizes the soul and facilitates its journey and the kind of unsatisfiable self-absorbed desire that leads to nihilistic despair.

In his recent book *Discernment and Truth*, Mark McIntosh cites the episode of Doubting Castle and its lord, Giant Despair, from *Pilgrim's Progress* as an example of the kind of desire that becomes self-annihilation. He notes of the character Pilgrim:

> It is as if the self, deprived of a real calling *beyond* itself, becomes the prisoner of its own anxieties and doubts. If the human will exists in a mere echo chamber of its own desires, in which the authentic voice

of the other has been silenced in favor of an 'other' that is merely my own self-interest projected outward, then my will becomes, paradoxically, self-annihilating.[7]

How does Pilgrim get to this point of believing despair? 'The voice that had continually *called* out to the self, made it alive and awake to a reality beyond itself, has been walled out, and the self now feels itself cut off and tyrannized by its own fears.'[8] One is reminded of Traherne's sensing and challenging his reader to sense, the call of 'Som great thing' at the beginning of his first *Century*, and the importance of retaining the ability to see and hear the call of an authentic other.

That this other must be real, and that Traherne sensed a critical need for an authentic other, is clear. Who that other is may be a matter for some discussion. There is the other who is the reader, the public one and the private one. The first he addresses in prefaces such as 'The Author to the Critical Peruser', in which he promises, among other things, to deliver in his poetry 'No curling Metaphors' but 'The naked Truth'. The preface to *Christian Ethicks* entitled 'To The Reader' similarly makes a promise, this time of leading his reader to blessedness by the study of virtue. In *Commentaries of Heaven*, his intended readership includes 'Atheists' as well as 'Divines', whereas the 'friend' of the *Centuries* is an intimate. In *Select Meditations* the ejaculations of 'O my T.G. O my S.H. O my Brother!'[9] and his admonitions to them as friends suggest the possibility of another intimate readership. And *Inducements to Retiredness* is written as an invitation to a specific kind of reader, one who has already embarked upon the pursuit of God. There is the encouraging reader of *The Ceremonial Law* and the 'critical reader' of the Lambeth manuscript, who corrected, advised and criticized his work at manuscript stage, and there is the wide audience for which a work such as *Roman Forgeries* was intended. Added to this there are the several others whose hands appear in the Traherne manuscripts, who worked alongside Traherne in the process of writing. But all of this may be no more than to say that a writer writes to be read by someone somewhere.[10]

---

7 Mark McIntosh, *Discernment and Truth: The Spirituality and Theology of Knowledge*, New York: Crossroad, 2004, p. 158.

8 Ibid., p. 159.

9 *SM*, II, 38. On the significance of these initials and speculations as to the identity of the persons indicated see *Select Meditations*, ed. Julia Smith, Manchester: Carcanet Press, 1997, p. 161, n. 38. See also Osborn, 'A new Traherne Manuscript', p. 928.

10 On the 'others' implied in Traherne's use of different personal pronouns and the divergence and merging of self and other in the *Centuries*, see Joan Webber, *The Eloquent 'I':*

DIFFERENCE

There is another Other in Traherne's work though, as we have noted: the 'Som Great Thing' of the first *Century*, also present in the poetry – that object of his desire whose attraction forms the basis of his very thought. It is to this object that his work constantly returns, whether that work be addressed to a broad or to an intimate audience. The 'Som Great Thing' functions both as a structural device and as a source of creative energy. It is from his desire for 'Som Great Thing' that his imagery of childhood gets its poignancy because his childhood, from the first recollection of it, is a vanished thing – his paradise, like Milton's, lost. This loss has been less fully explored than it deserves by most readers of Traherne. In fact, the loss of paradise, exclusion from it and the journey to regain a Promised Land is the whole subject of the unpublished manuscript *The Ceremonial Law*. This epic poem, which considers the books of Genesis and Exodus, recounts stories of elemental human experiences such as hunger, thirst, fear, danger, fire, water, gift and gratitude. Where one might expect a poem beginning with Genesis to abound in creation imagery, innocence and plenty, the poem begins instead with 'Adam's Fall' and banishment. From the outset the characters in the poem are displaced persons, outcasts, strangers, sojourners. The memory of paradise and the hope of the Promised Land may be its gilded frame but the poem's narrative sequences unfold largely in a wasteland. It is thirst that makes the outcasts know the worth of water; it is hunger that makes their manna meat. This is an epic poem about the loss of Eden, a public loss as poignant as Traherne's account of his own personal loss of innocence. The pull of 'Som Great Thing' of the *Centuries* derives its power from this very loss – the loss of childhood innocence, the loss of his people's paradise, a primal discord. The unity of object and desire described in that early state of innocence is as far removed as the state itself. His effort to be reunited with the object of his desire is, in one form or another, the force behind both his poetry and his prose. His writing on the soul, its powers and properties – reverting always to the recurring, sometimes erotic, image of the soul as a bride – is a reflection of that desire.[11]

In *Traherne in Dialogue*, Leigh DeNeef suggests that there is yet another Other beneath the object of Traherne's desire. This other is the Other of Traherne's own psychology, understood in a Lacanian model as 'the unnamed Other, whose desire Traherne seeks to incite and

---

Style and Self in Seventeenth-century Prose, Madison, WI: University of Wisconsin Press, 1968, pp. 226–38.

11 See especially *Seeds of Eternity*, *The Kingdom of God*, *Love* and *Select Meditations*.

address, who incites and is made answerable to Traherne's own desire, is the ground upon which the entire *epos* of linguistic re-creation is begun'.[12] It is because of the continually present absence of this other that DeNeef sees Traherne as 'preeminently a poet of desire'.[13] With DeNeef, I would assert that it is largely because of a failure to appreciate the centrality of desire in Traherne that he has been so widely misread as a poet of easy felicity. And with DeNeef I would argue that to understand Traherne in the light of desire is to bring important new insights to a misrepresented author. The work presented here on Lacan is not intended as a studied view of Lacan but as a helpful contrast to previous, mainly historical considerations of Traherne.

Perhaps the part of DeNeef's study most pertinent to this book is the attention that he gives to the notion of object/Other in Traherne. Where the psychologist Jacques Lacan writes, 'man's desire finds its meaning in the desire of the other, not so much because the other holds the key to the object desired, as because the first object of desire is to be recognized by the other'[14] and 'man's desire is the desire of the Other'[15] DeNeef follows: 'Man's desire is desire of the Other', desire of being recognized by the Other, of being the Other's desire, of being desirable to the Other, of desiring the Other. In Traherne's version of these dialectical and irreducible structures, the principal actors are man and God.[16]

Let us first consider God's desire for the Other. That Traherne's God desires has, I hope, been made plain in chapter one. God desires infinitely. And Traherne's recurring questions are questions of divine desire. *What* does God desire? *Why* does God desire? *How* does God desire? As DeNeef puts it, 'Insofar as God is perfect, he does

---

12 A. Leigh DeNeef, *Traherne in Dialogue: Heidegger, Lacan, and Derrida*, Durham, NC: Duke University Press, 1988, pp. 115–16.

13 Ibid., p.116. DeNeef offers a reading for the Dobell poems that sees them neither as mystical ascent (Clements) nor as a birth–fall–redemption narrative (Day) and so may offer a fresh insight to the sequence. Certainly his contribution to our understanding of desire in Traherne's poetry is very valuable. But the problems with DeNeef's reading are that it centres on the *psyche* at the expense of the *pneuma*, or perhaps makes no distinction between the two – this in appreciation of an author whose most central concern was the soul – and that it seems to contradict his own Lacanian model. When DeNeef contends that the Dobell sequence charts 'a course of psychic development into fully human maturity'(p. 109), he contradicts Lacan's own insistence that the three registers of real, imagined and symbolic do not represent developmental stages but co-exist at all times as structural relations in the ego.

14 Jacques Lacan, *Ecrits: A Selection*, trans. Alan Sheridan, London: Tavistock, 1977, p. 58.

15 Ibid., p. 264.

16 DeNeef, *Traherne in Dialogue*, p. 118.

DIFFERENCE

not need anything; but insofar as He is God, He demands all.'[17] But DeNeef would situate God's desire, with Lacan, in this gap between need and demand. And this gap is most often understood in terms of lack, absence, loss and want. Even in God there is something like lack. In *Christian Ethicks* Traherne describes divine wanting not only in terms of a longing outward towards its object but also, if denied, as an absence.

> Infinite Love infinitely desires to be beloved, and is infinitely displeased if it be neglected. GOD desires . . . the Love of his Beloved. And nothing in all Worlds but the love of that Person can be his satisfaction. For nothing can supply the absence or denial of that Love which is his end.[18]

Traherne's God is 'from eternity full of Want'.[19] This is not just the want of his lost and fallen creatures, though that particular loss enhances his desire,[20] but a want that is part of his eternal essence. And yet this want is not a want of being. Following Lacan's model, DeNeef identifies divine wanting with a *manque d'être*, which, Traherne insists, is entirely alien to the nature of God. That God's desire is 'infinite' is a mark of its capacity, not of its irreducibility. It is in this respect that God's desire is not like our desire. God's want is an act of freedom, performed in accordance with God's infinite goodness to the increase of his own and his creatures' delight. What DeNeef could not know because the work had not yet been discovered, is that Traherne clearly states in *The Kingdom of God* that there is no compulsion to God's desiring, there is no need or necessity in his act. In fact, necessity and desire are seen as opposite forces – to act by 'necessitie' is to act 'without Desire'. Necessity is the expression of compulsion, desire the expression of power and freedom to choose:

> It is the Glory of God, that he is a free, and eternal Agent. Had anything been before him to compel him, had he acted by an Inward Principle of necessitie, without Desire, and Delight, he had been Passiv, and dishonourable.[21]

---

17 Ibid., pp. 118–19.
18 *CE*, p. 251.
19 C, I, 42; 'Or else He would not be full of Treasure', Traherne adds. God's eternal fullness and his eternal want are spoken of in the same breath.
20 See C, II, 31; C, III, 83; C, IV, 26.
21 *KOG*, fol. 363r.

This is exactly where the desire of the human soul and the desire of God part company. For we are drawn by an inward inclination to the irrefutable beauty of our object, whereas God simply chose. Or, as Traherne puts it: 'But there is this Difference between God, and us; God was purely the first author of his own choise; nothing but its freedom and desire carried him to the Act, wherin he delighted.'[22]

So we may see divine desire as distinct from human desiring. According to Traherne, we may desire in the image of God – that is to say, not only infinitely but also freely – only because we are in the estate of trial. We are free to act, desire and choose only because we are shielded from complete vision of the divine. Were we to see fully, as God sees, the freedom of our actions would be subsumed in the irresistible draw of divine beauty. Hence our desiring is quite different from God's desiring. And yet at significant points the two types of desiring converge. Both human and divine desire are desire of the Other; it is in this sense that both the human and God need an object.

But how do we reconcile the necessity of an object that divine desiring implies with the assertion that all things exist in union with the divine? Traherne's answer is that all things are in God in their origin and in their end but that the soul does, nevertheless, have its own distinct existence. 'All Things are in God because they are in Eternitie; and his Omnipresence. All Things are in GOD, as in their Cause, and End. And Things are in him both realy, and by way of eminence', he claims in *The Kingdom of God*.[23] And yet several lines later he writes of the soul that 'Its own Existence is absolutely distinct from the Divine Essence'. We need to be distinct in order to enjoy ourselves and to enjoy God as an object of our desires: 'The Essence of God is allsufficient to make his Creatures Happy: yet without something more then his essence, no creature can be Happy . . . no creature can enjoy God, unless it hath it self to enjoy in like manner.'[24]

According to Traherne, this distinction of the soul from God is as necessary for God, in his chosen want, as it is for us. God wished us to be different or 'distinct' from him. 'He wanted Worlds, He wanted spectators', Traherne writes of God in the *Centuries*; 'He wanted Angels and Men, Images, Companions'.[25] Traherne circumnavigates

---

22 *KOG*, fol. 363r–v.
23 *KOG*, fol. 360r.
24 Ibid.
25 C, I, 41–2. As always, the want and supply are concomitant in God. Traherne continues, 'He wanted, yet He wanted not, for He had them.' For further explication of this see Ch. 1 above on God's wanting.

the problem of Divine all-sufficiency that this assertion raises by claiming, in *The Kingdom of God*, that the divine essence is all-sufficient by being able to create the means to satisfy its need to be enjoyed (*KOG*, fol. 360r). And so Traherne's God has prepared an answer to his own chosen need, an Other to be the object of desire and in whose eyes He may be an object of desire in return. This is the origin of all sense of object and Other in Traherne.

In the previous chapter we considered what Traherne's human is in terms of the capacities of the soul and in terms of humanity's unique position in the hierarchy of the universe. But what the human is may also be understood in terms of self and other. We may begin to know ourselves in the interplay of object and subject, in relation to an Other. In this sense, what a person is is as dependent upon the existence of the other as what he or she does. 'There is an instinct that carries us to the beginning of our Lives' writes Traherne in *Christian Ethicks*.[26] And that beginning is a beginning pregnant with desire. Desire is in the silence and in the chaos; in the expectation of 'Som great Thing' and in the abyss of nothingness. This is so for the individual human and for the whole human story because, right from the first pages of Genesis, the human experience is a creation *ex nihilo* followed shortly by a fall. It is as if we come out of nothing and fall into loss. And so the whole dynamic of desire is with us from the first. And it is in this sense that we may come to see the Fall in Traherne as more central than has been thought. For, as DeNeef notes, 'the Fall opens man's loss – his wants, and his lacks – to the desiring urgencies of restoration, recollection, recovery'.[27] What we are is constituted in desire.

It may be more in this sense than in any other that Traherne's humanity has inherited the effects of the Fall of Adam. For Traherne's human being is split between an inherited unity and an inherited disunity. By the divine light within us we sense we belong to the unified divine, but by our experience and reason we know our loss. This is in some sense similar to the position of the Lacanian infant who knows himself by alienation.

According to Lacan's theories of the formation of self and identity, the ego is irreducibly formed on a bipartition created by the false self the infant sees in the mirror. The child gestures and plays, observing the relation between its own movements and the movements assumed in the image and the reflected environment. This specular confusion of

---

26 *CE*, p. 212. Here he is referring specifically to memory, though this tendency to recollect one's origins may also apply to the quest for self-knowledge.
27 DeNeef, *Traherne in Dialogue*, p. 124.

reality with virtual reality initiates what Lacan calls *stade du miroir* (the mirror stage). Lacan records the event thus:

> Unable as yet to walk, or even to stand up, and held tightly as he is by some support, human or artificial (what, in France, we call a '*trote-bébé*'), he nevertheless overcomes, in a flutter of jubilant activity, the obstructions of his support and, fixing his attitude in a slightly leaning-forward position, in order to hold it in his gaze, brings back an instantaneous aspect of the image.[28]

For Lacan this activity 'discloses a libidinal dynamism' that is part of the 'ontological structure of the human world'.[29] The infant assumes an image or form that is separate from itself and in so doing etches its psyche with a kind of difference or discord. The purpose of the mirror stage is 'to establish a relation between the organism and its reality',[30] but because of the specular confusion between reality and virtual reality that occurs there is what Lacan calls 'a primordial Discord'[31] at the heart of the ego. The ego is set 'in a fictional direction, which will always remain irreducible for the individual alone', or rather, which will only be resolved asymptotically.[32] Ultimately, says Lacan of the infant, 'he must resolve as *I* his discordance with his own reality'.[33] Lacan's child, in the mirror stage, is already being psychologically formed along lines of alienation, lack of unified wholeness and an incipient longing for resolution. According to Lacan this primary discord arising from specular confusion marks the ego's entire development – a development irreducibly determined by lack.

In the mirror stage what the child sees is mistaken for what he is; his perception of reality is erroneous. Here we see one of the significant differences between Lacan and Traherne. Whereas Lacan sees the child's apprehension of the world as an error, Traherne sees it as the truth. For Traherne's infant, to perceive is to be. Sight and being are one and the sight that is beheld is one of unity rather than discord. Nevertheless, Lacan's emphasis on lack as a fundamental human experience that goes deeper into our psyche than our conscious lists of wants and dreams may suggest throws important light on the mechanics of desire in Traherne.

---

28 Jacques Lacan, *Ecrits*, pp. 1, 2.
29 Ibid., p. 2.
30 Ibid., p. 4.
31 Ibid., p. 4.
32 Ibid., p. 2.
33 Ibid.

DIFFERENCE

Lacan recognizes in the mirror stage 'the effect in man of an organic insufficiency in his natural reality . . . the mirror stage is a drama whose internal thrust is precipitated from insufficiency to anticipation'.[34] Here we have something that sounds very like Traherne's 'wanting', which springs from lack and stretches out in desire.

Traherne uses many terms such as want, desire, longing, appetite and thirst with easy familiarity, as if they were consanguineous. In contrast, Lacan uses three distinct and independent terms: desire (*désir*), need (*besoin*) and demand (*demande*). Lacanian desire is neither need nor demand. Where need is fundamentally biological, demand is strictly psychological. Where need is particular, demand is absolute. Desire, essentially in the singular, is born out of the gap between the two. 'Desire begins to take shape in the margin in which demand becomes separated from need',[35] writes Lacan. 'Let us articulate that which structures desire. Desire is that which is manifested in the interval that demand hollows within itself.'[36] Whereas need is satisfiable, demand remains forever unsatisfiable because it issues from a psyche fundamentally structured on separation and lack. So, states Lacan, 'the satisfaction of need appears only as the lure in which the demand for love is crushed, by sending the subject back to sleep, where he haunts the limbo regions of being'.[37] The unsatisfiable psyche shaped by lack reiterates an appetite for the Other that is neither pure need nor pure demand. DeNeef writes

> This means, I think, that desire is always situated in both a dependence upon demand and an imagined relation to need. That is, the subject must perceive a lack in the Other as the necessary precondition of the Other's desire. The appetite of the gaze, of the Other's eye, needs an object to see. So the subject responds to that appetite by objectifying himself in relation to a supposed lack. But the subject also recognizes, perhaps unconsciously, that the self he gives to be seen is not the self he wishes the Other to see. Indeed, demand is for the Other to see him as he really is, subjectively, not objectively. This wish, or demand, thus articulates a lack in the subject himself which the Other is then called upon to satisfy. Self and Other are

---

34 Ibid., p. 4.
35 'Desire begins to take shape in the margin in which demand becomes separated from need: this margin being that which is opened up by demand' (ibid., p. 311); 'Although it always shows through demand, as can be seen, here, desire is nonetheless beyond it' (ibid., p. 269).
36 Ibid., p. 263.
37 Ibid.

irretrievably caught in what Lacan calls a want-to-be, and desire as such is born from the discovery of a difference (between subject/object, presence/absence, self/Other, etc.) which situates all being in that *manque-d'être*, that lack of being. Neither the Other nor the subject is capable of satisfying this desire: I cannot be loved for what I am; I can only be loved as a signifier of what you lack. If, then, I am a metonym of your desire, you are a metonym of my want-to-be.[38]

In direct contrast Trahernean desire is ever satisfied, issuing from a human self essentially unifiable, if as yet ununified, and towards a unified object. The Other is not only recognized as essential lack or abyss but also as essentially full. And yet what Lacan is saying about the reciprocal nature of desire is very like Traherne. Traherne perceives a lack in his divine Other that is the precondition of divine desire; he perceives himself and all creatures as the object of that divine gaze; he is objectified in relation to the divine act. He wishes his truest self to be seen and desired by the divine Other, his wish or demand articulating a lack in him to which the other may respond. He becomes the desiring one and the divine Other the object of his desire. For Traherne, as for Lacan, desire is born out of a perceived difference.

In both Traherne and Lacan, desire as a constantly revisited process is necessary. Traherne speaks in terms of insatiability, infinite aspiration and eternal want – those faces of human desire with which we gaze upon our objects, by which we extend to the Other – the self at once extended and recipient. In Lacan, the Other is a structural necessity for the existence of a conscious self and for any and all human relations. All consciousness of self is irreducibly grounded in the condition of recognizing and being recognized by some other.[39] Therefore there can ultimately be no reconciliation between self and Other – the split or distinction, the separation between self and Other *is* the basic structure of the human being. That is how, for Lacan, all being can be founded in desire.[40]

---

38 DeNeef, *Traherne in Dialogue*, pp. 113–14.

39 See for instance 'the subject is subject only from being subjected to the field of the Other; the subject proceeds from his synchronic subjection in the field of the Other' (*The Four Fundamental Concepts of Psycho-analysis*, trans. Alan Sheridan, New York: Norton & Co., 1981, p. 188); and 'What I seek in the Word is the response of the Other. What constitutes me as subject is my question' (*The Language of the Self*, New York: Dell Publishing, 1975, p. 63). In the latter he is speaking particularly of linguistic discourse between self and other, whereas elsewhere he refers to visual identification.

40 The resulting theory leaves no room for the hope of ultimate unity, so dear to the likes of Day and Clements, who rightly saw its importance to Traherne; and it may be fair to

DIFFERENCE

For Traherne, as I have noted, being is not so much founded in as found in desire. This is where Traherne and Lacan fundamentally differ. For Traherne desire is not who we are but how we know who we are. From the *Centuries*:

> we search into the powers and faculties of the Soul, enquire into the excellencies of human nature, consider its wants, survey its inclinations, propensities and desires, ponder its principles, proposals, and ends . . . Whereby we come to know what man is in this world, what his sovereign end and happiness . . . by discerning man's real wants and sovereign desires.[41]

Let us, for a moment, consider what DeNeef calls the 'gaze' and Lacan calls *le regard* – that which 'cannot itself be seen but whose presence structures the entire act of seeing and being seen'.[42] The gaze is found in the split between need and demand, self and other, subject and object. It is the pre-existing lack or void that the eye, through seeing, tries to fill. It is the desire that is filled by sight: 'the gaze, withdraws into concealment the moment a given being is revealed, even though it is the necessary ground or condition of that revealing'.[43] For Lacan being is located in desire and desire is in the gaze, *le regard*, the thing that is not a thing but neither is it nothing. This is similar to what both A. L. Clements and Rosalie Colie suggest about where being is found in Traherne – it is in the middle ground along a continuum between subject and object. The experience is the concrete thing; the subject and object are abstractions.

'The self and the not-self, subject and object, as we ordinarily understand them, are, in actuality, opposite surfaces of the same coin, the reality of which lies in between', writes Clements.[44] And yet, for the purposes of knowledge, they need each other as separate entities:

> The real Self, as opposed to the ego, cannot, after all, be a separately, intellectually knowable object, for what, then, is it that does

---

say that DeNeef's work on desire explicates the mechanics of the process in Traherne more fully than it illuminates the end.

41 C, III, 42.

42 DeNeef, *Traherne in Dialogue*, p. 102.

43 Ibid., p. 104. DeNeef goes on to say of the gaze 'we speak universally of an evil eye but nowhere of a good eye. The evil eye is a metaphor for the subject's imagined condition of being subjected to the Other's gaze. The gaze makes the I desperate, suspicious, guilty, accountable. The gaze is heard as demand.'

44 Clements, 'Mode and Meaning', p. 505.

the knowing? The Self escapes itself into an infinite regress in its own attempt at definition. It can no more become its own object of knowledge than a thumb can catch hold of itself.[45]

While the rational mind reiterates both extremes – subject and object – the intuitive mind inhabits the middle ground or darts along the continuum, the rational mind setting boundaries or reference points that the intuition appears to ignore but upon which it depends. It is the relationship between the two extremes that is the reality.

Colie notes the significance of the two extremes of subject and object in terms of self-reference when she writes of self-reference as a mirror: 'The reflexive self-reference is, as the term suggests, a mirror image; as in mirror images, self-reference begins an endless oscillation between the thing itself and the thing reflected, begins an infinite regress.'[46] This infinite oscillation both confirms and questions the uniqueness of the self:

> The psychological effect of mirrors is that they both confirm and question individual identity – confirm by splitting the mirrored viewer into observer and observed, giving him the opportunity to view himself objectively, as other people do; question, by repeating him as if he were simply an object, not 'himself', as he so surely 'knows' himself to be, by repeating himself as if he were not (as his inmost self insists that he is) unique.[47]

Here Colie is writing of a re-created self, a 'separated and objectified' self, which she sees not as the 'real' self but as a 'threat to the self'.[48] And yet reflexive self-reference is the stuff of which any discussion about who we are is constituted. 'Man's relations with himself are inevitably paradoxical',[49] Colie writes. To suggest, then, that the object/subject distinction is necessary to self-knowledge while at the same time asserting that in their origin and end humans participate in the unity of God may not be counterproductive. Subject and object are necessary; they function as points of reference, two sides of the same

---
45 Ibid.
46 Rosalie Colie, *Paradoxia Epidemica: The Renaissance Tradition of Paradox*, Princeton: Princeton University Press, 1966, p. 355.
47 Ibid., pp. 355–6. Whereas for Lacan the mirror is the first step to self-knowledge, for Colie it is both helpful and deceptive.
48 Ibid., p. 356. For further discussion of the 'real self' see Traherne's 'The Preparative', and Clements, 'Mode and Meaning', pp. 504–6.
49 Colie, *Paradoxia Epidemica*, p. 355.

coin. The reality lies in the middle ground, in the act of perceiving, in the substance of their union. As Clements explains:

> Traherne's position [that subject and object meet together] does not constitute a denial of external reality or of an observing self. It merely asserts, affirms the truth, that object and subject exist only as abstractions from the concrete experience of perception, which experience 'includes' subject and object as the end limits of a single, integrated reality.[50]

Object and subject, self and Other, exist and must exist, not only for the purposes of self-knowledge but also for the purposes of action. Even when the human is not conscious of it, his or her need of an object is ever present because the human's re-creative action involves a conscious opposition of subject and object.

The re-creation in which we are to be employed is a returning of the world to its creator. 'The World within you is an offering returned', writes Traherne in the *Centuries*.[51] And thus returned to God it is more valuable to him than it was when first created. Not only is the world of our mind a creation that may delight God but God has also given the human being power to offer the created material world back: 'for God hath made you able . . . to give and offer up the world unto Him, which is very delightful in flowing from Him, but much more in returning to Him'.[52] Thus, according to Traherne, we may both create and re-create in our minds and in the world, respectively, offerings more pleasing to God than the initial creation.

This re-creative act is, Clements claims, the natural act of the infant whose 'simple act of perception re-creates the otherwise dead material world'.[53] In 'The Preparative', Traherne's bold claim that the infant is a 'Heavnly King' (l. 30) – as opposed to his brother Philip's correction,

---

50 Clements, 'Mode and Meaning', p. 505.
51 C, II, 90; cf. 'Is not then the Love which a man returneth a Magnifnicent thing! . . . it is the most great and marvellous thing in all the World, and is in its own place of all other things most highly desired by all Angels and Men; and is the greatest Gift which (in, and by that Soul) can possibly be given' (*CE*, p. 252).
52 C, II, 90.
53 Clements, 'Mode and Meaning', p. 514. In his notion of the elevation of the material world to spiritual, Traherne relies on Plotinus. Compare, for instance, the above quote and 'The material world is dead and feeleth nothing, but this spiriual world, though it be invisible, hath all dimensions, and is a divine and living Being, the voluntary Act of an Obedient Soul' (C, III, 90) with Plotinus' division of the intelligible and sensible world: *Enneads*, VI, 9.9, II, 4.4.8 and IV, 8.1.49.

which makes the infant, not King but heir[54] – suggests that the infant is empowered to act as lord. The infant is 'A Naked Simple Pure Intelligence' (l. 20), whose 'Simple Sence / Is Lord of all Created Excellence.' (ll. 39–40) and whose very act of perception is an act of creation. For the infant's simple sense, as a 'Pure Empty Power', is free to receive and re-create, as glass or polished brass may do, the image of all that it receives. In this case re-creation is like a mirror, the soul returns what it has first received, the quality of the image it returns entirely dependent upon the purity of the glass. The poem is primarily about the purity of infant sight but Traherne insists that this disentangled and naked sense may be retrieved, and the poem ends with a call to the mature human to 'Get free' (l. 70) and to perceive with infant purity again. It is in this most profound sense that Traherne's man is to be busy about the work of 'enjoying the world', where to enjoy is to take in to oneself and return again with praise. This is our active work:

> An Activ man is still employd;
> Till all things are enjoyd
> He never Rests . . .[55]

The enjoyment of all things and the transformation of the world is the work of bliss. In 'A Wise Man', the poem of fifteen stanzas from *The Kingdom of God* from which the above lines are taken, Traherne outlines the process by which the human may bring blessing to the material world. In the first six stanzas he describes the life of the wise, good, holy, righteous, pious, blessed and active person, concluding in the seventh stanza that:

> A Wise, a Good, a Holy Man,
> To end where we began;
> A lively, Righteous Grateful Soul
> A Pious Learned Wight

---

54 Where Thomas wrote 'And evry Thing / Delighted me that was their Heavnly King' (ll. 29–30), Philip corrected: 'And all things fair / Delighted me that was to be their Heir', at once both priviledging 'fair' things above 'all' things and disempowering the viewer. The implications of the changes Philip made to Thomas's manuscript work are as many as the changes themselves and I shall not explore them all here. It is generally agreed that Philip's changes were not improvements. For details of where this is so see, for example, Clements, 'Mode and Meaning', and idem, *The Mystical Poetry* pp. 105–7.

55 'A Wise Man will apply his Mind' (ll. 41–3). Note here that the work of the wise man is to enjoy; cf. *KOG*, fol. 334v, where the 'Power to enjoy is more desirable and Blessed then a Power to Create.' And *KOG* 340v in which Traherne claims that 'No Power can Creat, that cannot enjoy'.

> A Blessed man that doth controul
> The Powers of the Night,
> An Activ Heavenly Glorious Person is
> Employd, and Busy in the Work of Bliss.

That work of bliss is the transformation of the created world, an act of re-creation like that described earlier. With a certain boldness, Traherne claims of this wise man that 'Being transformd, himself he is / A very Spring of Bliss'. Everything he sees, touches, feels is transformed by its contact with his own transformed self: 'His fingers pierce, whatever thing they hold. / Like fire that alters evry thing / On which it passes' he brings his own blessed nature to bear on all things so that 'They also burn, and turn to fire, / Love, Pleasure, and Desire.'[56]

Re-creation is also inimical to the very structure of the *Centuries*, as Joan Webber notes: 'Of first importance to an understanding of the book's structure is the relationship between Traherne's view of the aim of God's creation of the world, and his own aim in writing the *Centuries*. According to Traherne, a part of God's creation – the human mind – was originally left blank in order that it might learn to reflect the whole creation. Such reflection – the idea of the world in man's thought – is the aim of creation, and more important than the world itself.'[57] Webber goes so far as to claim that the re-creative acts of the *Centuries* include not only the reflection of creation but also the author's own re-creation of himself and his reader who is to complete the book, 'thus recreating herself (as Cherub)'.[58]

Traherne is less concerned with self-creative action than he is with re-creative action, but either operation requires an interplay of subject and object and some sense of opposition of self and Other. William Craven, noting the contribution of the Renaissance humanist Pico, wrote that:

> Man's relationship to the world was changed because his self-creative action involved the conscious opposition of subject to object, which was not a once-for-all thing. This was why man's being and value

---

56 This and the preceding quotations are from ll. 81–2, ll. 88–90 and ll. 93–4 respectively.

57 Webber, *The Eloquent 'I'*, p. 226.

58 Webber, '"I and Thou" in the Prose of Thomas Traherne', *Papers on Language and Literature*, 2 (1966) pp. 258–64, 259. Webber refers here to the inscription at the front of the *Centuries*: 'This book unto the friend of my best friend / As of the wisest Love a mark I send, / That she may write my Maker's prais therin / And make her self therby a Cherubin.'

could only be defined dynamically. But it also contained the polarity on which was based the moral and intellectual tension characteristic of the Renaissance; man's will and knowledge turned towards the world but distinguishing themselves from it; duality but not dualism, relative and not absolute opposition, transcendence and participation in mutual determination. The relationship of man to the world was understood, therefore, as a *coincidentia oppositorum* after the manner of Cusanus.[59]

While I am not convinced that the main thrust of Pico's thought was self-creative action any more than was Traherne's, Craven's description of the opposition of subject and object as 'relative and not absolute' and of man in relationship to the world in the manner of Nicholas of Cusa is completely apposite to this study of Traherne. For in Traherne's human there is, on the one hand, the insistence that to perceive is to be the thing perceived and, on the other, that the perceiver receives the thing perceived as an object and returns it to God. Is this Traherne overcoming the normal subject/object relations? I do not think so. The tension in which Traherne holds himself as both recipient and co-creator is the tension of paradox, the *coincidentia oppositorum* or 'coincidence of contradictories' of Nicholas of Cusa:

> The place wherin Thou [God] art found unveiled is girt round with the coincidence of contradictories, and this is the wall of Paradise wherein Thou dost abide. The door whereof is guarded by the most proud spirit of Reason, and, unless he be vanquished, the way in will not lie open. Thus 'tis beyond the coincidence of contradictories that Thou mayest be seen, and nowhere this side thereof.[60]

For Nicholas of Cusa paradox is not just an intellectual necessity but a spiritual weapon. It is the tool by which proud reason is vanquished. Traherne's paradox continually cries 'both/and'. His human is both recipient and co-creator, both nothing and everything, the deep abyss and the pinnacle of creation.

---

59 William Craven, *Giovanni Pico della Mirandola: Symbol of his Age*, Geneva: Librarie Droz, 1981, p. 24.

60 Nicholas of Cusa, *The Vision of God*, trans. Emma Gurney Salter, New York: E. P. Dutton & Co., 1928, p. 44. Cusanus held that one could reach knowledge or union with God through achieving a resolution of opposites within the self. For details of the influence of Cusanus on the central issues of Renaissance thought (Cusanus came through the Florentine Academy) see Ernst Cassirer, *The Individual and the Cosmos in Renaissance Philosophy*, trans. Mario Domandi, New York: Harper & Row, 1963.

For Traherne a man or woman's being is defined dynamically in the kinds of paradoxes implied by the co-existence of, on the one hand, subject and object relations and, on the other hand, a unity that is the origin and end of all. Here, in the simultaneous concurrence of subject/object relations and ultimate unity, Traherne treads close to the central Christian paradox of the Trinity according to which doctrine God is three and God is one – unity and diversity existing simultaneously in the personhood of God. The importance of this Christian doctrine to Traherne may be glimpsed in his refutations of Socinianism (Unitarianism) in *Commentaries of Heaven*. What bothers him about the Socinians is that they deny the doctrine of the Trinity – to the Socinians God is Father but the Son, Jesus, though a model of goodness, is not divine, and the Holy Ghost is a kind of good presence washing over things. In his article 'Atonement' (in *COH*) he mentions the Socinians no less than six times, calling them 'The Abominable Socinians a sort of Christened Turks, or Baptized Infidels' and claiming 'Our Savior is evil requited by the Socinians for the Benefits of their Redemption: They rob him of his Nature, because he assumed theirs.' In the article 'Assumption' his whole concern is to uphold the belief that the divinity of Christ and the humanity of Christ go hand in hand and cannot be divorced one from the other. He quotes the early Greek father Athanasius:

> Being GOD from all Eternity, in the fullness of Time he took upon him the form of a Servant, & was made in the likeness of Man; being, as Athanasius saith, GOD of the substance of the Father, begotten before the World, & MAN of the substance of his Mother born in the World: Perfect GOD & perfect Man (*COH*, 'Assumption', fol 149r).

That Traherne is so vociferous in his attacks on Socinians suggests that he will not compromise on the doctrine of the Trinity however paradoxical and difficult it may be.[61]

So strong is Traherne's notion of the persons of the Trinity that he not only sees the Father, the Son and the Holy Spirit as separate but sometimes almost as at variance, as in this instance from the *Kingdom of God* in which he explores how great is God's love for his creation:

---

61 For further discussion of Traherne and Socinianism see Denise Inge, 'Thomas Traherne and the Socinian Heresy in *Commentaries of Heaven*', *Notes and Queries*, 252, 4 (December 2007), pp. 412–16.

> It seemeth as if God the Father Loved us better than his Son. For God so Loved the World, that he gav his only begotten Son that whosoever believeth on him should not perish; but hav Everlasting Life. It seemeth that the Son of God loved us better then his Father, for when Enmity and Variance fell out between us, he forsooke his Father, and did cleav unto us like a Bridegroom that forsaketh Father and Mother to cleav to his Wife. This is that we Know not how to Judg of.[62]

'Seems' is the significant word here, and Traherne's admission that both the love of God and the persons of God are unsearchable to us rescues his line of thinking from polytheism. There is no ultimate insurmountable difference between the persons of the Trinity, he concludes:

> He forsook not his Father, even while he forsook him . . . His Father was pleased, while he was displeased, and made him the object of his Anger, and gave him up onto Death, yet for this very caus also highly Exalted him and gav him a Name abov every Name, that at the Name of Jesus, Evry Knee should bow of things in Heaven, and things in Earth, and things under the Earth. His Lov was Wounded, and his Soul divided upon our Transgression. He hated us as Sinners, And there our Savior rather forsook him, then us, and undertook for us. He loved us as his Creatures, and there our Saviour and he were united. His only beloved Son was well-pleasing unto him, in Redeeming us: and yet in Redeeming us Endured the Wrath of his Eternal Father. That there should be Secrets enow in the Natur of Lov, to Justify these things is Strange . . .[63]

What interests me most here is that for Traherne love itself is by its nature full of contradictions. Right in the heart of God, who is love, he sees the battles of divided interests vanquished by a shared overarching desire for the redemption of the world. The persons of the Trinity are united not by a shared doctrine, a vow, a rule of life, but by their being one in essence and nature and by a common, undivided desire, the desire of God for God's creation. In this desire, the wooing of creation, the persons of the Trinity work together as the one that they in fact are. Where the Son sacrifices himself and the Father forgives, the Holy Spirit as a secret agent,

---
62 KOG, Ch 14, ll. 145–51 (here Traherne is quoting both John 3.16 and Gen. 2.24).
63 Ibid., ll. 156–70 (here Traherne quotes Phil. 2.9–10 and Isa. 53.5).

Speaks for GOD and whispers in the mind,
Kissing the Ear that to his Mouth's inclind.

(*COH*, 'Allurement')

The tension between unity and difference that exists within the doctrine of the Trinity, which Traherne sees as resolved by a unified desire, one essence, a single Love, informs his whole world-view. It is apparent in his treatment of the virtues in which each virtue remains distinct if it is to have any value yet all the virtues are one. It is echoed again in his insistence that everything participates in an ultimate unity, while insisting that each person, each thing, each creature is unique and treasured. Though explicitly defended only in particular writings, the doctrine of the Trinity shapes Traherne's whole cosmos. The allusively Trinitarian 'begetting, begotten, proceeding' love of the *Centuries* is the same Trinity that is the 'means, cause and end' in *Commentaries of Heaven*. Traherne's God, who cannot be the great One without being all three – Father, Son, Spirit; Maker, Redeemer, Sustainer – is the pattern for everything. We cannot 'enjoy the Deitie', Traherne insists, nor even be ourselves, without also being three by being the cause, means and end as God is, by participating in love begetting, love begotten, love proceeding. In 'Act' in *Commentaries of Heaven*, Traherne describes it as follows:

His face the Patern is, being one in Three,
Who without being Three, One cannot be.
Nor canst Thou Soul Enjoy the Deitie
Nor be thy self, without thy being Three.
Be caus means end; see Lov proceed and shine
On all, so Thou shall three in one Divine
Companions have; and being all alone,
Proceeder Parent Son be Three in one.

(*COH*, 'Act', ll. 28–35)

Traherne takes a Trinitarian God as the root of his model of a relational human self made in the image of God. His human is a self that, separated from the divine, knows itself both by the disunity inherent in subject/object relations and by its own hankering after the ultimate unity it senses as divine. The famous Rublev icon is perhaps one of the most easily accessible visual images of this Trinitarian unity in diversity – it shows the three persons of the Trinity seated at table together, each eye catching the others' in a single triangulated gaze – one God but a God for whom relationship is at the core of being. All of this informs Traherne's notion not only of subject and object relations but also of the relationship at the heart of the creation, the notion that 'All things allured God to make them' (*COH* 'Allurement'). Where there is creative energy there is either the presence or the present absence of an 'other'.

The object and subject need each other: light needs the eye in order to be seen, just as the eye needs light in order to see.[64] This interdependence of light and eye is a notion that is of course not uniquely Traherne's, though it may be traced in his poetry and his prose.[65] In *Christian Ethicks* Traherne writes: 'all satisfactions, joys and praises are the happy offspring of powers and objects well united. Both the one and the other would lie void and barren if they never met together.'[66] I suggest that not only do subject and object need each other but that, in Traherne, subject/object division and ultimate unity need each other too. By the one we are; by the other we come to know who we are. Ultimately what the human person is and what the person does and knows (what he or she perceives) are not discrete categories – the one affects the other.

We return again to the image of the infant, since that is the state to which Traherne insists that we must return ourselves. As Clements has observed 'the infant does not abstract from experience and divide it into subject and object. He simply perceives, experiences; he *is* the perception, the experience.'[67]

While the existence of an Other is a constant necessity for Traherne's structures and thought and for the working out of human self-knowledge and action, it is his belief that the soul participates in an original and final, an ultimate unity that gives his work its simple daring. This is what gives his infant-eye its re-creative power and his human soul its potential for transformation. The subject and object participate in a greater unity of perception and being.

The Other is a point continually revisited by Traherne. There is the other registered in the mechanics of reader and author, that other who

---

64 Clements goes so far as to say that 'the eye *is* the light, for without the other each is incomplete, unrealised' 'Mode and Meaning', p. 506, italics mine).

65 See for instance 'The Preparative', in which the soul is 'A Living endless Ey', simultaneously both '*Sphere of Light*' and '*Orb of Sight*'. In 'Mode and Meaning' Clements notes similarities between Traherne and both Plotinus and Eckhart on this subject ('Mode and Meaning', nn. 8, 9).

66 *CE*, p. 72.

67 Clements, 'Mode and Meaning', p. 505.

is both audience and co-creator. There is the great Other of our deepest desires figured in the divine. There is the other of Traherne's and of his reader's psychology, that sense of other by which we come to know a sense of self. And there is the other that functions as object, the thing known or perceived. All of these others are part of us, Traherne asserts, inasmuch as by them we know and are known. For Traherne, though all things may exist in an ultimate unity, we know and perceive in life through the vagaries of difference, a paradox that for him derives from the central paradox of a Trinitarian God. His opposition of subject and object, coupled with his notion of participation in an overall unity, leads us directly to theories of communication and circulation. By the one gifts are extended and received, and by the other they are returned again in a process that makes possible the fullness of final communion between a subject and its other.

Circulation and Communication

In Traherne's model of communication and circulation, the dynamic of gift and receipt is initiated by God, who communicates Godself in creation. Our human need to give and to receive, to live in communication with others, human and divine, begins here in the nature of God; for the human soul, writes Traherne, 'loves to *communicat* it self in the Image of the Deitie'.[68] In 'The Circulation' he explores this notion of gift:

> As fair Ideas from the Skie,
>   Or Images of Things,
> Unto a Spotless Mirror flie . . .
>   Just such is our Estate.
>   No Prais can we return again,
>   No Glory in our selvs possess,
> But what derived from without we gain . . .[69]

Traherne begins to speak of gift in 'The Circulation' by using the image of the mirror. This ability of the mind to mirror back to God what it receives is a function both of its lack of spontaneity and its capacity. And the clarity of the image it returns is a measure of its purity. In its capacious but unfilled primitive state the mind is 'like the fairest glass,

---

68 *SE*, pp. 239, 280–1.
69 'The Circulation', ll. 1–3, 10–13.

/ Or Spotless polisht Brass', which does itself in its 'Objects Image cloath'.[70] Most often, in both his poetry and his prose, Traherne emphasizes the positive aspect of this capacity and measure, expecting the soul to be its best: 'As a Mirror returneth the very self-same Beams it receiveth from the Sun, so the Soul returneth those Beams of Love that shine upon it from God.'[71] And so the soul may become 'A Mirror of all Eternity'.[72] Bacon, one of Traherne's sources, also used the image of the mirror but his soul is 'an uneven mirror', which 'distorts the rays of objects according to its figure and section'.[73]

For Traherne the fullness that he experiences by virtue of God's gift of light is, in him, 'the Mirror of an endless Life'.[74] In 'Thoughts IV' he prays to live with God's omnipresence in him so that he may mirror eternity to the world: 'O give me Grace to see thy face, and be / A constant Mirror of Eternitie'.[75] As his soul is a mirror to the universe, so thoughts are a mirror to his soul, by reflection making present what is past ('Thoughts I', ll. 13–18). Meanwhile, the world mirrors divinity to us. In *The Ceremonial Law* Traherne writes of the creation: 'And all these strange and Glorious works will be / A Sacred Mirror of the Deitie' ('[Manna] II', ll. 81–2). God also may mirror to us. Through him eternity (which would otherwise be impossible to see since it is endless) may be seen by reflection:

> Whose bosom is the glass,
> Wherin we we all Things Everlasting See.
> His name is NOW, his Nature is forever.[76]

And so may we see His wants and enjoyments, needs and joys together from all eternity and eternity and the present all at once. In all but the last of these images the return or reflection is, as in 'The Circulation' above, predicated upon gift.

The mirror is not an uncommon image of Traherne's period – all of the Neo-Platonists saw man as a receiver of images and Peter Sterry

---

70 'The Preparative', ll. 52–4.
71 C, IV, 84.
72 C, IV, 81.
73 Francis Bacon, *The Advancement of Learning*, Bk. I, Ch. I, 3. Traherne's notes on Bacon in the *Early Notebook* (Bod. MS.Lat.Misc.f.45) reveal an interest in Bacon's view of science (he quotes from *De Augmentis Scientarum* on fol. 71) and it is possible, rather than clear, that he read *The Advancement of Learning*.
74 'Fullnesse', l. 5.
75 'Thoughts IV'.
76 'The Anticipation', ll. 24–6.

was one who, like Traherne, made use of the mirror image in particular. In her study 'Thomas Traherne and Cambridge Platonism', Marks notes the similarities between Sterry and Traherne in their use of the mirror image. But she rightly sees Traherne as departing from Sterry and the other Platonists in his insistence that the human soul is more than just recipient. For Traherne's infinitely active soul sends out, communicating itself and an altered creation back to the divine giver, not just because it is 'fairest glass or polisht Brass' but also because it is essentially communicative, as God is. It is not merely recipient but recipient/transformer. Marks writes: 'Sterry's mirror reflected; Traherne's – somehow – projected as well.'[77]

Certainly, Traherne's soul returns more than it receives. The whole task of his poem 'Ammendment', for example, is to explain that God takes greater delight in his creatures when they are offered back to him as enjoyed by humankind than when they were first created.[78] 'That all things should be mine' is wonderful, writes Traherne,

> But that they all more Rich should be
>   And far more Brightly shine,
>   As usd by Me:[79]

is even more wonderful.

> That we should make the Skies
> More Glorious far before thine Eys,
> Then Thou didst make them, and even thee
>   Far more the Works to prize,
>   As usd they be,
> Then as they're made; is a Stupendious Work . . .[80]

God, Traherne asserts, finds the physical world useful only in its usefulness to humanity.[81] And because, as we have seen in chapter two,

---

77 Carol Marks, 'Thomas Traherne and Cambridge Platonism', *Papers of the Bibliographic Society of America*, 81 (1966), p. 533.

78 Alison Sherrington sees Traherne's emphasis upon the return of the world to God as an indication of his interest in the immanence rather than transcendence of God: 'the soul is a mirror relflecting God Himself . . . It is significant that Traherne's inclination toward the immanent rather than the transcendent God leads him to think of the soul as a mirror of the whole material creation also' (*Mystical Symbolism in the Poetry of Thomas Traherne*, St Lucia: University of Queensland Press, 1970, pp. 43–4).

79 'Ammendment', l. 1 and ll. 2–4.

80 Ibid., ll. 8–13.

81 'In himself he needeth not the sun nor sea nor Air nor Earth nor Gold nor Silver; he needeth them only for our sake and in us only enjoyeth the same' (*SV*, fol. 28v).

use and treasure are so closely linked, the world is really a treasure to God inasmuch as it is useful to us. In this act of return, which exceeds the original gift, Traherne's mirror is unique. He himself can hardly believe what he is saying:

> Am I a Glorious Spring
> Of Joys and Riches to my King?
> Are Men made Gods!

He exclaims.

> ... And is my Soul a Mirror that must Shine
> Even like the Sun, and be far more Divine?[82]

Fascinating as Traherne's mirror imagery is, however, the mirror is just one of the ways by which human beings enter into the process of gift, receipt and return. In 'The Circulation' Traherne begins, as we have seen, with the image of the mirror but he goes on from the most fundamental actions of human life – we breathe out only the air we first breathed in – to eucharistic images of offering – 'He must a King, before a Priest becom, / And Gifts receiv, e're ever Sacrifice'.[83] We may hear echoes of the liturgical prayer at the offering, 'All things come of thee O Lord, and of thine own do we give thee'. In fact, in the *Centuries* Traherne uses that very word 'offering' to describe man's return of the world to God: 'The World within you is an offering returned'.[84] What came from God goes back to God; everything owes its very existence to this principle of circulation. 'All Things to Circulations owe / Themselves', Traherne asserts; 'A Colour, or a Glimps of Light / The Sparcle of a Precious Stone' cannot show but by borrowed light. '[T]hey anothers Livery must Wear: / And borrow Matter first, / Before they can comunicat' ('The Circulation', stanza 3).

In all of this, return is predicated on gift: 'All things do first receiv, that giv',[85] Traherne insists. Only God can live from and in himself, whose 'All sufficient Love' is 'Without Original'. He is 'the Primitive

---

82 'Ammendment', ll. 29–31, 34–5.
83 'The Circulation', ll. 22–3. I have used Ridler's editing, which suggests that 'or ever sacrifice' read 'ere ever sacrifice'.
84 C, II, 90. He continues 'Which is infinitly more Acceptable to GOD Almighty, since it came from him, that it might return unto Him. Wherin the Mysterie is Great.'
85 'The Circulation', l. 71; this line begins the final stanza and draws the poem towards culmination.

Eternal Spring / The Endless Ocean';[86] we are the conduits of his bliss, which runs 'like Rivers from, into the Main'.[87]

That all things do first receive that give is not only the central argument in 'The Circulation' but a first principle in all of Traherne's thought.[88] Just as his man of the *Centuries* is unable to 'Breath out more Air then he draweth in',[89] so also is Adam, in the creation story, reliant on the first breath from God, and so must the disciples in the upper room wait for the breath of the Holy Spirit. The first principle of Traherne's circulation, the primacy of gift, reiterates the poet's dependence upon the divine.

I have taken 'The Circulation' as a model for Traherne's notion of circulation not just because of its obvious title but also because in it we see the whole movement of his 'circulation', from reflection on to what he calls 'transpiration'. Traherne may begin the poem with the image of the mirror but he quickly moves in the second stanza to the cycle of human breath and by the final stanza it is the image of the water cycle whereby he says of the soul 'And all it doth receiv [it] returns again'.[90] He has moved from reflection to images of inhalation, assumption, absorption. The thing received is not simply 'bounced back'; it becomes part of the very fabric of the recipient before it is returned. We are what we return, we return our very selves. By this we move from death to life, by this are we transformed from 'a Living Tomb / Of Useless Wonders' to 'a Womb / Of Praises'.[91]

The belief that this kind of transformative return can happen has been the informing notion of many writers, artists, musicians, philosophers and teachers. In his letters to his friend Arthur Greeves, C. S. Lewis asserts that any work to which one feels seriously impelled will have its effect precisely because it is a link in a larger chain of gift and receipt. Here he cites Traherne:

> Remember too what Traherne says that our appreciation of this world – and *this* becomes fully conscious only as we express it in

---

86 Ibid., ll. 78–79.

87 Ibid., l. 83.

88 Sandbank also asserts this point in his study when he states: 'The one principle that governs the endless transformations of the mind is its inability to be more than what it receives from without' ('Thomas Traherne on the Place of Man in the Universe', *Scripta Hierosolymitana*, 17 (1966), p. 124).

89 C, II, 94; cf. 'No Man breaths out more vital Air, / Then he before suckt in' ('The Circulation', ll. 15–16).

90 'The Circulation', l. 84.

91 'The Estate', ll. 6–7, 9–10. See also Stewart, *The Expanded Voice*, who notes (p. 190) echoes of the circulation theme in both 'The Estate' and 'The Enquirie'.

art – is a real link in the universal chain. Beauty descends from God into nature: but there it would perish and does except when a man appreciates it with worship and thus as it were *sends it back* to God: so that through his consciousness what descended ascends again and the perfect circle is made.[92]

Lewis had hit upon the centrality of the communicative circle in Traherne even before the most recent discoveries, which reinforce his claim. Reflection and transpiration, the two kinds of communication suggested above in 'The Circulation' and 'The Estate', are explored in greater detail in *The Kingdom of God*.[93] Reflection happens via light and eye. It is an exchange of image – as such an outward communication. Transpiration is 'a real communication of parts',[94] a deep and inward exchange of substance via emanations. The emanations of which Traherne speaks are exhalation and evaporation, inhalation and condensation, deterioration, decay and decomposition, by which one thing becomes another. That this second type of communication is the more 'real'[95] while at the same time the less visible is yet another source of blessing because in this we may also learn a moral lesson about seeming and reality. Reflection and transpiration are forms of communication 'Wherein there happens a Strange Deception. Or rather a Wonderfull and Happy Exchange, For that which is no part seems to be the whole Object, and that which is a real part is unseen' *(KOG,* fol. 252v).

Considering transpiration moves us towards what one might call 'circulation and science' in Traherne. In *The Kingdom of God*, Traherne invites his reader to 'single out any sand upon the Sea Shore' (fol. 222r). Those parts, he suggests, 'that we now behold in this sand, may herafter be dissolved. And when the particles are corrupted, or mouldred away, som of them may mingle with Water, others may turn into Earth, and become one with it' (fol. 222v). He further singles out this one particle that has become part of the earth:

---

92 *They Stand Together: the Letters of CS Lewis to Arthur Greeves (1914–1963)*, London: Collins, 1979, p. 396.

93 'The communication of all visible and corporeal Beings is two fold, either outward, and superficial, or Deep and Inward. The one is a Communication of figures and colours by reflexion, the other of Spirits and Interior Qualities by Transpiration' (*KOG*, fol. 251v).

94 *KOG*, fol. 252r–v.

95 'That these Inward communications are more real than the other, is manifest, because these are Communications not of Shadows and Images, but things of themselvs, substances being imparted in their own essential parts and spirits' (*KOG*, fol. 253r).

This one from the earth may be carried into a Root, or Seed, and breath up at last into a Spire of Grass, be eaten by a Beast, assist in the form of Nourishment, and pas into Flesh: that Flesh may be eaten by a Man, and become part of his, for a considerable season. Thence it may evaporate in a Steam, and continue in an exhalation, till it turn into Air. (fol. 223r)

From here, Traherne takes his particle on a tour of the universe, hypothetically stopping at the vortex of the sun, darting to a star, reflecting back via the moon to the earth, falling into the sea, from thence into a fish or a whale or a dolphin, at last escaping into an oyster. 'And mingling there in some transparent Drop, [it may] be fixed in a Pearl. It may come from so base an original to Ladie's Neck, sit at a King's Table, be advanced to his Throne, or Crown, or Scepter' (fol. 223r). Through the pearl, he at once returns to his familiar symbols of authority and power and plays on the irony of a grain of sand transformed. From sand it returns to sand and thence to pearl, but that final transformation could be considered trifling compared to the transformations this particle has already seen.

The circulation process as seen in the circulation of the blood also interests Traherne:

For as by the Systole and Diastole of the Heart all the pulses of the Body beat, and by the circulation of the blood (lately found out) all Lift and Motion is maintained: This in the Microcosm is answered with an Universal circulation in the Macrocosm: The Sun being as it were the Heart of the Univers, drinking the Blood, and sending it forth continualy to all the parts impregnated with motion and Refined, for the Conservation of the whole. By that circulation, which is Infinitly swift and Rapid, the Sun in an Instant transforming Aether into flame, and pouring it out in its Beams; a Gentle circulation is maintained. (*KOG*, fols 223v–224r)

Here he is citing Harvey's discovery that in systole the blood is driven from the heart and in diastole it flows back in.[96] Traherne was fascinated

---

96 See, for example, William Harvey, *The Circulation of the Blood*, trans. K. Franklin, Springfield, IL: Charles Thomas, 1963, pp. 13 and 59–69. Harvey wrote two anatomical essays addressed to Jean Riolan (Regius Professor of Anatomy and Botany in Paris) defending this assertion. The first, of 1649, was on the circulation of the blood; in the second, objections to the circuit were refuted. In neither essay does his tone show anything but the greatest of respect for his fellow medic and one may view them as much as colleagues as opponents. 'Prosper exceeding, most distinguished Riolan', Harvey concludes the first essay,

by this medical theory, but what interests him most in this case is the universal principle and its infinite applications: that the circulation of the blood may serve as a model for the pattern of the whole universe is more important to his purpose here than the details of Harvey's theory. He moves back to fire and sun and light, condensation, evaporation, exhalation, dispersion, rules of incidence and laws of motion, operations and emanations. 'I gallop over all, and hastily touch but the Tops of things', he admits with no shame.[97] Urgency fires his work. The sun has captured his imagination, light is in his eye and, in the words of St John, this Light is the Life of men.[98] Light is the model by which we may understand God's communication of himself 'from all parts and Quarters of the World . . . in every point and centre of his Immensity, without Confusion, Dislocation, Distraction, or Contradiction'.[99]

And so Traherne draws an extended, chapter-long parallel between God and the sun: 'As the Sun shines round about the univers, so doth he on evry side throughout all eternitie: His Beams are not one Way, but evry Way';[100] 'His Life is in the Act, & his Act in the essence. His Life is his Act'.[101] The Moon and the stars continue the allegory – 'The World is like heaven, God like the Sun; the moon and stars like Saints and Angels' reflecting his life and light.[102] All of this allegorical writing is fed by his knowledge of and enthusiasm for the historic and new scientific discoveries. From Archimedes' spheres and Hevelius' *Selenographia* to Robert Boyle's study of gases,[103] he moves in and out

---

hoping 'that all your [Riolan's] very distinguished writings may redound to your everlasting praise' (p. 28). Similarly he refers to Descartes as 'That very acute and ingenious man, Rene Descartes (to whom I am indebted for his honourable mention of my name)' (p. 65) before directly contradicting his observations on diastole and systole. This reference to Descartes in the present tense (see also p. 66) suggests that the second essay was written before Descartes's death in 1650, certainly before 1657, when Harvey himself died. In either case, Harvey's published writings would have been available to Traherne.

97 *KOG*, fol. 225r.

98 'το φωσ η ζωη. And the Light was the Life of Men' Traherne quotes from John 1.14. 'Thus speaketh the text of the holy Bible. An Allusion of Infinit depth; a divine and Eternal Mysterie, being painted out in a Temporal, and Visible, Created Wonder' (*KOG*, fol. 222r).

99 *KOG*, fols 228v–229r.

100 Ibid., fol. 232.

101 Ibid., fol. 233r; cf. 'The Anticipation', stanzas 11–12. In *KOG* Traherne writes that communication is requisite for goodness since, until it is communicated, goodness is not goodness even to itself. 'Having none in others, it hath none in it self. Should it pass on eternally without impressing in some other its own perfection it would be imperceptible. But meeting a receiver it instantly begets it self in another place, and is where it springs, and is where it endeth' (*KOG*, fol. 182v).

102 *KOG*, fol. 235r.

103 See *KOG*, fols 237r, 242v, 248v respectively.

of light and heat, 'Innumerable kinds of Exhalations, and Influences' all the while lending authority to his allegorical claims from the vast array of scientific knowledge available to him; and at the root of all this exploration is his belief in the basic principle of circulation and communication. Everything that is is communicated from God. And everything that receives communicates in turn, so that all creatures communicate with each other as well as with the divine: 'Evry thing therfore receiveth from all, and communicated to all, after its Kind and manner . . . all beings exchange themselves for each others sake to one another, and are united together'.[104] Traherne extends his notion of communication even to the stars, who 'shake hands and mingle rayes at all Distances, and are sweetly united in a fair Correspondence';[105] and from earthly creatures to the heavens – what is an exhalation here is an influence there.[106]

In all of this communication, circulation is implied. For Traherne, circulation and communication are not separate categories but parts of a single process of gift, receipt and return that is repeated over and over again; communication and circulation are, in fact, features of a cycle. Once again we are confronted by the figurative, symbolic, mythic imagery of the circle.

But what are we to think of a poet of circles, we who live in a 'post-circular' age, who can no longer believe in the 'circle of perfection'? Indeed, what are we to think of a theologian persisting in the image of the circle in a century when that very circle was broken? For, as Marjorie Nicolson asserts in her study *The Breaking of the Circle*, the scientific discoveries of the seventeenth century and the 'new Philosophy' that they spawned broke, once and for all, the old circle of perfection. When she writes:

---

104 *KOG*, fol. 251v. Communication as it is most commonly understood, in terms of verbal and non-verbal language, is not the primary meaning of the term for Traherne and so I have not treated the subject here. That kind of communication is not, however, a subject about which Traherne is silent. His whole work as a writer is predicated upon the importance of linguistic communication, in which he seemed to feel he fared better as a writer than as a speaker, since he criticized himself for 'Speaking too much and too Long in the Best Things'. For this and other difficulties he encountered in oral communication see *SM*, III, 65; the editor's introduction to *A Serious and Pathetical Contemplation* (1699) entitled 'to The Reader' (quoted in full in Margoliouth's editon of the *Centuries*, vol. I, pp. xxxi–xxxii); and Webber, *The Eloquent 'I'*, pp. 223–5.
105 *KOG*, fol. 254v.
106 'The transpirations of the Earth are called Exhalations here, where they exhale or breath out; and Influences there, where they are received in; be it in the Sun or moon, or other Creature' (*KOG*, fol. 254v).

> For three hundred years men have vainly tried to put together the pieces of a broken circle. Some have been poets, some philosophers, some artists. They have shared a common desire for a unity that once existed, and have sought a 'return to medievalism', when life seemed integrated about a strong center, whether of the Church or of a monarch,[107]

she sounds like she is describing Traherne. Then she continues:

> But all the king's horses and all the king's men cannot put Humpty-Dumpty together again. Mere fitting together of pieces may remake the picture in a jig-saw puzzle; it will not remake an egg. Nor can we reconstruct the old Circle of Perfection.[108]

Traherne comes into Nicolson's study not as a poet of the circle but as a poet of infinity – one whose imagination had been released by the breaking of the circle. Along with Henry More, Nicolson's Traherne has been liberated by 'the 'new Philosophy', which no longer called all in doubt but rather released human imagination to a spaciousness of thought human beings had not known before: 'The idea of infinity had utterly demolished the Circle of Perfection'.[109] Nicolson goes so far as to cite Traherne as 'the seventeenth-century climax of the poets of "aspiration"',[110] for whom infinity was a new sphere of imagination, whose imaginations 'could expand with the universe, whose soul[s] grew vaster with vastness'.[111]

Following Nicolson, Colie also saw Traherne's expansiveness as superseding the image of the circle. As Colie notes, 'Traherne found that the old images of a contained infinity, the sphere, the circle, the globe, and the ring, would not do: his concept of infinity forced itself beyond the "circle of perfection"'.[112] Colie contends that when, in the fifth Century, Traherne was 'ready to transcend human limitations' and to 'experience fully his own most intense perceptions of

---

107 Marjorie Hope Nicolson, *The Breaking of the Circle: Studies in the Effect of the 'New Science' upon Seventeenth Century Poetry*, Evanston, IL: Northwestern University Press, 1950, p. 105.
108 Ibid.
109 Ibid., p. 145.
110 Ibid., p. 173.
111 Ibid., p. 171. Nicolson cites 'Insatiableness', 'Contentment is a sleepy thing', the *Centuries*, 'Sight', 'The Anticipation', 'Felicity', 'News', 'The Preparative', 'My Spirit', 'Thoughts IV', 'Nature', 'Thoughts I' and 'Hosanna' as indicative of Traherne's adventures into infinity or exercises in capacity.
112 Colie, *Paradoxia Epidemica*, p. 167.

the metaphysics of Deity' he abandoned the circular image and resorted to 'real' spatial infinity which stretches out in every direction endlessly. And yet she herself ends the same chapter discussing the Trahernian soul in that most familiar of images, the infinite circle. Her own intelligent reading of Traherne brings her back to the circle. Certainly Traherne was never a slave to the image of the circle but he never abandoned it either. When the circle of perfection is broken we then have an extended spiral. The pattern of the circle remains, with its powerful cyclical force, though the closure of that circle has been breached. It is no longer a self-enclosed circle but a circle that extends into infinity. This is why Traherne can move his imagery of infinity from the 'circle of perfection' to 'real' spatial infinity and yet retain his cyclical imagery and style. He is not so much breaking the circular as stretching it.[113]

Barbara Lewalski is one critic whose reading of Traherne finds his circular imagery and his sense of infinite expansion to be in harmony. She treats the uninterrupted Burney manuscript as a sequence of poems not unlike the Dobell sequence, claiming that, in his treatment of its controlling figure, the infant eye, 'Traherne does not so much blur or undermine the sense of temporal development or progress as transpose such development from linear to spherical terms. ... The final poem, "The Review II", indicates that the spiritual pilgrimage is not a linear movement from Eden to the New Jerusalem, but a matter of ever-widening spheres whose expansion is forwarded by meditation upon the things seen and the ways of seeing in infancy'.[114]

Thus we may see that the expansive stretches of infinite space and the image of the circle are not necessarily mutually exclusive images. When, in *A Sober View,* Traherne calls the circle by which Love is both the Cause and End of all things convenient to itself as to its object, the 'Circle of Infinity',[115] he combines the idea of infinity and the circle, at first more confident in his belief that this is so than in his power to explain how it may be so. But as he continues his meaning becomes

---

113 Cf. ibid., p. 168.

114 Barbara Lewalski, *Protestant Poetics and the Seventeenth-century Religious Lyric*, Princeton: Princeton University Press, 1979, p. 364. Lewlaski notes light, sphere and temple as the three dominant tropes of both the Dobell and the 'Infant-Ey' sequences (pp. 379, 381). Stewart also suggests that the poems of the Burney MS, disentangled from the work of Philip, would read as a sequence similar to the Dobell sequence (*The Expanded Voice*, pp. 210–11).

115 *SV*, fol. 28r. In explaining how Love can be the 'End of its own Productions' and how 'That is Good Which is is Convenient to another', Traherne finds himself tangled in a trail of assertions, and his marginal note 'This Ring and Circle of Infinity varies more in Excess of Words, than in real Sense' reads like a plea to his reader to have patience.

clearer. The 'Circle of Infinity' is infinite love communicated and reciprocated, extended and returned again to its original:

> God ... infinitly Desireth to communicate himself, his Infinit Goodness infinitly delighting in anothers happiness, which without a Communication of itself can never be attained. Infinitly Desiring to Communicat Himself, with the same Measure he Desireth to be received. And the Work whereby God is received is Good, becaus it is convenient to Him: perhaps I may say infinitly convenient both to God and his Creatures. To God, because he infinitly Desires to be Enjoyed, to his Creatures, because they infinitly Desire to be Happy, ... which cannot be but by the fruition of His communicated Goodness.[116]

That this communicated goodness is spatially as well as conceptually infinite is part of Traherne's notion of universal communication. Along with Thomas Jackson, Traherne asserts that 'he [God] is every where, because no body, no space, or spirituall substance can exclude his presence, or avoid penetration of his Essence'.[117] Traherne's 'circle of Infinity', spatial as well as interior, is both ways infinite, filled with divine presence and with human and divine capacity. That God is 'universally' communicative is 'An Abyss of Wonders' (*KOG*, fol. 229r). Like rays of light that, 'coming from the East, fill the Hemisphere, and so do Rayes coming from the West, yet they do not clash, nor confound each other', so God's essence fills everything without hindering anything. It is absolutely necessary that universal communication should be thus infinite, for if just one corner were to be devoid of God's fullness his omnipresence would be shattered. Besides, urges Traherne, it is the nature of God to act and it is in the nature of God's goodness that this act should communicate goodness infinitely and satisfy infinite desire: 'Infinit Bounty must be infinitly Communicative, and Infinit Desire Satisfyed', he writes in *The Kingdom of God* (fol. 245v).

There are other circles in Traherne – recollection makes his life a

---

[116] *SV*, fol. 28r. Cf. 'all Nature heaves at and requires the Duty we have described. God desires in all things to be Enjoyed. Man desires to enjoy all Things' (*SV*, fol. 29r).

[117] Thomas Jackson, *A Treatise of the Divine Essence*, London, 1628, Part I, p. 53. In his *Commonplace Book*, when Traherne writes about God communicating himself to us, he quotes from Jackson's work: 'All the goodnesse man is capable of, doth but expresse Gods goodness communicative' (*CB*, under the heading 'Liberty', fol. 62v.i, citing Jackson, *Treatise of the Divine Essence*, Part I, p. 189).

DIFFERENCE

'Circle of Delights'.[118] More prolific and of similar significance, his favourite image of God from Hermes is as the sphere, and infinity as a circle brings us continually back to the circle motif. Traherne's use of this image puts him in the company of many other mystical writers, in particular Eckhart, Nicholas of Cusa and St Bonaventure, who try to discuss the negative attributes of God positively by also reverting to the hermetic image of the infinite circle whose centre is everywhere and whose circumference is nowhere.[119] Traherne's God is everywhere, his omnipresence wholly in every centre, communicating Godself there completely (C, II, 82). The image is one of immanence and of communication. And as such it marries, as we have seen in chapter one, his negative and affirmative theologies. The negativity or void, the abyss of the soul and of infinity, is filled with the omnipresence of God. Indeed, it is the great Abyss that is God – 'O what a Wonderful Profound Abyss is God!' cries Traherne in 'The Anticipation'.[120] God's own Nothing is a most essential Something.[121] Like the image of the circle itself, the affirmative and negative ways meet upon themselves in a ring of oneness. As Nicholas of Cusa wrote:

> all theology is said to be stablished in a circle, because any one of His attributes is affirmed of another, and to have is with God to be, and to move is to stand, and to run is to rest, and so with the other attributes.[122]

---

118 'Imaginations *Reall* are', which to his mind again repair, making his life a circle of delights, and 'An Earnest that the Actions of the Just / Shall still revive, and flourish in the Dust' ('The Review II', ll. 9–12).

119 Bonaventure: Being is 'entirely within and entirely without all things, and therefore, is an intelligible sphere whose center is everywhere and whose circumference nowhere' (*The Mind's Road to God*, trans. George Boas, New York: Liberal Arts Press, 1953, p. 38). Eckhart: the *Logos* is 'in the things, and indeed wholly in each one of them, in such a way that it is nevertheless wholly outside each, wholly within and wholly without' (James Midgley Clark (ed.), *Treatises and Sermons of Meister Eckhart*, New York: Octagon, 1983, p. 236). This image is also used by Dionysius the Areopagite, Nicholas of Cusa and Giordano Bruno, all of whom Traherne may have read. See Nicolson, *The Breaking of the Circle*, p. 107 and Queenie Iredale, *Thomas Traherne*, Oxford: Blackwell, 1935, pp. 52–3.

120 'The Anticipation', ll. 70–1.

121 Here I refer to Henry Suso, who describes the Godhead as 'unfathomable abyss'. He adds: 'by common agreement, men call this Nothing God; and it is itself a most essential Something. And here man know himself to be one with the Nothing, and the Nothing knows itself without the action of the intellect' (Henry Suso, *Little Book of Truth*, trans. James M. Clark, New York: Harper, 1953, pp. 178, 191–2).

122 Nicholas of Cusa, *The Vision of God* (1453), trans. Emma Gurney Salter, New York: E. P. Dutton, 1928, p. 12, quoted in Day, *Thomas Traherne*, Boston, MA: Twayne, 1982, p. 22.

Sandbank goes so far as to call Traherne's world picture a 'Circulation Doctrine'[123] and he notes the affinity this doctrine has with the thought of the Neo-Platonic Florentine Academy.[124] We have seen Traherne's use of Ficino in previous chapters and it is likely that Ficino's 'circuitus spiritualis'[125] – 'a single circle from God to the world and from the world to God',[126] whereby the world is returned to its intelligible form through the human mind and thence returned back to God – influenced the formation of the notion of circulation in Traherne. But Traherne's own version of the theory seems to me to take circulation further. He departs from Ficino here, just as he did from Sterry and the image of the mirror, by superseding the borrowed image. For not only does Traherne's man return a spiritual world for a material one but he participates in the transformation of the material world into a renewed material world as well. This is the bold claim Traherne makes that ultimately separates him from the Neo-Platonists. He is not just concerned with 'the spiritualization of the material world'[127] but with the transformation of the physical world here, now. This is partly reflected in his insistence, noted earlier, that heaven is here as well as hereafter.

Traherne's debt here is as much to the early Church Fathers as it is to the Florentine Academy. Their early tradition, developed fully in the Eastern Church and appearing in those writers whom Traherne loved, such as St Chrysostum, Irenaeus, Gregory of Nyssa, Gregory Nazianzus and others, also sees the fullness of God's work on earth in circular terms. Their teachings on *theosis*, which we have seen rooting his theory of man, resurface here in his theory of circulation. Christ became man so that all humanity might be lifted up to heaven. Salvation is not only about the state of an individual but about the redemption of the world. It is not so much about keeping people from hell hereafter but about bringing heaven to earth now. The Eastern Christian tradition

---

123 Sandbank, 'Thomas Traherne on the Place of Man in the Universe', p. 121.

124 Sandbank notes, for instance, though he does not trace in detail, the history of the doctrine of circulation, its origins in Plotinus and Proclus' dialectics of 'Remaining', 'Procession' and 'Reversion', and the importance it lent to Neo-platonism of the Italian Renaissance (pp. 121–2).

125 Marsilio Ficino, *Theologia Platonica*, IX, 4, in *Opera Omnia*, Basel, 1576, fol. 211.

126 Ficino, *Commentary on Plato's Symposium*, Second Speech, Ch. II, trans. Sears R. Jayne, Columbia, MI: University of Missouri, 1944, p. 134. See also Paul Oskar Kristeller, *The Philosophy of Marsilio Ficino*, New York: Columbia University Press, 1943, p. 109: 'Since the intellect enters into a real relationship with its objects, it can also give them something of its own essence. So the mind that thinks the corporeal objects changes their original quality in a certain sense and lifts them up to a higher grade of being by its thinking power.'

127 Sandbank, 'Thomas Traherne on the Place of Man in the Universe', p. 123.

reminds us that God's chosen home is not only heaven but also human flesh and this small globe of earth: it is this very refusal to abandon the material world that gives Traherne's work something of its immediacy. In Traherne the dualistic understanding, popular in the medieval mind, of heaven and earth as entirely separate and opposed entities gave way to an understanding of heaven and earth as two spheres linked by an ongoing motion of love from God to the world and from the world to God. And that motion of love has much more far-reaching effects than has been hitherto understood in the common readings of Traherne.

Most readings that concern either the return of an improved world to God by man or the 'spiritualization' of the material locate the centre of action in the mind. Redemption is cerebral; the work is the work of intellection. As Sandbank notes: 'The spiritualization of the world by the mind and the superiority of the "Thought of the World" (C, II, 90) to the world itself imply that by thinking it man improves it.'[128] This may be partly because, as we have noted, critics often refer back to Ficino's notions of the spiritualization of the material rather than to the Eastern Church Fathers for their reading of Traherne. But it may also stem from the fact that there is some ambiguity about the power of knowledge in Traherne. On the one hand, he claims '*Things tru* affect not, while they are unknown'.[129] On the other hand, he disagrees with 'a Maxime in the Scholes, That there is no Lov of a thing unknown', promising his reader to fill his book with 'those Truths you love, but know not' (C, I, 2). About this love, too, he seems to alternate. He calls the power of loving 'The most High and Noble of the Faculties', a faculty of the heart as well as of the mind, 'not seated by it self in the mind, but attended with a mighty Proneness and Inclination'; in other words, attended with desire (CE, p. 44). This appears in the opening paragraph of his chapter on Love in *Christian Ethicks*, yet he concludes the same chapter insisting that 'VERTUOUS Love is that which proceedeth from a well Governed understanding, and is seated in a Will that is guided by Reason.'[130] And so we may see that love and knowledge, while distinct categories, are not exclusive ones in Traherne. Love depends to some extent on knowledge, or perhaps it is more accurate to say that knowledge is implied in love: 'HAD

---

128 Ibid., p. 130. See also Sherrington, *Mystical Symbolism*, Clements, *The Mystical Poetry*, Franz Wohrer, *Thomas Traherne: Growth of a Mystic's Mind*, Salzburg Studies in English Poetry, Salzburg: Poetry Salzburg, 1982.

129 'The Inference', l. 9. He concludes the sentence 'But Thoughts most sensibly, when quite alone' (l. 10).

130 CE, p. 49. Similarly, in the *Centuries*, he asserts that love must be 'a Regulated well orderd Love Upon Clear Causes', a 'Rational Affection' (C, I, 91).

GOD limited and confined our understanding, our power of Loving had been shut up in Bounds'.[131] Inasmuch as love presupposes the existence of the 'idea' of the loved one in the lover's mind, love may be seen as dependent upon thought. But thought alone cannot redeem and restore; whereas in the *Centuries* it is 'By love alone' that God is apprehended, 'By Love alone is God enjoyed, by Love alone delighted in, by Love alone approached or admired.'[132] Both his nature and our nature require that it should be so.[133] Ultimately it is love that redeems and restores.

As Sandbank notes, 'The cosmic "circulation" is therefore activated by love . . . Love becomes a cosmic striving after perfection, the energy that makes the universe go. The Cycle of Being is a "circle of loves"'.[134] The first part of the circle is the love of the creator for the creatures – love extended to all and each everywhere, universal divine communication. The second part is the human being's return of an improved creation. The dynamic of the whole is a dynamic of love. This not only explains why knowledge alone is never enough but also makes sense of the return of the world as more than mirroring, since what we return is a world truly loved, a world by its many uses made part of our very selves. The motion of love also locates the energy of creation in desire. Traherne asserts in *Christian Ethicks*

> Had not GOD from all Eternity Loved, had he never desired, nor delighted in any thing; he had never exerted his Almighty Power, never communicated his goodness, or begot his Wisdom, never enjoyed Himself, never applied himself to the Production of his Works . . . (CE, p. 51).

In the year that he died, this same notion – that action springs out of desire – was being expounded by the sevententh-century non-conformist John Howe. 'Desire is love in motion, Delight is love in rest',[135] Howe

---

131 CE, p. 52. Here Traherne is explaining how perfectly matched is our love with its objects and our ability to enjoy them with their desirability.

132 C, I, 71. Traherne's 'apprehension' is not exclusively or even primarily an action of the mind; it is a 'taking hold of' which involves the whole self in a process of right sight, knowing, prizing, desiring, taking and returning.

133 'His Nature requires Love, thy nature requires Love' (C, I, 71).

134 Sandbank, 'Thomas Traherne and the Place of Man in the Universe', p. 132. On the term 'circle of loves' as Sandbank uses it see his reference to Leone Ebreo, *The Philosophy of Love (Dialoghi d'amore)*, trans. R. Friedberg-Seeley and J. H. Barnes, London: The Soncino Press, 1937, pp. 451–2.

135 John Howe, *A Treatise of Delighting in GOD*, London: A. Maxwell, 1674, p. 139. My thanks to Jeremy Maule who first introduced me to this treatise.

wrote. 'They are as the wings and arms of love: Those for pursuits, these for embraces.'[136] Desire is love 'tending to perfection': we move in order to rest, so also the spirit moves towards its object in expectation of satisfaction and enjoyment. Howe wanted to assert that desire is relevant to an imperfect state whereas delight is found in perfection; and yet the two refuse to be so neatly separated. Finally Howe admits, '*Desire* and *Delight* have a continual vicissitude, and do (as it were circularly) beget one another.'[137] Desire and delight self-perpetuating in love is exactly what the circle of desire is about in Traherne. In their common interest in the intuitive and personal encounter with God, the direct action of God in the soul that is at the heart of religion (in fact, Howe uses the term 'heart religion'), the two theologians are similar; but Traherne was much more the controversialist about doctrine and authority than Howe ever was. Whatever their obvious differences, here – in terms of delight and desire – there are striking parallels in their work. But where Howe cannot quite make sense of the contradiction that this implies between a perfect and an imperfect state, Traherne races ahead, out of time and into eternity, where all things co-exist simultaneously.

Nowhere is Traherne more insistent on the co-existence of desire and delight than, as we have seen in chapter one, in his depiction of a desiring God. Co-existing desire and delight are also the theme of 'The Anticipation', a poem about the circle of want in which God wants and has from all eternity, his wants perfecting his satisfactions: 'From Everlasting he these Joys did Need, / and all these Joys proceed / From Him Eternaly . . . His Endless Wants and His Enjoyments be / From all eternitie; / Immutable in Him' (ll. 19–21, 55–7). Everywhere in the poem we find completed circles. The end is, from everlasting, the fountain, having caused all to be: 'The End and the Fountain differ but in Name' (l. 36). The end being complete, the means must needs be so; the fountain, means and end at once complete, at once each other. Similarly, wants and enjoyments complete each other, God's wants lending value to all, his satisfactions delighting his wants. Taking this one step further, Traherne moves the business of desire and delight into the human realm and into the circle of gift and receipt. God's desire is 'To be by all possest; / His Love makes others Blest' (ll. 95–6). And so by receiving

---

[136] Ibid. Wings and arms, pursuits and embraces – this is strikingly similar to how Traherne describes affections: 'Affections are the wings and nimble feet / The tongue by which we taste whats good and sweet / The arms which a spirit doth embrace or thrust away, / The spurs which mend its pace' (*COH*, 'Affection').

[137] Howe, *A Treatise of Delighting in GOD*, p. 139.

we actually give to God – 'All Receivers are / In Him, all Gifts' (ll. 106–7). These circles of desire and delight, of end and fountain, of gift and receipt are manifestations of God's communicative nature, part of the very essence of God and his glory:

> His Essence is all Act: He did, that He
>   All Act might always be.
>   His Nature burns like fire:
> His Goodness infinitly doth desire,
>   To be by all possest;
>   His Love makes others Blest.
> It is the Glory of his High Estate,
> And that which I for ever more Admire
> He is an Act that doth Communicate.[138]

That in Traherne communication is God's glory is also noted by DeNeef, who defines 'glory' as synonymous in Traherne's mind with that giving/receiving motion of love that he calls circulation or communication. But DeNeef's understanding of communication and circulation, illuminating as it is, is (like Sterry's and Ficino's) essentially about reversibility or reflection rather than about transformation. DeNeef writes:

> God is the object of man's Eye, not because man can necessarily see God, but because he requires a mirror-object in order to see himself. What he sees, in fact, is himself reflected in the sight of God ... the power and capacity of man's Eye is the precise mirror-image of God's Eye. As Eye is to object, so Deity is to soul and so soul is to Deity. The reversibility of the optical operation structures all of Traherne's most important ideas and images: center and sphere, spring and fountain, origin and end, self and other, essence and act. Traherne calls the capacity of reversibility 'circulation' or 'communication'.[139]

To discuss divine communication in terms such as these seems to me to miss that most vital quality of divine communication – love. *Meditations on the Six Days of Creation* uses the image of breath to convey

---

[138] 'The Anticipation', ll. 91–9. See also *Christian Ethicks*, in which God desires love from us, his goodness desires to communicate itself, his blessedness is the pleasure of communication to all others and of receiving, his Glory desires to be seen, his love desires to be beloved and to make its object blessed (*CE*, p. 56).

[139] DeNeef, *Traherne in Dialogue*, p. 28.

the tender and passionate nature of God's communication of himself to his creation:

> The Breath which God inspired into the Soul of man, proceeded from him with so great a Love, as if he had drawn it from his very Bowels, and breathed his very Heart into the Body of Man ... Justly is the Soul of Man called the Breath of God, for he desireth, after a sort, to draw it in again, the soul issuing from him, and returning to him.[140]

Traherne uses this same image of blown breath in *The Kingdom of God* when he writes that 'Lov eflagitates and calls for our Return' (*KOG*, Ch. 32, l. 41). Circulation and communication as described here are neither optical nor illusionary but profoundly intimate and essential – a miraculous reality that should be answered with praise. And it is precisely this – praise – that follows in *Meditations on the Six Days of Creation*, since shortly after the passage cited above the author exclaims: 'O thou inexhausted, undrainable Ocean of everlasting Goodness, I praise thee for communicating unto us thine incommunicable Attributes, and making us Partakers of thine eternal Glory' (*MSD*, p. 88).

That praise is the appropriate response to the communication of divine goodness is equally clear in Traherne, but I do no more than note this here because I shall deal more fully with the issue of praise and gratitude in the next chapter. According to Traherne, the communication of his goodness is God's first and most urgent desire, the desire out of which all creation rises and in which creation is sustained. But capacity for communication is also a gift he has given to us: 'To receive all is sweet, but to communicate all is infinitely beyond all that can be sweet' (*CE*, p. 25). In fact, to be hindered from communicating is to be stifled and destroyed. Using again the image of breath to describe communication, Traherne writes in *Christian Ethicks*, 'Breath with the same necessity must be let out, as it is taken in. A man dies as certainly by the confinement, as the want of it. To shut it up and deny it are in effect the same' (*CE*, p. 259). In a little known poem in *The Kingdom of God*, it is confinement that kills:

> Like flame expend thy self to all thy Joys,
> Confinement is the only Thing destroys.

---

140 *MSD*, p. 81. Traherne also notes here the Holy Spirit as the breath of God filling the Apostles.

> . . . Our Joys
> Are no Impertinent and feeble Toys.
> They are Gods: and as they overflow,
> Return to him, to whom themselvs they owe.

The poem ends with the refrain of reciprocal possession from the Song of Songs, 'I my Beloveds am, and he is mine' (*KOG*, 'Who made it first?', Ch. 38, ll. 214–15, 240–3, 253).

Being vessels of the love we have received, we may and must give joy and feel joy in knowing that we occasion joy in others. In a circle that Traherne calls 'revolution' and 'reciprocation', the human being may enjoy his or her own emanations of love as God does, communicating something of the divine goodness he or she has received and so participating in circulation and communication not only as recipient/returner but also as giver unto others – to angels and humans and all creatures. This brings us finally to the idea of communion – that region where the circles of communication and circulation overlap so that the giver and the recipient enjoy and give, delight and desire in mutual benefit and bliss.

5

Communion

> Awake my soul, and soar upon the Wing
> Of Sacred Contemplation; for the King
> Of Glory wooes . . .
> His Soul, thy Soul, and all his Friends say Come;
> GOD is alone thy Glory and thy Home.
>
> (*COH*, 'Allurement')

This final chapter begins with a discussion of the soul as bride and wife, the differences between these two images and the way in which they invoke two models of ultimate felicity – union and communion. A fine distinction is noted between communion, which, requiring the presence of more than one, also requires the retention of separate selves, and union, which suggests the complete dissolving of boundaries. Both communion and union are commended as models for human and divine love as different points in the same circle or cycle of bliss.

The force of love that drives this cycle is exemplified most profoundly in Traherne by the cross of Christ. Its existence as an emblem of desire is noted, as is his use of the imagery of the phoenix that rises from the ashes. The burning nature of love is explored, and purgation and the fire of love are seen to be related in his imagery. That this love ultimately looks outward moves the discussion on to notions of communion with one another, self-love and love of others. Traherne's genius for felicity is seen in his placing happiness not in freedom from desire but in the very lacks and satisfactions from which and towards which desire flows. His felicity is neither an innocence lost nor a future end-point but a continuum in which God and the soul, and the soul with other souls, live in communion with each other: the circle of bliss and cycle of desire are the same thing. The chapter ends with a consideration of gratitude as an appropriate response to divine goodness and as a balance to insatiability.

Communion and Union

'Felicitie consisteth in two Joys, the Joy of communicating and the Joy of receiving', Traherne proclaims in *The Kingdom of God* (*KOG*, fol. 198v). And the mutual benefit and bliss of giver and receiver is nowhere more naturally and eloquently seen than in the image of the lover and the beloved, an image about which I wrote in chapter one and to which I now briefly return.

First let us consider the bride. Traherne's bride fills several roles, the most frequent being the role of recipient of what God has prepared, a kind of audience for divine expression and a receiver of divine gifts. Echoing the *Meditations on the Six Days of Creation* – 'As a King having builded his Palace, and furnish'd it with Provisions, bringeth in his Bride, even so God having finish'd the world brought in Man, to the Possession of it' (*MSD*, p. 72) – Traherne writes in *Select Meditations*, 'We [are] the Bride who He Designeth to Please and Delight, we the End to which He referreth and Disposeth all things.'[1]

Being the bride may give the supplicant the right to be heard. 'O remember how all Thy Lov Terminates in me: How I am made thy Bride', prays Traherne.[2] Or it may be a position we are given so that we may please God most fully by participating in his design of gift and receipt.[3] The fact that we have received may be what makes us capable of being the bride in the first place (*SM*, IV, 4). Traherne may use the term 'bride' in order to remind us of our worth and value: 'O Prize thy selfe as thy God prizeth Thee' (*SM*, IV, 50), he urges his reader. This is especially true in those extracts from *The Kingdom of God* already seen in chapter one, in which the bride is also the queen, exalted to a throne and honoured above all.

In all of this, the bride is marked by her difference from the bridegroom. As recipient, as supplicant, even as honoured and exalted one, her distinguishing characteristic is that she is something separate, a specific and distinct entity. She is something other. Traherne makes this explicit when he writes in *The Kingdom of God*: 'His Bride must hav som things peculiar to her sex, which God himself doth not enjoy, unless it be in her'.[4]

It is when Traherne speaks of the wife as opposed to the bride that

---

1 *SM*, IV, 7. On the gift of husband to wife of possessions see also *KOG*, fol. 199v.
2 *SM*, I, 82. A few lines earlier he has pleaded 'I beseech Thee to hear my Daylie prayers.'
3 'Being endued with power to keep his laws I am advanced to his Throne; and to do that which above all Things in Heaven and Earth he desireth: and therein I am made His Bride to Delight Him' (*SM*, II, 5). See also *SM*, III, 43; *ITR*, fol. 10v; 'The Recovery', esp. ll. 33–8.
4 *KOG*, fol. 364v. Cf. *CE*, Ch. 31, 'Of Magnificence', in which our greatness also lies in

the dynamic shifts from giver and receiver to a dynamic of union. In *The Kingdom of God* (fol. 200r), Traherne begins with an exposition of the Pauline advice on husbands and wives and then takes St Paul's line that 'He that loveth his wife loveth himself' as a springboard into the mystery of two becoming one:

> This is a great Mysterie, but I speak concerning Christ and the church. You see the apostle maketh use of this Instance, and leightly toucheth many Mysteries of Lov unto us . . . The Husband ought to giv himself to his Wife, and not his Gifts. (*KOG*, fol. 200r–v)

Ultimately, 'his Wife is himself' (*KOG* fol. 200v), Traherne concludes, seeming to collapse the distinction between the two. So, in this image of the soul as wife, the soul and God are united. That Traherne privileges neither the bride image, with its connotations of difference, nor the wife image, with its connotations of union, suggests that, when it comes to this central notion of a desiring God, he sees union and communion with God as two sides of the same coin.

I suggest that Traherne's refusal to abandon those images of the soul that describe it in terms of difference, efflagation, communion occurs not only because the bride/soul affords the prospect of divine courtship – and his God is 'a serious lover' (*COH*, 'Advocate' III) – but also because it is in this very stance of difference that the soul is able to offer back something amended rather than simply mirrored. Furthermore, for Traherne (in many ways a psychotherapist before the science was invented)[5] it is in the experience of difference, as in the vicissitudes of lack, that the soul comes to know itself and the disunities inherent in the self learn to be on speaking terms. This self communicative precedes the self in communion and is a first step towards that communion. Joan Webber's *The Eloquent 'I'*, an exploration of the self in seventeenth-century prose, may be of particular use here. Her concern is the development of a literary self-consciousness (that is, the awareness that the writer is the subject of his or her own prose whether he or she is writing autobiographically or not) on the part of the writers of that age.[6] In Traherne, authorial self-consciousness is the companion

---

being able to offer something distinctly separate to God: 'our Magnificence must be shewn in something he cannot do, unless he were in our Circumstance' (*CE*, pp. 252–3).

5 P. J. Kavanagh, review of Denise Inge (ed.), *Happiness and Holiness* in 'Books of the Year', *The Spectator*, 12 November 2008.

6 She sees this period as unique, since she claims that earlier writers, by and large, did not consider the nature of selfhood. The eight writers she considers (among whom is Traherne) 'are also different from writers of the Romantic age, who flaunt their lonely individuality,

to his reader's understanding of his/her own conscious self; his insights are our insights, his journey the journey he wishes us to make. Self-consciousness is vital to Traherne's whole project because it is only as a conscious self that his human can reach the kind of maturity necessary to become a vehicle for redemption. As Sandbank reminds us: 'The "Infant Ey" may be a perfect instrument of reception; it cannot, however, act upon the world and restore it back to God ... it is the active mind of the adult, that can perform that particular task which Traherne assigns to man.'[7]

It is of this mind maturing towards adulthood that Webber speaks when she notes that 'Traherne begins with disunities and disharmonies'.[8] These are not the first things he perceives in his infant state, but they are where his adult self, that re-creative self, must begin its work. The re-creative human must participate in God's act of continued creation, must feel the separations and yet from moment to moment hold the frame of things entire. Desire, I would suggest, is a primary tool in this reconstruction, for it acknowledges the real separate existence of a subject and object while at the same time urging the extension of each to fill the breach. Thus it may be that, out of the very separations and disunities of the world, rather than in spite of or in disregard of them, Traherne builds his felicity. Webber sees this overcoming of separation in many levels of Traherne's work:

> The physical and spiritual separation of man from God, writer from reader, man from man, moment from moment, meaning from meaning, and even clause from clause, is accepted and then transcended, as Traherne builds upon these separations the harmonies of his style.[9]

She notes that his prose is always a dialogue – in a process of communication – and that even the words are in communion with one another.[10] She notes the relationships between words and that there is

---

and from those after the mid-nineteenth century, whose thought is increasingly served by a highly technical vocabulary of self-analysis'. In Traherne and the other writers who are subjects of her study, 'individuality is real by limited, self-conciousness extreme, but untrained in modern techniques of introspection' (Joan Webber, *The Eloquent 'I': Style and Self in Seventeenth-century Prose*, Madison, WI: University of Wisconsin Press, 1968, introduction; see also the comments in her conclusion).

7 S. Sandbank, 'Thomas Traherne on the Place of Man in the Universe', *Scripta Hierosolymitana*, 17 (1966), p. 126.

8 Joan Webber, *The Eloquent 'I'*, p. 221.

9 Ibid.

10 Joan Webber, '"I and Thou" in the Prose of Thomas Traherne', *Papers on Language and Literature*, 2 (1966), pp. 258–64, 261–2.

communion in his paragraphs and sentences.[11] Webber goes so far as to assert that

> The urgency of this united theme [communion and the sustenance of reality from moment to moment] is wholly and uniquely revealed everywhere in his style, from its most obvious to its most apparently casual details – from imagery and wordplay to the rhythm and punctuation of his sentences.[12]

And that:

> The design of the *Centuries of Meditations* is wholly informed by the importance of communion, as is made apparent by the many ways in which the personae of the book – its 'I's and 'he's and 'Thou's – appear and meet and intermingle.[13]

This is not complete union but communication; the communion about which she writes is a unity that does not erase difference. Webber admits that things separate do sometimes become one another in his work but this, she claims, is only possible because of primary separation: 'Things separate are made to approve, affirm, become one another, but the merging can only be because the separation already is.'[14] One may discern echoes here of Ficino's theory of love according to which 'The two lives, God's and man's are made one while yet remaining two.'[15]

And yet in the *Select Meditations* Traherne also speaks of a union with God so complete that even here on earth we may experience something of it. In the sacrament of the Eucharist Traherne believes that God is communicated to us so fully that he becomes a part of us and we of him:

> Those that think our union with God so Incredible, are taught more in the Sacrament. He gives Himselfe to be our food. is united to us. Incorporated in us. for what doth he intimate by the Bread and wine, but as the Bread and wine are mingled with our flesh, and is

---

11 Ibid., pp. 262–3.
12 Webber, *The Eloquent 'I'*, p. 243.
13 Ibid., p. 226.
14 Ibid., p. 243.
15 Nesca A. Robb, *Neoplatonism of the Italian Renaissance*, London: G. Allen & Unwin, 1935, p. 68. Here the author is expanding Ficino's theory of love.

nourishment diffused through all our members, So he is Lov mingling with our Lov as flame with flame, Knowledge shining in our knowledge as Light with Light, an omnipresent sphere within our sphere. (*SM*, II, 66)

Several meditations later Traherne cries 'O my soul admire the Perfection of thy union with God' (*SM*, III, 94). When he writes of this kind of union it is most often in the context of love:

But the union of our Soul with God is the more Sublime. He being more us by the force of Love then our very selves . . . By seeing and Loveing Him we are Transformed into Him, become his Similitude, feel his Blessedness, Enjoy his Glory, possess his Treasures and become his own. (*SM*, III, 93)

Such love

maketh the Lover infinitly Subject to [the] Person beloved, it maketh them both Supremely each others. We Lov him so much that we magnifie and Adore Him, and annihilate our selves and all our delights to be Delightful to Him. The Beloved of God is a God unto Him: (*SM*, III, 93)

One is reminded of those immortal lines from Emily Brontë's novel *Wuthering Heights* when the protagonist Cathy tries to describe her wild and abandoned love for the undeserving and utterly desired Heathcliff. There are no words adequate; she is lost in love, where one is no longer half of two but two are halves of one.[16] 'Love him?' she cries; 'I *am* Heathcliff.' I suggest that this is a picture of Traherne's loving God who comes to us in the incarnation. For his theology is set within the context of the story of God and humanity that begins with creation as desire, in which all things allured God to make them (*KOG*, Ch. 15), followed by rejection, deceit, banishment from Eden and exile. The Old Testament unfolds as the story of a people in exile, which Traherne explores in *The Ceremonial Law*, a story of a God who is seeking his beloved, God's jealousy and forgiveness bearing all the hallmarks of a lover's tale. Between paradise lost and paradise savoured there is the long expanse of paradise sought. Never does

---

16 'One is not half two it is two are halves of one' (e. e. cummings, first line of Poem 74 in *100 Selected Poems by e. e. cummings*, New York: Grove Press, 1959).

desire fail; even when Traherne's God says 'I will spew you out of my mouth'[17] it is said not for want of desire but for the frustration of it. This God is the one whose desire, when all tokens and signs of love had failed, is expressed by becoming us. Not primarily to teach us anything, or even to be nearer to us, but to *be* us. This is Traherne's radical understanding of the incarnation, in a model that casts God boldly as lover.

So far does Traherne's notion of unity go in *Select Meditations* that in it not only are we 'raised', exalted almost to divinity, but God seems to be 'lowered' in a gesture of total self-abandon: 'The Lover abandoneth Himselfe to the disposeall of his Beloved, is absolutely his Subject, and infinitly delighteth to be commanded by Him' (*SM*, III, 93). All of this self-abandon is written in the context of passionate love. When we are united to God, it is by love alone that we are so united. Again from *Select Meditations*:

> All exterior works will I Performe to Please Thee: but by Delighting in thy Love will be united to Thee. Thy Lov to me Shall Dwell within me, Return againe, be Lov unto Thee, Transform my soul, and make us one. O my Father and the Bridgroom of my soul. All these are Treasures, and thy palace wonderfull, but thy Person is the Joy and Happines of my Soul. (*SM*, IV, 39)

God's nature and person is love. The implication is that we may never be one with him until we are not only improved by love but made love as he is love: 'Other Persons are made amiable by Lov. Thy Person is Lov' (*SM*, IV, 39). So there seem to be two models of ultimate felicity. In communion, God communicates himself to us and we offer back to him a world transformed. We live in a dynamic of continuing desire and satisfaction, of repeated gift and receipt, in communion with each other and with him. In union, we become one with him by love, following the model of the wife and husband, the lover and the beloved. Union and communion – in the one we are lovers; in the other we are friends. In fact, Traherne uses the two terms not inseparably and without contradiction – together, singly and separately.[18] In the same sentence we are called to 'be Amiable as Brides, Live in communion with Him as friends'.[19] This coupling of the two together suggests that

---

17 Rev. 3.16.
18 See, for example, 'Next unto Retiremt, A Stable Reflection is required in ye Soul to dedicate it self to God, in an Individual union & communion with him' (*ITR*, fol. 2v).
19 *SM*, IV, 4; 'Brides and Friends' are also coupled in *SM*, III, 43.

neither state is privileged above the other.[20] Each speaks of a particular stage or place in the cycle of desire and felicity. It is an ever fuller participation in that cycle that is the real destination of the soul in Traherne. In *A Sober View* he describes it as follows:

> our Act of Enjoying is the End for which the World is made; & that by which we imitat God who rejoyceth in all his Works, live in Communion with him, and inherit all his Benefits, fulfilling all his Laws to wit the laws of Nature, & making ourselves Happy. Enjoying Him in them, & pleasing Him by Enjoying them. For the more we prize him the more we honor him; & the more we honor the more we Glorify him: the more we Glorify the more we Delight in him; & the more we delight in him the more we Enjoy him, & the more we enjoy him the more delightful we are made unto him. Nay and the more we Enjoy him, the more we prize him. These things being one and compleat in a Circle. (*SV*, fols 28v–29r)

An earlier manuscript version read 'These things being one & the circle compleat'; Traherne's editorial change suggests that the circle is part of the perfection of the thing rather than a sign of its completion. Things are, in a circle, one and complete rather than one, and so the circle is complete; it seems that he wanted to make this distinction clear. The implication is that the circle continues. Indeed, its very continuance is part of its virtue because this circle is concerned with more than simple self-perpetuation. As Traherne's repetition of 'the more' above makes clear, each action provokes another action of more intensity and fervour or of greater depth of delight. And so the circle might more appropriately be described as a kind of upwards spiral ever ascending into felicity.

On Communion and the Cross

The perpetual motion of this circularity relies on the force of love and desire. We are drawn by the force of some great thing. Initially we do not know what that is but, even after we do know the force to be love, the draw of that love does not diminish. For Traherne this force of love is manifest most profoundly in the cross of Christ: 'When I am lifted

---

20 Lest the implication be that being lover or wife is more intimate than being a friend, I should note that, in *ITR*, Traherne calls marriage second to friendship in terms of the intimacy that it requires.

up, saith the Son of Man, I will draw all men unto me . . . But by what cords? The cords of a man, and the cords of Love.'[21] His discussion of the cross in the *Centuries* is curiously limited to about ten meditations in the first *Century*[22] but the imagery he uses here of being drawn by cords is not. Elsewhere in the *Centuries* we see also ligatures, bonds, cement, cords and sinews.[23] Always they speak of desire between the human soul and God. Where for many theologians the cross is the place of substitution and sacrifice following the model of substitutionary atonement, for Traherne, in the *Centuries* at least (though he employs the substitutionary model elsewhere[24]), an appeasement of God's wrath is not what the cross is about. He is not primarily concerned with God the Father drawing a line through a now-paid debt but with the human response to what is seen there; the cross, despite its gore, functions as an object of desire that draws the human witness to the giver of such immense love. In these meditations from the *Centuries*, the draw of the Cross is magnetic: 'As eagles are drawn by the scent of a carcase, as children are drawn together by the sight of a lion, as people flock to a coronation, and as a man is drawn to his beloved object' (C, I, 57) so are we drawn to the cross. 'If Love be the weight of the Soul, and its object the centre, all eyes and hearts may convert and turn unto this Object: cleave unto this centre, and by it enter into rest' (C, I, 59). We are drawn to the bloody sufferings of Christ, 'our eye must be towards it, our hearts set upon it, our affections drawn, and our thoughts and minds united to it' (C, I, 56). So the lodestone is the Rock of Ages:[25]

> See how in all closets, and in all temples; in all cities and in all fields; in all nations and in all generations, they are lifting up their hands and eyes unto His cross; and delight in all their adorations.[26]

---

21 C, I, 56. Cf. C, I, 57, where Traherne continues the image: 'What visible chains or cords draw these? What invisible links allure?'

22 I use the term 'curiously' because most of his topics are revisited, revised and discussed across several genres and works. Why the cross is treated differently could make an interesting point of discussion but it would be a departure from the purpose of this work and so I do not treat it here.

23 'Wants are the bands and cements between God and us. . . . Wants are the ligatures between God and us, the sinews that convey senses from Him into us' (C, I, 51).

24 For more on Traherne's theories of atonement see *COH*, 'Atonement' and selections from *CE*, *TCL*, *C*, *SM* and *KOG* in Denise Inge (ed.), *Happiness and Holiness: Thomas Traherne and his Writings*, London: Canterbury Press, 2008, Ch. 3, readings 6–12.

25 C, I, 59 continues 'There [in the cross] we might see the Rock of Ages, and the Joys of Heaven.'

26 C, I, 85. Cf. 'As on every side of the earth all heavy things tend to the centre; so all nations ought on every side to flow in unto it' (C, I, 56).

What is it that draws them? Desire. '[N]othing compels him [to look upon the cross], but... Commodity and Desire' (C, I, 57). In fact the cross is the centre of all desires. *Century*, I, 58 is dense and brief; the whole of it reads:

> The Cross is the abyss of wonders, *the centre of desires*, the school of virtues, the house of wisdom, the throne of love, the theatre of joys, and the place of sorrows; It is the root of happiness, and the gate of Heaven. [italics mine]

Belden Lane's insights are helpful in seeing how this may be so. The cross may be (among the other things listed) the centre of desires not just because it has, according to Traherne, the drawing force of a lodestone and so becomes a focus of desire but also because it teaches us about the fruitfulness of not having (we already understand the fruitfulness of having) and in so doing how to participate beneficially in the perpetual cycle of desire. Lane writes of the cross:

> Here lies the key to understanding the dark side of a universe filled with competing wants of every sort. The eagle's desire for food and the ground squirrel's longing for life are not easily reconciled apart from the cross. Only there do we learn how to fathom wanting-and-not-having as an exercise of love.

Through the cross, says Lane, we learn to focus on desire less as an exercise in acquisition and more as a 'circle of interconnectedness that binds us strangely and inseparably to each other'.[27] According to Traherne, the cross is at once the most peculiar and the most exalted of all objects, an ensign, the only supreme and sovereign spectacle in all worlds. In the cross opposites unite in paradox. God's mercy and his anger, man's sin and infinite value go hand in hand. The hope and fear, misery and happiness of the human soul are there displayed. 'There we may see a Man loving all the world, and a God dying for mankind ... An innocent malefactor, ... There we may see the most distant things in Eternity united: all mysteries at once couched together and explained.'[28]

Traherne moves from paradox to metaphor: 'The Cross of Christ is Jacob's ladder'. It is 'a tree set on fire with invisible flame... The flame

---

[27] This and the previous quotation are from Belden Lane, 'Thomas Traherne and the Awakening of Want', *The Anglican Theological Review* 81 (1999) pp. 651–64, 658.
[28] C, I, 59.

is Love: the Love in His bosom who died on it' (C, I, 60). It is a throne of delights. Above all other objects of contemplation, it is 'that Centre of Eternity, that Tree of Life in the midst of the Paradise of God!'(C, I, 55).

'The centre of eternity' is a term used several times by Traherne to describe the cross.[29] I think he means by it that the cross is the centre of all centres, the supreme centre from which everything else radiates. 'The centre of eternity' suggests timelessness, or the superseding of temporal notions of time and space, and places the cross in infinity. Webber claims that 'the Cross is made the symbol of communion, and thereby negates time and space'.[30] I suggest that it simply supersedes them, renders them aspects of a less relevant and less accurate vision, relics of partial illumination. As Webber rightly notes, 'Traherne uses the word "centre" to apply to anything that can be said to have a core (as, for example, the earth), but he prefers it to mean something which can organize and shed light on what lies around it.'[31] The cross becomes the measure of all other things; all must be interpreted in relation to it.

The centrality of the cross can be seen in the image of it not just as the centre of eternity but also as the Tree of Life. In the image of the Tree of Life, Traherne draws together the desire of the human, divine desire and the cross. The first *Century* begins with the desire of 'some great thing' and desire structures much of the first *Century*'s exploration of enjoyment.[32] Nearly halfway through the first *Century*, Traherne proclaims '*The Desire Satisfied is a Tree of Life.*' And God's desire is also that tree: 'God was never without this Tree of Life'.[33] In this instance, desire is life-giving because by it we learn our wants, because it 'imports something absent', it makes our wants our treasures. And so the Tree of Life becomes a symbol of desire ever present and ever satisfied. Several meditations later, when the cross becomes 'that Tree of Life in the midst of the Paradise of God!'(C, I, 55), displacing the tree from which Eden's fatal fruit was taken, we may come to see the fully vitalizing force of the cross for Traherne. It totally rewrites the human script. As Day attests, 'the Cross is the most profound example of satisfied desire and the deepest expression of the "Great thing" with

---

[29] C, I, 54; C, I, 55.
[30] Webber, *The Eloquent 'I'*, p. 233.
[31] Ibid.
[32] Malcolm Day argues this structure persuasively. See *Thomas Traherne*, Boston, MA: Twayne, 1982, pp. 119–21.
[33] This and the preceding quotation are both from C, I, 43.

which the *Century* began, the archetype by which we learn what we must know about loving all things properly'.[34]

Webber also sees the vitality of the cross: 'The Cross is distinctly a vitalizing force, not the instrument of penitence that it had often been in earlier meditational writing.'[35] This vitality of the cross is where Traherne's imagery of it most nearly approaches his concept of desire, for desire too is a vitalizing force. In *The Kingdom of God* Traherne writes of desire as a 'spring of motion':

> The Soul when made like a Watch wound up is apt to go of it self; if the wheels be not entangled with grit and their teeth full of filth, the Spring that Commands them, will draw them about by a Gentle Threed, and direct the Hand to point out the Hours for a Day together, as if the Dead Workmanship were endued wih understanding ... Appetite and Desire are the Spring that urge it, the Wheels are the Affections and powers of the Mind; Its Inclination is the Thred that draws them about ... Being endued with Life, the Soul can feel the Absence, and the presence of all Objects. Being capable of Pleasure and Affected with its desire, it loves it self, and is ambitiously carried to all Enjoyments.[36]

That desire has a kind of mechanical quality is also suggested in the *Centuries* where, again, the figure of wheels set in motion by a spring is used to convey the vitalizing force of desire:

> Can all these things move so without a life, or spring of motion? But the wheels in watches move, and so doth the hand that pointeth out the figures: this being a motion of dead things. Therefore hath God created living ones: that by lively motion, and sensible desires, we might be sensible of a Deity. (C, II, 2)

The Cross is that 'centre of desires' (C, I, 58) from which this energy springs. Furthermore, desire is one of the effects that the cross has on its viewers. We have noted how people are drawn to the cross. Traherne uses images of hunger and feeding, suggestive of the Eucharist – eagles drawn to a carcase (I, 56), the hungry to a feast (I, 57) to describe the reaction that the cross invites. And this hunger is answered several meditations later when Traherne refers to Christ as 'wholly fed upon

---

34 Day, *Thomas Traherne*, p. 121.
35 Webber, *The Eloquent 'I'*, p. 234.
36 KOG, fols 158v–159r.

by every Christian' (I, 86), those who are enabled 'to digest the nourishment' (I, 87) to their souls. Thus the cross is the centre of desires in terms of both its vitality and its attractiveness. In being the centre of desire, the cross is also the central inspiration for this poet of desire. It is the well from which many of his images spring and it is profoundly connected to his theories surrounding the function of desire, and, as we shall see, his concern with learning virtue.

Like desire, the cross also burns. It is not only 'that Tree of life in the midst of the Paradise of God' (I, 55) but also 'a tree set on fire' with the flame of Love (I, 60). This flame is both passionate (love in the bosom of him who died) and illuminating (an invisible flame that illuminates all the world). In *The Ceremonial Law*, in which Traherne writes about Moses' call in the burning bush, the burning bush, though symbolic of the Church rather than the cross, is similarly illuminating and alluring. The burning bush is not the only thing that ravishes the sight by its brightness. God's grace also shines brightly in every age; but what ravishes Traherne about this grace is that it shines for him.[37] By grace all things relate to him and are his just as they are God's:

> Who would expect that from the very first,
> Even from the Time the World for sin was curst,
> All thing to one new born should so relate,
> And all the Ages be his own Estate?
> A Wide Possession! And a Joy Divine!
> That's wholy thine, O Lord, yet Wholy mine.
>
> (*TCL*, 'Moses Call', ll. 31–6)

The realization of so great a grace should move the soul to a new intensity of love:

> Oh how should this my Soul transform to Lov
> What flames, what fires, what Halelujahs mov!
>
> (*TCL*, 'Moses Call', ll. 41–2)

And so, soul by soul, the whole Church becomes alight with fire. The Church is the burning bush, a thorny bramble converted by love, so that the barren bush bears 'Even in the midst of fire. What fruit? Her

---

37 'Lord I am ravished the Grace to see, / In evry Age so Brightly shine for me' (*TCL*, 'Moses Call', ll. 29–30).

Tears' (*TCL*, 'Moses Call', l. 46). As burning branches weep in a fire, so the Church in tears confesses its enmity and begins to bear fruit:

> And in this Heavenly Light she strangely bears
> All Kind of fruits, as well as Watery Tears.
> Which, while her peircing Thorns do prick her eys,
> Out of her Burning Lov to Thee Arise.
> Hope, Patience, Glory, Faith and Charity
> Within the Splendor of her flames we see
> And while in stranger fire she seems to burn
> She Joy conceivs, and Praises doth return.
>
> (*TCL*, 'Moses Call', ll. 61–8)

The fire 'Calcines her only', her flames 'aspire' to heaven and purify her so that, burning, she is a light alluring all the world, just as the burning bush allured Moses to a vision of God. So Traherne concludes on both a personal and a corporate level:

> And I O Lord pull off my shoes, and com
> With Reverence unto Thee, my shining Sun . . .
> Send me unto thy Church, and let her prov,
> To me and Thee, a burning Bush of Lov.
>
> (*TCL*, 'Moses Call', ll. 75–6, 81–2)

Right through this stanza of the poem the imagery is working at several levels. The bush burns as a sign to Moses, it burns as a sign for the poet and it burns in its love for God. All of these burnings signal to each other. The sign to the individual becomes the sign to the whole Church, and that same fire that is a sign is also the fire by which the Church itself burns and is purified – its barrenness turned into fruitfulness, its thorns the place of bounty. The fire that signalled the need for change becomes both the vehicle of that very transformation and the sign of love returned back to God. In all of this movement the flames work much as does desire. There is the initial calling to something greater or higher, that striking difference between the fire and the empty land around it. There is a movement of aspiration towards heaven accompanied by a sense of distance from that heavenly end (that part of the poem in which the Church confesses its enmity). There is purgation, purification, suffering, repentance followed by joy, fruitfulness and transformation. The fire of purgation becomes, finally the fire of love and an expression of continued desire, 'a burning Bush of Lov'.

In *The Kingdom of God* divine goodness is also seen as a fire: 'His Infinit goodness being infinitly Ardent is infinitly Bright, because Infinitly Glorious. It is compared to Fire in the Holy Scripture' (*KOG*, fol. 183r). In this passage Traherne makes no distinction between divine goodness and divine love – the two are represented together in the image of fire. He cites Moses and the bush, the descent of flames on Mount Sinai, Christ's baptizing with fire in the descent of the Holy Spirit, the coal of fire pressed to the lips of Isaiah, Ezekiel's vision of glory in the wheels of fire and Daniel's description of the throne of God as 'like the Fiery Flames, and his Wheels as a Burning Fire'.[38] As in 'Moses Call' in *The Ceremonial Law* above, this fiery love purifies.[39] This fire shares many of the qualities that we have seen in Traherne's notion of desire – it is 'Activitie, vigor, Violence, Ardor, Impatience, Zeal, Irresistible Speed, Perfection, Purity, Glory' (*KOG*, fol. 183v). Traherne does not call this loving fire 'desire'[40] but, like desire, it too is 'love in motion': 'What is more glorious, then that which is most Active? Light and Fire!'(*KOG*, fol. 183v). This activity promptly leads him back to his recurring theme of communication and the need of divine goodness to be communicated. Divine goodness 'loves to be delighted in' (*KOG*, fol. 183v). From simple communication he moves on to relationship, for divine goodness travels on a two-way street; it not only affects but is also affected by its recipients: 'if it sees another dissatisfied with its own miscariage, it is confounded with Affliction'.[41] Goodness is by its nature communicative. It is no surprise then that Traherne moves on, in the subsequent folios of the manuscript, from the fire of divine goodness and love and its need to be received to our duty to communicate this goodness to others.

---

38 *KOG*, fol. 183v. In the margin Traherne notes: 'Daniel 7.9.10'.

39 'What Purifies the Rust of Idleness, or Death or consumes the Earthiness of a Dull estate, but the fire of Activitie, and Zealous Love' (*KOG*, fol. 183r).

40 In fact, in the list of what this fire is (cited above), 'Desire' was edited out of the manuscript. I take this not as an indication that desire is not relevant to his description of the fire of divine goodness and love but that the treatment of it is deferred, since he devotes several subsequent paragraphs to the desire of goodness to be communicated, its need to participate in the life of others and its inability to be full (i.e. its lack) without this necessary communication. In other words, the fire is a quality of desire rather than desire being a quality of the fire.

41 *KOG*, fol. 183v. Several folios later Traherne writes: ' He is so deeply concerned in them, that his is persecuted[,] Imprisoned, Wounded, flouted and Killed in his servants' (*KOG*, fol. 185r).

Another fire that moves through purgation to renewal of life occurs in the legendary fire of the phoenix, an image that also appears in *The Kingdom of God*, in the *Centuries* and in the *Select Meditations*. The 'celestial stranger', whose hypothetical arrival on earth instigates Traherne's great catalogue of creation in chapter 25 of *The Kingdom of God*, would believe himself 'faln into the Paradise of God, a phoenix nest, a Bed of spices', so astonishingly full is this pleroma of creation. If in the fourth *Century* 'Love is a Phoenix that will revive in its own ashes', a love that can attempt all and suffer all (C, IV, 61, 62), in *The Kingdom of God* creation is the nest of that phoenix. To have fallen into a phoenix nest and a bed of spices sounds luxurious, sensual, reminiscent of the lovers' bed of spices in the Song of Songs.[42] If love is the phoenix are we to understand that nest as the cradle of love, the place in which love is nurtured and grows? In fact, the phoenix nest *is* made of spices; the bed of spices and the nest are one and the same. The nest, however, is the place of sacrifice: the phoenix builds her spice nest, fans the nest into fire with her own wings, dies and arises sweet-smelling, renewed from the ashes. In the *Select Meditations* Love, Christ and the phoenix are one. Or, perhaps more precisely, Love is the meaning, the phoenix the symbol, Christ the person. They are each their own altar, perfume and flame:

> Love is the onely sacrifice. It is Like our Saviour its own Preist, and its own Alter, Perfume and Flame. A Prophet Preist and king. O my God it is like thy son, the Phœnix of the world, Its comprehensiv sphere, a flaming Temple . . .

But for Traherne, Love, the antitype, supersedes the type. Love is:

> The Antitipe of her who is the faigned Miracle of all the Birds and more then so. Its own Alter fire nest and Sacrifice. O Thou nest, and Bed of spices! In its Highest Agonies, ever Dying, Expiring and Reviving every moment.[43]

Where the phoenix reaches her life span and is renewed, Love is ever dying, expiring and reviving, as Christ, the personification of Love, continually creates and re-creates in his own image. In *The Kingdom of God* Traherne has set the fiery nest right in the centre of paradise, where the Tree of Life was in Eden, and exactly where the cross of the

---

42 S. of Sol. 5.13, 6.12.
43 *SM*, II, 77. I am indebted to Alison Kershaw for first directing me to this passage.

Centuries also resides. The place in which we live may also be such 'a nest of sweet perfumes' (C, I, 80) when we see the cross in its place on fire.

Traherne's cross is not only a tree set on fire and the centre of desires but it is also a mirror of the truest reality. It not only shows us the life of heaven but the trial and triumph of earth too, in its true colours: 'It is a Well of Life beneath in which we may see the face of Heaven above: and the only mirror, wherin all things appear in their proper colours'.[44] Furthermore, it shows us how to live in the world. The cross is 'the school of virtues' (C, I, 58): 'Here you learn all patience, meekness, self-denial, courage, prudence, zeal, love, charity, contempt of the world, joy, penitence, contrition, modesty, fidelity, constancy, perseverance, contentation, holiness and thanksgiving'.[45] Lest his reader think that the virtues learned at the cross are private virtues, Traherne ends the meditation with: 'Here we learn to imitate Jesus in His love unto all.'

We receive God's love that we may give it. So strong is Traherne's desire to imitate Christ's love that he prays to apprehend this love with each of his five senses:

> O that I could see it through all those wounds! O that I could feel it in those stripes! O that I could hear it in all those groans! O that I could taste it beneath the gall and vinegar! O that I could smell the savour of thy sweet ointments, even in this Golgotha, or place of a skull. (C, I, 63)

This passionate plea is both preceded and concluded with the same theme: 'O Thou who art most glorious in Goodness, make me abundant in this Goodness like unto Thee. That I may as deeply pity others' misery, and as ardently thirst for their happiness as Thou dost' (C, I, 63). When he writes: 'I pray Thee teach me first Thy love unto me, and then unto mankind!'(C, I, 63), the whole purpose of his prayer is that by being so united he may be able also to imitate God's love to all persons. In this love, as in all else, divine gift is primary. Traherne wants to receive as fully as possible, be filled and overflow. 'Abide in me and I in you', said Jesus Christ to his followers in St John's Gospel,[46]

---

44 C, I, 59. See 'On Leaping over the Moon', in which heaven is in the puddle beneath the poet's feet.
45 C, I, 61. That Traherne ends this list of virtues with thanksgiving is typical of his study of the virtues, a point to which I shall return in the final section of this chapter.
46 John 15.4.

and it is this very Johannine sense of abiding that Traherne is suggesting here. The one who abides bears fruit; the ones who abide live in God and God lives in them; they live towards each other and lay down their lives with joy. Here, in this recurring theme of receipt and gift, the cycle of desire is looking outward: 'for we must be Beloved, that we may lov. And lov, that we may be Glorious.'[47]

On Communion with One Another

Traherne's claim in the fourth *Century*, 'That Pool must first be filled, that shall be made to overflow',[48] is simple logic. You would not ask a beggar to dispense wealth; you would not ask a dead man to breathe. To talk of overflowing until all our emptiness and capacity be full within is 'impertinent' and 'unseasonable' (*CE*, Ch. 32). But there is more going on here than simple logic because Traherne's theory of fullness poses a serious challenge to those images that separate love into exclusive categories of selfless and selfish love.

There is a strand in Christian theology that would see love divided into three types: *eros*, *philia*, or brotherly love, and *agape*, or what St Paul calls 'charity', the selfless, giving love. In this model *agape* is often seen as divine love; *eros* and *philia*, though not detrimental, belong to lower orders of loving. Søren Kierkegaard, for example, wrote that one should take pains to make it clear that erotic love belonged to paganism and that the love of one's neighbour belonged to Christianity.[49] Eros and love of neighbour are in opposition and self-love 'in the strictest sense has been characterized as self-deification . . . love and friendship . . . are essentially idolatry'.[50] This separation of loves received weighty backing in the twentieth century from Anders Nygren's influential book *Agape and Eros*, in which *agape* is universal and all-embracing while other loves are particular and exclusive. While Nygren admits that *eros* is much more than the erotic, tracing it back to Plato as 'love for the beautiful and the good', he still contrasts *agape* and *eros* as 'Christian and non-Christian fundamental motifs';[51] this fundamen-

---

47 KOG, fol. 166v. Cf. 'For all Pleasures will naturaly flow & overflow in ye Soul, where once it enjoy wth such Circumstances ye pleasure of Loving & being Beloved' (*ITR*, fol. 10v).
48 C, IV, 55. On the overflowing of love from a satisfied heart see also C, IV, 60.
49 S. Kierkegaard, *Works of Love*, trans. Howard and Edna Hong, New York: Harper & Row, 1964, p. 58.
50 Ibid., p. 68.
51 Anders Nygren, *Agape and Eros*, London: SPCK, 1932, p. 94.

tal division between loves has shaped much of twentieth- and early twenty-first-century thinking about love in God. However, the classification of loves, though it has shaped much of current thinking about the nature of divine love, is not a recent notion. In Traherne's day, too, there was within the tradition a strand that would oppose Christianity and self-love. Traherne himself asks 'How can God be Love unto Himself, without the imputation of self-love?' (C, IV, 65), aware of the Christian admonition to prefer others above oneself. His answer lies in understanding love less as a formula and more as a series of streams whose waters commingle. Do not be mean-minded with love, he would say. Categorize it less, spill it more. That God should be 'Love unto His beloved, Love unto Himself, love unto His creatures' (C, IV, 64) is all part of God's essential being.

For Traherne personal fulfilment and self-giving are as inextricably tied up with each other for us humans as they are for God. They are not the same thing, but neither do they function in isolation. The modern theologian Helen Oppenheimer's words echo Traherne's when she says:

> Self-giving and fulfilment are not, of course, synonyms. They do stand for distinct ideas. The point is that they need each other. On the one hand, self-giving on its own does not make as much sense as Christians are apt to think. One cannot give from emptiness. One cannot give to someone who is too selfless to receive. Relentless competitive unselfishness is a ghastly caricature of Christian love. Selfish fulfilment, on the other hand, does not make as much sense as unregenerate humanity is apt to think.[52]

Just as God's self-love increases rather than diminishes his love for us, so our self-love should overflow into love for others. At a time when Hobbes was proclaiming self-preservation as the foundation of society, Traherne suggests that the love of other things runs even deeper than self-preservation; self-love in the end cannot be divorced from the love of others:

> We feel it [self-preservation] first, and must preserve our selves, that we may continue to enjoy other things: but at the bottom it is the love of other things that is the ground of this principle of Self-preservation. And if you divide the last from the first, it is the poorest Principle in the World. (CE, pp. 259–61)

---

52 Helen Oppenheimer, *The Hope of Happiness: A Sketch for a Christian Humanism*, London: SCM Press, 1983, p. 115.

In *The Kingdom of God* he reminds us that 'Duties towards our selvs and Neighbors may be united. For Infinit Goodness hath made us one' (*KOG*, fol. 184v). The implication is that our interests should be so united to the interests of others that the two loves are indistinguishable.

Just so is it also, Traherne argues, between God and humanity. The dichotomy that many believers sense between 'our will' and 'God's will' or between human interests and divine interests should really be seen as ultimately artificial, or at least temporary. In fact, one of the most scabious qualities of piety is when pious persons fear rather than embrace God's generosity in the divide that they create between human interests and divine interests. As Traherne writes in *The Kingdom of God*:

> They are highly Mistaken that think it dangerous for Goodness to be Infinit. Some there are that like pusillanimous niggards (who think they shall be undone by Liberalitie) fear least God also should over Act himself in Bounty . . . When Men once pin their base and penurious excuses upon God's shoulders, and think him such an one as themselves, their horrid maximes and covetous Providences may pass then for good Divinitie . . . It is a trick that Satan taught them, but God was never acquainted with it, to divide his own Interest from that of others. (*KOG*, fols 180v–181r)

He continues, 'His Interest is most promoted in that of his Creatures, and only in theirs it is secured'. With God, as with each other, we are 'individually one', not merged and yet united, as in the fourth *Century* where, pouring phrase upon phrase, Traherne cannot say it often enough:

> They are individually one, which it is very amiable and beautiful to behold, because therein the simplicity of God doth evidently appear. The more He loveth them, the greater He is and the more glorious. The more He loveth them, the more precious and dear they are to Him. The more He loveth them, the more joys and treasures He possesseth. The more He loveth them the more He delighteth in their felicity. The more He loveth them the more He delighteth in Himself for being their felicity. The more He loveth them, the more He rejoiceth in all his works for serving them: and in all His kingdom for delighting them. And being Love to them the more He loveth Himself, and the more jealous he is lest Himself should be displeased, the more He loveth them and tendereth them and secureth their welfare.

And the more He desireth His own glory, the more good He doth for them, in the more divine and genuine manner.

Love, delight in, possess, give. Jealousy runs alongside tenderness here; the divine lover loves himself as well as his beloved. Again we see Traherne saying of love – categorize it less, spill it more. Yet he concludes all of this with the challenging admonition: 'You must love after His similitude.'[53]

That we human beings are tied in such bonds of unity and community means that our actions have real power, and the damage or good that they do reaches far beyond the one upon whom the action is initially acted. Traherne reminds us that what we do to each other we do to all and to God. In words that are a fusion of Scripture and poetry, Traherne asserts that to hurt a brother or sister is to hurt God himself:

'Verily in as much as ye did it to the least of my Brethren,' saith our Savior, ye did it unto me.
Saul, Saul. Why persecutest thou me?
A Christian is not only his, but He!
He that toucheth you, toucheth the Apple of mine eye.[54]

Conversely, in *Christian Ethicks*, when we love our neighbour we love God. In fact, loving our neighbour is the best way to love God (*CE*, p. 144). In living in communion with God and one's neighbour, one is at once going out of oneself and coming home, at once acting freely and nobly and answering a deep-seated need. We best enjoy the treasures we give away; we enrich ourselves by donation rather than accumulation, says Traherne. We are to 'posess all in Such a manner as to be the Joy of all. Be Like God by Lov a Lone' (*SM*, II, 65).

In the light of this kind of outstretched love we may see all creatures as servants of our happiness, as we are of theirs. It is not until every person is a treasure to us that we may be co-enjoyers of their joys and co-possessors of their delights. And Traherne writes 'treasure' here not in a sentimental tone but with august desire and utmost reverence for the other. Every man must be a god unto his soul 'or Like a God, a Living Treasure, a friend, a joy, an Immortal Lover', for 'Lov a Lone

---

53 This and the previous quotation are from C, IV, 65. Again Traherne's repetition of 'the more' indicates the perpetually intensifying nature of this love. He has used the same structure for the same purpose in SV, fols 28v–29r.

54 KOG, fol. 185r, citing Matt. 25.40; Acts 9.4, 22.7, 26.4; Zech. 2.8.

maketh me the possessor of all their joys, lov aLone maketh me a Joy and a Delight to them'.[55]

This is what it means to live in communion. Traherne's communion is not about living in complete agreement; it is not a companionable co-existence but a profound exchange of needs and sufficiencies, a kind of essential co-reliance in which wholeness cannot be found in oneself alone but only through mutual generosity. Karl Barth wrote 'There can be no question of an extension in principle of the concept of Christian love for the neighbour into a universal love of humanity unless we are to radically weaken and confuse it'.[56] For Traherne this universal love is not watered down by being widely spread but, fired by a love that has as much to do with the needs and lacks of *eros* as with the plenitude of *agape*, it retains the passion of the particular. In *Inducements to Retiredness* he wrote that he aimed to love the whole world as much as he would a wife or a dearest friend.

Traherne admits that this is difficult, confessing that 'there are many Disguises, that overcast the Face of Nature with a vail . . . and Eclipse this Glorious Duty, and make it [loving our neighbour] uncouth and difficult to us'. But 'all these Disorders came in by sin . . . In the Purity of Nature, Men are Amiable Creatures and prone to Love' (*CE*, p. 145). We must look with the eyes of Eden. There was no law there that compelled Adam to love Eve – 'His Appetite and Reason were united together, and both invited him to lose himself in her Embraces' (*CE*, p. 145). Traherne calls this appetite and reason together 'a silent Law', which we too may follow, not regarding 'the Malevolence of Men' (*CE*, p. 145) but looking instead upon what good might have been achieved if that silent law had never been broken. We are given the chance to be the new Adam and the new Eve and to observe the law of love. And so Traherne's invitation to communion with our neighbour is not only an invitation to personal fulfilment but also to participation in a larger scheme of redemption. We are to break the cycle of disobedience and division and open up a whole world of possibility.

We have seen Traherne's description of love in *The Kingdom of God* as 'at once a freedom from all law, and the severest law in the World, but a willing and delightfull law of the most constraining, and Indispensable Necessitie' (*KOG*, fol. 186v). He constantly reminds his reader of the importance of freedom, that 'No action can be Delightful that is not our Pleasure in the Doing', that the soul's 'Honour [is]

---

55 *SM*, II, 83. Cf. 'For Two persons to love each other in all this Grandure, clothed with the Heavens . . . is to Liv towards each in Glory' (*SM*, II, 96).
56 Karl Barth, *Church Dogmatics*, III/2, Edinburgh: T&T Clark, 1958, p. 807.

founded in the freedom of its Desire' (*CE*, p. 149). That freedom, however, is most expeditously exercised in an ordered manner. The law of love, which is so severe and total, is also irresistible: Traherne cries of divine love, 'O sweet and eternal Violence! O healing fire, O Lawfull and Irresistible Charm! To be a slave Unto thee is perfect freedom ... O make me a happy Captive, and lead me captiv allwayes!' (*KOG*, fol. 187r–v).

According to Traherne, if an individual's interests and the interests of love were one 'there would be so Divine a Sympathie between GOD, and the Soul, that it would read all its own Desires in his Bosom, all its own Joys in his Desires'.[57] This is the fullness of felicity – to delight and desire with God. In this felicity, happiness and holiness are the same thing. One's own happiness is the happiness of others and it is also the glory of God since God has so extended himself towards us that he has made the happiness of his creatures his own highest desire. 'He infinitely desires', Traherne reminds us. His God desires glory and human goodness,[58] the happiness of his creatures and their love.

'Love teacheth more in one day then Books can in a thousand years' (*KOG*, fol. 187r). It teaches, unites, makes us possessors of each other's happiness; but the value of love is more than educational. There is an intrinsic worth to love – love for love's sake. 'Naked love', as Traherne calls it in *The Kingdom of God*, *Inducements to Retiredness* and here in *Select Meditations*:

> All security and Power are in Lov ... yet all these reach not the Inward parts and Depths of love. There is something beside for which these are valued. Namely the sweetnes of naked Love, and unexpressible sweetness and Intrinsick Joy and pleasure which we feel in Naked Lov. Which God doth So strongly covett and Delight in, that for the sake of it He created the world and all. (*SM*, II, 86)

This 'naked love' is the same desire and delight that is behind all of creation:

> Naked Lov is the cause of all things, and naked Lov is the End of all Things ... Till therefore we see the Inward Blessednes of being

---

57 *KOG*, fol. 187r. Cf. 'For he is to dwell in us, and we in Him, because He liveth in our knowledge and we in His. His will is to be in our will, and our will is to be in His will' (*C*, IV, 72).

58 Human goodness is so like God's that nothing can be more like it than it is. 'And yet that it is distinct from His, is manifest because it is the return or recompense of it: the only thing which for and above all worlds He infinitely desires' (*C*, IV, 85).

Beloved we can never Enjoy the Palaces and Temples of those that are to Lov us: nor God who hath made them to Lov us.[59]

Could we see Love itself, we should see God (*SM*, II, 86).

'It remaineth therfore that I retire into God', writes Traherne in *Inducements to Retiredness*, 'And lov all Mankind in Him, after His Similitude. That is, evry person in the whole World, with as near & violent affection, as I would my Wife, or my Dearest Friend' (*ITR*, fol. 10r). Since giving love is such a joy to all, we should be as ready to be beloved as we are to love. Our employment is both to 'Lov to be Beloved' and 'To Lov'. Until we can see this, felicity is 'a Broken Circle' (*SM*, II, 87).

Desire and Satisfaction in the Circle of Bliss

To love and be beloved is the circle of felicity – desire and delight feeding and filling each other in love, human and divine. In all of this, satisfaction is always implied: the ways of God 'Prevent, fulfill, exceed my whole Desire', Traherne writes in *The Ceremonial Law* ('The Introduction', l. 26). And in this simple statement we see the pattern of desire as a whole – desire goes before, is the means and overflows. Desire informs the sight: 'For Want preceding makes us cleerly see / Both End and Fountain of Felicitie' (*TCL*, '[Manna] II', ll. 23–4). Desire is also the engine and the path that we travel into emptiness and nothing in order to find fullness and everything, into lack and need to find satisfaction and plenty. In the process of desiring, Traherne suggests, we find heaven within while looking for it without:

> Lets sojourn in the Desert Wilderness
> Of long and uncreated nothing, guess
> What may the Dismall Chaos be, and view
> The vacant Ages, while he nought did doe.
> Those Empty Barren Spaces will appear
> At last as if they all at once were here
> The Silence Darkness and Deformitie
> In which we nothing plainly nothing see
> Will make the Univers enlightning them
> Even like unto the new Jerusalem.

---

59 *SM*, II, 84. On 'naked love' see also *KOG*, Ch. 32, 1. 52; *ITR*, l. 248.

> And while we wisely seek for Heaven there,
> Twill clearly make us find our Heaven here.
>
> (*TCL*, '[Manna] II', ll. 69–80)

What matters is our hunger. To the hungry, all is manna;[60] to the one who prizes all is treasure. Want is the fountain of felicity.

Just as delight and desire are the two faces of love, so possession and want are two faces of God's fullness. Both are held simultaneously, distinctly and eternally. In 'The Anticipation' Traherne writes of God:

> He's not like us: Possesion doth not Cloy,
>   Nor Sence of Want Destroy.
>   Both always are together:
> No force can either from the other Sever.
>   Yet theres a Space between
>   Thats Endless. Both are seen
> Distinctly still, and both are seen for ever.
>
> ('The Anticipation', ll. 82–7)

God is like us, inasmuch as God is the mirror in which we may see how the co-existence of desire and delight function – desire lending greater intensity to delight, delight feeding the next desire (stanzas 7–8). And yet God is not like us. We

>   ought to have a Sence
> Of all our Wants, of all His Excellence,
> That while we all, we Him might comprehend.
>
> ('The Anticipation', ll. 124–6)

God is the fountain and end; he is also the means. And, as we have seen, God's desiring, in which God both has and wants with neither cloying nor ceasing, is to be the model we follow. God desires infinitely; and what he desires in return is desire itself.[61] This is why desire in Traherne is not something temporary. It is not, as many Eastern religions

---

60 'All will be manna to the Hungry Soul, / Or Living Waters in a Chrystal Bowl' (*TCL*, '[Manna] II', ll. 87–8).

61 It was not so much the performance of Solomon as the passionate purpose of David that pleased God, writes Traherne: 'Infinite desires and intentions of Pleasing him are real objects to his Eye ... His desire is, that the Soul would ... delight in him freely' (*CE*, pp. 252–3).

suggest, the primary distraction we must leave behind. Neither is it a transitional state that we pass through on the way to final fullness but a site that we revisit again and again in the continuing cycle of want and satisfaction. Notwithstanding his many valuable chapters spent discussing the ins and outs of Calvinism, his disputational addresses to dissenters and atheists, his traceable concern with the shape and formation of the English Church after the Reformation, his clear passion for the peace and security of his nation and its people, this theme of desire is the one to which Traherne reverts like a wanderer to water. His deep exploration of desire and its place in the heart of God and thereby in the heart of Christianity is perhaps the most significant theological contribution he has made. Certainly it is the most timeless. Felicity is not about regaining childhood innocence, or about deferring happiness to an afterlife, or about negating or subjugating the plethora of human desires. Because desire exists in God, felicity is about living in lack and longing, being simultaneously needy and filled. Final fullness *is* this interplay of want and satisfaction, heaven here and hereafter, having and wanting from and into eternity.

This is a very different picture of bliss from that suggested by harp-playing angels on clouds or even from images that connect final bliss with eternal rest, peaceful sleep, a kind of cushioned limbo. It also differs from notions of a bliss that is to be found in annihilation of self or a removal of the soul/psyche from all that is earthbound. It differs most profoundly from an idea of bliss as nirvana, extinction, the flame blown out. For Traherne the fire of desire is a fire of life, creation called into being by the overflow of divine desire itself. Because of this and because for him heaven is here as well as hereafter, the idea that there is no desire in heaven is an absurdity.

There is one place where this seems not to be true – a passage from the *Centuries* in which the idea that there is no want in heaven is predicated on an uncharacteristic division between this life and the next:

> Here upon Earth, it [love] is under many disadvantages and impediments that maim it in its exercise, but in Heaven it is most glorious ... There it appeareth in all its advantages, for every soul being full and fully satisfied, at ease, in rest, and wanting nothing, easily overflows and shines upon all. (C, IV, 60)

Throughout the meditation, 'Here upon Earth' is opposed to 'but in Heaven' whereas, in most of his writing, heaven is a continuation of felicity on earth; felicity is both here and hereafter. Towards the end of the meditation it becomes clear why Traherne has used this division. He is writing about the specific power of love under trial, and the estate of trial, though it may be where felicity is learned, though it may make us fit to be the bride, does not continue in Heaven: 'remember that this and the other life are made of a piece, but this is the time of trial, that, of rewards' (C, IV, 60). The reason he emphasizes the satisfaction, ease and rest of heaven here is so that we might appreciate the high value of love shown without these advantages. Those who are 'wanting nothing' may love easily, whereas those who love in the midst of want show love 'in this world more glorious' because it exerts itself 'in the midst of these disadvantages' (C, IV, 60). The point of the meditation is not so much to describe the nature of desire in the afterlife as it is to make plain that 'The greatest disadvantages of love are its highest advantages. In the greatest hazards it achieveth to itself the greatest glory' (C, IV, 60).

Far greater in number and force are Traherne's statements that portray heaven as partially present now and desire as eternal. Not only is desire a divine attribute, thereby making it eternal, but its function as a purveyor of treasure and as an enhancer of delight is an ongoing function. Were there no desire there would be no treasure, and were there no treasure heaven would not be heaven. Eternal delight is not a static state but a 'succession of delights'. God's perfection is 'a Propertie that propagates infinit Numbers, and Successions of Delight and naturaly proceeds to Measures Illimited, and everlasting' (*KOG*, fol. 196v), is what Traherne claims. And desire fulfilled begets more desire. Just as there is a circular generation in ice and water so is there a perpetual and eternal reciprocation in desire:

> For as Water begets Ice, and ice begets Water; the perfection we receive from God makes us to admire, and love his perfection, and the love of his perfection increases ours; and the more our perfection is increased, the more we admire his, and the more we admire it, the more perfect we are. Which manifestly tends to an Illimited Growth of Happiness and Pleasure. (*KOG*, fol. 196v)

This 'circular generation' is like the 'circular progress' of 'Seed from Trees, & Trees from Seed' in the *Commonplace Book*,[62] in which desire is also self-perpetuating.

In his *Commonplace Book* entry on desire, Traherne notes that love

---

62 *CB*, fol. 35, col. 1.

and knowledge are implanted in the soul as seeds. Our desire for knowledge or true happiness draws us so that the soul 'ayms or levells at som particular objects', at first guided by sense rather than choice. The first thing that the soul apprehends is 'its own Attractions or impulsions', eventually moving on to 'the exercise of its own Acts or choice . . . now using sense as a servant, which before did lead it as a guide'.[63] Desire is not taught. The origins of desire are with us from birth and the knowledge that feeds it comes from without. Even the best teacher is but a midwife. As Traherne writes in his *Commonplace Book*:

> As food received by the mother doth only nourish, not give life to the fruit conceived in her womb, so the most pregnant suggestions of some, do only feed, not beget the informall desire of knowledge or happiness. The best Instruction or precepts of tutors, of parents, or the experimts we get ourselves are but as so many offices, or Rules of midwivrie, for bringing forth what was before conceivd.[64]

Knowledge is love restored, desire focused on its proper object, 'So that knowledge properly is but our naturall desire, or implanted blind lov restored to sight.'[65]

So much writing surrounding Traherne's famous theme of felicity or happiness – the blessed life – has construed felicity as a return in one form or another to childhood innocence. This return is so palpably implausible, if not impossible (and in any case not entirely desirable because it suggests a denial of all that the adult has learned), that it has left most readers with little alternative than to relegate Traherne, appealing though his words may be, to the realm of whimsy along with Santa, Rudolph and the Easter Bunny. But what if Traherne's admonition to 'become a child again' is less about returning than it is about rejuvenation, not going back but going forward renewed. In the Gospel of John, Jesus invites Nicodemus to 'be born again'. Traherne's admonition has a similar ring. It is a call to a new beginning; this is about letting our minds be renewed and our desire be educated so that we see the world not so much as a child but as an adult who has been challenged by a child's simplicity. The clear call to unlearn – to become, as it were, a child again – may not be a call to abandon the responsibility of the adult at all, but to regain the ability that the child has to see through the phoney and peripheral to the heart of things. It

---
63 Ibid.
64 Ibid.
65 Ibid.

is often said that love is blind. Here Traherne is saying that love sees, understands, accepts, forgives, speaks the truth, does not hide. For him knowledge is not attaining another layer of sophistication, gaining some archane gnosis; it is love reinvigorated, hope that had gone to seed restored, desire educated, sight renewed.[66] It is about a return, certainly, but a return to clarity of vision and clarity of desire. Here the undivided passion of the child and of the adult may be indistinguishable from one another. Where we begin by groping after the unknown 'som great thing', we learn that that great thing is none other than God Almighty, who is also reaching out to us, seeking reciprocity. This is what the education of desire is; educated desire is not desire repressed but desire that is focused, knows itself to be connected to the eternal longing of God and to the creative urge of the universe. Such desire knows that it is most usefully employed not in the stashing of treasure but in the dispersal of its wealth; it makes the ordinary a gift and illuminates the meaning of things, and in so doing brings home the bounty to all and to each. Although such an educated desire is poised, it is no less full of energy than uneducated or blind desire. In fact, its force or drive keeps increasing with use, so that what we grope towards in the dark we desire more intensely when we see it. Traherne follows his maxim that 'knowledge properly is but our naturall desire, or implanted blind lov restored to sight' with the assertion: 'And nature doth as it were first grope after that which at length she comes to see, and having seen desires to embrace or kisse.'[67] The more educated our desire and the more exercised it becomes, the more passionate it is and the more likelihood it has of being fulfilled because it aims after ever clearer ends.

So the soul progresses in ever enlarging circles of desire that multiply into infinity:

> As there is a circular progress of Seed from Trees, & Trees from Seed: so is there a reciprocall production of desire or lov in one & the same man: for mens Actions of this kind are immanent and multiply within himself.[68]

Ultimately, felicity and the circle of desire are the same thing. In *The Kingdom of God* Traherne describes the circle of felicity as precisely

---

[66] See Timothy Gorringe, *The Education of Desire: Towards a Theology of the Senses*, London: SCM Press, 2001, Ch. 4.

[67] CB, fol. 35, col. 1. Or as Augustine puts it in his *Commentary on St. John's Gospel*: 'Everyone is drawn by his own dear delight.'

[68] Ibid.

this circle of desire, in which desire is magnified and multiplied infinitely into all eternity. In this circle the human soul is the end of all, the sole object, the bride, the sovereign, able to love because she is loved, participating in a dynamic that never ends because it is in itself the motion of love. 'The more he Loves us, we Lov him the more . . . Thus backward and forward there is a perpetual Growth of Excellencies',[69] he writes,

> And the greatness of our Reciprocall Love growes everlastingly till it be consummate with its Period, which is never attained, as long as there is Room or Time for Actions to be multiplied which being renewed, and Repeated to all Eternitie, makes the greatness of our Lov and pleasure infinitely infinite. (*KOG*, Ch. 13, ll. 176–80)

This is true of all things spiritual; in them there is 'a Continual Growth'. Take, for instance, knowledge, wisdom and goodness, which when exercised are self-perpetuating: so love is 'augmented by its own operations . . . our Desires are fed by their Satisfactions, and our Delights redoubled by their Continual Exercise' (*KOG*, Ch 13, ll. 205–9). Composed of both delight and desire, this divine/human love is both ever satisfied and never satisfied, so that 'neither is there stop nor stay'. The soul and God are both always jealous of love and love again, impatient of delay, violently transported by love and reduced to a desperate state at any perceived mitigation of that love. God's fervour is as severe as ours. In fact the very jealousy of human love may serve as a picture of divine love. Traherne extends this metaphor in *The Kingdom of God* when, layering phrase upon phrase and 'more' upon 'more', he writes:

> If it be lawfull to Compare Cottages with Towers, and little Villages to Imperial Cities, full of Temples and palaces; we may transfer this [the account of a jealous husband] in a figure, to God and the Soul. And indeed to this Intent was the place in Solomon's Song first uttered. It being a Song of Love between Christ and his Church. For her Affection and his are equaly Compared to Perfumes and Spices of such Orient Sweetness, and fragrant Smell, that neither of them can ever be satisfyed with Loves. The more he Loves, the more he Desireth her Affection: The more she Loves, the more she desireth his. The more he Loves, the more Lovely he is. And the more she Loves him, her lips drop as an Honey Comb the more Honey and Milk are under her Tongue, and the further allways their Lov's proceed,

---

[69] *KOG*, Ch. 13, ll. 157–60.

they are still the Sweeter; So that neither there is stop, nor stay, till the Measure be Infinit; the deeper the Sweeter, the last, and Highest Degree, being the Crown of all. By how much the more excellent and dearly beloved, by so much the more precious and esteemed. By how much the more esteemed, by so much the more Jealous is the Soul that esteems, at least the more desirous of Lov again: By how much the more Infinitly it cavels the perfection of Lov, by so much the more impatient is it of Delay. So that God being infinitly Excellent, and Infinitly beloved, we are infinitly Jealous of his Glory, yet infinitly more violently transported with his Love and reduced to a desperate Estate and Condition if we perceiv any Mitigation, or coolness in it, nor is God behind with us, his earnestness and fervor is as severe as ours. There is no Attribute more forcibly urged, than his Jealousie to us. Hereupon it is, that we must needs be the end of all, evry one the sole Object, the Bride; the Sovereign exalted. (*KOG*, fol. 166r–v)

This is Traherne's felicity. In this circle of desire does the sphere of felicity consist. In the end felicity is not so much a destination as it is a process or a way of life:

And of This Circle does the Sphere of felicite consist. This is the Circuit of Heaven against which there is no Inchantment; this the communion between God and us, this the cause, and the end of all. (*KOG*, fols 166v–167r)

Traherne concludes his discussion of desire, replete with its almost incantatory repetition of 'more' and 'more', in this final statement, eloquent and simple. As a piece of prose it is masterful. He begins with lofty metaphor and more complex grammatical constructions. With each of the three regular rhythmic repetitions 'this is . . . ', the statement simplifies itself, so that by the time he reaches his final phrase there is no adornment at all. The final phrase is a simple statement composed of single syllable words. The circular imagery – circle, sphere and circuit – consistent with itself and with what he has written elsewhere, reminds us of the other cycles in his work: innocence/fall/redemption, or sight/custom/sight regained. 'Circuit of Heaven' and 'Inchantment', following so soon after the circle and sphere, allude to the hermetic circle, so ubiquitous in his work, whose centre is everywhere and circumference nowhere. The whole statement both refers back to his central theme of felicity and directs his reader to the ultimate goal of his faith (communion with God) while employing familiar scholastic terms (cause and end), themselves laden with layers of meaning. In the end, less is more.

The whole thing acts as a funnel – expansive at the top, condensed at the bottom – or as a lasso, circling round in the air before finally tightening in to the clinch. The cycle of desire is the circle of bliss.

Gratitude

A perpetual cycle of desire may sound to some not dissimilar to the misery of mice on treadmills. Traherne wrote in the *Centuries* about the despair of those who live in a state of desiring yet never possessing,[70] and desire that constantly recurs without reference to an 'other' outside the self is stifling. One becomes a prisoner of one's own inward-looking desire, focused on lack rather than capacity, and in such a state nothing can please or satisfy. We have seen in chapter four that healthy desire in Traherne avoids solipsistic despair by its attention to authentic objects. Having authentic objects, true desire is always intended for satisfaction; and gratitude is intended as a counterweight to insatiability. Just as hope is a virtue of belief and desire,[71] so gratitude is a virtue of satisfaction and praise. Desire without satisfaction is despair; desire satisfied without gratitude is despicable. And so Traherne may well assert that insatiability is good but that Ingratitude is bad.[72] ingratitude is bad for several reasons: it kicks against heaven, it is unbecoming but, more importantly, it is a kind of blindness that cannot see its treasures.[73]

As we have seen, understanding the worth of a thing is not just about feeling its usefulness to oneself but also about appreciating its place and purpose in eternity. In failing to prize rightly, ingratitude fails to be righteous. True gratitude relies on right sight, on right esteem or prizing rightly and so is connected with the whole notion of righteousness as established in chapter two. Gratitude is a choice, as the existence of its opposite, ingratitude, implies; as such it is exercised in that sphere of power and act inhabited by the human soul as set out in chapter three. 'Base', 'odious' and 'abominable' are some of the adjectives that Traherne uses to describe ingratitude (*CE*, p. 272), whereas gratitude

---

[70] See, for instance, *C*, I, 48, 49.

[71] 'Hope is a Vertue mixt of Belief and Desire, by which we conceive the Possibility of attaining the Ends we would enjoy, and are stirred up to endeavour after them' (*CE*, p. 117). Cf. p. 132, 'Hope'.

[72] See *C*, I, 21–2; *C*, III, 59.

[73] 'Two things there are, that make the kingdom of Heaven Desolate upon Earth. The one is the Blindness of those Profane ones that cannot See celestial Joys, the other is the Ingratitude of those Holy ones that kick at Heavenly Treasures' (*SM*, III, 23).

is a thing of beauty. And this beauty is not just a reflection of the greatness of the gift, though there is a correlation between magnitude of gift and degree of thanks.[74] Gratitude has its own beauty distinct from the goodness of the received benefit to which it refers: there is 'a certain beauty in the act of Gratitude, distinct from the goodness of the Benefit, that is so naturally sweet to the goodness of the Soul, that it is better to die than renounce it'.[75] Traherne asserts this with such force that it is clear that gratitude is more than an adjunct to the gift received, a kind of afterthought or reflex. Yet it is a response, and as such is always reliant upon the act that precedes it. Gratitude cannot exist outside the process of gift and receipt of which it is a part, and so it has its place in the whole dynamic of communication and communion set out in chapter four. In many ways, then, gratitude mirrors the patterns, shape and sequences that we have seen in the cycle of desire.

Traherne writes of gratitude 'One of the greatest ornaments of this *Vertue*, is the *Grateful Sence* of Benefits received ... All Gifts are but *Carkasses* devoid of Life, unless inspired with that *Sence*, which maketh them *Delightful*' (CE, pp. 269–70). One may be surrounded by causes of delight but not be blessed unless one is full of joy and gratitude. Along with prizing, gratitude is that which makes the gift a treasure, and perhaps this is so because gratitude is a kind of acknowledgement of previous need. Gratitude, as a habit, repeatedly reminds one of needs that have been satisfied, one's own or others'. By addressing a donor, the act of gratitude presupposes a donor's involvement, thus drawing one out of isolation into relation. It also requires at least a minimal distance from the moment of need, which may afford the chance to reflect on desire's root and call.

Gratitude is that poise of the soul that is aware both of its need and of its satisfaction. In gratitude the soul is retrospective and present at once, aware that it has needed, is full, and will need again. In fact, the cycle of desire, in which we want, have and overflow, is the root of gratitude according to Traherne:

> when that want is satisfied and removed, another appeareth, of which before we were not aware. Till we are satisfied we are so clamorous and greedy, as if there were no pleasure but in receiving all: When we have it we are so full, that we know not what to do with it, we are in danger of bursting, till we can communicate all to some fit and

---

74 See CE, pp. 272–3.
75 CE, p. 272. See also 'All acts of Gratitude have a great deal of sweetness in their own nature' (CE, p. 273).

amiable Recipient, and more delight in the Communication than we did in the Reception. This is the foundation of real Gratitude. (CE, p. 258)

Gratitude issues forth as contentment and praise and thanksgiving:

In the utmost height of our Satisfaction there is such an infinite and eternal *force*, that our Gratitude breaks out in exulting and triumphing Effusions; all our Capacities, Inclinations, and Desires being fully satisfied, we have nothing else to do, but to Love and be Grateful. (CE, p. 273; see also p. 275)

Note that Gratitude happens 'In the utmost height of our Satisfaction' (CE, p. 273). Traherne is not speaking here only of the satisfaction of a particular desire but of the larger promise that all our capacities, inclinations and lacks will find their eventual and continuing satisfactions. So sure is he of this abundant satisfaction that he writes of it as a thing already achieved. Here satisfaction is neither a passive state nor an end of story but a condition of 'infinite and eternal *force*' of exultation and effusion. We can do nothing but love and be grateful. Our sense at that point is 'to receive no more, but overflow for ever' (CE, pp. 273–4). This is where we want to remain, at the point of overflowing. In fact, gratitude is so full and so filling that we want to *become* all gratitude. As Traherne describes it, 'Pure Gratitude is so divine a thing, that the Soul may safely wish to be turned *all* into Gratitude' (CE, pp. 275–6). And what kind of state would this be? Certainly not a quiet or a passive one. Traherne writes of the grateful soul that 'The pleasure of Loving is its only business; it is turned all into flame, and brightness, and transportation, and excess. It infinitely passes Light and Fire in quickness of motion: all Impediments are devoured, and GOD alone is its Life and Glory' (CE, p. 274).

One of the clearest expressions of this gratitude is found in a life turned towards virtue. Traherne asserts 'That all the business of Religion on GODS part is Bounty, Gratitude on ours, and that this Gratitude is the sphere of all Vertue and Felicity, easily is discerned after the first intimation' (CE, p. 284). For Traherne all religion is about gratitude. Not only are all praises, ecstasies, adorations and offerings the feathers and wings of angelic gratitude,[76] but the virtues of repentance, obedience, hope, patience, courage – any desire to please – are

---

76 Gratitude is a seraph and all of our praises are 'but the Feathers and the Wings of that Seraphim in Glory' (CE, p. 284).

'but Gratitude in several dresses, as Time, Place, and Occasion require' (*CE*, p. 284). The public forms of religion are all about gratitude too: 'Sermons are to inform and assist our Gratitude, Sacraments to revive and exercise its vertue' (*CE*, p. 28).

Day writes of a 'rhetoric of gratitude'[77] and gratitude is not simply a virtue but a way of seeing, a way of life. We are to see clearly what we have been given, not praising God only for our health, food and raiment but for all the bounty and causes of joy that we find in the whole creation, angels and humans. In so doing the soul is enlarged and participates in the dynamic of gift, receipt and return that marks the Christian life:

> HE that praiseth God only for his Health, and Food, and Rayment, and for his blessing on his Calling (as too many only do) either is very ignorant, or upon a strict scrutiny, will be detected for upbraiding GOD, for the meanest of his bounty ... He that sees not more Causes of Joy than these, is blind and cannot see afar off: The very truth of Religion is obscure to him, and the cause of Adoration unknown ... No man can return more Blessings than he receiveth: nor can his Praises exceed the number (and greatness) of his Joyes. A House is too little, a Kingdom is too narrow for a Soul to move in. The World is a confinement to the power, that is able to see Eternity, and conceive the Immensity of Almighty GOD! (*CE*, p. 276)

One can only be grateful in as much as one is aware of the greatness of the gift that has been received. But the point of all this is the soul's expansion towards the divine. 'The clothing of the soul with the habit of Gratitude is identical with the soul's union with God', writes Day.[78] Gratitude is the soul, fed by knowledge, extending itself in love towards its benefactor. And so it is a position, a poise of the soul, an attitude, as well as being a virtue.

That is not to say that gratitude is a speculative or meditative virtue. Gratitude may be an attitude of life, a poise of the soul, but its direction is towards action. Sincere thankfulness, like true holiness, must be thankfulness of life, and the thankful life issues its most eloquent praises in its actions.[79] Over and over again in the *Thanksgivings*, Traherne's

---

77 Day, *Thomas Traherne*. p. 41.
78 Ibid., p. 36.
79 'Thus ought we to the best of our power to express our gratitude and friendship to so great a benefactor in all the effects of love and fidelity, doing His pleasure with all our might, and promoting His honor with all our power' (C, III, 93).

plea is for an active life, a life that is useful to others.[80] 'Throughout the *Thanksgivings* the reader is assailed less with an image of the beauteous world', McFarland reminds us, 'than with an onslaught of verbs and verbals: . . . praising . . . silencing . . . flight . . . demolishing . . . transforming . . . exalting . . . concerning . . . reaching . . . begetting . . . propagating . . . enlivening . . . cherishing . . . preserving. Until finally, in the "Thanksgiving and Prayer for the NATION", we are reminded that the world is "A Theatre for Actions", and it is into that great epoch of activity, bustle, and ado that this work leads us'.[81]

It is no accident but a reflection of Traherne's general tone that his longest, most frequent and most highly developed prayers are *Thanksgivings* – thanksgivings for the body, for the soul, for God's works and ways and laws, for God's providence and his Word, and for the nation. Much of his theology is reflected in these prayers: his belief in the goodness of creation, in the infinite capacity of the soul and its propensity for desire, in the infinite and intimate love of God, and his belief that the welfare of the person and the welfare of a people are inextricably linked. In his final *Thanksgiving*, 'Thanksgiving and Prayer for the NATION', Traherne asks God to make him a leader in the 'Theatre of Actions':

> Moses
> Make me a Nehemiah, to thee & them.
> Ezra, David
>
> (*Thanksgivings*, ll. 51–3)

In the *Centuries* Traherne repeatedly identifies himself with David.[82] Here he continues the image and expands it:

> As *Moses* did the *Israelites*, *David* his *Jews*; *Jesus* Sinners:
> Give me wide and publick Affections;
> So strong to each as if I loved him alone.
> Make me a Blessing to all the Kingdom,
> A peculiar Treasure (after thy similitude) to every Soul.
>
> (*Thanksgiving and Prayer for the Nation*, ll. 386–90)

---

80 See for instance, *Thanksgivings*, pp. 236, 267, 284 285.
81 Ronald McFarland, 'Thomas Traherne's *Thanksgivings* and the Theology of Optimism', *Enlightenment Essays*, 4, no. 1 (1973), pp. 3–14.
82 A substantial part of the third *Century* (C, III, 70–96) concerns Traherne's exploration of the psalms and his particular identification with David is hinted in Meditation 70. In *Thanksgiving for the Body*, too, he cries 'O that I were as *David*, the sweet Singer of Israel!' (l. 341).

As McFarland points out, in this *Thanksgiving* Traherne's words comprise a social ethic of gratitude in action such as is not uncommon in devotional writing of the age. That thanksgiving should be transcribed as action is also found, for example, in Bishop Reynolds, who, in his 'General Thanksgiving' added to the *Book of Common Prayer* in 1661, includes a supplication for the ability to 'show forth thy praise, not only with our lips, but in our lives'. For Richard Baxter in the *Christian Directory* (1673, p. 167), words alone are not enough to express thanks: 'Let Thankfulness to God thy Creator, Redeemer and Regenerator, be the very temperament of thy soul, and faithfully expressed by thy Tongue and Life.' John Arrowsmith makes the connection between gratitude and action even clearer when he asserts: 'He is the most thankful that is the most fruitfull Christian. There must be *Gratiarum actio* a doing of thanks.'[83] This 'doing of thanks' is exactly what Traherne is suggesting. As McFarland concludes, Traherne's view of thanksgiving 'is clearly within this tradition of gratitude in action'.[84]

This *gratiarum actio*, doing of thanks or thanks in action, could provide the subject of a whole further study of Traherne, so serious and hitherto largely underestimated is Traherne's notion of gratitude.[85] The *Thanksgivings* themselves have received relatively little attention. Stewart calls the collection 'a marvelous little work';[86] Harold Fisch claims that they are in places 'little more than a pastiche of Psalm-poetry'.[87] Day devotes a chapter to them in *Thomas Traherne*, in which he notes, with Sauls, the roots of Puente in the *Thanksgivings*, their structure and, most insightfully, that they are a kind of laboratory of style, a 'workshop' in which Traherne was forging the most characteristic devices of his style.[88] Their similarity to Lancelot Andrewes' *Preces Privatae* is clear, as is their relation to the psalms, but no work has been done on their similarity to Traherne's other psalmic resolves in *Inducements to Retiredness* and *The Kingdom of God*. In their bracketing style the *Thanksgivings* intimate the simultaneity of all things,

---

83 From a sermon preached before Parliament, quoted in McFarland, 'Thomas Traherne's *Thanksgivings*', p. 14.

84 McFarland, 'Thomas Traherne's *Thanksgivings*', p. 14.

85 One exception to this would be Malcolm Day's study, *Thomas Traherne*, which recognizes the significance of gratitude in Traherne.

86 Stanley Stewart, *The Expanded Voice: The Art of Thomas Traherne*, San Marino, CA: Huntington Library, 1970, p. 97.

87 Harold Fisch, *Jerusalem and Albion: The Hebraic Factor in Seventeenth-Century Literature* (New York: Schocken Books, 1964), p. 53, cited in Day, *Thomas Traherne*, p. 67.

88 Day, *Thomas Traherne*, pp. 68–71. See also Lynn Sauls, 'Traherne's Debt to Puente's *Meditations*', *Philological Quarterly*, 50 (1971) pp. 161–74.

Traherne's vision of all things existing in what Day calls the 'eternal now'[89] and what Selkin terms 'the eternal and infinite One that underlies the apparent multiplicity of phenomena'.[90] But more pertinently to this project, at the heart of the *Thanksgivings* is the dynamic of human need and divine plenitude and the overflowing of gratitude.

Gratitude, like love, is a free operation. In words that echo his earlier statements about love, Traherne writes of gratitude that 'the essence of Gratitude consists in the freedom of its operation' (*CE*, p. 271). And the expression of gratitude is an exercise in that freedom by which, as set out above in chapter three, we are fully human. The joy of the donor is gratitude freely given, 'Of which to rob GOD is a kind of *Spiritual Sacriledge*' (*CE*, p. 271), whereas to feel gratitude is to redouble the joy of the giver. This same principle is at work in our communication with each other. Another's joy is 'an Object and a Cause of ours ... when we are the Authors of it' (*CE*, p. 271). And so gratitude effects greater communion.

Just as love is increased by being given away, so, too, possession is multiplied to each and to others by its own exercise. Because each soul may participate in the happiness of every other soul, each soul's possession of the world increases the possession of every other soul. Stewart sees this as a form of narcissism; Day sees it as exactly the opposite – a forgetting of the ego and an absorption into the divine. However you look at it, the idea that possession may be increased by its own exercise makes every treasure a treasure upon treasure and gives grounds for the reduplicaton of gratitude.

So also may gratitude multiply the depth of our communion with God. Our gratitude is love returned, the appropriate answer to God's desire:

> These are the Things wher with we God reward.
>   Our Love he more doth prize:
>   Our Gratitude is in his Eys,
>   Far richer than the Skies.
> And those Affections which we do return,
> Are like the Lov which in Himself doth burn.
>
>   ('The Estate' ll. 51–6)

---

89 Day, *Thomas Traherne*, p. 79.
90 Carl M. Selkin, 'The Language of Vision: Traherne's Cataloguing Style', *English Literary Renaissance*, 6 (1976), pp. 92–103, **94**.

Sandbank sees thanksgiving in Traherne as a part of 'the doctrine of circulation' whereby all things that give must first receive. Gratitude returned for blessings given is evident in the poems 'The Circulation', 'Amendment' and 'The Recovery'. In the last of these three, we may see one of Traherne's most forceful assertions that gratitude is what God expects and desires. Right apprehension may be the beginning of gratitude but God seeks the full-bodied thing itself, the whole heart returned in praise:

> Tis not alone a Lively Sence
> A Clear and Quick Intelligence
> A free, Profound, and full Esteem:
> Tho these Elixars all and Ends to see
> But Gratitude, Thanksgiving, Prais,
> A Heart returnd for all these Joys,
> These are the Things by Him desird.'

('The Return' stanza 6)

This gratitude is described most simply as 'One Voluntary Act of Love' ('The Return', l. 68). By this is the world returned. By gratitude and love does the human soul completely fill its central position in the cosmological design. And so thanksgiving is a significant part of what Sandbank calls 'a dynamic cosmos, a motion of love . . . the returning of the physical world to God through its restoration to its initial intelligibility'.[91]

Gratitude is the concluding virtue in *Christian Ethicks*. It is not a separate virtue tacked on to the end as an addendum but a culmination of the virtues. It is, as Day argues, 'the final virtue'.[92] Not only is it the last virtue that Traherne considers in the long list of virtues that culminates in chapter 32, 'Of Gratitude', but its finality takes on greater significance when, in chapter 33, Traherne goes on to explore 'The Beauty of Gratitude'. To this he adds a further appendix to declare 'how Gratitude and Felicity inspire and perfect all the Vertues'. Day suggests that Traherne may have only realized the significance of gratitude as his work in *Christian Ethicks* progressed, 'as though in his own writing he is undergoing a process of discovery'.[93]

Gratitude is 'the final virtue' in the fullest sense of the word; it is that

---

91 Sandbank, 'Thomas Traherne on the Place of Man in the Universe', pp. 122–3.
92 Day, *Thomas Traherne*, p. 36.
93 Ibid., pp. 36–7.

virtue to which all the others tend. But as much as gratitude is the final virtue, it is also the first. Here, in the estate of grace and trial, gratitude is a virtue learned and practised, but it was not always so.

> Before I learned to be poor,
> I always did the Riches see,
> And thankfully adore[94]

Traherne writes with regret. In the estate of innocence, thankfulness is natural to the soul. For the estate of misery one can only be grateful in retrospect. In the estate of grace, one may learn gratitude as the poise of the soul. In the estate of glory, all will be praise. Gratitude, like love, desire and satisfaction and all that makes the soul divine, is natural in the first and final estates.

There is a kind of retrospective or intuitive thanksgiving implied in much of the poetry and most especially seen in those poems of wonder such as 'The Salutation' and 'Wonder'. And we may see that gratitude in the regenerate is a kind of relearning of what was lost in the innocent. In 'Silence' the prelapsarian soul had only this work to do:

> The first and only Work he had to do,
> Was in himself to feel his Bliss, to view
> His Sacred Treasures, to admire, rejoyce
> Sing Praises with a Sweet and Heavnly voice,
> See, Prize, Give Thanks within, and Love
> Which is the High and only Work, above
> Them all.
>
> ('Silence' ll. 21-7)

Thankfulness here includes sight, prizing and love, and illustrates the notion of gratitude as not an utterance but a process or an attitude within a larger frame of action. This attitude of thankfulness, and the appreciation of treasure that it implied, was not the work of an infant because it was so small as to be suited to an infant's capacity; it was the work of the infant because only the soul unpolluted by custom was capable of so high and single a task.

Here, in the estate of grace and trial, gratitude is an expression of the soul engaged in the divine dynamic of gift and receipt. As McFarland writes, 'There is a response especially suited to the estate of grace, and

---

94 'The Return', ll. 14-16.

that response is thanksgiving or gratitude, which is, in effect, a return of love for love given.'[95] True to form, Traherne does not separate the act of gift and the act of receipt. The act of return by which we complete our purpose in the divine scheme of things is also the same act by which we receive, that by which we gain: 'Now Love returned for Love is the Soul of Gratitude. In that act, and by it alone, we gain all that is excellent' (*CE*, p. 266). Well then may he assert that 'Gratitude is all that is to be expressed here upon Earth, and above in Heaven' (*CE*, p. 284).

This gratitude is the first and final virtue, the correct poise of the soul, relating it both to other souls and to God in desire and thankfulness and in continued satisfaction of ever-present wants. In Traherne, gift and receipt are so intimately related that even as we give we desire, and as we desire we thank: 'We see the Beauty and Glory of all, and offer it all up to him, with infinite Desire, our selves also with infinite Gratitude' (*CE*, p. 252).

---

95 Ronald McFarland, 'Thomas Traherne's *Thanksgivings*', p. 4.

Epilogue

The beginning of this book mentioned new discoveries that have required and will continue to require new readings of Traherne. A brief description of the newest of Traherne's works may be found in the appendix at the end of this volume. Never before in the study of Traherne has so much new material been available all at once; never before have we had so many new works of sustained prose, never before so much of his theology at our fingertips. A new Traherne emerges, no naive optimist or rural songster but a serious thinker, debater, theologian and visionary. Here we see a man of his time, not only grappling with issues of his day, theological and political discussions that were shaping the future of his Church and his society, but also open to questions that concern us now, deep questions about who we are, about what it means to be human, our place in the universe, about our hopes and aspirations, our insatiable demands, our destinies.

We see a churchman at the formation of the Restoration Church making his own contribution to the development of that church's doctrines and apologetics. We see a keen reader fascinated by the emerging sciences, the new infinities of microscope and telescope, aware of the directions in which these discoveries might take us all, away from the old certainties, and still fearless in his faith. We see a priest in his parish, practitioner of the theology that he could not help proclaiming of a God in love with his creation, longing for reciprocity. We catch glimpses of a person who is friend and brother, pastor, scholar, colleague. We see a man offering himself to his work, desiring to be loved, looking for salvation. It is in this context that we may understand Traherne's felicity not as an achieved state but as a participation in the dynamic of desire and satisfaction that for him marks the relationship of God and the soul. Traherne's felicity has never been about arrival at a fixed point, nor about the memory of a lost state, confident though he is in his experience and hopes of felicity. His felicity, both here and hereafter, is an ongoing pursuit, a dance of gift and receipt, otherness and union that exists between God and the soul and between one soul and another.

EPILOGUE

In Traherne's theology of desire, his encounter with God is primarily as with a creator yearning toward his creation, then as a lover seeking his beloved. His world is an alluring one filled with delights and pleasures, every hunger an indication of some awaiting feast and every creature hungry to be satisfied. According to *The Kingdom of God*, all things allured God to make them and God's power allured him to make all things.[1] Even before the advent of the human, desire was. Into this desiring milieu God came as creator, later as man in the incarnation, hallowing this world and proclaiming again that the human soul may be a worthy companion for the divine. Into this world came a wanting God.

Traherne's 'want', with its implications of both lack and longing, can be seen in his poetry as well as his prose. The infant self so celebrated in the Dobell poems and in the *Centuries* is, from the moment it is written, a separate self divided from the writer, both an expression of lack and an object of longing. We look to Traherne's 'happy infant' and know what we are not, what we have lost and may try to regain. The 'Desire of Som Great thing' that speaks from the opening lines of the *Centuries* right through its meditations is a powerful, less visible face of Traherne's want. *Christian Ethicks* praises desire, drawing even its ugly sisters, ambition and avarice, into the circle of virtues. And when we look at Traherne's notions of desire in detail, at what they suggest and demand in terms of power, consent and union, we see once again the importance of human choice in his scheme of things. Wanting like a God is not just about august desire and infinite longing but also about being a creature capable of choice – capable of discerning real from imagined treasure, endowed with power to act and freedom to decide. This volume has traced the origins of that high view of humankind in Renaissance humanism, in the Hermetic writings and in the Patristic teachings of the Early Church.

Freedom and choice in the pursuit of truth are defended fiercely in *A Sober View* and *Roman Forgeries*. Where *Roman Forgeries* defends the right of the national Church to decide its own affairs and debate its doctrines, *A Sober View* argues that both those who are and those who are not chosen by God retain the right to their own subsequent choices and that the whole reason why some are chosen is so that they

---

1 'All the Pleasure of Life, all Worlds allured him to make them. all Angels and Men, all Beauties and perfections all Delights and Treasures, all Joys and Honors allured him to make them. All that he Saw his Omnipresence and Eternitie Capable of, Invited him unto them. His own Wisdom, and power allured him: So did the Hallelujahs, and praises of all his Creatures' (*KOG*, Ch. 15, ll. 144–8).

themselves may then choose. According to Traherne, freedom is one of the qualities that elevate the human soul sufficiently to be considered an appropriate spouse of the divine; correspondingly, it is the freedom of the soul's choice, that fact that she acts with volition, that pleases the divine lover. Love is a free emotion, according to Traherne; and desire must be without compulsion (*SV*, fol. 26r: 'Now Love is a free Affection wch cannot be compelled').

Desire percolates throughout his writings. In *The Select Meditations*, the notebooks, *The Church's Year-Book*, *The Kingdom of God* and *Love* we see in formation and in fruition images of the soul as bride, of an allured creator and his high creation, or of a pilgrim people and the joys of a Church restored. Where *The Ceremonial Law*, infused with lack and longing, recounts the story of pilgrims on a journey through a barren land, *Inducements to Retiredness* urges the reader towards the clear-focused desire that withdraws from the world so as to heighten the experience of God for better re-engagement. Here we may hear a call not dissimilar to the desire of lovers for privacy and exclusion. The exploration of the capacity of the soul that Traherne follows in *Seeds of Eternity* is important precisely because he is trying to answer the question of the soul's fitness as divine consort and mate. *The Kingdom of God*, premised entirely upon a God desiring his creation, is a tale of divine disclosure and divine love outstretched. This is the dance, with its rhythms of longing and reciprocity, that moves beneath the surface of all of Traherne's work.

I have attempted to explicate the theory and the working out of desire in Traherne, show the roots of his theories of Man, the longing or *eros* that informs many of his images, the balance that his notion of prudence gives to his praise of unbridled passion. This study has flagged his attraction to infinity and his praise of insatiability as correlated to his high notion of the capacity of the human soul. It has suggested the importance of prizing and of discernment in determining objects of desire and measures of worth, and offered the practice of gratitude as an answer to insatiability's incessant demands. In all of this the most important insights return again and again to questions of self and identity which dispel the previous models that associated Traherne with naive optimism. In these questions of being – what kind of God Traherne believes in, who we are as humans, what we may become – we find ourselves circling around profound issues of power, volition and act that are at the heart of human identity and that resonate deeply with human experience.

There remains another question, less well answered by Traherne, relating to want. Traherne insists that we are creatures of desire, made to desire infinitely and insatiably, and that we are designed for satisfaction and for renewed desire. But what about those people whose wants never seem to be satisfied or those whose satisfactions inevitably occur as the destruction of another's hope? What about whole nations so exposed and desolate? At a practical level Traherne's response to the demands of poverty and deprivation are found not so much in his writings as in his life, in his recorded generosity and in his final testimonial will. In this he models for his readers a life tuned to the needs of others. Theologically, the question of unanswered need is addressed by Traherne in the illogicality of the Christian cross on which the most powerful is crucified, Life is killed and love continues to hope in the face of utter loss. The cross may be, as Traherne calls it in the *Centuries*, 'the centre of desires' not just because it has the drawing force of a lodestone and so becomes a focus of desire but also, as I discussed in the previous chapter, because it teaches us about the fruitfulness of not having, and in so doing how to participate beneficially in even the shadow side of the perpetual cycle of desire. For Traherne satisfaction is never promised in the sense of our every wish being granted by a fairy God. Traherne's understanding of the human spirit is modelled on his understanding of the divine. Our human desires find their satisfactions as do God's desires in the process of loving and being loved, by stretching out in longing towards the draw of Som Great thing, by 'adventuring' the possibility of failure as well of as success in our longing. Traherne's God makes himself vulnerable to his own creation, experiencing frustration and loss as well as delight. In the end it is participation in the process of desire that matters, rather than the list of wishes that we hope may be fulfilled, since what we most desire is to be transformed. Even when our needs are met we keep on desiring. Ironically, although we are designed for satisfaction, it is in the periods of longing and lack, when our experience of desire is most acute, that desire is also most instructive and most transforming. It is then that we learn to focus on desire less as an exercise in acquisition and more as a 'circle of interconnectedness that binds us strangely and inseparably to each other'.[2]

What of social justice? Traherne's answer is found in the life transformed by this vision of inseparability, the life that will not sit comfortably alongside its fellow's discomfort, that cannot live abundantly in the shadow of another's deprivation. If a person truly catches this

---

2 Belden Lane, 'Thomas Traherne and the Awakening of Want', *The Anglican Theological Review*, 81 (1999), pp. 651-64, 658.

vision of herself or himself in profound relation with others, if it once becomes true that 'All! all! all the souls in Heaven and earth Shall Dwell in Him. And He in them, and they in God, and God in Him, and He in God forevermo[re]', then Traherne's conclusion that 'they limmit not each other' (*SM*, II, 27) makes perfect sense. In *The Kingdom of God* Traherne writes that love is 'at once a freedom from all law, and the severest law in the World, but a willing and delightfull law of the most constraining, and Indispensable Necessitie' (*KOG*, fol. 186v). This law of love is his answer to social injustice, a soft option only to the hardhearted.

'Want is the universal, alluring activity that permeates the entire cosmos',[3] wrote Belden Lane after a week in the wildernesss with Traherne. It is not surprising that he should make this claim, for Traherne's world and his God and his very notion of self are unified in one word: 'Want'. In a world that 'allured' God to make it, Traherne commands his reader to want. 'You must Want like a GOD that like GOD you may be Satisfied'; 'He is from Eternity full of Want. He made us Want like GODS.'[4] Not aquiring but holding, not grasping but savouring, knowing the treasures that are before and behind us, around and within. Once having the basic necessities of life, then living in lack and in longing; richer for both, despairing in neither. This is what Traherne asks his reader to do, to live a wanting life – pierced by an awareness of one's own lacks, taking pleasure in the delights that are near and ambitious for delights that may come, for Traherne's wanting is its own felicity. 'Be Sensible of your Wants, that you may be sensible of your Treasures', he writes, 'Wants themselvs being sacred Occasions and Means of Felicitie.'[5]

---

3 Ibid., p. 656.
4 C, I, 44, 42, 41.
5 C, I, 45, 43.

Appendix 1
Manuscript Discoveries

The fascinating story of the first discoveries of Traherne manuscripts on two London book-barrows at the turn of the twentieth century has often been told and is ably recorded[1] so I will do no more than recount the story briefly here.

The first editor of Traherne's poetry, Bertram Dobell, describes how, after Traherne's death, his largely unattributed manuscripts fell into the hands of those 'ignorant of their value' and how, by the later part of 1896 or the early months of 1897, they had 'descended to the street bookstall, that last hope of books and manuscripts in danger of being consigned to the wast-paper mills'. Here two (the *Centuries* and the Dobell *Poems*) were found by a friend of Dobell's, a Mr William Brooke, who purchased them in April 1897 for a few pence and, noticing a similarity in sentiment and subject with Henry Vaughan, became convinced they were Vaughan's. Brooke sold them to the famous collector Dr Alexander Grosart, who was about to have them included in a new complete works of Henry Vaughan but whose untimely death stopped the project in its tracks. Dobell eventually acquired the manuscripts from the late Grosart's dispersed library, did some sleuthing and discovered a poem in one of the manuscripts to be almost identical to one in Traherne's *Christian Ethicks*, which had been published the year after Traherne died. (Curiously, this poem, 'For Man to Act', is the very same poem that proved conclusively to Jeremy Maule, roughly a century later in 1997, that *Lambeth Palace MS 1360* was Traherne's, since it also appears in the last work in that manuscript, *The Kingdom of God*.) Dobell became the first editor of Traherne's poetry when *The Poetical Works of Thomas Traherne* was published in 1903;

---
1 See Bertram Dobell, 'Introduction', *The Poetical Works of Thomas Traherne*, London, 1903. See also Hilton Kelliher, 'The Rediscovery of Thomas Traherne', *Times Literary Supplement*, 14 September 1984; Peter Beal, *Index of English Literary Manuscripts*, vol. 2 (1625–1700), part 2, Lee–Wycherley, London: Mansell, 1993.

his account of the finding and subsequent sleuthing is recorded in the introduction to that work. Dobell published the *Centuries of Meditations* in its entirety in 1908. Hilton Kelliher notes that at least one of these manuscripts had passed through London auction rooms half a century earlier and had already once been owned by Grosart himself. The *Commentaries of Heaven*, which was 'discovered' on a burning rubbish heap in Lancashire in the late 1960s, had also coincidentally passed through the same London salerooms as the 'Dobell Folio' in 1844 and 1854 without being identified.

As Peter Beal notes, Traherne is one of the most interesting British authors not only because he is noted for what in the seventeenth century would have been 'an almost unprecedented number of original, chiefly autograph MSS' but also because the chance findings and very near losses of his work are unparalleled anywhere in the history of English literature. The *Select Meditations* (1997) was badly mutilated with whole sections of the book cut out. The *Commentaries of Heaven* was rescued from a burning rubbish heap by a Mr Wookey who had gone to the tip to look for spare parts for his car. He scooped up the manuscript and batted out the flames, stored it in his suburban loft, took it to Canada when he moved there and stored it in his loft there. It was identified when a student from the University of Toronto who was helping him lay insulation noticed it and wondered what it was. He asked permission to take it to the university, where it was identified by Alan Pritchard. It is now in the British Library. Despite its dance with death, it is one of the most entire of the manuscripts, with two pins of the kind used in the seventeenth century to hold in extra pages still intact.

In 1997 *Select Meditations*, edited by Julia Smith, was published. A *Complete Works* is currently underway, edited by Jan Ross and published by Boydell and Brewer. Volumes I–III of the *Works of Thomas Traherne* have already been published and contain Lambeth Palace 1360 and *Commentaries of Heaven*. Both the *Select Meditations* and *Commentaries of Heaven* are ably introduced at the front of these volumes by their respective editors, so I offer no introduction to them here.

The newest manuscript discoveries – the Lambeth Manuscript[2] and *The Ceremonial Law* – have spawned a new and fast-growing interest in Traherne's writings. The sheer volume of new material presented in them is staggering and the range of themes covered, as well as

---

2 For a fuller description of the Lambeth Manuscript see Denise Inge and Calum Mcfarlane, 'Seeds of Eternity: A New Traherne Manuscript', *Times Literary Supplement*, 2 June 2000, p. 14.

APPENDIX I

the range of writing styles that are evident therein, will continue to attract interest for many years to come. Although the introduction to the Lambeth Manuscript includes a brief description of each work, the publication did not afford space for more. I have therefore included a more leisurely introduction to each work below as well as a description of *The Ceremonial Law*. My intention with these introductions is not to attempt an exhaustive description but to give information that may begin to place each work in the reader's mental map of the period, to give an idea of the concerns of each work, its shape and themes, and to suggest some of the questions that the works raise.

The Ceremonial Law

The Ceremonial Law, discovered in 1997 at the Folger Shakespeare Library in Washington, DC, by Julia Smith and Laetitia Yeandle,[3] though not insignificant with its 1800 lines of rhyming couplets, is an unfinished poem written in a notebook large enough to contain a poem three times its length. In it Traherne considers the Old Testament books of Genesis and Exodus in short narrative sections, retelling the stories as types that might inspire and instruct the reader of his day. There is a down-to-earthness about this typological poem that makes it seem more the work of a teacher than of a mystic. Not only is it less ecstatic than, for instance, the Dobell poems but it is also rooted in a strong narrative uncharacteristic of much of his other work. Its concerns are not remote or philosophical. The stories deal with elemental human experiences: thirst, hunger, fear, fire, water, danger, deliverance. By deprivation, by journeying 'through this Wide Abyss Of Desert Horors',[4] the Israelites learn to prize the joys they posess in Elim and to taste the sweetness of manna. So, too, the reader is urged to travel into the desert of uncreated nothing in order to see the sweetness of the created world:

> Lets sojourn in the Desert Wilderness
> Of long and uncreated nothing, guess
> What may the Dismall Chaos be, and view
> The vacant Ages, while he nought did doe.

---

[3] See Julia Smith and Laetitia Yeandle, '"Felicity disguisd in fiery Words": Genesis and Exodus in a newly discovered poem by Thomas Traherne', *Times Literary Supplement*, 7 November 1997, p. 17.

[4] 'Elim' ll. 120–1.

Those Empty Barren Places will appear
At last as if they all at once were here
The Silence Darkness and Deformitie
In which we nothing plainly nothing see
Will make the Univers enlightening to them
Even like unto the new Jerusalem.
And while we wisely seek for Heaven there,
Twill clearly make us find our Heaven here.[5]

Traherne interprets the types at several levels. In common with other seventeenth-century readings of Scripture, the Old Testament stories and figures are seen as types of the New Testament but Traherne also reads the Church and sometimes himself into the stories, becoming Moses whose shoes must be removed in front of the burning bush and whose transfigured face terrifies befores it pleases. Hence the types are not remote; his reader may enter into the stories as he does and find himself or herself alive to Scripture, but even those less imaginative or less sophisticated readers will find the intended lessons intelligible, since the moral of each story is clearly indicated.

Curiously, for those readers expecting a poem springing from Genesis to abound in Traherne's customary praise of creation and of original innocence, there is not a prelapsarian moment to be seen. The poem begins with 'Adam's Fall'. It carries on with the Old Testament account until 'The Inside' where, just after Moses descends from Mount Sinai, the poem breaks mid-line with the tantalizingly enigmatic: 'Men promise to themselves Som great Delight, / Could they but once enjoy the Glorious Sight / Of God on Earth . . .'[6] The poem never reaches the Promised Land. Its recurring motif is that of journey; the people are, from the moment the poem begins, displaced persons, outcasts, sojourners, strangers looking for home. The memory of paradise and the hope of the Promised Land may be its gilded frame but the poem's narrative sequences unfold largely in a wasteland.

Julia Smith dates the poem some time after the Restoration in 1660. It is written entirely in Traherne's own hand and seems to be a working copy with editorial additions and deletions running freely between the lines. Whether Traherne lost interest or confidence in the work or was prevented from finishing it by ill health or was simply working on too many projects at once, we may never know. But the fact of its incompletion was already a cause for concern in his own day. 'I like

---

5 [Manna] II, ll. 69–80.
6 'The Inside', ll. 9–11.

APPENDIX I

this mightily but I pray prosecute it', wrote the reader to whom Traherne submitted the work in progress on the flyleaf. It seems this reader wanted the whole project to be enlarged, writing: 'I would you would goe thorow the whole Sacred Story. God direct & Inspire you.'

The Lambeth Manuscript

The Lambeth Manuscript (MS 1360), discovered at the Lambeth Palace Library in London by Jeremy Maule in 1997 and recently edited by Jan Ross, contains five new works, or four and a fragmentary fifth: *Inducements to Retiredness*, *A Sober View of Dr Twisse*, *Seeds of Eternity*, *The Kingdom of God* and *Love*. There is no thematic progression in the manuscript. Each work is distinct, though the first two, *Inducements to Retiredness* and *A Sober View*, bear the comments of the same critical reader. *Seeds of Eternity* bears minor additions in a similar hand. Definitive dating of the manuscript is, as Ross notes, not yet possible, though source material for *A Sober View* dates the completion of that treatise some time after 1660. Traherne used part II as well as part I of Theophilus Gale's *Court of the Gentiles* in *The Kingdom of God*, most heavily in chapters 20–23, which renders a completion date for that work no earlier than 1670.

The manuscript may be a compilation of treatises copied into a single pre-sewn manuscript, or the treatises may have been written separately and sewn together at a later date. *The Kingdom of God* bears the kind of editorial adjustments and arrangements that are consonant with preparation for publication, and it is likely that this treatise at least was intended for a wider audience.

Although Maule never published the details of his discovery of the manuscript, the tale of its discovery as recounted to his friends and colleagues tells how, finding himself with time on his hands on a wet and rainy day in London, he called in at the Lambeth Palace Library to look at the *Catalogue of Manuscripts in the Lambeth Palace Library*, hoping to unearth a discovery of some sort, though not necessarily Traherne's. Perusing the catalogue his eyes fell upon the entry for MS 1360, entitled simply 'Theology'. The entry made reference to 'three theological treatises' that had been composed 'in and after 1660', the second of which caught his attention. It was entitled *Seeds of Eternity or the Nature of the Soul in which Everlasting Powers are Prepared*, and it was those first three words – *Seeds of Eternity* – that made him think that the manuscript might be one of Traherne's. However, it was not until he travelled to Lambeth Palace again a few weeks later that he was able to summon the manuscript and, on close inspection, verify that Traherne was indeed the author. Traherne's hand is found in many parts of the manuscript, his themes and idiosyncratic spellings appear and significantly, in the final work of the manuscript, *The Kingdom of God*, a version of the poem 'For Man to Act' is written out. This poem, also occurring in Traherne's posthumous *Christian Ethics*, gave Maule the conclusive evidence of authorship for which he was looking.

Inducements to Retiredness

In the opening words of the first untitled autograph work, given the modern title *Inducements to Retiredness* by Jeremy Maule, Traherne invites his reader to retire from the world 'for the better Introversion of Spirit' and in so doing sets the tone for the work as a whole. For Traherne's concern is particular, his invitation to a life set apart is not an invitation to denial for the sake of mortification but for the sake of greater joy and fruitfulness. His denial is a kind of spiritual and physical pruning, in which everything is ordered to its proper place so that the soul may be 'sweetly disposed and Composed for Devine Enjoyments'.[7]

In its praise of strict solitude and prayerfulness *Inducements to Retiredness* echoes the traditional monastic wisdom uttered again and again in Thomas à Kempis's *The Imitation of Christ*.[8] This is not surprising since it is à Kempis whom Traherne cites in the first *Century* when he considers the religious impulse to condemn the world that does not sit easily alongside his famous admonitions to enjoy the world. 'Give all (saith Thomas a Kempis) for all. Leave the one that you may enjoy the other',[9] writes Traherne.

Traherne's aversion to marriage in *Inducements*, and his insistence on celibacy as the better way for clergy, is reminiscent of St Paul. However, there is no sense that it is 'better marry than burn'.[10] Traherne

---

7 ITR, ll. 5–6 of the abstract to the first section.
8 See for instance 'If thou wilt stand as thou oughtest, and make a due progress, look upon thyself as a banished man, and a stranger upon earth' (Book I, Ch. 17), 'Seek a proper time to retire into thyself, and often think of the benefits of God . . . The greatest saints avoided the company of men as much as they could and chose to live to God in secret' (Book I, Ch. 20). These are two among very many such admonishments.
9 C, I, 7.
10 1 Cor. 7.9.

APPENDIX I

is not concerned with marriage as a means of sexual containment. His concern is purely practical: marriage is a distraction. Like St Paul, Traherne regards celibacy as a gift – a gift that affords freedom to belong to all and to be concerned with many that is the strength of the public minister. Traherne's discussion of singleness in *Inducements* may also be traced in the voluminous extracts and notes from Bacon found in his *Early Notebook*. Among the extensive notes on Bacon's *De Augmentis Scientiarum* and fragments of *Apotegms* and *Essays* that appear over 101 pages of the *Notebook* are extracts from Book II of *De Augmentis* in praise of Queen Elizabeth's celibacy.[11] Traherne goes on to quote from Bacon's essay 'Of Marriage and Single Life' but where Bacon calls wives 'Companions for middle Age' Traherne writes 'burdens of middle age'. More significantly, Traherne singles out a remark from Bacon that applies to him personally: '& Amongst the rest a single life is proper for Church men: for Charity will hardly water the ground where first it must fill a poole'.[12] He expands this sentiment in *Inducements*, concluding that, although celibacy is not a universal rule, yet 'it holdeth infallibly in Publick Ministers'.[13] In his insistence that retirement is a necessary precursor to useful public service, that this kind of emptying leads not to nothing but to great fullness, Traherne is also a voice among voices. Yet the work remains distinctly his. His common themes – eternity, infinity, felicity – appear as the ends towards which retiredness aims; the world is to be avoided not because it is inherently evil but because it is a distraction from these aims. And the language he uses when he describes retirement as a freedom and a glory, 'the Paradice or Palace of Pleasure',[14] is characteristic of his work elsewhere.

In 1665 George Mackenzie's *A Moral Essay, Preferring Solitude to Publick Employment, And All it's Apannages; such as Fame, Command, Riches, Pleasures, Conversation, etc.* appeared, thrived and was reprinted. Two years later John Evelyn responded with *Publick Employment and an Active Life, Prefer'd to Solitude, and all its Apannages, Such as Fame, Command, Riches, Conversation, etc. In Reply*

---

11 *EN*, p. 113; Francis Bacon, *De Augmenti Scientiarum*, Bk. II, Ch. 1. As Carol Marks has noted, Traherne had 'a talent for extracting the pith of Bacon's argument, as well as a frequent disregard for Bacon's main points and priorities' ('Thomas Traherne's Early Studies', *Papers of the Bibliographic Society of America*, 62 (1968), p. 520).

12 *EN*, p. 113; Francis Bacon, *Essays*, ed. Geoffrey Grigson, London: Oxford University press, 1937, p. 30. This problem of filling the pool is resolved in Traherne's work; cf. 'That Pool must first be filled, that shall be made to overflow' (C, IV, 55).

13 *ITR*, l. 461.

14 Ibid., ll. 805, 926.

to a late Ingenious Essay of a contrary Title. This debate about the relative value of the private and contemplative life as opposed to the public and active one, though popular in the seventeenth century, was not a new debate, having its antecedents in Scripture, in the Church Fathers and in medieval monastic writings. That Mackenzie and Evelyn were debating this in Traherne's lifetime gives a helpful context to *Inducements to Retiredness*; and it has been suggested that Traherne's treatise was a specific or deliberate response to that debate.[15] This may be so, although it was common for seventeenth-century works written in response to be so addressed in their titles or to mention clearly in the body of the text the writers and works specifically being addressed. Both these strategies were favoured by Traherne, as we may see in his response treatise *A Sober View*. Curiously, neither is used in *Inducements*. The influences that Traherne does note in *Inducements* are largely patristic and medieval. Whether or not *Inducements* was written as a direct response to the Mackenzie and Evelyn texts, the existence of that debate will be useful for anyone studying *Inducements* in its wider context.

Inducements to Retiredness is written in five relatively short sections, each of which (except for the fourth) is preceded by an introductory abstract. Section one is an invitation to withdrawal from the world. Section two calls for a stable resolution in dedicating oneself to God. In section three the will is transformed so that the holy person becomes qualified for service in the world. Section four considers retirement as the citadel of truth and the centre of rest, the necessary home of the holy. Section five studies the example of holy persons. The work is a study of holy living and in its structure we see a pattern familiar in spiritual writings about holiness, in which the person who would be holy is called away from the world that he/she may re-enter it more usefully, and in which the holy person, though called to separateness, is called in a community of saints and fellow-seekers. All of this sounds deeply theoretical but in *Inducements to Retiredness* one feels that Traherne is speaking from experience – his own as well as that borrowed from the monastic tradition. However, its tone is testimonial rather than confessional; what he is saying is prepared, poised as if intended to instruct. *Inducements* is addressed to 'the pious soul'; the work treats issues of celibacy, friendship and public ministry that are of particular concern to clergy but *Inducements to Retiredness* is also addressed to a wider audience. Since the fruit of retirednesss is public

---

15 See Ross, 'Introduction', in *The Works of Thomas Traherene*, vol. 1, Cambridge: D. S. Brewer, 2005, p. xxi.

service, one feels that he is writing not only for the clergy but also towards a more public audience. In the midst of his clerical concerns, he has a great deal to say about human nature and human relationships. *Inducements to Retiredness* is rich with practical wisdom, like the suggestion, in the fourth section, that it is not scarcity but service that maketh jewels and that 'we are to grow Rich, not by seeking what we Want, but by Enjoying what we have'.[16]

Like the third *Century*, *Inducements* is punctuated by quotations from the Psalms and each section ends with a psalmic resolve similar to those in parts of *The Kingdom of God*. Each resolve is a sustained cry to God, reflecting those of the biblical Psalmist, composed of lines appropriated from Scripture, most often from the Psalms, altered and blended in a way that is reminiscent of the various *Thanksgivings*.

A Sober View of Dr Twisse

The second work in the Lambeth Manuscript, *A Sober View of Dr Twisse*, is a long work of academic theology written in 28 sections. It is an important text showing, as mentioned earlier, Traherne's commitment to theological study and a lively interest in the important debates of his day. It also shows him engaged in the messy business of working out, alongside his fellow theologians, the way forward for the newly restored English Church. During the Commonwealth the king had been beheaded and the Church broken; nothing could be the same again. Traherne was finding his way not just in a new theological world but in a new political, social and philosophical world. The men and women of Traherne's day had gained certain freedoms and lost precious certainties. In this intellectually provisional world one had to work out where one stood, where one's loyalties lay and the direction in which one was pointed without the comfort of clearly marked maps. This is the ground on which the Calvinist/Arminian debate was staged and it was a debate that raged in retaliatory discourse and heated language. Consider William Prynne's searing criticism in *Anti-arminianisme* of Thomas Jackson, one of Traherne's sources and, like Traherne, an Oxford man as

> a man of great abilities . . . till of late he hath been transported beyond himself with Metaphysical contemplations to his own infamy

---

16 *ITR*, ll. 859–60.

and his renowned mother's shame, I mean the University of Oxon, who grieves for his defection; from whose dugges he never sucked his poysonous doctrines.[17]

Traherne well knew the temperature of the debate he was entering and the kind of criticisms he might face. The Calvinist/Arminian debate, as noted earlier, was a battle about God's decrees, the decisions he had made before the foundation of the earth; but this politically charged battle mattered so much precisely because at its heart lay burning questions about human choice and liberty, and about the position of the individual in the scheme of things, questions that had implications for the whole way in which the country was to be governed. This is what *A Sober View* is really all about. It follows a popular and particular theological and political debate in immense detail while at its core runs a parallel and broader debate about the importance of human freedom.

The texts that Traherne uses in *A Sober View* range over two generations of a dispute that was complicated by the fact that some manuscripts of the 1630s were published again in the 1650s and so rekindled old arguments. The texts considered are Samuel Hoard's *Gods Love to Mankind. Manifested by dis-prooving his absolute decree for their damnation* (1633, 1656, 1658); William Twisse's posthumous *The Riches of Gods Love* (1653), which answers Hoard; and Henry Hammond's *Pacific Discourse* (1660), containing long extracts from a letter by Robert Sanderson.

During the first five sections Traherne focuses his attentions on the writings of Dr Twisse.[18] At section VI he begins his consideration of the writings of Dr Hammond and Dr Sanderson, preceded by a clear disposal of the doctrines of the Church of England on the matter of

---

17 William Prynne, *Anti-arminianisme*, London, 1630, p. 270. William Twisse was one of Jackson's worst enemies. On Twisse and Jackson see Sarah Hutton, 'Thomas Jackson, Oxford Platonist, William Twisse, Aristotelian', *Journal of the History of Ideas*, 34 (1978), pp. 635–52.

18 Twisse (1578–1646) was of English and German descent, educated at Winchester and Oxford, and appointed by James I to be chaplain to Princess Elizabeth in Heidelberg in 1612. He declined other preferments and remained rector of Newbury. He made his reputation as a rigid Calvinist for his defence of the Sabbath, his report on the Synod of Dort and his defence of the Calvinist doctrine of predestination. His attack on the Jesuits brought him fame in Europe. Ever one to arouse passions, he was buried with great pomp in Westminster Abbey, but his bones were exhumed and tossed into a communal grave outside at the Restoration. His scholastic attack on Thomas Jackson (1631), accusing Jackson of Arminianism leading to Pelagianism, loses some credibility when it confronts metaphor with exact literalness and quibbles over wording. See Hutton 'Thomas Jackson, Oxford Platonist'.

APPENDIX I

election as laid out in Article Seventeen of the Thirty-nine Articles and in the liturgy of the Church. Alongside Article Seventeen, which allows that God does choose or elect some, he considers the Comfortable Words said before communion, a prayer from Ash Wednesday and the Thanksgiving at a public baptism, all from the *Book of Common Prayer*. Traherne was a conforming minister and it is a testament to his commitment to the Restoration Church that he judges the orthodoxy of his sources against the doctrines of the Church of England rather than against any other creed or against his own isolated reasoning: 'He [Dr Sanderson] had the Advantage on Dr Hammond in that he perfectly conformeth to the Ch. of England', Traherne writes. Nevertheless he will dismiss neither reason nor experience; he continues: 'for he that denieth the Article of Election, loppeth away one great Branch from the Doctrine of the Ch. of England: as he that denieth the Gift of Liberty doth violate a great part of Experience and Reason'.[19] Once again we see him firmly placed in the Anglican position of deriving authority from a balance of Scripture, reason and tradition.

However true to Church doctrines Traherne remains, he is not comfortable with the darker side of the doctrine of election – that God hates some just as he loves and chooses others – and says that we should not think about election in those terms or it will drive us to despair. To those who quote Romans chapter nine, a central text in the argument for election – 'Jacob have I loved, Esau have I hated'[20] – Traherne replies that one must be wary of how one applies a particular text. Using an image of Sanderson's, he writes: 'Fire is the same, put it where you will: yet in the Chimney it will warm you, or roast your meat; if you appy it to a Weinscoat Wall, it will consume the Dwelling.'[21] Traherne points to the ameliorating tenth chapter of Romans and he later groups the Romans 9 text alongside the passage from Luke's Gospel in which Jesus declares that any following him must 'hate' their father and mother, sister and brother for his sake as a text that cannot be taken literally, and goes on to claim that, in Scripture, hate is a term for lesser love. In his conclusion to *A Sober View* Traherne again affirms the love of God, asserting that

---

19 *SV*, VII, 19–22.
20 Rom. 9.13; see also Mal. 1.2–3.
21 *SV*, XXVII, ll. 113–15. In his sermons Sanderson describes Puritan zeal as 'a kind of fire' whose right use is valuable, though 'blind or indiscrete zeal, like fire in the thatch will soon set all the house in a combustion' (*Thirty-four Sermons*, fifth edition of the 1657 collection of sermons, London, 1671, part 2, p. 159).

that Doctrine which some suck from this [Romans] Text, That God from all Eternity simply and without Caus hateth any, and that there are Multitudes of Reprobates so hated, is a Damnable poyson as can that way be put into the mouth of a Christian . . . The first thing the Devil persuaded our first Parents in Paradice was that God did not love them Enough.[22]

Ultimately, Traherne adopts a both/and position, as does the Church of England. He seems to put as much weight behind Article Two of the Thirty-nine Articles (which, following the Council of Chalcedon, decrees for the redemption of the whole human race) as he does to Article Seventeen regarding election, even though this doctrine of universal redemption seems counter to the doctrine of election. But 'all verity fitteth in the Golden Mean' says Traherne,[23] and to err on either extreme is equally dangerous.

There is a tension here that Traherne must live with. It is as if what he calls 'the lovely and Amicable contention' between Dr Hammond and Dr Sanderson is a contention that he sees also in the Church and feels in himself. Time and time again in this section, as elsewhere, Traherne returns to the principle 'that above all things in the World God desires that men should turn of themselves and that having all Means and Motives thereunto, should repent and believ of their own Accord'.[24] God's action in drawing people to himself, though prevenient, is not exclusive. In either the case of the elect or the reprobate, the end of divine initiative is that the human soul should act of its own accord: 'For that they may herafter do Good Works of their own Accord are the one [the Elect] now Invaded: and that in this Act the other might be righteous of their own Accord are the other omitted'.[25] Traherne cites the Gospel text that 'many are called but few are chosen' as instance of God's preference for the reprobate, his chief desire and greatest longing fulfilled in the conversion of the lost. While Traherne affirms that God creates grace irresistibly in the heart of the elect, it is the reprobate who seems the most interesting to Traherne, for it is the person who has the greater choice to make whose actions may be considered righteous.

Traherne's use of the Thirty-nine Articles as a doctrinal guide is not surprising but the length of discussion over one single matter may strike some readers as disproportionate. He considers the debate at

---

22 *SV*, XXVIII, ll. 142–5, 149–50.
23 *SV*, VI, l. 44.
24 *SV*, IV, ll. 196, 197.
25 *SV*, IV, ll. 28–30.

length partly out of respect for the authors represented, partly because the debate had such political significance, but chiefly out of his own love of truth,[26] an earnest pursuit in which no matter is too small to admit consideration. In *Commentaries of Heaven*, his poem 'Article', which follows a diatribe against the Quakers, describes each of the Thirty-nine Articles as 'a little joint'of the whole body. In matters of doctrine, all the Articles must be united since relation and proportion are what give symmetry to the whole. So assembled, Traherne says, they strike the viewer dumb as God is seen in perspective, alive as if in bodily form in the Thirty-nine Articles. Such is his reverence for the doctrines of the Church of England.

The intense examination of doctrine in *A Sober View* may draw scholars back to reconsider *Roman Forgeries*, not only because the two works signal a similar interest in matters doctrinal but because they both make the same kind of claim to an earnest pursuit of the truth derived from the examination of texts and because they both indicate the degree to which Traherne was willing to engage in inseparably linked theological/political controversies of his day. In these two works, as elsewhere, Traherne criticizes Roman Catholicism and non-conformity alike; taken together they may chart a middle way between extremes. The whole work lodges Traherne securely in post-Dort theology[27] and in the Church of England; as such, *A Sober View* is primarily of theological rather than philosophical interest. But the questions that he raises and the parts of the questions that he chooses to emphasize highlight his overarching philosophical concerns regarding freedom, choice and action seen elsewhere in his work. In *A Sober View* Traherne is more detached than in many of his other works. There are no rhapsodic exaltations, no lofty flights into mystical vision. He is concentrated, busy, trying to find a simple answer. Calvinism and Arminianism – in *A Sober View* Traherne puts two pins in the map of post-Reformation theology and charts a tricky path between them as he asks the question: How free are we?

---

26 Traherne writes that 'Dr Hammonds Scruples are learned, and his objections important. But that which principaly moveth and prevaileth with me is Love to the Truth' (*SV*, VII, ll. 41–3).

27 That is, the theology that followed the Synod of Dort (1618–19), convened by the Netherlands to end the bitter controversy over Arminianism, in which followers of Arminius (d. 1609) were summoned as offenders rather than as representatives. At the synod the Five Points of Arminianism were condemned and the Five Points of Calvinism were stated explicitly. Representatives from England were present. The Decrees of Dort gained wide approval in the Reformed Churches. For a concise account see J. T. McNeill, *A Dictionary of Christian Theology*, London: SCM Press, 1969, p. 99.

Love

A beautiful and engaging fragmentary start to a larger, unfinished work, *Love*[28] begins with the words: 'To Speak fully and distinctly concerning Lov is impossible'. Traherne wisely sets parameters for the work: 'Four Cares and concerns it has, which abov all other I shall chuse to speak of'.[29] But here the reader is teased since not only does he get no further than the first concern, which is that love desires to beautify itself, but he also fails to tell us what the other three concerns were going to be. What we have is a tantalizing beginning. He starts by contemplating 'the illimited Sweetness of Tyrannical Love',[30] in which an Empress, admired and adored by many, surrenders herself to the love of one, greedily desiring his embraces and prodigally bestowing her own. Traherne is telling a story that reads as remarkably real for one who claims to disown such experience: 'Such fancies and descriptions have I seen in Playes and vain Romances.'[31]

The themes in *Love* are similar to those in the ending of *The Kingdom of God* where, in an extended metaphor in the final chapter, we again see the soul as bride. This image of the soul/bride is not unusual in Traherne. It recurs several times in *Commentaries of Heaven* and in the *Select Meditations* and, less forcefully, in chapter 18 of *Christian Ethicks*. In each of these works the soul is the beloved wooed by a divine Lover, but here in *Love* the allegory is sharper. Gone are the notions of benevolence and complacency that mark the relationship of God to the soul in *Christian Ethicks*; superseded are the distant longings of *Select Meditations*. Instead we have greedy desire and wild abandon as the lovers surrender to their great passion. The exploration of the theme is striking in its intensity, making this fragment interesting to scholars in general but of particular use to those concerned with Traherne's theories of desire in the love of God, as this study has shown.

Seeds of Eternity

Seeds of Eternity or The Nature of the Soul in which Everlasting Powers are Prepared is a short theme (12 pages) exploring the powers of the soul, by the greatness of which the human is made capable of union

---

28 The treatise is untitled in the manuscript. *Love* is the modern title given to it by Jeremy Maule.
29 *Love*, ll. 5–6.
30 Ibid. ll. 35–6
31 Ibid. ll. 71–2.

with the divine. It is one of the three titled works in the manuscript that appears in the 1972 Lambeth Palace Library catalogue of manuscripts under the title: 'Three theological treatises of the 1660's'.[32] The catalogue noted only those works in the manuscript that were titled, and it was the phrase 'Seeds of Eternity' that caught the eye of Jeremy Maule as he perused the catalogue of acquisitions. The phrase struck him as reminiscent of Traherne and he asked to inspect the manuscript; so it is in some part to this short treatise that a whole discovery is due.

Written in Traherne's own hand, the treatise is redolent with themes, phrases and stylistic features that are typical of the author. *Seeds of Eternity* opens with the words: 'Humanity, which is the Handmaid of true Divinity, is a noble Part of Learning, opening the best and rarest Cabinet in nature to us, that of our Selvs';[33] in many ways this is just what the treatise is – an exploration of the self. The soul, says Traherne, 'naturaly desires to see the Lineaments of its own face'.[34] True humanity, being not the study of exterior actions but the interior endowments and inclinations of the soul, is the most certain of all sciences 'becaus we *feel* the Things it declares'.[35] Cosmography, medicine, anatomy, rhetoric, poetry and history touch the skirts of true humanity, Traherne says, but all the examples of these in the world will not penetrate to the centre. So it was that he was largely disappointed in learning because it did not answer his thirst for knowledge of the soul. He writes:

> Nay, when I heard the Lecture of Humanitie in our Scholes, I was frustrated in my expectation, and tho Aristotle hath written a book of the soul, opening many Faculties and Powers in it yet because he shewd not the uses of those Faculties at least not so as to make me see the Pith of that perfection and glory I expected, to me he was defective.[36]

Traherne saw in Aristotle the parts of the soul 'like a broken monument whose fragments are seen, but lying in the Rubbish';[37] it was for

---

32 E. G. Bill, *Catalogue of Manuscripts in Lambeth Palace Library: MSS 1222–1860*, Oxford: Clarendon Press, 1972, pp. 78–9.
33 See also C, III, 41–2, in which Traherne discusses the excellency of 'Humanity': 'By humanity we search into the powers and faculties of the Soul ... Whereby we come to know what man is in this world.'
34 *SE*, l. 18.
35 *SE*, l. 22.
36 *SE*, ll. 155–60. Similarly, Traherne's disappointment with his scholastic education is recorded in C, III, 37.
37 *SE*, ll. 191–92.

him a reading of the soul that contained many excellent things but left him dry and empty. Like Thomas Jackson, who derided Aristotle for dealing with neither 'the first cause or last end of all things',[38] Traherne also grew impatient with Aristotle's treatment of the soul. What he longed for was to see the end for which the powers of the soul were created. This, he says, Aristotle 'buried in Silence'.[39] The powers and inclinations of the soul, Traherne asserts, must be viewed in symmetry and proportion, the inclinations coming 'from GOD to GOD'.[40]

In *Seeds of Eternity*, the desire to see the excellence of things and the covetousness that longs to have possession of them are two high and soaring inclinations that make us capable of bliss. These two inclinations are implanted in order that they might be satisfied by a God willing to communicate himself to his creation. This notion of communication is central to the project of *Seeds*. The whole point of gazing on the beauty of the soul is not to become proud (which, Traherne reminds us, was the fall of the Angels) but so that one might be moved to repentance at having defiled so excellent a creature as the soul. The end of these two implanted desires – to see the excellence of things and to possess them – is God's glory. 'He desires to be Delightfull, and to be enjoyed: he is infinitly Good and communicative . . . That therfore we might be capable of all Enjoyments, in communion with him, he made us like him self',[41] who also desires the most excellent things and enjoys them. Nothing can be a treasure that is not possessed and the divine nature therefore 'desires Application, as well as Excellency'.[42] For a thing may be capable of being a treasure that is not a treasure until it be enjoyed.

Traherne's stylistic quality is consistently good in *Seeds of Eternity*. He is fluent, confident and logically ordered. A quarter of the way through his argument there appears a page and a half on the Coimbran scholars – Jesuits of Coimbra University in Portugal whose Latin translations of Aristotle and others who wrote on the soul were very popular among advanced scholars of the seventeenth century. This interlude provides an interesting and detailed list of Classical and Patristic treatment of the soul in the Aristotelian *de anima* tradition. However, having noted these 'Learned Commentators' and acknowledged the

---

38 Thomas Jackson, *The Eternal Truth of the Scriptures*, London, 1613–14, p. 112; see also his *Treatise of the Divine Essence and Attributes*, London, 1628, 1629, p. 31. Jackson is one of Traherne's sources in his *Commonplace Book*.
39 *SE*, l. 183.
40 *SE*, l. 187.
41 *SE*, ll. 93–4, 96–7.
42 *SE*, ll. 100–1.

APPENDIX I

excellency of their work, Traherne steps to one side at the point at which he feels their contribution becomes a diversion – a gathering of 'Criticismes and Niceties'. What he wants to do is to reach a clear understanding of the soul's capacity for union with the divine that resonates with experience – to *feel* the things that humanity declares.[43] And so he picks up the thread of his earlier argument on communication: the soul is infinitely communicative in the image of God. Thus the 'ΓΝΩΘΙ ΣΕΑΥΤΟΝ' [sic] of Delphi – the admonition to know oneself – becomes an oracle of deepest wisdom because 'in the knowledge of one self, the Knowledge of God, and all things appeareth'.[44] *Seeds of Eternity* goes on to consider the body as a glorious companion to the soul and to assert the superiority of humankind over animals. The treatise ends with the inquisitiveness and restlessness of human nature that needs to know the Original and End of creation. It concludes by stating briefly that it is by all the powers of the soul and superiority of the human position that the soul is made capable of union with God.

There are no catchwords or pagination in the manuscript that would suggest preparation for publication, though this does not necessarily indicate an absence of intent to publish. A few revisions in darker ink with a wider nib are not dissimilar to the wider nib of the 'Critical Reader' of the first two works in the Lambeth Manuscript. There is a clear break where the writing changes and is smaller after folio 141r, and Jan Ross's suggestion that he may have broken off writing *Seeds of Eternity* and resumed it later seems entirely plausible; although, in fact, the size of the writing after this point is not dissimilar to that at the very beginning of the work (fol. 135r) and it may be that the changes in font size have to do with simple fatigue or with freshness of application in approaching the work on a new day – it is difficult, on the limited information available to be clear about what these changes in handwriting signify. Editorial deletions and additions grow less frequent after folio 138v and seem to dwindle towards the end of the work. Most of his emendations have to do with redundancies, errors of expression, clarification and simplification, but some have to do with tone. For those readers of Traherne familiar with his ecstatic exclamations, it may be interesting to note that in *Seeds of Eternity* he seems to be making an effort to edit some of the personal and ecstatic out of the text. Thus on folio 136r he moves from the first person to the third person:

---

[43] This is similar to his complaint in C, III, 37 that what he studied was always studied 'as *aliena*': information was gained but meaning was missed.
[44] *SE*, ll. 299–300.

> Since therefore O my Soul, thou art so great a Lover of thy Self & so mightily delightest in thine own Beauty, how Happy art thou that thou art so Glorious! Nay O my Soul, whereas all other Things are most truly Glorious, that tho art most Exceedingly so! And how much owest thou unto God Almighty, that by his Wisdom and Power he hath make those things that are most excellent, most Essentialy, thine, & seated them within! I am amazed when I consider the perfections of my Soul

becomes

> Since therefore the Soul, is so great a Lover of it Self, and so mightily delightest in its own Beauty, how happy is it that it is so Glorious! How much owest thou unto God Almighty, that by his Wisdom and Power he hath made those things that are most excellent, most Essentialy, thine, and seated them within! I am amazed when I consider the Perfections of the Soul.

Traherne's considered detachment here is interesting. As well as wanting to simplify, he may have been wanting to make this passage fall in line with the prevailing academic tone of the work. He may have been conscious of those critics who censured him for speaking in the first person;[45] perhaps he was also heeding his own warning a few lines later against the kind of pride that caused the fall of angels.

In *Seeds of Eternity*, Traherne expounds Christian humanism using a long line of ancient and Patristic sources, and in so doing he quotes freely, often not identifying his source until some lines later if at all; many of his sources are quoted second hand.[46] The work resonates with his exposition of the utility of humanity and the surpassing significance of felicity in the third *Century*[47] and with parts of *Christian Ethics*.[48] In its high view of humanity *Seeds* echoes the Neo-Platonist ideals that we see in his poetry and prose, particularly in his quotations from Pico in the *Centuries*.[49] In its themes of insatiability and the capacity of the soul it is reminiscent of the lofty *Thanksgivings for the Soul*. But, although his subject is marvellous, he refrains from ecstatic

---

45 'Here I am censured for Speaking in the Singular number, and Saying I' (*SM*, III, 65).
46 For specific examples see Ross, 'Introduction', p. xxiii.
47 See C, III, 41–6.
48 See most significantly CE, Ch. 4, 'Of the Powers and Affections of the Soul' and to a lesser extent Ch. 20 'Of Prudence'.
49 See C, III, 74–8.

utterances. Just as *Christian Ethicks* aims to draw the reader towards a life of virtue by considering the beauty of the virtues, so *Seeds of Eternity*, in its consideration of capacity, studies the glory of the soul rather than its capacity for evil; it aims to draw the reader to repentance by focusing not on his or her sins but on the great beauty of the original that has been marred.

The Kingdom of God

This is Traherne's longest work of philosophical theology: a 42-chapter study of God and his creation – God as creator first of all, then the creation as an expression of himself. It is a story of divine disclosure and of divine goodness extending in love.

The title of the work suggests that it may have a place among those millenarian writings common in the seventeenth century that explored the biblical promise of God's thousand-year reign on earth.[50] Even before *The Kingdom of God* was discovered critics had made attempts to locate Traherne within this millenarian tradition. Nabil Matar and Michael Ponsford both discuss Traherne in millenarian terms but, whereas for Ponsford Traherne's new Jerusalem is not a literal event but a foretaste of bliss, an allegory, Matar claims that the eschatological promises of the Reformation were realized for Traherne by the Restoration of the King in 1660, an event that, according to Matar, turned Traherne into a man with a prophetic mission who 'presented the eschatological vision more persistently and politically' than any other divine in the Church of England.[51] There is indeed much in *The Kingdom of God* that points towards a realized eschatology; and there can be little doubt that Traherne was aware of the millenarian writings that abounded in his day.[52] It may be that the work was written in part as a response to some of these texts; it is certainly a text aware of

---

50 Millenarians believed that the approaching thousand-year reign of Christ on earth prophesied in Scripture would be ushered in by divine, probably apocalyptic means; but their interpretations of how and when this would occur, and who would benefit or suffer from the arrival of the 'new heaven and new earth' or the 'new Jerusalem' differ widely. At different points the millenarian banner was taken up by Puritans, radicals, Restoration divines and latitudinarians alike.

51 Michael Ponsford, 'Thomas Traherne, the New Jerusalem, and Seventeenth Century Millenarianism', *Durham University Journal*, 87 (1995), pp. 243–50; Nabil Matar, 'The Anglican Eschatology of Thomas Traherne', *Anglican Theological Review*, 74 (1992), pp. 289–303, 302.

52 He also shares the millenarian fascination with the book of Revelation, evident in his long entry 'Antichrist' in *COH*, in which he cites George Downham's 'Treatise Concerning Antichrist' (1603) which named the pope as antichrist and refuted Bellarmine.

its cultural and intellectual surroundings. Littered with various asides addressed to Atheists or 'Deicides', to heretics of varying sorts, to the 'Wits of the Age', to the pusillanimous, the timid and the self-deluding, *The Kingdom of God* is consciously aimed to convince and to correct: the kingdom is now; the kingdom is here as well as hereafter. And yet, in the work, Traherne seems to suffer a certain amount of dis-ease about his own inclination towards what might be seen as a completed eschatology: 'Neither would I be mistaken, as if there were no Heaven in another place. My Meaning is, that all is as delightfull, and happy here, as if all were intended for this alone' (*KOG*, Ch. 25, ll. 204–6), he writes, qualifying his four preceding pages in praise of a heavenly creation. If *The Kingdom of God* is as much of a direct attack on the preoccupation with the hereafter evident in many of his fellow seventeenth-century theologians as it seems to be, perhaps he qualifies his assertions to mollify the anticipated voice of critics who could argue that he veers off into the opposite extreme. Or perhaps the other image of a kingdom laid waste in need of redemption that is the premise of *A Sober View* is in the back of his mind. It seems that Traherne is neither wholly satisfied with a 'realized' eschatological promise, as Matar claims, nor is he as completely allegorical in his understanding of the kingdom of God as Ponsford suggests. With the later millenarians (some of whom were latitudinarians), who believed in a mathematically regulated universe that would at an appointed time physically expire, Traherne has very little in common indeed.[53] For Traherne the New Jerusalem is neither wholly spiritual nor is it discovered most spectacularly in the temporal reigns of king or commonwealth; it is discovered in the marriage of Heaven and Earth:

> The Celestial City is not as far from us, as Heaven from the Earth, but Infinitly more remote, if we neglect it . . . The distance is not to be Measured by the length of spaces, but by the Institution of our lives, and the Affections of our Minds, As that Holy father Saith. We come by Endeavour, we Approach by Desire, we Enter by Faith, we Enjoy by Love. (*KOG*, Ch. 4, ll. 107–8)

---

53 Among those who held such millenarian views were Isaac Barrow, John Tillotson, Richard Baxter, Bentley and Newton himself. For more information on latitudinarians and the notion of a mathematically regulated universe see Margaret C. Jacob, 'Millenarianism and Science in the Late Seventeenth Century', *Journal of the History of Ideas*, 37 (1976), pp. 335–341; for Newton's views see H. W. Turnbull, ed., *The Correspondence of Sir Isaac Newton*, Cambridge: Cambridge University Press, 1961, vol. III, p. 245; James E. Force and Richard H. Popkin (eds), *Newton and Religion: Context, Nature and Influence*, Dordrecht: Kluwer Academic Publishers, 1999.

Here he is quoting John Chrysostom. We enter the kingdom when the kingdom enters us. In this sense the kingdom is within, but it is also without us. The physicality of life and its concomitant choices matter: 'this life is the most precious season in all Eternity, because all Eternity dependeth on it' asserts Traherne, our actions now are 'piecing this life with the life of Heaven' (C, IV, 93). With heaven and earth seamlessly stitched one to the other, the kingdom of God becomes not so much a final apocalyptic event as a means of grace, a channel of communication between God and us. However political its application may have been, Traherne's eschatology derives as much from the ancient Church Fathers and their view of a grace-filled earth as it may have done from the millenarian movements of his own age. In the midst of competing claims, his work alludes neither to an exclusively heavenly realm beyond this one nor to a New Jerusalem gained either by apocalypse or the Restoration but to a new way of seeing, to *'things that have been kept secret from the foundation of the World*. Things strange yet Common',[54] to the Word incarnate continually creating, to what Traherne calls infinite goodness manifest in the common, the known and the plain.[55] Rooted in the millenarian disputes of its day but towing neither party line, *The Kingdom of God*, as Alison Kershaw notes, is not simply a piece of devotional writing – 'it earnestly seeks to win its reader away from competing points of view'.[56]

In *The Kingdom of God* many of Traherne's sources are those also found in other works, especially *Commentaries of Heaven*, but there are some that are new. Set out in an Aristotelian fashion, but often dealing with Platonic notions, *The Kingdom of God* seems equally indebted to both traditions. In this balance between Plato and Aristotle, as in many of his theological theories, Traherne shares much with his fellow theologian 'the judicious [Richard] Hooker',[57] who was also deeply imbued with the Platonic/Aristotelian combination and with the work of the Church Fathers.

Maule describes the work as an early work of physico-theology – in

---

54 C, I, 3. See also Alison Kershaw, 'The Poetic of the Cosmic Christ in Thomas Traherne's *The Kingdom of God*', unpublished PhD thesis, University of Western Australia, 2005, p. 24.

55 C, I, 3; *KOG*, Ch. 8; chapter two of this book argues that Traherne's treasures are always those things that are simple, common and useful.

56 Kershaw, 'The Poetic of the Cosmic Christ', p. 26.

57 *KOG*, Ch. 22, ll. 1–4: 'The judicious Hooker, that Glorious Beam of the English Church, and the admired Star of all his Nation, wading into the spring and fountain of Laws, and digging neer into the root of things, hath some Sage and important Maxims which he casteth up like Sparkling Jewels.'

many ways an apt term despite being one that Traherne would not have used, since it appeared in the eighteenth century and derives in part from John Ray's series of lectures in 1713, 'Physico-theology: or, a Demonstration of the Being and Attributes of God, from His Works of Creation'. The thinking behind the term, however, has antecedents in earlier works,[58] among which are some of the Cambridge Platonists with whom Traherne was familiar. His physico-theological argument for the existence of God is not isolated to *The Kingdom of God*; it recurs in the *Centuries* and in the *Select Meditations*, where it is again offered as a direct hit on atheism: 'God in Assuming the world for His Body, hath out don all that the Atheist can wish or desire.'[59] In fact, Traherne's natural world rebuttal of atheists, or 'Deicides' as he also calls them, is part of a popular genre noted by Maule in works such as Bishop John Wilkins's *Dialogues of Natural Religion* (1675) and Stillingfleet's *Origines Sacrae* (1662), as in Isaac Barrow's *The Being of God proved from the Frame of the World*. The latter two theologians are men from whom we know Traherne read and copied. In works of this genre, the utility and beauty of creation are the chief characteristics thought to reveal divinity and the writers are keen to examine the most minute and the most extensive parts of creation, their singular attributes and the fruitfulness of their relation each to the other: here again Traherne is no exception.

However, as is often the case with Traherne, although *The Kingdom of God* can be placed in the context of physico-theological writings, it does not entirely fit this genre; and Maule himself noted the work's refusal to be genre-bound. What seems, especially in those chapters from 17 onwards – Traherne's section on 'the Material Causes' – to look very like what Maule calls a 'creed commentary' describing the attributes of God, ends up exploring the nature of human experience, the depths of love and longing, the soul as bride and humankind's capacity to sense, enjoy and offer back to God a transfigured creation. *The*

---

58 William Derham's *The Wisdom of God Manifested in the Works of Creation* (1691) and earlier Cambridge Platonist writings such as Ralph Cudworth's *The Intellectual System of the Universe* (1678) and More's *An Antidote Against Atheism* (1652). More's use of the creation as an argument against atheists is similar to that which appears in Ch. 17 and 27 of Traherne's *The Kingdom of God* with such lines as: 'It is Impossible to See the Kingdom, but we must believ, and admire the King' and ' The World is the Glorious Body, which he hath assumed to make himself Famous. Nor only to make it Known, that he is: but to make it Known, what he is.' More's connections with Traherne are well documented by Carol Marks, in 'Thomas Traherne and Cambridge Platonism', *Proceedings of the Modern Language Association*, 81 (1966), pp. 521–34; and 'Thomas Traherne's Commonplace Book', *Papers of the Bibliographic Society of America*, 60 (1966), pp. 458–65.

59 *SM*, IV, 34. See also C, II, 20.

Kingdom of God, although showing a sustained interest in arguments from design, posits neither the distant creator nor the divine architect/master-craftman that is often characteristic of later physico-theology. Traherne's creator is intimate with, even immanent in his creation. In terms of tone *The Kingdom of God* bounces out of the physico-theology box; in terms of structure Traherne designates the Aristotelian Causes.

Traherne begins this ambitious work with careful clarity, setting out the efficient (Chs 1–16), material (Chs 17–30), formal (Chs 31–42) and final causes (never in fact considered in a separate section) of God's kingdom.[60] He is aware of the enormity of the work he has set himself, admitting from the start that neither he nor anyone else is sufficient to the task; and it is in a spirit of endearing humility that he sets about this demanding project. For the kingdom he is about to consider is not just the kingdom of God on earth, all of creation animate and inanimate, but it is a kingdom that marries earth with heaven and time with eternity. It is a kingdom of angels as well as of men, in which all ages are present together and all territories animated with the divine life. Well then may he be daunted by the task ahead of him. It is as if he is already expecting the work to exceed the careful boundaries he has set for it before he begins; and it may be this anxiety that, throughout the work, draws his thoughts back again and again to the scholastic framework with which the work opens. Traherne knows he is attempting an immeasurable and untameable magnificence; and although the first chapter begins with the firm structural foundation it ends with the searching question 'What footing Can we Expect, what limit, what foundation, what Shore . . . where all is Infinit and Eternal?'

Nevertheless, Traherne feels bound to attempt this consideration of the kingdom of God 'for that which discourages Timorous Spirits, animates the Couragious';[61] it is the very incomprehensibleness of God's kingdom that is part of its allurement. In this he echoes the voices of Gregory of Nyssa (whom he also cites in the *Centuries*) and Gregory the Great (cited in *Commentaries of Heaven*), who each conceived God as essentially unknowable. Here too we may hear echoes of the

---

60 The terms 'efficient', 'material', 'formal' and 'final' refer to Aristotle's four causes necessary for producing a result. They concern questions of origin and process as follows: efficient – where things come from or that which originates the process; material – of what they consist, the matter from which a thing is made; formal – how things operate, what form they have, the shape or design that is imposed on the materials; final – the end towards which they aim. in the case of a house, for example, the efficient cause might be the builder or architect, the material cause the bricks, the formal cause the architect's drawings or the builder's plans, the final cause shelter and comfort.
61 *KOG*, Ch. 2, ll. 4–5.

'Som great thing' of the first *Century* that also allures Traherne and his reader. But here, as in the *Centuries*, the call that Traherne is answering is more than curiosity; he wants to 'consider and feel, and see, and prie into the Bottom'[62] as far as he can, not just because he loves prying but because, along with many fellow theologians, he believes that this kingdom is a mirror of the divine essence in which 'God himself, and the Eternal Generation of his Son, are made Known by his Works'.[63] This kingdom of God is 'the Center of our Union, and the sphere of our Communion with GOD'.[64] Clearly Traherne is hoping for more than knowledge as the fruit of this project. In *The Kingdom of God*, as elsewhere, what he seeks to find and to convey is an unfolding of the mystery of divine abundance and divine longing. In his first chapter, he describes this kingdom as both the 'subject of his discourse' and the 'object of his contemplation' and this gives the reader a clue to the style that is to follow, since he alternates between scholastic analysis and wondering contemplation throughout the work.

Traherne begins the third chapter by collapsing the distinction between heaven and earth, time and eternity. There is another life and another food, another liberty and another bondage, another want and another abundance, another conversation and another world running parallel to the one in which we find ourselves – we are in God's kingdom even now, if we have eyes to see it. This here and hereafter heaven is characteristic of Traherne's eschatology. He writes of heaven 'Even here on Earth' in the *Select Meditations*, saying 'I do not See a Carter on the Road, nor a carpenter Building a Little Cottage, but in the Light of Heaven they are before mine eyes. Deep Misteries are beneath the Surface of common works.'[65] Similarly, in the beginning chapters of *The Kingdom of God* he reflects on the spiritual nature of God's kingdom, which is to be discovered not by eschewing the world but by apprehending the spiritual in the everyday. The Celestial City is remote if we neglect it and near at hand if we consider it. 'The Distance is not to be Measured by the length of spaces, but by the Institution of our lives, and the Affections of our Minds' writes Traherne; and he goes on to quote John Chrysostom: 'We come by Endeavour, we approach by Desire, we Enter by Faith, we Enjoy by Love.'[66]

Chapter five moves from a discussion of the spiritual nature of the

---

62 Ibid., Ch 2, ll. 64–5.
63 Ibid., Ch 2, ll. 54–5.
64 Ibid., Ch 2, ll. 57–8.
65 *SM*, III, 20. See also *SM*, II, 19; *SM*, III, 59–60; *SM*, IV, 27; C, I, 46–7, 54.
66 *KOG*, Ch. 4, ll. 111–14.

kingdom into a philosophical account of the powers of the soul that overlaps in thought with much of *Seeds of Eternity*. Included in the discussion are notions of liberty and the importance of volition, which are similar to those found in *A Sober View*. Chapter six explores the theme of the soul/bride that also occurs in *Select Meditations* and *Love*, in which divine desire seeks a bride. We see the soul loving and being beloved in a circle of felicity that is the communion between God and his creatures; for without the gift of himself, God's kingdom would be an empty house, heaven 'a Nest without the Birds'.[67]

So far, the account of God's kingdom has largely been drawn from human experience, from the capacities, desires and needs of the soul. Traherne shifts his account in chapters seven and eight to that drawn from the attributes of God's self. Here we have infinite wisdom and infinite goodness communicating themselves in a good creation, principally in the creation of humans as free agents who may become authors of their own actions. Chapter nine considers three types of goodness: physical, moral and divine. In chapter ten, the active nature of goodness and the human duties that spring from divine goodness are considered. This chapter, steeped in Scripture, culminates in a poem on the passion and death of Christ, whose love is a piercing sweetness. In this remarkable poem, which will be of great interest to those studying the themes of sin and salvation in Traherne, it is God's love rather than his wrath that is too severe.

Chapter 11 overflows in its exposition of love. Threaded with scriptural phrases from the Old and New Testaments, this chapter is bold with assertions such as 'It is only Sin that Crumples up the Soul, which were it freely Spred abroad, would be as Wide and as large as the Univers',[68] and it explodes with psalmic exclamations addressed to divine love. It is as if Traherne takes a break here from strict analysis of the kingdom of God and, overwhelmed by his subject, revels in the magnitude and bounty of love shown in God's kingdom.

When chapter 12 begins 'the Glory of the Efficient Cause of the World is Love', Traherne seems to be attempting to rein himself in, to root his study back in its scholastic framework. In patristic fashion he celebrates Love as the original of all things, the first spring of all action; he also celebrates the unity in diversity that sees Love and the beloved as inseparable with the striking comment 'we truly are, what we seem

---

67 Ibid., Ch 6, l. 125.
68 Ibid., 305, Ch. 11, ll. 31–3. This is a phrase that Traherne took from Ralph Cudworth, *Sermon preached before the Honourable House of Commons, at Westminster, March 31 1647*, Cambridge: Roger David, Printer to the universitie, 1647, p. 78.

to God'[69] and the quirkily appealing thought that infinite love is so intimately a part of us that it even 'Strengtheneth our Ankle Bones' and 'is hid in the Labyrinth of our Ears'.[70] There is nowhere in us that love is not, Traherne is saying, and again he bubbles up as the chapter ends with a cocktail of praises from the Psalms.

Chapter 13 calmly considers attributes of God – wisdom, goodness, holiness, love – as 'divine and single perfections' that, being known, beget a kind of perpetual growth of virtues in the soul. As water begets ice and ice begets water, so there is a continual growth with regard to things spiritual so that, for instance, 'the more we exercise Wisdom, the more Wise we are, Our goodness is Increased by the use of Goodness, and our Lov augmented by its own operations'.[71] This chapter, like the ones immediately preceding it, ends with a recitation from the Psalms.

In chapter 14, God's kingdom is his bride, and the vehemence and self-giving of divine love is expounded. Traherne looks, for one example of divine love, to the husband of the adulterous wife who forgives and loves and lives again happily with his wife: 'So deeply is it Engraven in the Nature of som, . . . that they can more Easily ceas to liv, then Love.'[72] This vehement love is necessary in God because, as chapter 15 asserts, whatever God does must be infinitely complete and perfect – his holiness and righteousness require it. The fervour of his love, which carries him to infinite perfection, is his real purity; all the things in the world allured him to make them. Almighty power must exert itself infinitely. Traherne's assertions here correspond with those in his extensive treatment of Act in the *Commentaries of Heaven*.[73] Both originate in the scholastic and Thomist traditions that understood God's actions to be one with God's nature.[74]

In Chapter 16 the nature of divine infinity is explored, beginning with infinite bounty. Here, as in the *Centuries*, Traherne considers the

---

69 *KOG*, Ch. 12, l. 117.
70 Ibid., ll. 162–3, 164.
71 Ibid., Ch. 13, ll. 205–7.
72 Ibid., Ch. 14, ll. 180–1. See the story of the prophet Hosea in the Old Testament.
73 His entry 'Act' is some six folios in length, followed immediately by nearly four more on 'Action' and three on 'Activity'.
74 While Mark McIntosh is right to note that Traherne is 'following a long tradition in Christian neoplatonism' when he 'holds that it is the very nature of such a freely given goodness to diffuse itself to the widest possible extent', it is also true that Traherne's technical understanding of 'Act' contrasts with that part of Neo-Platonism that conceived God as a source of Being that is itself beyond Being. See Mark McIntosh, *Discernment and Truth : the Spirituality and Theology of Knowledge*, New York: Crossroad, 2005, p. 245; and Paul Cefalu, 'Thomistic Metaphysics and Ethics in the Poetry and Prose of Thomas Traherne', *Literature and Theology*, 16 (2002), pp. 248–69.

perversity of human nature that prefers things rare and scarce, things little and vain, which are not given to us, before all the great and glorious blessings of God and Nature that are bestowed on us. Because what is given is taken for granted, God's generosity is lost to us by its very freedom. God's bounty hides itself in its own infinity. The infinity of God's act, Traherne goes on, is not to be measured in successions of addition but in the whole creation at once and together infused; for God's being wholly everywhere includes being in all times as well as in all places. We enjoy the elements of creation in time but his act of creation is everlasting and exerts itself infinitely. Repeatedly in this chapter Traherne illustrates the problems of drawing an understanding of God from human experience. The reader feels Traherne's frustration as he prepares to close this first section.

Chapter 17 begins Traherne's study of the material causes of the kingdom. Here he moves from considering the nature of God's kingdom based either on our needs and experience of God or on his attributes to examining in parts the physical creation. He begins the chapter 'It is Impossible to See the Kingdom, but we must believ, and admire the King'. This is in effect what he has been doing so far, trying to explicate the kingdom by admiring the king, but chapter 17 marks a transition. 'A King's Highness is in the Kingdom', he continues, and so it is the separate elements of the physical creation that are now to be examined. Here Traherne suggests what he further develops in subsequent chapters – the extraordinary and striking notion of the physical creation as God's body. God inhabits his creation: 'He dwelleth in his Kingdom, not as in other Temples, where he is the object of the Adorers Thoughts and Affections only.' He continues,

> But as the Skill of an Architect dwelles in his Work, and the Face of a Spectator in the Mirror he beholds. As the virtu of the Sun dwels in the Trees and Herbs it inspireth, and a fountain in the Stream, so does the Fullness of the Godhead lodg in his Kingdom.[75]

He restates the spiritual nature of the kingdom, that all possibles, actuals and impossibles are included in it, 'All Eternitie and the Amplitude of Illimited Space';[76] and he restates the value of contemplating the efficient cause of the kingdom (that is God, his nature and attributes). Traherne's first principles are spiritual, but in the subsequent chapters he is to choose the actual and particular because, he claims, things

---

[75] *KOG*, Ch. 17, ll. 31–7.
[76] Ibid., ll. 68–9.

actual are better than things possible because they are pleasing, glorious and blessed. They are what we know as real. They are capable of use and pleasure.

The chapters in the late teens and twenties are the 'scientific' chapters of the work alluded to earlier. In chapter 18 Traherne's studies of the matter of the universe include a treatise on atoms. Chapter 19 treats Harvey and the circulation of the blood, the circulation of atoms, the laws of motion and the nature of light. Chapter 20 considers the sun, its ever replenished self-giving an emblem of the Trinity. Chapters 21 and 22 consider the moon and the stars, taking on the discoveries of telescopes and the speculative scientific theories of his day and positing even the inhabitation of other planets, all of which, in his view, enrich rather than threaten his notion of heaven. Chapter 23 sets out ancient and modern theories of the nature and influence of the sun. In chapter 24 he asserts the interconnectedness of things seen in the communication between particles, atoms, bodies, rays and emanations, including the influences of the moon and planets. Chapter 25 moves on to the globe of earth and asks how this earth would seem to a celestial stranger first visiting it. He contrasts earth's littleness and baseness with the dignity and glory of its creatures – plant, animal and human – and asserts its place in the centre of the universe, not geographically but metaphorically. Taking a closer look at this globe of earth, Traherne goes on in chapter 26 to consider the wealth in seas and rivers, trees, herbs and flowers, minerals and precious stones. The water cycle is seen as another example of the circulation of all things. Heaven and earth and sea conspire together to make one drop of water; and Traherne restates what he has suggested earlier, that the real treasures are those things most useful and common rather than the most rare. Chapter 27 sees the development of an idea glimpsed earlier in the *Centuries* and in chapters 16 and 17 of the *Kingdom of God*, that the earth is God's body, a way of making himself visible. Traherne considers weather – rain and hail, snow, clouds and meteors – and how the nature of God is seen both in the exercise and in the restraint of these conditions. The chapter ends with a poem of 15 stanzas, beginning 'A Wise man will apply his Mind', that describes the power of a person who sees the world through the eyes of wisdom and love, who rightly esteems the gifts of creation and transfigures the ordinary by his enjoyment of it. This poem, with its extraordinary sense of deified humanity, beatific vision and the restless employment of the happy, should spark further study and will be of immediate interest to those scholars concerned with Traherne's theory of transfiguration. Chapter

28 celebrates Life, that great mystery at the centre of creation that defies explanation, animates all that is and evades Traherne's neat categories of efficient, material, formal and final. Much in the ebullient and abundant way that he gave himself up, in chapter ten, to Love, here he gives himself over to Life, the darling of God and nature. 'Give me a life Extensive like thine', he prays, 'so vast a Measure of it, that all the Waters in the Sea, might be but Drops in Comparison.'[77]

Chapters 29 and 30 explore this theme of life in greater detail, looking at the different kinds of life – vegetable, animal and human, limited and illimited, mortal and immortal. This ends his considerations of the material causes of the Kingdom of God.

Chapter 31 begins Traherne's study of the formal causes of the kingdom – how that kingdom is constituted, its laws, the relationships between creatures and their creator and their relation to each other. In this kingdom all things find value in their relation to each other. The sun, for instance, matters because of its influence on earth and earthly creatures: 'if it be not Good to other things it is good for Nothing',[78] writes Traherne; 'Use gives to things their Worth'.[79] At first glance this rendition of the formal causes of the kingdom, which sees the kingdom as relational, seems very pragmatic, though a more complicated and deeply theoretical side to the discussion swiftly emerges. During Traherne's discussion of the material causes – the matter of the universe, from atoms to astronomy – his subject was somehow tangible; however here, in the formal causes, where the kingdom is about relationships of need and satisfaction, of law and obligation, grace and gift, we find that temporal boundaries are eroded. The kingdom is no longer concentrated in the created world but in a way of being with each other that transcends time and place. In one atypical opposition Traherne specifically contrasts 'the created world' with 'the kingdom', writing 'It is the first and the last of all possible Kingdoms. For be ther never so Many Worlds, there is but one Kingdom.'[80] And he begins to use the traditional language of those whose heaven is not here but hereafter: 'O my Joy and mine Inheritance, when Shall I Enjoy thee! What Reason hav I to Watch and Pray, and Labor, and Endure that I may attain thee! What are all the Pleasures upon Earth in Comparison of thee!'[81] This

---

77 Ibid., Ch. 28, ll. 416–17.
78 Ibid., Ch. 31, ll. 145–6.
79 Ibid., l. 165.
80 Ibid., ll. 124–5.
81 Ibid., ll. 133–6. The heaven/earth opposition can also be found in C, IV, 60, 70; SM, III, 65.

placing of heaven in the hereafter contrasts with much of Traherne's thinking in the rest of *The Kingdom of God*, in most of the *Centuries* and elsewhere. It is as much an admission of the idealized nature of his understanding of the kingdom as it is an expression of hope.

The kingdom is so constituted that Love is to the kingdom as the soul is to the human body, Traherne goes on to claim. This 'Lov which is the great Soul and Dæmon of the World',[82] is the breath of God. And in a line that is reminiscent of a line from 'The Circulation' – 'No man breaths out more vital air than he at first suckd in' – Traherne writes of the breath of God: 'Love efflagitates and calls for our Return'.[83] Love is primary, the life giving force of the entire kingdom. Here, as in the *Select Meditations*,[84] 'Naked Love' is the cause and the end of all things, and the thing that God desires above all – that is, a love that is generous and free, unadulterated, unencumbered, a voluntary choice. Traherne goes on to consider love as a creation of God so like God as to be thought to be God. It is (in the imagery of the ancient hermetical writings) 'Great without Bulk, an Infinit Sphere without Dimensions, A Centre Comprehending the very Heavens, apparently here, yet Secretly present in other Places ... Potent without a Body, Beautifull without a Face ... Loves Eternaly, yet is never old.'[85] And so he prefaces all his study of the formal causes of the kingdom with love. Subsequent chapters go on to consider all created things as treasures in their usefulness and ability to be enjoyed, with God as the first enjoyer and humankind created to enjoy in his image. In the image of God also the human soul may be present in all times and in all ages. Traherne takes this idea from the hermetical writings of Hermes Trismegistus, 'who if were a Heathen, was the Strangest sort of Heathen that ever the world produced',[86] to whom he is indebted, along with St John Chrysostom, for long portions of chapter 37. Chapters 38 and 39, which concern enjoying God, lead inevitably to the final chapters, which celebrate the physicality of creation, embodiment, with the human person (in the Renaissance humanist ideal) as the golden clasp between the visible and invisible worlds, uniting material and spiritual:

> Our Bodies are not, as Som Imagine them, Enemies to be used, with all kind of Rigor ... They are Vessels worthy of the Treasures they

---

82 Ibid., Ch. 32, l. 58.
83 Ibid., l. 41.
84 *SM*, II, 83–4.
85 *KOG*, Ch. 32, ll. 184–90.
86 Ibid., Ch. 37, ll. 119–20.

inclose; and you must believ they are very Dear to the Power, which Created them. (*KOG*, Ch 41, ll. 1–3)

Without bodies how could we enjoy the creation? How could we become a second creator, an 'Assistent Form' begetting offspring and works, laborious and faithfull in our virtue, offering real gifts of more worth than the gifts of the unencumbered and undistracted angels? This conviction of the superiority of humankind over angels is reiterated in the subsequent poem 'For Man to Act', which also appears in *Christian Ethicks*. That this poem appears in both these accomplished works suggests something of its importance to Traherne. Here in *The Kingdom of God* it draws the whole work towards its expansive conclusion celebrating the human's unique position in creation: the soul is once again the bride and God the great lover. The virtue of struggle is extolled, as is the benefit of trial, by which the soul may not so much win its own perfection as offer gifts of real value to its beloved. The soul may be perfected by trial but this happens as a side effect. The real aim is to please the divine lover. It is the very otherness of the human soul as much as its capacity to be a mate fit for divine love that makes it attractive to God, according to Traherne: 'His Bride must hav som things peculiar to her Sex, which God himself doth not Enjoy, unless it be in her' (*KOG*, Ch 42, ll. 341–2). But, in a surprising denouement, Traherne's soul is no whimsical maiden waiting to be chosen; the bride is a magnificent warrior armed with knowledge and appetite, an Amazon equipped for battle, with a will that is all her own.

What are we to make of this ending to what is one of Traherne's most highly developed works? With a great sense of humility and insufficiency, he sought, at the beginning of the work, to impose on his huge exploration into all created space in all ages the Aristotelian causes as a framework and guide. Yet his map-and-compass scholastic structures seem to have been abandoned at various stages; not only does his tone differ, in many places throughout the work, from the kind of cool analysis that his structure leads us to expect but his ideas do not keep within their apportioned space. Although his movements from efficient to material and material to formal causes are clearly marked, the expected fourth section on the final causes never materializes. Is this because, since the first and final causes are the same – 'The Efficient and the final Cause is God himself' (*KOG*, Ch 1, l. 10), writes Traherne at the outset – the whole category of 'final cause' is by implication included in the first discussion of the efficient cause? Could the work be unfinished? Possibly, although, as Jeremy Maule noted in his first lecture on the discovery,[87] the work shows the kinds of editing that are consonant with an intention to publish – hints that are not conclusive. Could it be that Traherne knew himself to be running out of time? There is a kind of urgency to the final three chapters that is hard to ignore. From chapter 40 onwards the surge of a wave builds up as he writes about the physicality of being human, our sensible pleasures, our needs and appetites, our trials, hazards, ardours and the glory of our limited success, a wave that surges most forcefully in the final chapter. Does the force of his revelation mean that he simply abandoned the structures that held the work from the beginning? Are the final chapters a great letting go? Is he, at the end of the work, reaching a great conclusion or a new point of departure – the end, in a way, a new beginning that he had no time to develop? Was he simply in a rush? These are among the many questions with which new readers of this text may want to grapple.

The Kingdom of God is a philosophical study of divine interaction with creation. It is a treatise designed to correct specific theological misconceptions and to convince its readers of the possiblility of the life of heaven beginning here on earth. It may also be a response to the specific social and political changes of Traherne's day. But it is also in another sense a love story, which begins with a display of a king's dominion and ends with his betrothal – a revelation of God's outstretched longing to communicate his love and a desire that his love should be reciprocated. In this work God always longs to reveal himself as fully and intimately as it is possible he should. It is interesting to note that *The Kingdom of God* reads less as testimonial than some of Traherne's other works. Only in the two chapters on 'Love' and 'Life' does he allow himself an overflow of rapture. The moments of annunciation or epiphany that we find in *The Select Meditations* or the *Centuries* are largely absent here. The revelation is of Godself in the world, the world to the self, God to the self, the self to God. In chapters 16, 17 and 27 the creation is God's body by which he seeks to show himself. In chapter 41 Traherne conceives the creation as a love letter from God to the human soul, personal but not exclusive, written and copied, as were most works in the manuscript culture in which Traherne wrote, to be distributed to humankind, his bride. For God had

---

[87] 'Five New Traherne Works: The Lambeth Manuscript', unpublished paper given at Thomas Traherne Conference, Brasenose College, Oxford, 30 July 1997.

made an Epistle of his Lov. He had written it upon the Earth in knots and flowers, in Letters of Gold, in the Sun, in Silver Copies in the Stars, in Bloody Characters, in the Living Creatures which was in more Bloody ones afterwards Copied in the Death of his Son. (*KOG*, Ch. 41, ll. 193-7)

Throughout the work the soul is God's potential mate and finally his Amazon bride. What is the voice inside Traherne that constantly calls him back, in this work as in others, to the themes of longing, desire, communication, reciprocity, communion and union? One cannot help wondering whether the fragmentary *Love* could have been the beginning of a deeper exploration of the themes that he approaches at the end of *The Kingdom of God*.

There is, in *The Kingdom of God*, a recurring motif of circularity. The Circle of Felicity that Traherne names in chapter six resonates with the circular progress of infinite goodness of chapter seven, which 'is able to giv one thing intirely to Innumerable persons' and give all things to one (*KOG*, Ch. 7, ll. 74-5), and with infinite wisdom, which knows 'how by communicating, to receiv Infinit Glory: to make it self the End of all things by making others so' (*KOG*, Ch. 7, ll. 97-8). Sometimes this motif occurs in pithy statements of contrast as above, sometimes in extended lists of the ways and means by which the circle is achieved. Sometimes the simple statement is followed by illustrations that pile upon each other until the reader's head spins; then the list comes to a consolidating stop (*KOG*, Ch. 7, ll. 203-15). This kind of writing and thinking, stating and restating, listing and consolidating occurs again and again in *The Kingdom of God*. It is as if, throughout the work, as Traherne seeks to describe what the kingdom of God is, its parts and causes, and its concerns, he finds that everything is connected. His categories are not exclusive; his lists grow long and longer, yet never manage to be exhaustive. Despite the structure he seeks to impose on the work, it occasionally doubles back on itself. In the end, what we are given as a systematic account feels more like a magnificent mountain of interlocking thoughts conveyed with a great deal of energy. Nevertheless, as I have noted, the work is by no means without form. In fact, the reiterative elements of the work may be seen as completing Traherne's theme of bounty. Nowhere in *The Kingdom of God* is this more evident than in the great catalogue of creation that we find in chapter 25. Alison Kershaw describes this catalogue as 'one of the most exhilarating', its prose 'oiled with alliteration and repetition'.[88] It forms a litany of celebration and praise, in which the richness of the kingdom suggests the phoenix nest, the bed of spices, the lover's bed.[89] If the text is replete sometimes to the point of bulkiness, those catalogues are a characteristic of Traherne's replenishing style.[90] The use of the threefold Scripture, rumination and aphorism that Stanley Stewart notes in *Christian Ethicks*[91] is also used here in *The Kingdom of God*; as all good teachers do, Traherne states and restates, repetition being foundational to his art.

There is a deeply courteous, almost apologetic tone to the use of the first person in such phrases as 'If I may speak my mind freely' and 'I shall detain you no longer'; Traherne writes of what he dares to and dare not say, once even putting himself into the third person ('I know a stranger' who), as he does in the fourth *Century*,[92] as if he is aware of a critical reader. This often has the opposite effect to apology, making his point at once both more personal and more powerful. As Esther De Waal asserts, 'he wastes time with words',[93] and all his promises to detain us no longer amount to this – that he believes what he has to say is worth the time it takes to say it. In *The Kingdom of God* Traherne is a visionary working the vision into a mystical theology and he seems to write his way to greater clarity as the work progresses. The chapters in the twenties, when he is dealing with science, are particularly clear. He is fully aware of the science/religion divide that is beginning to be felt in his day and, while he sees this divide as a false one,[94] he is not so naive as to imagine that it will not matter to scientists, philosophers and theologians alike. It seems interesting that this particular work should be found now, at the beginning of the twenty-first century, when this divide appears in many ways to be beginning to close as the latest theories of physics bring us back to the brink of wonder.

---

88 Kershaw, 'The Poetic of the Cosmic Christ', p. 80. Kershaw's study of the catalogue of creation (pp. 80–7) is well worth reading.

89 For further discussion of these images see chapter five above.

90 Carl Selkin calls the catalogue 'the most distinctive feature' of Traherne's 'redeemed language': 'The Language of Vision: Traherne's Cataloguing Style', *English Literary Renaissance* 6 (1976), pp. 92–103. See also Louis Martz, *The Paradise Within: Studies in Vaughan, Traherne, and Milton*, New Haven: Yale University Press, 1964.

91 Stanley Stewart, *The Expanded Voice: The Art of Thomas Traherne*, San Marino, CA: The Huntington Library, 1970, pp. 72–3.

92 See *KOG* Ch. 19, l. 78; Ch. 20, l. 220; Ch. 25, 144–5; Ch. 33, 26–7; Ch. 40, ll. 107, 140–1; Ch. 42, l. 240.

93 Esther De Waal, *Lost in Wonder: Rediscovering the Spiritual Art of Attentiveness*, Norwich: Canterbury Press, 2003, p. ??.

94 Indeed many scientists (such as Boyle, whom Traherne cites) wrote theologically, just as he wrote about science.

APPENDIX I

In publishing this material, Jan Ross's new edition of the Lambeth Manuscript, including *The Kingdom of God*, makes available to the public what has only hitherto been read by a handful of scholars. *Commentaries of Heaven* has now been published in two volumes in the *Complete Works*. Selections from remaining unpublished manuscripts appear along with readings in Denise Inge (ed.), *Happiness and Holiness: Selected Readings from Thomas Traherne*, Norwich: Canterbury Press, 2008). However, *The Church's Year-Book*, the *Ficino Notebook*, the *Early Notebook* and the *Commonplace Book* remain unpublished as entire units. These books and notebooks are not without interest and should be considered in the ongoing effort to publish a complete works.

Appendix 2
Folios and corresponding chapters for *Inducements to Retiredness*, *A Sober View of Dr Twisse*, and *The Kingdom of God*

Inducements to Retiredness

Folio	Section
1r	I
2v	II
7r	III
9r	IV
11r	V

A Sober View of Dr Twisse

Folio	Section
22r	I
24r	II
27r	III
31v	IV
36r	V
40r	VI
44r	VII
47r	VIII
51r	IX
54r	X
58r	XI
62r	XII
67r	XIII
70v	XIV
74r	XV
77r	XVI
81r	XVII
83v	XVIII
86r	XIX
88v	XX
92r	XXI
94r	XXII
99r	XXIII
101v	XXIV
106r	XXV
187r	XXVI
112v	XXVII
116v	XXVIII

The Kingdom of God

Folio	Chapter
148r	1
149v	2
151v	3
155v	4
158v	5
164r	6
167v	7
173r	8
177r	9

APPENDIX 2

181v	10	269r	27
186r	11	275v	28
189v	12	285v	29
193v	13	289r	30
198v	14	296r	31
203r	15	301r	32
206v	16	307v	33
211v	17	314r	34
215v	18	320r	35
221v	19	324v	36
229v	20	329v	37
235r	21	335v	38
241v	22	340v	39
247v	23	346r	40
251r	24	352v	41
258r	25	358r	42
264r	26		

Bibliography

A. M. Allchin, *The Joy of all Creation: An Anglican Meditation on the Place of Mary*, London: New City, 1993.
——, *Landscapes of Glory: Daily Readings with Thomas Traherne*, London: Darton Longman and Todd, 1989.
——, *Participation in God: A Forgotten Strand in Anglican Tradition*, London: Darton Longman and Todd, 1988.
John Stewart Allitt, *Thomas Traherne: Il Poeta-Teologodella meraviglia e della felicità*, Milan: Edizioni Villadiseriane, 2007.
Robin Attfield, 'Thomas Traherne and the Location of Intrinsic Value', *Religious Traditions*, 6 (1983), pp. 66–74.
James J. Balakier, 'Thomas Traherne's Dobell Series and the Baconian Model of Experience', *English Studies*, 70 (1989), pp. 233–47.
Jacob Blevins (ed.), *Re-reading Thomas Traherne: A Collection of New Critical Essays*, Tempe, AZ: Arizona Center for Medieval and Renaissance Studies, 2007.
David Buresh (ed.), *Waking Up In Heaven: A Contemporary Edition of Centuries of Meditations*, Spencerville, MD: Hesed Press, 2002.
A. L. Clements, *The Mystical Poetry of Thomas Traherne*, Cambridge, MA: Harvard University Press, 1969.
Stephen Clucas, 'Poetic Atomism in Seventeenth-century England: Henry More, Thomas Traherne and "Scientific Imagination"', *Renaissance Studies*, 5 (1991), pp. 327–40.
Patrick Collinson, *From Cranmer to Sancroft*, London: Hambledon Continuum, 2006.
Malcolm M. Day, *Thomas Traherne*, Boston, MA: Twayne, 1982.
A. Leigh DeNeef, *Traherne in Dialogue: Heidegger, Lacan, and Derrida*, Durham, NC: Duke University Press, 1988.
Esther De Waal, *Lost in Wonder: Rediscovering the Spiritual Art of Attentiveness*, Norwich: Canterbury Press, 2003.
Graham Dowell, *Enjoying the World: The Rediscovery of Thomas Traherne*, London: Mowbray, 1990.

BIBLIOGRAPHY

T. S. Eliot, 'Mystic and Politician as Poet: Vaughan, Traherne, Marvell, Milton', *The Listener*, 2 April 1930, p. 90.

David Ford, *Christian Wisdom: Desiring God and Learning in Love*, Cambridge: Cambridge University Press, 2007.

——, *Self and Salvation: Being Transformed*, Cambridge Studies in Christian Theology, Cambridge: Cambridge University Press, 1999.

Patrick Grant, *The Transformation of Sin: Studies in Donne, Herbert, Vaughan and Traherne*, Amherst, MA: University of Massachusetts Press, 1974.

Christopher Hill, *Collected Essays: Writing and Revolution in Seventeenth Century England*, Amherst, MA: University of Massachusetts Press, 1985.

Sarah Hutton, 'Thomas Jackson, Oxford Platonist, and William Twisse, Aristotelian', *Journal of the History of Ideas*, 34 (1978), pp. 635–52.

Denise Inge, *Happiness and Holiness: Thomas Traherne and His Writings*, Norwich: Canterbury Press, 2008.

——, 'Thomas Traherne and the Socinian Heresy in *Commentaries of Heaven*', *Notes and Queries*, 252 (2007), pp. 412–16.

—— (ed.), *Thomas Traherne: Poetry and Prose*, London: SPCK, 2002.

Margaret Jacob, 'Millenarianism and Science in the Late Seventeenth Century', *Journal of the History of Ideas*, vol. 37 (1976), pp. 335–41.

C. A. Johnston, 'Heavenly Perspectives, Mirrors of Eternity: Thomas Traherne's Yearning Subject', *Criticism*, 45 (2001), pp. 377–405.

Alison Kershaw, 'The Poetic of the Cosmic Christ in Thomas Traherne's *The Kingdom of God*', unpublished PhD thesis, University of Western Australia, 2005.

Belden Lane, 'Thomas Traherne and the Awakening of Want', *Anglican Theological Review*, 81 (1999), pp. 651–64.

Barbara Lewalski, *Protestant Poetics and the Seventeenth-century Lyric*, Princeton: Princeton University Press, 1979.

Nicholas Lossky, *Lancelot Andrewes le predicateur (1555–1626)*, Paris: Editions du Cerf 1986.

Nabil Matar, 'The Political Views of Thomas Traherne', *Huntington Library Quarterly*, 57 (1994), pp. 241–53.

Mark McIntosh, *Discernment and Truth: The Spirituality and Theology of Knowledge*, New York: Herder and Herder, 2004.

Marjorie Nicolson, *The Breaking of the Circle: Studies in the Effect of the 'New Science' upon Seventeenth Century Poetry*, Evanston: IL: Northwestern University Press, 1950.

Michael Ponsford, 'Thomas Traherne, the New Jerusalem, and Seventeenth Century Millenarianism', *The Durham University Journal*, 87 (1995), pp. 243–50.

Anne Ridler (ed.), *Poems, Centuries and Three Thanksgivings*, London: Faber & Faber, 1966.

Jan Ross (ed.), *The Works of Thomas Traherne*, vols I and II, Cambridge: D. S. Brewer, 2005, 2007.

D. L. Sayers, 'The Beatrician Vision in Dante and Other Poets', *Nottingham Medieval Studies*, 2 (1958), pp. 3–23.

Alison Sherrington, *Mystical Symbolism in the Poetry of Thomas Traherne*, St Lucia: University of Queensland Press, 1970.

Julia Smith, 'Thomas Traherne and the Restoration', *The Seventeenth Century*, 2 (1988), pp. 203–22.

———, 'Thomas Traherne', *Oxford Dictionary of National Biography*, vol. 55, Oxford: Oxford University Press, 2004, pp. 205–8.

——— (ed.), *Select Meditations*, Manchester: Carcanet Press, 1997.

——— and Anne Ridler, 'Thomas Traherne: Some Extracts from *Commentaries of Heaven*', *PN Review*, 18, no. 6 (July/August 1992), pp. 14–20.

Stanley Stewart, *The Expanded Voice: The Art of Thomas Traherne*, San Marino, CA: Huntington Library, 1970.

Thomas Traherne, *Centuries, Poems, and Thanksgivings*, ed. H. M. Margoliouth, 2 vols, Oxford: Clarendon Press, 1958.

———, *Christian Ethicks*, ed. Carol L. Marks, Ithaca, NY: Cornell University Press, 1968.

Nicholas Tyacke, 'Religious controversy', in *The History of the University of Oxford: vol. IV. Seventeenth-century Oxford*, Oxford: Oxford University Press, 1997, pp. 569–620.

Joan Webber, *The Eloquent 'I': Style and Self in Seventeenth-century Prose*, Madison, WI: University of Wisconsin Press, 1968.

Franz Wöhrer, *Thomas Traherne: The Growth of a Mystic's Mind*, Salzburg Studies in English Literature, Salzburg: Universität Salzburg, Institut für Anglistik und Amerikanistik, 1982.

Index

accounts 111–12
action, springing from desire 216–17
Adam and Eve 137, 178
affections 217
agape 238–9
Allchin, Donald 21
Allestree, Richard 21, 55
Allitt, John Stewart 103
allure 27, 38, 200
almshouses 91
Amazon 297
ambition 64, 172
Anabaptists 155
Andrewes, Lancelot 132
angels 76, 134–5
Antichrist 131
appetite 30, 41, 64
Aquinas *see* Thomas Aquinas
Aristotle
 on choice 47
 on exchange value 116–17
 on the mind 149
 on prudence 42–5
 on the soul 281–2
 on virtue 39, 49
 on wisdom 46
Arminianism 15, 124, 154–7, 275
Arrowsmith, John 257
astronomy 52–4

Athanasius 139, 197
atoms 96–7
Aubrey, John 6
Augustine 21, 36, 38, 69
authority 127, 130–1
avarice 172

Bacon, Francis 202, 273
Barrow, Isaac 288
Baxter, Richard 257
Beal, Peter 268
beauty 36–7, 148
Berkeley, George 147
Blake, William 2
bliss 246
body, human 93, 134, 296–7
Bonaventure 213
Boyle, Robert 208
Brasenose College 19, 91
breath 219
bride/soul imagery 32–3, 35–6, 164–6, 221, 222
Bridgeman, Orlando 6, 10
Brontë, Emily 226
Brooke, William 267
Bruce, Donald 26
Bunyan, John 113, 181–2
burning bush 233–5
Bush, Douglas 22–3

Calvinism 15, 124, 154–7, 275

307

Cambridge Platonists 20-1, 99-106, 288
Casaubon, Isaac 136
celibacy 273
Charles II (king) 83, 85-6
choice 47, 124-74, 140, 145, 148, 263-4; *see also* free will
Chrysostom 286-7
Church of England 16, 18, 276-9
circle
  of bliss 244-52
  of desire 249-50
  of infinity 59, 211-13
  spiritual 214
circulation 201-20
  of the blood 54, 207-8
Clements, A. L. 59-60, 176, 179, 191-3, 200
Colie, Rosalie 56, 60-1, 191-2, 210-11
communication 201-20, 282
communion 221-61
conservation 94-5
contentment 55
conversion 159; *see also* new birth
cords of love 229
Corpus Hermeticum see hermetical writings
councils of the church 128-9
Countryman, William 31, 73-4
covetousness 64, 121
Cragg, G. R. 101-2
Cranmer, Thomas 132
Craven, William G. 143-4, 195-6
creation
  and allure 263
  as desire 226
  enjoyment of 93-4
  and mutuality 133
  and praise 134
  preservation 94-5
  purpose 37, 77-8
  and revelation 102
Credenhill 6, 10, 11, 15-16
cross of Christ 221, 228-38, 265
Cudworth, Ralph 132
Culverwell, Nathaniel 21, 65, 68-9, 99, 101
custom 95, 116-18, 130

David (king) 85, 134
Day, Malcolm 23, 176, 257, 258, 259
death 98
delight 217, 243
DeNeef, Leigh 183-5
  on desire for the Other 189-91
  on the Fall 187
  on glory 218
  on historicizing Traherne 2
desire
  and action 216-17, 232
  and choice 148, 187, 263
  and creation 26-7, 124, 226
  education of 249
  etymology 30
  by God 4
  and God's freedom 164, 243, 245
  human and divine 186-7
  and infinity 50-72, 76
  and knowledge 247-8
  necessity of 121
  and re-creation 224
  and satisfaction 244-52
  sexual 31
  and the soul 152
  and will 26
difference 175-220

INDEX

Diggers 177
Dionysius the Areopagite 31
discernment 98–106
divine light *see* natural light
Dobell, Bertram 1, 126, 147, 267–8
Dodd, Nigel 115
Donne, John 6, 40, 52–3
Dort, Synod of 279
Downham, George 131, 285
Dreher, Diane 141

Eales, Jacqueline 14
Eckhart, Meister 180, 213
Eden 137, 183, 242
ego 188
election 154, 156–60, 277–9
Eliot, T. S. 3, 26
Ellrodt, Robert 60
enclosures 176–7
enjoyment 194, 203
  of creation 93–4
erotic imagery 31–3
erotic love 238–9
eschatology 285–6
esteem 107–8
eternal life 70
eternity 58–9, 149
Eucharist 225–6
Evelyn, John 273–4
excess 47–9
exchange-value 116–18
excommunication 128–9

faith, and reason 100
fall, the 109, 156, 187
fasting 82
felicity 22–4, 243, 262
  as a circle 25–6
  and communion with God 221, 222, 227
  and desire 249–50
  early interpretations 1–3, 248
  and satisfaction 246, 250–1
  two models 227
  as unity 176–81, 227
Ficino, Marsilio 20, 132, 136, 139–41, 153, 214
Filmer, Robert 88–9
fire 233–7
Fisch, Harold 257
free trade 112
free will 125–6, 145, 153–62
  and election 154
  risk 165
freedom *see* liberty
friendship 11–12

Garin, Eugene 142–3
giving and receiving 203–4, 217–18
glory 162, 218
God
  as creator 77–8
  his freedom and desire 164, 185, 245
  his infinity 51–2, 62, 68–70
  his love for his creation 197–8, 203
  his wanting 72–80, 185
  holiness 76
  as king 82, 89
  omnipresence 59
  passionate nature 40, 75
  perfection 76
  revealed in creation 103–5
  union with 180–1
  as wanting 28
Golden Link (Golden Clasp) 131–46, 148
Good, Thomas 13
Goodenough, Ursula 27

goodness 167–8
  of God 235
grace 157–8, 162–9, 233
gratitude 252–61
Greenberg, Lynne 177
Gregory the Great 36, 65
Gregory of Nyssa 36, 65–9, 80
Grosart, Alexander 267

Hammond, Henry 155–7, 276–7
happiness 49, 243; *see also* felicity
Harley, Edward 13
Harvey, William 54, 207–8
Hawkes, David 111, 112–13, 117
heaven 49, 110, 157, 214–15, 244–7
Herbert, George 22, 71, 71–2, 171
Hereford 6, 10, 14
Hermes Trismegistus 136–40, 153
hermetical writings 132, 136–46, 213
Hill, Christopher 177
Hoard, Samuel 157, 276
Hobbes, Thomas 28, 88, 89
holiness 75–6, 125, 160, 243
Hooker, Richard 21, 132, 287
hope 169–74
Hopton, Susannah 13
Howe, John 216–17
human dignity 164
human nature 149, 187
humanity, greatness 148–9

image of God 145–6, 148–9, 153
imagination 88
incarnation 226
infants 263
  as heavenly king 193–4

intuition 100
  perception by 187–8, 200, 224
  receptivity 150–1
  union with God 63
infidelity 36
infinity
  circle of 211–13
  and desire 50–72
  of God 51–2, 68–70
  of God's kingdom 82
  and the imagination 210
  and land boundaries 179
  nature of 50–1
  of space 52–9
inheritance 87, 91, 177–8
innocence 162
insatiability 64–6, 68, 79–80
intuition 100
Itrat Hussain 60

Jackson, Thomas 212, 275–6, 282
Jesus Christ *see* cross of Christ; incarnation
John Chrysostom 286–7
Johnston, Carol Ann 86
Jordan, Richard 121, 162

Kelliher, Hilton 268
Kershaw, Alison 287
Kierkegaard, Søren 238
king, imagery 84–9
King, Francis 23
kingdom of God 286–7, 289–301
kingship 14, 86, 88–90
knowledge 215

Lacan, Jacques 175, 184–5, 187–91
Lake, Peter 155

Lambeth Manuscript 271–301
land enclosures 176–7
Lane, Belden 26–7, 230, 266
law of love 242–3
Lewalski, Barbara 211
Lewis, C. S. 205–6
liberty 125–31, 143
  and authority 130–1
  and choice 263–4
  and desire 243
  and goodness 167–8
  and grace 162–9
  and redemption 133
  and trial 168
light of nature *see* natural light
loss 61–2
lost innocence 109
lost paradise 183, 226
love 25, 148, 296
  and free will 153
  for God 48–9, 165, 216
  God's 37–9, 48–9
  and knowledge 215–16
  and law 242–3
  purpose of creation 37
  three types 238–9
loyalty 83

McFarland, Ronald 256–7, 260–1
McIntosh, Mark 181–2, 292
Mackenzie, George 273
magnanimity 153–4
Malynes, Gerard de 112
market economics 110–23
Marks, Carol 2, 138, 141, 203
marriage 272–3
Matar, Nabil 65–6, 83, 86, 285, 286
Maule, Jeremy 267, 271, 281, 287–8

Maximus the Confessor 102–3
meditation 102–3
millenarianism 285–6
Miller, Justin 23
mind 149
mirrors
  and giving back to God 201–4
  and infants 187–8
  and the self 192
misery 162
Misselden, Edward 112, 117
monarchy 85, 88
money 115–19
moral goodness 167
Moses 233–5
mutuality 133

natural light 20–1, 99–106, 140, 151, 187
negative theology 60–2
Neo-Platonism 99–106, 147
  and union with God 180
new birth 150, 248
Nicea, Council of 128
Nicholas of Cusa 196, 213
Nicodemus 150, 248
Nicolson, Marjorie Hope 55–6, 209–10
Nygren, Anders 238

Oppenheimer, Helen 239
other *see* difference
Owen, Catherine 141

paradise lost 183, 226
passion 37–49, 75
patience 87, 162
Patrick, Simon 104
perfection 75–6, 217
Petty, William 112
phoenix 236–7

Pico della Mirandola, Giovanni 20, 132, 139, 142–5, 195–6
Plato 20, 104
Plotinus 20, 105, 180
political economy 110–23
Ponsford, Michael 285, 286
possessions *see* property ownership
poverty 265
praise 134, 219
present moment 58–9
prizing 106–10
Promised Land 183
property ownership 90–1, 118, 177–80
providence 101
prudence 41–9, 72
Prynne, William 275–6
Puritanism 113, 155
Puritans 15–16

reason 100, 104, 148
re-creation 195, 224
redemption 131–3, 215; *see also* salvation
reflection 206, 218; *see also* mirrors
religion, form and heart 155
reprobate souls 157–8, 161–2
restlessness 170–1
retirement from the world 70
Reynolds, Edward 257
righteousness 107
risk 165
Roman Church 126–31
Ross, Jan 271, 301
Rublev icon 199

Salter, Keith 19
salvation 90; *see also* redemption
Sandbank, S. 205, 214, 215–16, 224, 259
Sanderson, Robert 154–7, 276–7
satisfaction 244–52
sciences 17–19, 52, 101, 208–9
Seelig, Sharon 73
Selby, Peter 114–15
self and identity 187–91
self-knowledge 108–9, 137
self-love 238–9
self-preservation 239
Selkin, Carl M. 258
sexual desire 31
sexual imagery 72, 181
sight 54, 105
Simmel, Georg 115
sin 168–9
Smith, John 65, 67–8
Smith, Julia 270
social contract 88
social justice 265
Socinianism 197
soul 59–63, 70
  in Aristotle 281–2
  as bride 32–3, 35–6, 164–6, 221, 222
  contemplation of 108–9, 121
  and desire 152
  destination 228
  in hermetic writings 137
  omnipresence 138–9
  potential 150–3
  received from God 149, 219
  as wife 221, 222–3
space, infinite 52–9
spirit, human 59–60
spiritual discernment 98–106
Staley, Thomas F. 124–5
Sterry, Peter 65–8, 103–5, 202–3
Stewart, Stanley 108, 126, 127, 128, 176, 179, 257, 258
subject/object 200–1

INDEX

sublapsarians 156
supralapsarians 156
Swimme, Brian 26

Taylor, Jeremy 21, 132
theosis 32, 131–3, 214
Thomas à Kempis 271
Thomas Aquinas 37–8, 74
trade 112
Traherne family 7, 14
Traherne, Philip 6, 10, 14
Traherne, Thomas
  historical context 3–4
  imagery 31–2
  life 6–13
  ordination 16
  prose style 224–5, 257, 282–4
  reading 19–22, 102, 142, 288
  Centuries: on beauty 36; on the created world 82, 94, 102; on creation 77–8, 104; on the cross 229–31, 232–3, 237; on custom 95, 117, 118; Davidic imagery 83; on desire 252, 263; on the fall 109; on God's wanting 186; on heaven 110, 246–7; on hope 170; on infinity 56–8, 68–9, 72–5, 77–80, 93, 210–11; on knowledge 215; on liberty 169; on love 229, 236–7; on the natural world 94–5; and Pico 142, 144, 148; on private ownership 90–1; on private property 90–1; on prizing 109–10; on re-creation 195; on reason 18; on science 101; on the soul 59–63, 61, 150–1; on treasures 93, 114, 122–3; on union with God 240–1; on value 113, 119–20; on want in God 72; on wanting 25, 27, 30, 38; on wealth 92–3
  The Ceremonial Law 268–71; on the burning bush 233–5; on the creation 202; on desire and satisfaction 244; on God's wooing us 165–6; on paradise lost 183, 226; on prizing 110
  Christian Ethicks: on ambition 64; on ambition and avarice 172; on communication 219; on covetousness 64; on custom 116; on desire 187, 243, 263; on desire and action 216–17; on the estate of trial 163; on esteem 107–8; on excess 47–9; on faith and reason 100; on free will 153, 160–1; on goodness 167–8; on gratitude 253–5, 258, 259–60, 261; on Henry Hammond 157; on Hermes 137; on holiness 76, 125; on hope 172–4; on human greatness 153–4; on love 215–16, 241; on patience 162; on prudence 42, 46; on religion 155; on righteousness 107; on satisfaction 254; on self-preservation 239; on sin 168–9; on treasure 106; on wealth 90–1; on wisdom 46, 102
  The Church's Year-Book 21, 142, 301
  Commentaries of Heaven 268; 'Accounts' 111–12; 'Adoration' 178; 'Adultery' 36, 41; 'Affection' 37; 'Allurement' 27, 38, 200; 'Antichrist' 131; 'Appetite' 30, 41, 55, 106; 'Assumption' 197; 'Atom' 96; 'Attire' 116; 'Baptism' 90, 155

313

Traherne, Thomas *continued*
Commonplace Book 142, 301; on desire 247-8; on natural light 99-100
Early Notebook 273, 301
Ficino Notebook 140-2, 142, 301
Inducements to Retiredness 272-5; on property law 118; on the soul 70; on treasures 121
The Kingdom of God 15, 17-18, 82, 89, 271, 285-301; on allure 27; on atoms 96-7; on the breath of God 219; bride imagery 222; bride/soul image 32-3, 35-6; on communication 206-9, 212; on creation 263; on desire 26, 164, 232, 266; on enjoyment of the world 194; on the estate of trial 163; on free will 125, 165; on God revealed in nature 103-4; on God's desiring 185-7; on God's goodness 235; on God's infinity 76-7; and the hermetical writings 136; on hope 171-2; on the human body 93; on human greatness 146; on infinity 50-1, 54; on joy 56-7; on land enclosures 176; on love 236-7, 240, 242-3, 243, 250-1; sexual imagery 72; on the soul 150-3; on treasures 97-8, 106, 114; on treasures in the world 82; on value 95-6; wife imagery 223
Love 33-6, 280; sexual imagery 72
Meditations on the Six Days of Creation 134, 172, 218-19, 222
poems: 'Affection' 75; 'The Anticipation' 217; 'Blisse' 178; 'The Circulation' 201, 204-5; 'Contentment is a Sleepy thing' 171; 'Desire' 64, 71, 171; 'Dissatisfaction' 64, 170; 'Ease!' 87; 'The Estate' 205, 258; 'For Man to Act' 267, 272, 297; 'The Inference' 215; 'Insatiableness' 68; 'Love' 31; 'Misapprehension' 86; 'The Odour' 111; 'The Person' 94; 'The Return' 259; 'The Review II' 211; 'Right Apprehension' 111; 'Solitude' 61; 'Thoughts IV' 202; 'A Wise Man' 194
Roman Forgeries 15, 126-31
Seeds of Eternity 271-2, 280-5; on restlessness 171; on the soul 108-9, 121
Select Meditations 15, 268; bride imagery 222; on desire 121; on felicity 227; on human limitations 149; on kingship 86; on love 243-4; on prudence 41-2; on treasures 93, 122; on union with God 225, 227
A Sober View 15, 153-62, 271, 275-9; on choice 263-4; on the circle of infinity 211-12; on the estate of trial 166-7; on goodness 167-8; on grace 163; on leadership 256; on prizing 108; on the soul 62, 125-6, 228; and virtue 168
Thanksgivings 257-8; on action in the world 255-6; on God's risk 125-6, 165; on the soul 61-2, 257-8
transpiration 205, 206

INDEX

treasures 81–123, 106, 110, 114
  definition 97–8, 106
  enjoyment of 79
  and needs 122
Tree of Life 231
trial 163, 166–7
Trinitarianism 175, 199, 201
Trinity 197–200
Twisse, William 15, 157, 276
types 269–70

unboundedness 176–7, 179
union with God 180–1, 222–8
unity 176–81
unlearning 150

value 95–6, 111–13, 119–20
Vaughan, Henry 3
virtues 39, 93, 259–60
  and free will 168
  and gratitude 254
  our expectations of 44–5
  see also prudence

Wade, Gladys 1, 14, 104–5, 126
want 266
  etymology 28–30
  in God 28, 30
wanting 25–80, 72–80
wealth 90–2, 113
Webber, Joan 195, 223–5, 231–2
Whichcote, Benjamin 100
Whitman, Walt 2
wife imagery 221, 222–3
Wilkins, John 288
will *see* free will
Winstanley, Gerrard 177
wisdom 46
Wood, Anthony a 6
Wordsworth, William 2